Business Intelligence

Business Intelligence

The Savvy Manager's Guide

Second Edition

David Loshin

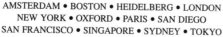
AMSTERDAM • BOSTON • HEIDELBERG • LONDON
NEW YORK • OXFORD • PARIS • SAN DIEGO
SAN FRANCISCO • SINGAPORE • SYDNEY • TOKYO

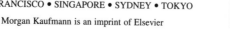
Morgan Kaufmann is an imprint of Elsevier

Acquiring Editor: Andrea Dierna
Development Editor: Robyn Day
Project Manager: Danielle S. Miller
Designer: Greg Harris

Morgan Kaufmann is an imprint of Elsevier
225 Wyman Street, Waltham, MA 02451, USA

Notices

Knowledge and best practice in this field are constantly changing. As new research and experience broaden our understanding, changes in research methods or professional practices, may become necessary. Practitioners and researchers must always rely on their own experience and knowledge in evaluating and using any information or methods described herein. In using such information or methods they should be mindful of their own safety and the safety of others, including parties for whom they have a professional responsibility.

To the fullest extent of the law, neither the Publisher nor the authors, contributors, or editors, assume any liability for any injury and/or damage to persons or property as a matter of products liability, negligence or otherwise, or from any use or operation of any methods, products, instructions, or ideas contained in the material herein.

Library of Congress Cataloging-in-Publication Data
Loshin, David, 1963-
   Business intelligence : the savvy manager's guide / David Loshin. – 2nd ed.
     p. cm.
   ISBN 978-0-12-385889-4
   1. Business intelligence. 2. Information technology–Management. 3. Management information systems. I. Title.
   HD38.7.L67 2012
   658.4'72–dc23

                                                           2012032793

British Library Cataloguing-in-Publication Data
A catalogue record for this book is available from the British Library.

ISBN: 978-0-12-385889-4

Printed in the United States of America
12 13 14 15 10 9 8 7 6 5 4 3 2 1

Working together to grow
libraries in developing countries

www.elsevier.com | www.bookaid.org | www.sabre.org

ELSEVIER   BOOK AID International   Sabre Foundation

For information on all MK publications
visit our website at www.mkp.com

Contents

Preface

Introduction

It has been nearly ten years since I began the process of writing the first edition of this book; in some ways that span of years seems like an eternity, while in others, a blink of the eye. At that time, business intelligence (BI), business analytics, OLAP, and data mining were still maturing techniques. But one interesting observation, looking back at the text of the first edition: our objective in developing the book (titled *Business Intelligence – The Savvy Manager's Guide*) was to provide an overview of a collection of techniques that were gradually being adopted to help business understand ways to work better, and this objective anticipated the eventual democratization of the capabilities for repurposing information from many sources in ways that could lead to business value. At that time, I suggested that:

The boundary that divides business and technology is a fuzzy one, and this border erodes more and more as organizational managers recognize how integral knowledge and information management are to the bottom line. A natural development of this is the concept of business intelligence (BI), which (loosely defined) incorporates the tools, methods, and processes needed to transform data into actionable knowledge.

What I find curious about BI is that it is not just technology, nor is it just practices and methods. It is more a combination of the best of both the business world and the technical world—using advanced algorithms and data management techniques to better implement the way a business works. But what prevents BI programs from being successful is precisely what forms the dividing line between business and technology. If we are moving toward a business environment where profits are driven by the exploitation of information, then it is critical for those who run, or, more properly, improve, the business to understand what kinds of value lie within a company's information and how to unlock that value and transform it into profits.

As I was completing my previous book, *The Practitioner's Guide to Data Quality Improvement*, I was approached by Rick Adams at Morgan Kaufmann (MK) to revise the material in the first edition into a second edition, which I agreed to do because I thought that many things had changed in the ways that we guide our customers in implementing a BI program. I embarked on the set of tasks of updating the material in the book as well as adding material about what has changed in the industry and **xix** expanding sections and chapters about things and ideas that have changed over time. But what I found interesting is that as I reviewed the material, I was struck by how much of the first edition has remained relevant, which I believe has contributed to the long shelf-life of the original version.

And in turn, it seems that Morgan Kaufmann's interest in business intelligence has matured as well; I was invited to be the series editor for the business intelligence series, and (after some fits and starts) found a strong MK editor partner, Andrea Dierna. At the same time that I have been revising this book, Andrea and I have been diligently working at laying the foundation for expanding the catalog of books to guide data management and business intelligence professionals. A lot of the material that is introduced in this book is, or will be treated in much finer detail in the upcoming books of the series. This book is intended to be a cornerstone piece of that strategy. My overall goal is to paint a broad-brush overview of the objectives and practices for designing and deploying a BI program, and other books in the series will provide greater depth about many of the topics we discuss here.

What This Book Is

There is a logical sequence to understanding the basics of a BI program. This book will progress through that sequence, starting with the value of information, the mechanics of planning for success, data model infrastructure, and data preparation, followed by data analysis, integration, knowledge discovery, and finally the actual use of discovered knowledge. My goals for this book include:

- Providing a knowledge base for the decision maker to determine the value of integrating business intelligence, querying, and reporting technologies into the company;
- Providing a high-level description (i.e., not deep with technical jargon) of technical concepts targeted at the knowledgeable reader, followed by more in-depth descriptions;
- Providing summary information about technology concepts and their advantages and disadvantages;
- Providing leadership concepts associated with implementing or integrating these technical components;
- Acting as a multiple-use text that doubles as a detailed explanatory guide and as a quick reference;
- Providing a clear explanation of the *utility* of technology without trying to explain how to implement that technology.

As an example, there are some very good resources on developing a business intelligence roadmap, "big data analytics," or data mining and knowledge discovery that may cover the same topics covered here at a high level, but whose authors provide much greater depth in the techniques or algorithms. Just as someone watching a television doesn't need to know how to build one, a data analyst, IT manager, or business user does not need to know how to build an association rule discovery system to take advantage of the results of using one.

Each chapter in this book is meant to stand on its own, and although the sequence of the chapters relates to a typical implementation sequence, you should not feel constrained by that sequence. My intention is to provide a book that can be referred to for guidance during the entire process of building and improving a BI program.

Why You Should Be Reading This Book

You have probably picked up this book for one or more of these very good reasons:

- You are a senior manager seeking to take advantage of your organization's information to create or add to corporate value by increasing revenue, decreasing costs, improving productivity, mitigating risks, or improving the customer experience.
- You are the Chief Information Officer or Chief Data Officer of an organization who desires to make the best use of the enterprise information asset.
- You are a manager who has been asked to develop a new BI program.
- You are a manager who has been asked to take over a floundering BI program.
- You are a manager who has been asked to take over a successful BI program.
- You are a senior business executive who wants to explore the value that a BI program can add to your organization.
- You are a business staff member who desires more insight into the way that your organization does business.
- You are a database or software engineer who has been appointed a technical manager for a BI program.
- You are a software engineer who aspires to be the manager of a BI program.
- You are a database or software engineer working on a BI program who aspires to replace your current manager.
- You are a business analyst who has been asked to join a BI team.
- You are a senior manager and your directly reporting managers have started talking about BI using terminology you think they expect you to understand.
- You are a middle-level manager or engineer and your manager has started talking about BI using terminology you think they expect you to understand.
- You are just interested in BI.

How do I know so much about you? Because at many times in my life, I *was* you—either working on or managing a project for which I had some knowledge gaps. And at the time, I would love to have had a straightforward book to consult for a quick lookup or a more in-depth read, without having to spend a huge amount of money on a technical book that only briefly addressed a topic of interest. Instead, I have a wall full of technical books that cost a fortune, and because they never really addressed my real needs, they just sit there gathering dust. So I have decided to take a stab at writing the book I wish I had twenty years ago when I first embarked on a career in information utilization.

Organization of the Book

The book is organized into 21 chapters that cover the business intelligence and analytics program from developing a value proposition, and planning, through design and development, then focusing on preparation, integration, and then use of the business intelligence results. The chapter descriptions are provided in greater detail in Table P.1.

TABLE P.1 Layout of the Book

Chapter	Title	Description
1	Business Intelligence – An Introduction	This chapter provides a definition of business intelligence, provides an overview of the drivers for business intelligence and analytics activities, and suggests the capabilities that would be included as part of a business intelligence and analytics program.
2	Value Drivers	This chapter provides a description of how business intelligence can improve the ways that business is done. This includes both "horizontal" applications that can be applied across many different types of organizations and "vertical" applications associated with specific industries.
3	Planning for Success	This chapter was reengineered to concentrate on assessing organizational preparedness for exploiting the results of a business intelligence program—establishing performance measures while instituting changes to the organization that allow action to be taken as a result of analytics. This chapter also provides an overview of the success factors for the business intelligence program.
4	Developing a Business Intelligence Roadmap	This short chapter provides a high-level overview and example ordering of the tasks to be performed as business intelligence is deployed across the organization.

(Continued)

TABLE P.1 Layout of the Book (*Continued*)

Chapter	Title	Description
5	The Business Intelligence Environment	This chapter provides a high-level overview of capabilities within a business intelligence environment. Here we review the fundamentals of business intelligence: architecture, design, data modeling, data preparation, integration, data quality, along with the different methods and styles of delivering actionable knowledge.
6	Business Models and Information Flow	This chapter describes approaches for modeling the flow of information across cross-functional business processes, the desire for performance measurements along those processes, and their need for reporting and analytics.
7	Data Requirements Analysis	This chapter provides suggestions and guidelines for engaging business data consumers, understanding the types of business problems they are looking to solve, and soliciting data requirements for reporting and analytics.
8	Data Warehouses and the Technical Business Intelligence Architecture	This chapter focuses on the platforms for analysis, largely focusing on data warehouses, operational data stores, and associated data models supporting the business intelligence activity.
9	Business Metadata	The topic of metadata is important enough to warrant its own chapter in which we look more closely at the concepts of business metadata, business term glossaries, definitions, and semantics.
10	Data Profiling	Here we look at the beginning of the data preparation phase and data discovery, where candidate data sources are subjected to statistical analysis to identify potential anomalies that would compromise the level of trust in the final information products.
11	Business Rules	We refer to the separation of business logic from logic implementation as *the business rules approach*. The simplest way to describe a business rules system is as a well-described set of environment states, a collection of environment variables, a set of formally defined rules that reflect business policies, preferences, guidelines, and such, indicating how the environment is affected, and as a mechanism for operationalizing those rules.
12	Data Quality	This chapter centers on the importance of defining data quality expectations and measuring data quality against those expectations. We will also look at the general perception of data quality and what the savvy manager needs to know to distinguish between data cleansing and data quality.

(Continued)

TABLE P.1 Layout of the Book (*Continued*)

Chapter	Title	Description
13	Data Integration	The next step is to understand how information can be shared across the enterprise, both flowing into and out of the analytical environments. This chapter discusses the broad spectrum of details surround data extraction, transformation, loading, as well as data virtualization.
14	High-Performance Business Intelligence	This chapter looks at the need for high-performance analytical platforms, and discusses parallelism and other approaches for hardware-based or commodity-based BI appliances, as well as alternates such as Hadoop.
15	Alternate Information Contexts	This chapter considers the aspects of incorporating external data sets and how data sets are used for enrichment and enhancement.
16	Location Intelligence and Spatial Analysis	This chapter looks at the emerging broad use of geographic information in a variety of contexts to provide actionable intelligence based on location intelligence and spatial analytics.
17	Knowledge Discovery, Data Mining, and Analytics	This chapter provides details on the use of data mining techniques and predictive analytics to develop predictive models to help automate decision-making in many operational applications.
18	Repurposing Publicly Available Data	In this chapter we look at ways to evaluate additional data sets, particularly ones that are publicly available (such as government-provided data sets) as a way to enhance your corporate data asset.
19	Knowledge Delivery	This chapter looks at methods for delivering business intelligence, ranging from reports, ad hoc queries, to scorecards, dashboards, and mash-ups.
20	New and Emerging Techniques	Here we provide some review and some deeper dives into emerging technologies such as text analytics, sentiment analysis, ESP and complex event processing, and social media and network analytics.
21	Quick Reference Guide	This final chapter of the book is dedicated as a quick reference guide for selected BI terminology. Each important topic mentioned in the book is given an entry in this section in summarized form for a quick refresher of the named topic.

Our Approach to Knowledge Transfer

As I have mentioned in the prefaces to both *Master Data Management* and *The Practitioner's Guide to Data Quality Improvement*, I remain devoted to helping organizations strategically improve their capabilities in gaining the best advantage from what might be called "information utility." My prior experiences in failed data management activities drove me to quit my last "real job" (as I like to say) and start my own consulting practice to prove that there are better ways to organize and plan information-oriented program.

My company, Knowledge Integrity, Inc. (www.knowledge-integrity.com), was developed to help organizations form successful business intelligence, analytics, information quality, data governance, and master data management programs. As a way of distinguishing my effort from other consulting companies, I also instituted a few important corporate rules about the way we would do business:

1. Our mission was to develop and popularize methods for enterprise data management. As opposed to the craze for patenting technology, methods, and processes, we would openly publish our ideas so as to benefit anyone willing to invest the time and energy to internalize the ideas we were promoting.

2. We would encourage clients to adopt our methods within their success patterns. It is a challenge (and perhaps in a way, insulting) to walk into an organization and tell people who have done their jobs successfully that they need to drop what they are doing and change every aspect of the way they work. We believe that every organization has its own methods for success, and our job is to craft a way to integrate performance-based information quality management into the existing organizational success structure.

3. We would not establish ourselves as permanent fixtures. We believe that information management is a core competency that should be managed within the organization, and our goal for each engagement is to establish the fundamental aspects of the program, transfer technology to internal resources, and then be on our way. I often say that if we do our job right, we work ourselves out of a contract.

4. We are not "selling a product," we are engaged to solve customer problems. We are less concerned about rigid compliance to a trademarked methodology than we are about making sure that the customer's core issues are resolved, and if that means adapting our methods to the organization's, that is the most appropriate way to get things done. I also like to say that we are successful when the client comes up with our ideas.

5. Effective communication is the key to change management. Articulating how good information management techniques enhance organizational effectiveness and performance is the first step in engaging business clients and ensuring their support and sponsorship. We would invest part of every engagement in establishing a strong business case accompanied by collateral information that can be socialized within and across the enterprise.

With these rules in mind, our first effort was to consolidate our ideas for semantic, rule-oriented data quality management in a book, *Enterprise Knowledge Management – The Data Quality Approach*, which was published in 2001 by Morgan

Kaufmann. I have been told by a number of readers that the book is critical in their development of a data quality management program, and the new technical ideas proposed for rule-based data quality monitoring have, in the intervening years, been integrated into all the major data quality vendor product suites.

The first edition of this book, *Business Intelligence – The Savvy Manager's Guide*, was released in 2003, and has been noted by many industry experts as a great introduction to business intelligence. That was followed by *Master Data Management* in 2009 and *The Practitioner's Guide to Data Quality Improvement* in 2011. Over the span of time, we have developed a graduate-level course on data quality for New York University and multiple day-courses for The Data Warehousing Institute (www.tdwi.org); presented numerous sessions at conferences and chapter meetings for DAMA (the Data Management Association), and course and online content for DATAVERSITY (www.dataversity.net); provided columns for Robert Seiner's Data Administration Newsletter (www.tdan.com) and monthly columns for DM Review (www.dmreview.com); provided a downloadable course on data quality from Better Management (www.bettermanagement.com); and host an expert channel and monthly newsletter at the Business Intelligence Network (www.b-eye-network.com) and TechTarget (www.TechTarget.com).

We are frequently asked by vendors across the spectrum to provide analysis and thought leadership in many areas of data management. We have consulted in the public sector for both federal, state, and other global government agencies. We have guided data management projects in a number of industries, including government, financial services, health care, manufacturing, energy services, insurance, and social services, among others.

Since we started the company, the awareness of the value of information management has been revealed to be one of the most important topics that senior management faces. In practices that have emerged involving the exploitation of enterprise data, such as Enterprise Resource Planning (ERP), Supply Chain Management (SCM), Customer Relationship Management (CRM), among others, there is a need for a consolidated view of high-quality data representing critical views of business information. Increased regulatory oversight, increased need for information exchange, business performance management, and the value of service-oriented architecture are driving a greater focus on performance-oriented management of enterprise data with respect to utility: accessibility, consistency, currency, freshness, and usability of a common information asset.

Contact Me

While my intention is that this book will provide an overview of a business intelligence and business analytics framework and program, there are situations where some expert advice helps get the ball rolling. The practices and approaches described in this book are abstracted from numerous real client engagements, and our broad experience may be able to jump-start your mission for data quality improvement. In the spirit of openness, I am always happy to answer questions, provide some additional details, and hear feedback about the approaches that I have put in this book and that Knowledge Integrity has employed successfully with our clients since 1999.

We are always looking for opportunities to help organizations establish the value proposition; develop the blueprint, roadmaps, and program plan; and help in implementing the business intelligence and information utilization strategy; and would welcome any opportunities to share ideas and seek out ways we can help your organization. I mean it, I really want to hear from you.

I can be reached via my email address, loshin@knowledge-integrity.com; or through Knowledge Integrity's company website, www.knowledge-integrity.com, via www.davidloshin.info, or through the web site I have set up for this book, www.businessintelligence-book.com.

Acknowledgements

What is presented in this book is a culmination of years of experience in projects and programs associated with best practices in employing data management tools, techniques, processes, and working with people. A number of people were key contributors to the development of this book, and I take this opportunity to thank them for their support:

First of all, my wonderful wife Jill deserves the most credit for perseverance and for her encouragement in completing the book. I also must thank my children, Kira, Jonah, Brianna, Gabriella, and Emma for their help as well.

Richard Ordowich, one of the principal consultants from Knowledge Integrity, has contributed a significant amount of ideas for helping our customers, and for a number of years has acted as both a springboard and a critic.

Critical parts of this book were inspired by works that I was commissioned to assemble for vendors in the data quality and master data management spaces, such as SAS/DataFlux, Informatica, IBM, Microsoft, Pitney Bowes Software, SAP (and Sybase), CA, Embarcadero, Composite Software, Kalido, Information Builders, MelissaData, as well as material presented through my expert channel at www.b-eye-network.com; and adapted from presentation material at conferences hosted by Wilshire Conferences, DATAVERSITY, DebTech International, The Data Warehousing Institute (www.tdwi.org), and vendor-hosted webinars and live events.

My involvement with the folks at TechTarget/The Business Intelligence Network (www.b-eye-network.com), especially Hannah Smalltree, Ron Powell, and Jean Schauer, has provided me with a firm basis of material developed over time in my series of articles on "Straightforward Analytics." I have worked with Mary Jo Nott and Eric Kavanagh from The Bloor Group in different places over time, and they have also acted as springboards for developing ideas fleshed out in this book.

Special thanks to Tony Shaw at Wilshire Conferences, presenters of the annual DAMA/Meta-Data and Data Governance conferences, The Data Warehousing Institute, and Davida Berger at DebTech International for allowing me to develop and teach courses supporting good data management practices.

Last, special thanks to the Morgan Kaufmann Elsevier editor for this book, and my partner in developing the business intelligence series, Andrea Dierna, who has a personal dedication to seeking out talent and developing high-quality content to expand the universe of thought leadership in the business intelligence and data management space.

Foreword

David Loshin has done it again!! A home run, clean out of the park!!

It is hard to imagine that one man could accumulate this broad spectrum of information in the detail he has presented. This book ranges from the definition of Business Intelligence, its value, its creation with all of the intricacies of its meaning and quality, its depiction and management, both internal and external data, the presentation and visualization as well as the analytical strategies and predictions of the future. In regard to the future, he has some very practical observations on the increasingly popular "big data" subject.

Having observed the spectrum of this book's coverage, David's prose is readable by the non-technical observer but comprehensive for the technical implementer. He covers an exhaustive array of subjects vital to the successful experience of a sophisticated enterprise as well as providing foundational orientation to the enterprise beginner.

I loved the *The Business Value of Intelligence* chapter. As a CEO, it gave me a multiplicity of great ideas on intelligence strategies I can pursue to improve my business that I had never considered.

I also appreciated this sentence: "… acquiring tools to perform these functions is of little value in the absence of professionals who understand how to use them and how to get the right kinds of results." It was Tim Lister, one of the sages of the Structured Methods generation, who said, "A fool with a tool is still a fool." Nothing has changed. Somehow, the world has a penchant for "silver bullets." People are grasping at straws, looking for the next technological innovation to solve all their problems. Take some friendly advice from David Loshin and me: money is not going to fix the problems. Actual work is required. David has spelled out, in great detail, for the novice and the professional all of the relevant factors that must be considered to successfully exploit the value of Intelligence.

At the mention of "silver bullets," I can't help but remember the article *There Are No Silver Bullets* by Fred Brooks. That article has been reprinted in his seminal piece of work, *"The Mythical Man Month"* which he wrote having managed the OS 360 project at IBM between 1962 and 1964. David deftly reinforces Fred Brooks' observations about "silver bullets" and catalogs the significant issues that need consideration for successful experiences in the field of Business Intelligence. **xxix**

This book is not useful only to the Business Intelligence community. It is an excellent accumulation of most of the issues relevant to the data community in general. The discussions of the identification of data requirements, data modeling and design, as well as data quality, integrity, mining, warehouses, and other vital topics is lucid and helpful to every data professional. In fact, for management folks, it is a very readable, comprehensive discussion of Business Intelligence and has an abundance of good ideas that can be embraced by every business enterprise, public and private.

The last chapter is a quick reference guide of exceptional utility and value to Business Intelligence professionals.

I have known David Loshin for many years and I am always impressed with his meticulous technical understanding and ability to articulate technical issues—especially data-related subjects—to amateurs, but more importantly, to pros.

I think you will like *Business Intelligence: The Savvy Manager's Guide*, Second Edition, by my friend, David Loshin!

John A. Zachman
Glendale, CA 2012

Chapter 1

Business Intelligence and Information Exploitation

Over the past few decades there has been a monumental transition regarding the creation, collection, and use of data. While great strides have been made in data management, there is always the desire to extract business value hidden within the piles (or rather "mountains") of bits and bytes that today are not only stored within structured data systems, but are captured, stored, managed, shared, and distributed across different file formats, representative structures, and even as unstructured data assets.

But imagine if you had the power to filter out and deliver the gems of knowledge to the right decision-makers that can trigger the right kinds of choices and actions at the optimal times. For example, imagine if you could:

- Identify who your company's best customers were, predict the amount of money they would be willing to spend over the next three months, and engage your best sales people to contact those customers;
- Predict energy consumption over the next two weeks based on average demand over similar time periods modulated by the different weather patterns so as to best negotiate energy generation, acquisition, and delivery contracts;
- Automatically assess global commodity prices and dynamically balance high net worth client investment portfolios to reduce risk while maintaining a high rate of return;

- Continuously review product profitability and eliminate the worst performing items from the catalog;
- Compare supplier performance based on credit-worthiness, product availability, compliance with contract terms, and product pricing to reduce the number of approved vendors;
- Figure out underserved geographic regions and the relative costs for entering local markets to identify best opportunities for expansion;
- Monitor key aspects impacting customer satisfaction among a collection of traditional sources coupled with social media streams to identify and correct issues in a rapid and effective manner; or
- Provide accurate audit trails demonstrating regulatory compliance to prevent fines and bad publicity.

All of these scenarios share key characteristics: the results of analyzing data suggest actions for specific individual roles that can lead to business advantage. And these are just a few examples of the kind of knowledge that can be exposed and exploited through the use of business intelligence (BI).

There is significant value embedded within the collective of sets of information at our disposal, waiting to be discovered and exploited. But to access this hidden treasure, we must first adjust the way we think about data, information, and ultimately, actionable knowledge. Historically, data is the raw material that fueled operational activities and transaction systems. Today, different data sets are used and then repurposed multiple times, simultaneously feeding both operational and analytical processes intended to achieve different business objectives. Limiting the use of those data sets to their original purposes is a thing of the past. Today, and for the foreseeable future, data utility expands to support operational activities as well as tactical and strategic decisions.

Improving the Decision-Making Process

Almost every business process presents a situation in which information is collected, manipulated, and results are presented to help individuals make decisions. Some decisions are significant, driving broad organizational strategies; some are business-critical, but may be operational and narrower in scope, such as selecting the most cost-efficient containers that best accommodate the products within each customer's order. Other decisions may be narrower, such as determining which product advertisements are to be placed in which positions on a web page served to a specific user.

Every business process has its associated measures of performance, and in a perfect world, each decision would be the *optimal* one—the decision whose results lead to the best overall performance. But those decision-makers are sometimes prevented from making the optimal decision because they are not provided with the information they need. Providing more information does not necessarily address the situation. When large amounts of unfiltered data are made available across the organization, overwhelmed individuals may be stunned into "analysis paralysis"—the compulsion to delay decision-making while waiting for just a *little bit more data* that can simplify (and perhaps justify) that impending decision.

This paralysis can be diminished if instead of delivering *all* the data, the information overload is reduced by distilling out the specific information needed to help make the optimal decision so that specific actions can be taken. Delivering trustworthy intelligence to the right people when they need it short-circuits analysis paralysis and encourages rational and confident decisions.

From the comprehensive strategic perspective, the senior management team can review overall company performance to consider any alternatives for adjusting corporate strategy for long-term value generation. From the immediate, operational perspective, day-to-day activities can be improved with specific pieces of intelligence suggesting adjustments for optimizing activities in real time. In the best scenario, business processes are augmented with the ability to incorporate information that is actionable—streaming the results of analyses directly into the process, tracking performance measures, and indicating when better decisions are being made.

In the best scenarios, reporting and business analytics contribute to a continuous virtuous cycle between operations, analysis of operations, modifications to business processes driven by the analysis, and then changes to the operational business processes and corresponding applications. Actionable information informs both strategic and operational processes, and its delivery to staff members up and down the organizational chart can facilitate a transition from reacting to what has happened in the past to streamline making the optimal decisions in the future.

Why a Business Intelligence Program?

What drives the desire for instituting a BI program? And more to the point, what are the primary drivers for business analytics and how can the benefits be effectively communicated to the important organizational stakeholders?

A straightforward approach for considering the value of a BI program looks at business processes, their source of derived or generated value, performance measures, and where the absence of knowledge impedes the complete achievement of business success. By categorizing dimensions of business value, we can then evaluate the ways that BI can contribute to increased performance along those dimensions. A high-level overview suggests at least these dimensions of value:

- Financial value associated with increased profitability, whether derived from lowered costs or increased revenues;
- Productivity value associated with increased throughput with decreased workloads, diminished time for executing end-to-end processes (such as manufacturing or operational workflows), and increasing the percentage of high quality products or outcomes;
- Trust value, such as greater customer, employee, or supplier satisfaction, as well as increasing confidence in forecasting, maintaining consistent operational and management reports, reductions in time spent in "analysis paralysis," and better results from decisions; and
- Risk value associated with improved visibility into credit exposure, confidence in capital and asset investments, and auditable compliance with jurisdictional and industry standards and regulations.

Of course, there are many other benefits to building a BI practice within an organization. Some benefits are focused on the ability to answer what might be considered the most basic questions about how a company does business. For example, it is surprising how few senior managers within a company can answer simple questions about their business, such as:

- How many employees do you have?
- For each product, how many were sold over the last 12 months within each geographic region?
- Who are your 10 best customers?
- What is the value of any particular customer?
- Who are your 20 best suppliers?

What is even more interesting is that in some organizations, not only can we not *answer* these questions, there may not even be a framework in which someone can even *ask* these questions. There is a critical point to be made here: Starting a well-conceived and comprehensive BI program that engages both the technical practitioners and the business consumers will not just provide the physical tools for answering these kinds of questions, but, more importantly, should be a catalyst for changing the way team members think about doing business and about how information is a critical catalyst for closing the loop by taking action and measuring the outcomes of those actions.

For example, before we can determine who the 20 best customers are, we must be able to articulate the difference between a "good" and a "bad" customer, as well as be able to identify a collection of metrics used to measure goodness, what data sets need to be collected for measurement, establish and integrate the methods for collecting and aggregating the data used for measuring, establish the processes required for conducting the measurement, ensure the quality of that data so as to not draw faulty conclusions, package the results into a reasonable report, and find a method to quickly and effectively disseminate the results of this process.

Although a lot of this process may be automated using off-the-shelf technology, the most important part (i.e., asking the right question) needs input from individuals with expertise and a stake in the result. It again reinforces the need for supporting the growing utility of multipurposed data. Correspondingly, there is a growing community of individuals willing to consider data as a corporate asset that can be manipulated in different ways to derive benefit along the key value drivers.

Taking Advantage of the Information Asset

Anybody involved in the BI process is concerned about the ability to take advantage of information in a way that can improve the way the organization operates. Yet the ultimate goal of BI is powered by the ability to manage access and availability of necessary information—to assess business needs, identify candidate data sources, and effectively manage the flow of information into a framework suited for reporting and analysis needs.

Although a significant amount of money has been invested in attempts at building and launching BI frameworks and applications, most of that money has been spent in infrastructure, whereas very little has been invested in managing and exploiting a valuable corporate asset—a company's data. And in some arenas, the concept of what constitutes "business intelligence" is so poorly defined that the business users' expectations are set based on what they are told by their incumbent contractors or the continuous parade of tool vendors.

Getting the most advantage from a data analysis means evolving good business processes in lock-step with establishing good practices for data management. The ability to design and build analytical platforms must dovetail with assessing business process performance expectations, determining the information requirements to address business needs, and establishing clear success criteria to ensure that the actual implementation meets business user expectations.

On the other hand, there are a number of organizations that have started to view their data as a corporate asset and to realize that properly collecting, aggregating, and analyzing their data opens an opportunity to discover bits of knowledge that can both improve operational processing and provide better insight into customer profiles and behavior. In these environments, there is a clear agreement on the management, governance, and technical disciplines designed to exploit actionable knowledge discovered from the company's information asset that constitute the BI program.

One of the objectives of this book is to discuss the fundamental concepts for taking advantage of the information asset. That merges the information management capabilities, the technical descriptions, how each is manifested in the business environment, along with some of the aspects involved in managing the technical, political, and personal issues that can pose a challenge to a successful implementation.

Business Intelligence and Program Success

The fact that you are reading this book implies that you are somehow involved in some aspect of BI. You may be just curious and looking to learn more, or you may be actively involved in some phase of a BI activity: the discovery phase, justification, analysis of requirements for design, creation, management, maintenance, or development of a BI program. And it may also be likely that somewhere within your corporate senior management hierarchy, there are individuals who have been convinced of the value of starting a BI program. Unfortunately, the disparate perceptions of what "business intelligence" means and how (or perhaps even "if") the knowledge derived through BI is to be employed can contribute to delays, stalls, and in some cases, overall program failure.

As with any technology investment, when we look at organizations that have started implementing reporting engines, developing data warehouses, or have purchased large-scale data mining software suites without any program management, change agents, or business goals, we see high expectations and many disappointments related to the failure in the way that data warehouse projects are conceived, designed, architected, managed, and implemented, for any, if not all, of these reasons:

- The amorphous understanding of what BI methods and products could do resulted in an absence of a proper perception of the value proposition on behalf of the business sponsor.
- The absence of clear measures of success masked the value of specific milestones and deliverables.
- A communications gap between the implementers and the end users prevented the integration of information requirements into the system development life cycle.
- The scope of the project was not fully understood, causing delays in delivering to the business sponsor.
- Insufficient technical training prevented developers from getting software products to do what the vendors said they do.
- Attempting to incorporate many inconsistent data sources failed because of variance in formats, structures, and semantics.
- Poor understanding of technology infrastructure led to poor planning and scheduling.
- Business users were unable to trust results due to poor data quality.
- The lack of a clear statement of success criteria, along with a lack of ways to measure program success, led to a perception of failure.

The goal of this book is to provide a high-level overview of the technical (and some political) concepts for which a savvy manager must have awareness when involved in a BI or information exploitation project in order to make that project successful. The material is intended to cast interesting technology in an operational business framework while providing the introductory technical background and highlighting important topics such as:

■ Management issues
■ Managing change
■ Technical issues
■ Performance issues
■ Complexity

This book will describe the basic architectural components of a BI environment, beginning with traditional topics, such as business process modeling and data modeling, and moving on to more modern topics, such as business rule systems, data profiling, information compliance and data quality, data warehousing, and data mining. My hope is that this will be a valuable introduction to the technology, management issues, and terminology of the BI industry. But first, let's settle on a definition of *business intelligence*.

Business Intelligence Defined

The Data Warehousing Institute, a provider of education and training in the data warehouse and BI industry defines *business intelligence* as:

> *The processes, technologies, and tools needed to turn data into information, information into knowledge, and knowledge into plans that drive profitable business action. Business intelligence encompasses data warehousing, business analytic tools, and content/knowledge management.*[1]

This is a great working definition, especially because it completely captures the idea that there is a hierarchy imposed on the different scopes of intelligence. In addition, this definition also exposes two critical notions:

■ A BI program encompasses more than just a collection of software products and visualization tools. The value of BI comes from the processes for delivering actionable knowledge to the end users, the processes for acting upon that knowledge, and the right people willing to take action. This means that without the processes and the right people, the tools are of little value.
■ The value of BI is realized in the context of profitable business action. This means that if knowledge that can be used for profitable action is ignored, the practice is of little value.

Unfortunately, the words *data* and *information* are frequently used interchangeably. At the risk of clashing with any individual's understanding of the terms *data*, *information*, and *knowledge*, for the purposes of this book we will use these conceptual definitions:

■ **Data** is a collection of raw value elements or facts used for calculating, reasoning, or measuring. Data may be collected, stored, or processed but not put into a context from which any meaning can be inferred.

■ **Information** is the result of collecting and organizing data in a way that establishes relationships between data items, which thereby provides context and meaning.

■ **Knowledge** is the concept of understanding information based on recognized patterns in a way that provides insight to information.

TURNING DATA INTO INFORMATION

The process of turning data into information can be summarized as the process of determining what data is to be collected and managed and in what context. A good example is the process of designing a database that models a real-world set of entities, such as *parties,* which is a frequently used term that refers to people and organizations, along with the roles taken on by those parties.

Out of context, the individual bits of data, such as names and birth dates, are of little value. Having established which bits of data are to be used to configure a description of a party, as well as creating instances and populating those instances with the related data values, we have created the context for those pieces of data and turned them into a piece of information.

We might say that this aspect of BI involves the infrastructure of managing and presenting data, which incorporates the hardware platforms, relational or other type of database systems, and associated software tools. This aspect also incorporates query and reporting tools that provide access to the data. Last, this part of the process cannot be done without experts in the area of data management integrating and coordinating this technology.

THE FLASH OF INSIGHT: TURNING INFORMATION INTO KNOWLEDGE

Sometimes it happens when you wake up in the middle of the night or perhaps while you are stuck in traffic or even while you're daydreaming in the shower. I am referring to that flash of insight that almost magically appears that provides you with the answer to that particularly nasty problem over which you've been agonizing. I like to compare the concept of turning information into knowledge to that flash of insight. We accumulate piles of information, which are then analyzed in many different ways until some critical bits of knowledge are created. What makes that knowledge critical is that it can be used to form a plan of action for solving some business problem.

We can say that this aspect of BI involves the analytical components, such as online analytical processing (OLAP), data quality, data profiling, business rule analysis, predictive analysis, and other types of data mining. Again, acquiring tools to perform these functions is of little value in the absence of professionals who understand how to use them and how to get the right kinds of results.

TURNING KNOWLEDGE INTO ACTIONABLE PLANS

This last aspect is probably the most important, because it is in this context that any real value is derived. If you are using BI for micromarketing, finding the right customer for your product is irrelevant if you do not have a plan to contact that customer. If you are using BI for fraud detection, finding the pattern of fraud is of little value if your organization does not do something to prevent that fraudulent behavior.

Being able to take action based on the intelligence that we have learned is the key point of any BI strategy. It is through these actions that a senior management sponsor can see the true return on investment for his or her information technology (IT) spending. A BI program provides benefits that increase business efficiency, increase sales, provide better customer targeting, reduce customer service costs, identify fraud, and generally increase profits while reducing costs. Because of this, we might say that when implemented properly, BI is one IT area that can be a profit center instead of the traditional cost center.

Actionable Intelligence

That last point is so critical that it is worth mentioning a second time: Discovered knowledge is of little value if there is no value-producing action that can be taken as a consequence of gaining that knowledge. This means that the business-technology partnership must work together not just to act on discovered intelligence but to do so in a timely fashion so as to derive the greatest benefit. This reinforces the sentiment that BI can succeed as the result of cooperation between technical developers and their business clients.

The Analytics Spectrum

The concepts of "business intelligence" and "analytics" include tools and techniques supporting a collection of user communities across an organization, as a result of collecting and organizing multiple data sources to support management and decision making at operational, tactical, and strategic levels. Through the capabilities of a BI discipline, actionable intelligence can be delivered to best serve a wide range of target users. Organizations that have matured their data warehousing programs allow those users to extract actionable knowledge from the corporate information asset and rapidly realize business value.

But while traditional reporting engines and data warehouse infrastructures support business analyst querying and canned reporting or senior management dashboards, a comprehensive program for information insight and intelligence can enhance decision-making processes for all types of staff members in numerous strategic, tactical, and operational roles. Even better, integrating the relevant information within the immediate operational context becomes the differentiating factor. On the one hand, customer analysis that reports general sales results provides some measurable value. On the other hand, real-time actionable intelligence can provide specific alternatives to a sales person talking to a specific customer based on that customer's interaction history in ways that best serve the customer while simultaneously optimizing corporate profitability as well as the salesperson's commission.

Maximizing overall benefit to all participants and stakeholders will lead to business process optimization—improvements in sales, increased customer satisfaction and employee satisfaction, improved response rates, reduced overhead costs, and so on. There are many different types of analytical capabilities provided by BI, and all help suggest answers to a series of increasingly valuable questions. These questions are both increasingly complex and add greater cumulative value. Here are the questions in increasing order of complexity:

- **What?** Predefined reports will provide the answer to the operational managers, detailing what has happened within the organization and various ways of slicing and dicing the results of those queries to understand basic characteristics of business activity (e.g., counts, sums, frequencies, locations, etc.). Traditional BI reporting provides 20/20 hindsight—it tells you what has happened, it may provide aggregate data about what has happened, and it may even direct individuals with specific actions in reaction to what has happened.
- **Why?** More comprehensive ad hoc querying coupled with review of measurements and metrics within a time series enables more focused review. Drilling down through reported dimensions lets the business client get answers to more pointed questions, such as the sources of any reported issues, or comparing specific performance across relevant dimensions.
- **What if?** More advanced statistical analysis, data mining models, and forecasting models allow business analysts to consider how different actions and decisions might have impacted the results, enabling new ideas for improving the business.

- **What next?** By evaluating the different options within forecasting, planning, and predictive models, senior strategists can weigh the possibilities and make strategic decisions.
- **How?** By considering approaches to organizational performance optimization, the senior managers can adapt business strategies that change the way the organization does business.

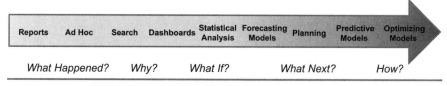

Figure 1.1   A range of techniques benefits a variety of consumers for analytics.

Information analysis makes it possible to answer these questions. Improved decision-making processes depend on supporting BI and analytic capabilities that increase in complexity and value across a broad spectrum for delivering actionable knowledge (as is shown in Figure 1.1). As the analytical functionality increases in sophistication, the business client can gain more insight into the mechanics of optimization. Statistical analysis will help in isolating the root causes of any reported issues as well as provide some forecasting capabilities should existing patterns and trends continue without adjustment. Predictive models that capture past patterns help in projecting "what-if" scenarios that guide tactics and strategy toward organizational high performance.

Intelligent analytics and BI are maturing into tools that can help optimize the business. That is true whether those tools are used to help

- C-level executives review options to meet strategic objectives,
- Senior managers seeking to streamline their lines of business, or
- Operational decision-making in ways never thought possible.

These analytics incorporate data warehousing, data mining, multidimensional analysis, streams, and graphic visualizations to provide a penetrating vision that can enable immediate reactions to emerging opportunities while simultaneously allowing us to evaluate the environment over time to discover ways to improve and expand the business.

Taming the Information Explosion

Technical analysts have been speculating for years about the explosive growth of data volumes. A 2010 article suggests that data volume will continue to expand at a healthy rate, noting that "the size of the largest data warehouse … *triples approximately every two years.*"[2]

The data explosion is globally recognized as a key Information Technology (IT) concern. According to a Gartner study in October of 2010, "47% of the respondents to a survey conducted over the summer ranked data growth in their top three challenges."[3] As an example of rampant data growth, retailer Wal-Mart executes more than 1 million customer transactions every hour, feeding databases estimated at more than 2.5 peta-bytes. Persistence is not a requirement either—a 2012 report suggests that by 2016, the amount of traffic flowing over the Internet annually will reach 1.3 zettabytes![4]

Structured information in databases is just the tip of the iceberg; some important milestones document the explosive growth of unstructured data as well: by the end of 2009, the amount of digital information was estimated to have grown to almost 800,000 petabytes (or 800,000,000,000 gigabytes), with an expectation that by the end of 2010 that amount would total approximately 1.2 million petabytes! At this rate, the amount of digital data could grow to 35 zettabytes (1 zettabyte = 1 trillion gigabytes) by 2020.[5]

Complex business processes are increasingly expected to be executed through a variety of interconnected systems. Integrated sensors and probes not only enable continuous measurement of operational performance, the interconnectedness of many systems allows for rapid communication and persistence of those measures. Every day, it is estimated that 15 petabytes of new information is being generated, 80% of which is unstructured.[6]

What does this really mean? Just looking at this set of "predictive snapshots" providing evidence of the rapid expansion of the amount of digital information leads us to conclude that incredible new vistas can be opened up as never before through combined analysis of structured and unstructured data. Business intelligence and its accompanying approaches to widespread analytics allow organizations to identify new business trends, assess the spread of disease, or even combat crime, among a plethora of other opportunities for creating value. We are beyond the point where data is used to just run the business. Rather, information is becoming the most significant focus of the business, where "statisticians mine the information output of the business for new ideas."[7] And new ideas are not just lurking in structured databases, but are envisioned through analyses that combine structured with unstructured data also.

The complexity of discovering actionable knowledge grows in lock-step with the volume of data. The issue is no longer the need to capture, store, and manage that data. Rather, the challenge is the need for distilling out and delivering the relevant pieces of knowledge to the right people at the right time to enhance the millions of opportunities for decision-making that occur on a daily basis. This can be summa-rized as the desire to integrate all aspects of collecting, consolidating, cleansing, aggregating, and summarizing massive amounts of data and presenting the resulting actionable intelligence into both the strategic and the operational processes across all functions and levels of the organization.

Considerations

The emergent recognition of the value of BI and analytics might be seen to conflict with rampant data volume growth. Competitive organizations are evolving by adopting strategies and methods for clearly specifying business objectives, assessing business information requirements, selecting and vetting the expansive set of potential data sources, developing an analytical framework, and providing a variety of means for analyzing data and delivering results to the correct individuals who are willing to take actions when they lead to business benefit.

In other words, these organizations are integrating BI and analysis in a way that supplements the spectrum of decisions that are made on a day-to-day and sometimes even moment-to-moment basis. Individuals overwhelmed with data may succumb to analysis paralysis, but delivering trustworthy actionable intelligence to the right people when they need it short-circuits analysis paralysis and encourages rational and confident decision-making.

Continuing Your Business Intelligence Education

There are a number of good online resources that provide a large amount of material on data warehousing, BI, predictive analysis, and many of the other ideas discussed in this book. I am providing an online resource site, http://www.businessintelligence-book.com, where I will continue to share ideas as well as provide additional links and suggestions!

Endnotes

1. "The Rise of Analytic Applications: Build or Buy," TDWI report series, Wayne Eckerson, 2002.
2. Merv Adrian, "Exploring the Extremes of Database Growth" IBM Data Management, Issue 1 2010.
3. Lucas Mearian, "Data growth remains IT's biggest challenge, Gartner says," Computerworld Nov 2, 2010, (downloaded from http://www.computerworld.com/s/article/9194283/Data_growth_remains_IT_s_biggest_challenge_Gartner_says).
4. The Economist, "Data, data everywhere," Feb 21, 2010, (downloaded from http://www.economist.com/node/15557443?story_id=15557443).
5. Gantz, John and Reinsel, David, "The Digital Universe Decade – Are You Ready? The IDC 2010 Digital Universe Study," May 2010 (downloaded from http://gigaom.files.wordpress.com%2F2010%2F05%2F2010-digital-universe-iview_5-4-10.pdf).
6. Bates, Pat, Biere, Mike, Weideranders, Rex , Meyer, Alan, and Wong, Bill, "New Intelligence for a Smarter Planet," ftp://ftp.software.ibm.com/common/ssi/pm/bk/n/imm14055usen/IMM14055USEN.PDF.
7. Op. cit., The Economist.

The Value of Business Intelligence

Chapter 2

In spite of the continuous drumming of the idea of considering "data as an asset," it would still be rare for data or information to appear as a line item on a corporate financial balance sheet with specific monetary amounts tied to its value and/or associated costs. Some experts might try to convince you to treat information as an asset, but what does that really mean?

From a practical standpoint, it might instead be worth examining information use in the context of how value is created within an organization. We might simply look at three different perspectives on information value versus use:

- **Functional perspective.** From this point of view, processes focus on the tasks relating to a particular business function such as sales, marketing, finance, and such. Functional processes have a reliance on data within standard operating business activities to "run the business." Transactional or operational applications can execute and successfully complete when they have the data specific for the immediate task. When the transaction or process is completed, the associated data may be archived or logged for future reference.
- **Cross-functional perspective.** In reality, most businesses are run as a conglomeration of functional processes, and this is often reflected in more complex information technology applications (such as Enterprise Resource Planning, or ERP systems) to oversee the end-to-end processing of a sequence of operations. **15**

An example is the "order-to-cash" cross-functional process, which reflects the sequence of activities from the time a customer places an order, through the credit evaluation and finance processes, then fulfillment, shipping, then on to invoicing and collecting customer payments. From this perspective, the activity is successful when *all the tasks* have completed; by its very nature, this process involves sharing information across different functions, and success is measured both in terms of successful completion as well as characteristics of the overall performance, such as shortening the duration between shipping the order and collecting the payment. Here data is not only used to run the business, it is also used to monitor how well the business is run.

■ **Enterprise perspective**. From an organizational perspective, observing the reported performance characteristics of cross-functional processes can inform enterprise architects and business analysts as to ways that the organization can change and improve the way things are done. By reviewing a collection of key performance indicators, the senior managers can seek to understand where bottlenecks or challenges are and determine approaches to alleviate their root causes. In this point of view, we might say that data is not just used to run the business, data is used *to improve the business.*

The notion of using data to both *run* and *improve* the business suggests a different approach to thinking about the value of information: by taking a forward-looking view of data, the key business stakeholders can internalize the notion that strategic knowledge is embedded in the collection of a company's data and that extracting actionable knowledge will help a company *improve* its business. And this suggests an intriguing notion that an organization may acquire a competitive edge by viewing itself as an information business instead of taking the traditional industry view.

Consider this: Is a supermarket chain a business that sells food, or is it a business that exploits knowledge about customer preferences, geographical biases, supply chain logistics, product lifecycle, and competitive sales information to optimize its delivery, inventory, pricing, and product placement as a way to increase margin for each item sold? The answer to that question (and its corresponding versions in any industry) may ultimately determine your company's long-term viability in the Information Age.

So how do you transform data into a strategic resource? A part of that process involves properly applying new technology to your data, but the most important part is being able to understand and subsequently build the business case for the value of information. This is partially an abstract exercise and partially a discrete one, and in this chapter we look at the value of information in particular contexts, its related costs, and the difference between the traditional use of data in a transactional environment for the purpose of effecting operational side effects and the modern view of data as a valuable resource that can be used for analytical purposes. The chapter also reviews a number of different business intelligence (BI) use cases, both in a horizontal (i.e., generally applied in many industries) and a vertical (i.e., industry-specific) context.

Value Drivers and Information Use

There are different ways of looking at information value, yet most look at simple views of the costs of information rather than the potential upside. For example, we might consider the cost of data acquisition (i.e., the data is worth what was paid for it) as opposed to its market value (i.e., the data is worth what we are willing to pay for it).

Yet as discussed in Chapter 1, there is a transition to an environment in which data is not just created, stored, and immediately processed. Increasingly data sets are exchanged, shared, aggregated, and reused, possibly many times. In this context, the value of information lies in its utilization, and the greater the number of ways that the information can be put to use for multiple purposes, the greater its value. "Information utility" value can be linked to different aspects of the business, both operational and strategic. Examples can range from identifying opportunities for increased productivity, where greater effort is necessary to execute business processes (which can be streamlined), to optimizing budget allocations to increase overall profitability by both increasing revenues while decreasing costs.

Attempting to assign a monetary value to a single piece of information might be a challenge, but there are general value drivers within an organization that establish a foundation for generally assessing the corresponding information utility value. Identifying organizational business objectives and then examining how (and what!) information is needed to meet those goals is a good first step, beginning with an enumeration of key business value driver vectors, as shown in Figure 2.1.

These four value drivers are:

- **Financial value**, associated with improved profitability through a combination of increased revenues and decreased costs;
- **Productivity value**, derived from increased throughput, improved process speeds, decreased manual intervention, and increased volumes;
- **Trust value**, which relates to customer, market, employee, or supplier satisfaction; and
- **Risk value**, associated with improved customer and market visibility, reduced capital risks, regulatory compliance, as well as reducing risks associated with leakage and fraud.

These value drivers are typically relevant at the enterprise level, yet they should permeate activities and performance measures across the entire organization. While

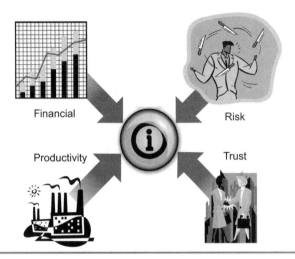

Figure 2.1   Corporate value drivers.

the CEO might be interested in a rolled-up report of corporate profitability, the manager of each line of business (who is responsible for the profit and loss of that line) would be interested in a profitability report for his or her own area of the organization.

Alternatively, different functional managers would be informed by reports of their own specific drivers. These categories help the business analysts understand how performance measures relate up and down the management chain, and provide a framework for mapping specific business objectives (associated with anyone in the organization) to the delivery of actionable knowledge.

Performance Metrics and Key Performance Indicators

Performance metrics measure how well we perform within a particular business context. A performance metric relates an objective "score" (with a specific unit of measures) within a subjective scale of success. As an example, we might have a measure of the number of calls handled by each call center representative per hour. The unit of measure is the "number of calls," but this measure provides only an objective score, but does not provide any subjective insight. Assessing comparative performance means determining the expected number of calls to be handled per hour, as well as specific target goals. To continue the example, the expected number of calls to be handled is 10, while the target could be set at 15.

In the best scenarios, performance metrics are associated with every business process. In turn, these performance metrics can be accumulated or aggregated into higher-level metrics that describe a broader view of corporate success. The highest level of metric is the key performance indicator (KPI), which is some objective measurement of an aspect of a business that is critical to the success of that business.

KPIs can be collected together to provide a conceptual scorecard for a business and can be associated with a number of different business activities, especially within our four value driver areas such as financial value, productivity, risk, and trust. In fact a large number of KPIs can be defined in terms of measuring performance associated with many different BI analytical activities.

Another conceptual value of BI is the ability to capture the business definitions of the key performance indicators, manage those definitions as part of the corporate knowledge base, and then provide a visualization dashboard that reflects those KPI measurements, presented in a form for management review. This BI dashboard displays the results of the analytics required to configure the KPIs in a succinct visual representation that can be understood instantaneously or selected for drill-down. A BI dashboard will not only provide real-time presentation of the selected KPIs, but will also hook directly into the BI components that allow for that drill-down.

By looking at some sample performance metrics, we can become comfortable with engaging the business users to assess their query and reporting needs as well as determine the degree to which existing data sets can address those needs. And the categorization of business value drivers that has been presented earlier in this chapter supports the BI process by helping to clarify general business objectives and corresponding performance metrics and indicators.

Improving the way the business is run as a result of integrating a BI framework goes beyond the technology—key stakeholders must specify what their perception of "performance" is, provide the performance measures, and then define achievable targets and use the tools to inform the decision-making processes. These measures are put in place to assess, measure, and control the degree to which the business objectives are being met. Specific programs can be designed and developed around improvements within any of these key categories. Consider these examples:

- **Revenue generation via customer profiling and targeted marketing**. Business intelligence reports and analyses reflecting customer transactions and other interactions enable the development of individual customer profiles incorporating demographic, psychographic, and behavioral data about each individual to support customer community segmentation into a variety of clusters based on different attributes and corresponding values. These categories form the basis of sales and profitability measures by customer category, helping to increase sales efforts and customer satisfaction.
- **Risk management via identification of fraud, abuse, and leakage**. Fraud, which includes intentional acts of deception with knowledge that the action or representation could result in an inappropriate gain, is often perpetrated through the

exploitation of systemic scenarios. Fraud detection is a type of analysis that looks for prevalent types of patterns that appear with some degree of frequency within certain identified scenarios. Reporting of the ways that delivered products and services match what had been sold to customers (within the contexts of their contracts/agreements) may highlight areas of revenue leakage. Both of these risks can be analyzed and brought to the attention of the proper internal authorities for remediation.

■ **Improved customer satisfaction via profiling, personalization, and customer lifetime value analysis.** Customer lifetime value analysis calculates the measure of a customer's profitability over the lifetime of the relationship, incorporating the costs associated with managing that relationship as well as the revenues expected from that customer. Employing the results of customer profiling can do more than just enhance that customer's experience by customizing the presentation of material or content. Customer profiles can be directly integrated into all customer interactions, especially at inbound call centers, where customer profiles can improve a customer service representative's ability to deal with the customer, expedite problem resolution, and perhaps even increase product and service sales.

■ **Improved procurement and acquisition productivity through spend analysis.** Spend analysis incorporates the collection, standardization, and categorization of product purchase and supplier data to select the most dependable vendors, streamline the RFP and procurement process, reduce costs, improve the predictability of high-value supply chains, and improve supply-chain predictability and efficiency.

Each of these examples can be viewed in both the operational and the strategic business perspectives. The operational view provides insight into existing conditions and performance comparing existing activities to expectations. From the strategic perspective, we can evaluate the degree to which any potential measurements impact future corporate value.

Using Actionable Knowledge

It is important to recall that you can only derive the value from information if you are able to make positive changes based on that information. This means that some investment will be required to build the environment where data can be turned into knowledge, but the real benefit occurs when that knowledge is *actionable*. That means that an organization cannot just provide the mechanics for creating knowledge; it must also have some methods for generating value using that knowledge.

This is *not* a technical issue—it is an organizational one. Delivering actionable knowledge is one thing, but to take the proper action requires a nimble organization with individuals empowered to take that action. And despite the costs, the senior managers must be convinced that the investment will yield results. Therefore it is in the best interests of the organization to consider the types of costs inherent in developing a BI platform for comparison with the anticipated benefits.

This includes analyzing costs in relation to increased performance for any value driver related to the activity, such as:

- The fixed costs already incorporated into the BI infrastructure (e.g., database or query and reporting tool purchases);
- The variable costs associated with the activity (e.g., are there special software components required?);
- The ongoing costs for maintaining this activity;
- The value of the benefits derived by taking actions when expected knowledge is derived from the activity;
- The costs and benefits of other BI components that need to contribute to this business activity;
- The value model expected from this activity;
- The probabilities of successful applications of these actions to be applied to the expected value;
- The determination of the time to break even as well as a profitability model.

Let's look at a simple example: building a CRM data warehouse for the purpose of increasing the lifetime value of each customer within a company's customer base. The goal is to build a data warehouse that encapsulates all the data related to each individual customer. Building this data warehouse incurs costs associated with physical computational hardware, a database system, additional software tools, and integrating those components into the enterprise. Next there are the additional costs associated with the design and implementation of the warehouse model(s), as well as identifying the data sources, developing the processes for extracting data from its sources and loading it into the data warehouse, and ongoing maintenance of the data warehouse. The expected benefit of the data warehouse is a 30% increase in each customer's lifetime value by the end of the third year following the launch of the data warehouse into production. This anticipated "lift" must offset the costs with the overall benefit value associated with the increase in lifetime value. If there is no breakeven point, the cost to build the data warehouse is more than the value derived from it; in that case, it is probably worth looking for additional value that can be derived from the project before pitching it to senior management.

Horizontal Use Cases for Business Intelligence

It is interesting to note the different uses of data and the contexts of each use as it pertains to the advantageous use of information. As previously noted, data use can be segmented into operational and analytical activities, and organizations are increasingly seeking ways to transition from being solely operational to embracing both operational and strategic use of information. This section enumerates some typical strategic uses of information that are not specific to any industry. The types of analyses presented here are useful for many different businesses. Note that although many of these analytic applications may be categorized within a specific business domain, many of them depend on each other within the business context.

CUSTOMER ANALYSIS

The intent of the original batch of *customer relationship management* (CRM) applications was to provide a means for capturing information about customer contacts as a way to solidify the company–customer relationship and thereby lead to increased sales, volumes, and satisfaction. However, the perceived value of CRM may actually lie in the ways that customer interactions can be analyzed to drive increased value coupled with process improvements suggested by the analyses. As a result, we can segregate the analytics associated with customer interactions and feed the recommendations to other functional activities such as marketing and sales, or even blend the results into operational processes that are directly exposed to the customer.

Following are different aspects of customer analytics that benefit the sales, marketing, and service organizations as they interact with the customers.

- **Customer profiling**. Marketing traditionally casts a wide net and hopes to capture as many qualified prospects as possible. Companies are realizing that all customers are not clones of some predefined market segment; instead, the characteristics of the "best customers" almost reflect a self-organized categorization. This means that profiling the customers and identifying the key characteristics that differentiate the different *de facto* segments can guide the marketing and sales teams to better identify qualified prospects while reducing effort spent on nonproducing communities. To this end, customer analytics encompass the continuous refinement of individual customer profiles that incorporate demographic, psychographic, and behavioral data about each individual.
- **Personalization**. Online businesses enable a direct-to-customer interface that goes way beyond the traditional customer segments. With an Internet browser acting as the primary face to the customer, personalizing the browsing experience can help streamline the sales process. Personalization, which is the process of crafting a presentation to the customer based on that customer's profile, is the modern-day counterpart to the old-fashioned salesperson who remembers every-thing about his or her individual "accounts." Web site personalization exploits customer profiles to dynamically collect content designed for an individual, and it is meant to enhance that customer's experience.

- **Collaborative filtering**. We have all seen e-commerce web sites that suggest alternate or additional purchases based on other people's preferences. In other words, the information on a web page may suggest that "people who have purchased product X also have purchased product Y." These kinds of suggestions are the result of a process called *collaborative filtering,* which evaluates the similarity between the preferences of groups of customers. This kind of recommendation generation creates relatively reliable cross-sell and up-sell opportunities.
- **Customer satisfaction**. One benefit of the customer profile is the ability to provide customer information to the customer satisfaction representatives. This can improve these representatives' ability to deal with the customer and expedite problem resolution.
- **Customer lifetime value**. The lifetime value of a customer is a measure of a customer's profitability over the lifetime of the relationship, which incorporates the costs associated with managing that relationship and the revenues expected from that customer. Customer analytics incorporates metrics for measuring customer lifetime value.
- **Customer loyalty**. It is said that a company's best new customers are its current customers. This means that a company's best opportunities for new sales are with those customers that are already happy with that company's products or services, so analyzing customer loyalty models as a way of flagging sentinel events leading to attrition can improve loyalty and extend customer lifetimes.

REVENUE GENERATION

The flip side of customer analytics is using the acquired knowledge by sharing it with the different front-end teams such as marketing and sales as a way to encourage methods for increasing revenues, using techniques such as:

- **Targeted marketing**. Knowledge of a set of customer likes and dislikes can augment a marketing campaign to target small clusters of customers that share profiles. In fact, laser-style marketing is focused directly at individuals as a by-product of customer analytics.
- **Cross-selling and up-selling**. Increasing same-customer sales is somewhat of an art, but involves advising customers of opportunities for getting better value from an increased order (up-selling) or by purchasing complementary items (cross-selling). This involves analysis of transaction histories and customer predispositions, evaluating success patterns, and looking for common behaviors to find affinities between customer profiles and products and opportunities to make additional sales or sales of higher-end products.
- **Market development**. This activity allows analysts to evaluate those demographic characteristics of individuals within particular regions as a way of

understanding geographic dependencies to drive more efficient marketing programs targeted at geo-demographic profiles based on physical location.

■ **Loyalty management.** Determining when a customer is about to shutter their relationship provides a great opportunity to reestablish ties by providing discrete offers to stay. This type of analysis helps in reducing the loss of customers while providing profiles that can help in avoiding customers with a predisposition to defection.

HUMAN RESOURCES AND STAFF UTILIZATION

One way to attain value internally from BI is to be able to streamline and optimize the way that people are integrated and operate within the organization. Some uses include:

■ **Salary and compensation modeling.** This seeks to find the best ways to compensate staff in a way that encourages high productivity in the manner that is the most cost-effective for the organization.

■ **Productivity and utilization.** Here managers look to maximize staff throughput and productivity by better allocation of material resources over time.

■ **Improved project delivery.** This process analyzes overall staff performance to enable more efficient project planning to increase predictability for delivery.

■ **Call center utilization and optimization.** The value of analyzing call center utilization comes from improving call throughput while decreasing customer waiting time. This type of analysis can lead to increased customer satisfaction, improved support, and possibly increased sales.

■ **Production effectiveness.** This includes evaluating on-time performance, labor costs, production yield, and so on, all as factors of how staff members work. This information can also be integrated into an information repository and analyzed for value.

PRODUCT MANAGEMENT, PRODUCTIVITY ANALYSIS, AND COST MANAGEMENT

Business intelligence, reporting, and analysis contribute to assessing the performance characteristics of the product development, pricing, productivity management, as well as acquisition of materials, with techniques such as:

■ **Price modeling**, used to analyze the price point that will encourage the largest number of customers while maximizing profitability;

■ **Product customization**, where specific product features are provided for sale to specialized customer segments;

■ **Distribution analysis**, used to optimize product delivery and supply-chain logistics as a way to maintain consistent and predictable product availability;

- **Manufacturing efficiency**, in which manufacturing processes are analyzed to find opportunities for streamlining;
- **Spend analysis**, which incorporates processes to help evaluate sources of increased costs in relation to acquisition of goods, products, and services from different vendors and suppliers, and helps to organize views of products acquired by supplier price, and provides visibility into spending patterns to identify opportunities for negotiation for better vendor contract terms and performance;
- **Asset management and resource planning**, where utilization, productivity, and asset lifecycle information can be integrated through business analytics to provide insight into short- and long-term resource planning, as well as exposing optimal ways to manage corporate assets to support the resource plan.

OPERATIONS

Another popular analytic realm involves business productivity metrics and analysis, including:

- **Defect analysis**. While companies struggle to improve quality production, there may be specific factors that affect the number of defective items produced, such as time of day, the source of raw materials used, and even the individuals who staff a production line. These factors can be exposed through one component of business productivity analytics.
- **Capacity planning and optimization**. Understanding resource utilization for all aspects of a physical plant (i.e., all aspects of the machinery, personnel, expected throughput, raw input requirements, warehousing, just-in-time production, etc.) through a BI analytics process can assist management in resource planning and staffing.
- **Site location**. This is a process that organizations use to identify retail locations most suitable to the constituent customer profiles.
- **First-call resolution**. Interaction patterns are mined to provide insight into ways to resolve customer complaints during the first call.

FINANCE AND RISK MANAGEMENT

A large part of running the business involves financial reporting, especially to comply with regulatory expectations and requirements. Alternatively, slicing and dicing the financial information can help in determining opportunities for improving corporate practices. Some examples include:

- **Financial reporting**. Stricter industry regulatory constraints may force companies to provide documentation about their financials, especially in a time when companies are failing due to misstated or inaccurately stated results. In addition, financial reporting analytics provide the means for high-level executives to take the pulse of the company and drill down on particular areas.

■ **Risk management**. Having greater accuracy or precision in tracking business processes and productivity allows a manager to make better decisions about how and when to allocate resources in a way that minimizes risk to the organization. In addition, risk analysis can be factored into business decisions regarding the kind of arrangements that are negotiated with partners and suppliers.

■ **Fraud and abuse detection**. Fraudulent (or abusive) behavior frequently is manifested in patterns. For example, there are many popular health insurance fraud schemes involving making claims with inflated charges or practitioners prescribing expensive medications or procedures that may not be necessary. Behavior analytics can be used to seek out patterns of suspicious behavior by provider, geographical region, agent, and so on.

■ **Credit risk analysis**. These are processes to assess individual or organizational credit risk, for underwriting insurance, and determining payment scenarios.

SUPPLY CHAIN MANAGEMENT

Supply channel analytics are used to characterize and benchmark a company's supply channels from its various vendors and suppliers, through internal inventory management and ultimately aspects of delivering products to its customers. Aspects of supply chain analytics involve the following:

■ **Supplier performance**. Another aspect of spend analysis involves evaluating the performance of your company's suppliers, reviewing variables such as consistency in pricing, speed of order delivery, credit ratings, and general compliance with contract terms.

■ **Just-in-time**. The concept of just-in-time product development revolves around the mitigation of inventory risk associated with commodity products with high price volatility. For example, the commodity desktop computer business is driven by successive generations of commodity components (disk drives, CPUs, DRAM memory chips, to name a few). Should a vendor purchase these items in large quantity and then come up against a low-sales quarter, that vendor might be stuck with components sitting on the shelf whose commodity value is rapidly declining. To alleviate this, the knowledge of how quickly the production team can assemble a product, along with sales channel information and supplier can help in accurately delivering products built to customer order within a predictable amount of time.

- **Portfolio/demand/inventory analysis**. These methods include assessment of product demand across temporal, geographic, and demographic variables to see how that can help in manufacturing, inventory, and supply chain optimization.
- **Supplier and vendor management**. Many organizations are unable to identify who their vendors are or how many vendors are supplying products or services. Supply chain analytics allow a company's management to track performance and reliability by supplier, evaluating and rating the quality of the products supplied, as well as help to optimize supplier relationships with respect to spending, procurement, and risk.
- **Shipping**. There are different methods by which a company delivers its products to its customers, each with its own cost schedule. For example, it may be more expensive to ship products by air than by truck, but the products will arrive at the destination faster if shipped by air. A company can minimize its delivery costs by being able to select the most efficient delivery method for any specific business arrangement, but knowing whether the products can be available within the right time schedule is a difficult problem, especially if your production depends on external suppliers. Therefore, merging supplier and inventory information with productivity data lets management accurately determine the best way to move product.
- **Inventory control**. Maintaining an inventory of commodity products that exhibit volatile pricing *and* limited useful life creates a market risk if those products cannot be used before their obsolescence. Alternatively, we would not want to keep the shelves empty, because parts are needed to build the products that are in the order-and-fulfillment cycle. Between the sales channel information, the productivity data, and the supply chain data, it is possible to make more precise predictions about inventory requirements. It is also possible to determine the best way to quantify and mitigate risk, especially through the development of financial products (such as barrier options) to limit financial losses.
- **Distribution analysis**. Imagine that your company has a large number of retail outlets, a smaller number of regional warehouses, and a very small number of factories. The optimal distribution model would arrange for the delivery of the exact number of products from each factory to its closest warehouses so that each warehouse could deliver the exact number of products to each of the retail stores. Unfortunately for both companies and customers, this optimal distribution is pretty rare. If a company can predict demand for specific products within certain areas, though, the managers can not only distribute the product to the right locations in the right quantities, but also minimize shipping costs by ramping up product creation at the factories most economically geographically located at a rate that matches the consumer demand.

SALES CHANNEL ANALYTICS

We might consider sales channel analytics a subset of business productivity analytics, yet there is enough value in segmenting this area of application:

- **Marketing**. Both the ability to fine-tune a marketing program and the ability to determine marketing effectiveness can be derived through sales channel analytics. A typical iterative process would be to identify a marketing strategy based on an analysis of a clustering of customers by profile and then to implement that strategy. The effectiveness of the strategy will ripple through the sales channel data, which can then be used to compare the actual results with expectations. The degree to which those expectations are met (or exceeded) can be fed back into the analytical processing to help determine new strategies.
- **Sales performance and pipeline**. Data associated with the sales staff can be analyzed to identify variables that affect the efficiency of the sales cycle, such as individual sales staff member, region, industry, contact people, contact times, and contact frequency.

BEHAVIOR ANALYSIS

Most of the analytical applications we have reviewed so far deal with "drillable" data that a manager can use to optimize some kind of process, such as sales, utilization, or distribution. Another area of analytics deals with a more fluid view of activity as a way to predict trends or capitalize on identifying specific kinds of behaviors. In general, any behavior pattern that presages significant business events is worth noting and then seeking. This type of analytical processing makes use of historical data to look for behavior patterns that take place before the significant event (whether or not they are causal) and then try to identify those behavior patterns as they are taking place. This allows for the following kinds of analytics:

- **Purchasing trends**. Although many product lifecycles can easily be predicted and charted, there are apparent nonlinear trends that elude predictability, the most notable cases being toy sales around winter holiday time. Yet not being able to identify a warming (or heating!) product may result in the inability to ramp up production to meet demand or the inability to move products from factory to store shelves, which can effectively dump a glass of cold water on that hot product. Behavior analytics can be used to identify purchasing patterns that indicate a growing trend that can be used to adjust a company's reaction to customer trends.
- **Web activity**. In the world of e-commerce, the ability to draw and maintain customers to a web site and then encourage them to commit to purchasing

products is not only critical to success, but also much more difficult than doing the same in a brick and mortar environment. Different kinds of content presentation may lead different kinds of consumers to behave differently. It is interesting to identify patterns that lead to committed business (e.g., product purchase)—let's call them "success patterns." Then perhaps including some personalization (see Customer Analysis on Page 22), the content presentation can be crafted to direct the web site visitor into these success patterns, which in theory should improve the probability of making a sale.

- **Customer attrition**. Another serious problem for many businesses is customer attrition, when a company's customers decide they no longer want to remain affiliated with that company. In competitive industries, it is much easier to convince a customer to stay with the company before the decision has been made to leave rather than afterwards. For example, offering a long-distance telephone customer a better offer than can be gotten from a competitor can recapture that customer, but it is not to the company's benefit to make this offer to (higher valued) complacent customers. Therefore, it is important to recognize the signs that a customer is ready to cease being a customer. This can be done by evaluating patterns of behavior before previous attritions (such as a history of customer service complaints) and then using those patterns for ongoing customer behavior analysis.
- **Social network analysis**. Sometimes it is important to identify relationships between specific entities within a system and to analyze their behavior as a group. For example, a component of criminal intelligence is finding collections of individuals whose individual behavior may be nondescript yet who act suspiciously as a group. This kind of analytical processing is valuable to law enforcement, regulatory compliance (think of insider trading), marketing (consider *viral marketing,* which is a strategy that encourages individuals to pass your marketing message to all of their contacts), as well as sales optimization (by finding a contact path of people to find the right audience).
- **Sentiment analysis**. Sentiment analysis combines text analytics, event analysis, and social network analysis to continuously monitor customer feedback from customer service notes, online postings, and via social media channels and be proactive in quickly addressing negative perceptions.

Vertical Use Cases for Business Intelligence

Opportunities for improvement manifest themselves in different ways and at different times, often depending on the industry in which the organization operates. We can adopt the same set of corporate value drivers and still determine ways the company can benefit from reporting and analytics specifically tuned to its industry, such as these "vertical" examples:

■ **Health care**. Monitoring business process performance permeates all aspects of quality of care. For example, understanding why some practitioners are more successful at treating certain conditions can lead to improved quality of care. Analytics can help to discover the factors that contribute to success of one approach over others, and see whether those successes are dependent on variables within the control of the practitioner or factors outside their control. Improved diagnostic approaches can reduce the demand for high-cost diagnostic resources such as imaging machinery, and better treatments can reduce the duration of patient stays, freeing up beds, improving throughput, and enabling more efficient bed utilization.

■ **Logistics/supply chain**. Integrated analysis for transportation and logistics management sheds insight into evaluation of many aspects of an efficient supply chain. For example, BI is used to analyze usage patterns for particular products based on a series of geographic, demographic, and psychographic dimensions. Predictability becomes the magic word—knowing what types of individuals in which types of areas account for purchases of the range of products over particular time periods can help in more accurately predicting (and therefore meeting) demand. As a result, the manufacturer can route the right amounts of products to reduce or eliminate out-of-stocks. At the same time, understanding demand by region over different time periods leads to more accurate planning of delivery packaging, methods, and scheduling. We can map the sales of products in relation to distance from the origination point; if sales are lower in some locations than others, it may indicate a failure in the supply chain that can be reviewed and potentially remediated in real time.

■ **Telecommunications**. In an industry continually battling customer attrition, increasing a customer's business commitment contributes to maintaining a long customer lifetime. For example, examining customer cell phone usage can help to identify each individual's core network. If a customer calls a small number of residential land lines or personal mobile phones, that customer may be better served by a "friends and family" service plan that lowers the cost for the most frequently called numbers. Identifying household relationships within the core network may enable service bundling, either by consolidating mobile accounts, or by cross-selling additional services such as landline service, Internet, and other entertainment services. On the other hand, if the calls from the customer's individual mobile phone are largely to business telephone numbers and have durations between a half hour to an hour, that customer may be better served with a business telephony relationship that bundles calling with additional mobile connectivity services.

- **Retail**. The large volume of point of sales data makes it a ripe resource for analysis, and retail establishments are always looking for ways to optimize their product placement to increase sales while reducing overhead to increase their margins, especially when market baskets can be directly tied to individuals via affinity cards. Understanding the relationship between a brick-and-mortar store location and the types of people who live within the surrounding area helps the store managers with their selection of products for store assortment. Strategic product placement (such as middle shelf or end-cap) can be reserved for those items that drive profitability, and this can be based on a combination of product sales by customer segment coupled with maps of customer travel patterns through the store. Product placement is not limited to physical locations; massive web logs can be analyzed for customer behavior to help dynamically rearrange offer placement on a web site, as well as encourage product upselling based on abandoned cart analysis, through collaborative filtering, or based on the customer's own preferences.
- **Financial services/insurance**. In both insurance and banking, identifying risks and managing exposure are critical to improved profitability. Banks providing a collection of financial services develop precise models associated with customer activities and profiles that identify additional risk variables. For example, analyzing large populations of credit card purchases in relation to mortgage failures may show increased default risk for individuals shopping at particular shopping malls or eating at certain types of fast food restaurants. In turn, recognizing behaviors that are indicative of default risk may help the bank anticipate default events and reach out to those individuals with alternate products that keep them in their homes, reduce the risk of default, and improve predictability of the loan's cash flow over long periods of time.
- **Manufacturing**. Plant performance analysis is critical to maintaining predictable and reliable productivity; tracking production line performance, machinery downtime, production quality, work in progress, safety incidents, and delivering measurements of operational performance indicators along the management escalation chain so that adverse events can be addressed within the proper context within a reasonable timeframe.
- **Hospitality**. Hotel chains assess customer profiles and related travel patterns, and know that certain customers may be dividing their annual "night allocation" among the competitors. By analyzing customer travel preferences and preferred locations, the company may present incentive offers through the loyalty program to capture more of that customer's night allocation.
- **Energy services**. Increasing deployment of "smart meters" not only enables comparative reporting and analytics with customers to reduce demand while increasing efficiency through utility-managed powering of residential machinery (such as air conditioners), but understanding demand and usage patterns can help

drive acquisition and delivery strategies as well as help in identifying scenarios driving maintenance activity such as transient "flickers" indicative of imminent outages (dues to trees or animal damage).

The examples for these industries are similar in that the analysis ranges from straightforward reporting of key business performance indicators to exploring opportunities for optimizing the way the organization is run or improving interactions with customers and other business partners. Investigation of the business processes and performance measures from any industry will yield suggestions for ways to specifically benefit from reporting and analytics.

Business Intelligence Adds Value

We can confidently say that knowledge derived from a company's data can be used as if it were an asset, as long as senior managers understand that an investment in turning data into actionable knowledge can have a significant payoff. It is important to recognize that this problem cannot be solved solely by the application of technology. In truth, the technology must augment a more serious senior-level management commitment to exploiting discovered knowledge and having a way to measure the value of those activities.

There are a number of BI analytics that provide business value. Selecting and integrating these analytic functions depends on the ability to effectively build the underlying information infrastructure to support the applications as well as the ability to configure reporting and visualization of the discovered knowledge.

Chapter 3

Planning for Success

Introduction

We have taken the first two steps in establishing a program for business intelligence (BI): defining what BI is, and determining the value it can provide. Yet despite the promise of taking advantage of actionable knowledge, many BI programs do not succeed in delivering on the promise. Whether you and others in your organization are exposed to BI through popular technical media outlets, hardware and software vendors, internal developers, your organization's system integrators, or external consultants, the promise of BI is often presented as a black box full of incredible technology that cranks out profits by the cartload.

Unfortunately, the reality is a bit different, and that promised benefit is often left unachieved as escalating costs, limited benefits, and missed expectations become synonymous with your comprehensive BI program. Individual constituents are driven by different motivating factors; while vendors are often seeking to extend their product and license penetration, developers may be motivated by new and different technologies, and system integrators and consulting firms often look to extend their service contracts.

And while a truly enterprisewide BI strategy encompasses multiple years to mature, many corporate compensation programs do not tie developer remuneration to long-term project success, especially when the typical annual review process is based on only the previous nine months of an employee's service. In essence, though, most failures are systemic, and are indicative of the inability to translate a high-level vision into a clear strategy that can be operationalized and executed.

Any manager planning for a successful BI implementation must always maintain an awareness of how the results of the BI program are contributing to corporate value. Whether that means improving profitability, reducing risk, increasing productivity, or building trust, no BI program will succeed without continuously reminding senior management of the value in building and maintaining the program.

In this chapter we'll look at some of the critical factors you must know for the planning and execution of a successful BI program. This includes the first important steps in achieving senior-level support and sponsorship for a BI program, assessing and documenting the value proposition, exploring the partnership between the business user and the information technology development staff, and general organizational preparedness. In addition, we will also look at how to establish and formally define success factors and how to measure against those factors and maintain the partnership relationship between business and IT. Last, we consider some ideas associated with building the implementation team and how to leverage short-term tactics to ensure the continued development of a long-term BI strategy.

Organizational Preparedness for Business Intelligence and Analytics

Often, organizations have committed to implementing a BI and analytics project yet still face barriers and delays in executing the program. The barriers to success are not isolated, but rather are rooted in a general lack of organizational preparedness to take advantage of the value of an integrated framework for evaluating, reporting, and changing based on performance measures.

What is meant by organizational preparedness? At the highest level, it is a state within the organization in which both management and staff are prepared to:

- Execute performance improvement measurement
- Identify opportunities for benefits
- Make changes to processes
- Make changes to behavior as a result
- Monitor improvement in relation to process and behavior changes

There are different aspects of organizational preparedness; we can get a sense of how prepared an organization is based on three areas of concentration: *organizational*, *programmatic*, and *operational* readiness.

ORGANIZATIONAL READINESS

From the *organizational readiness* perspective, you want to assess alignment between the (stated and *de facto*) objectives at different levels of management and the overall mission of the company. When the interests of the middle managers or the staff members in a particular group differ from those of the organization, it is challenging to even recognize that their behavior is motivated by alternate factors.

MANAGEMENT READINESS

It would be difficult to inspire any significant change to the organization without involvement from key individuals. We can assess the degree of programmatic preparedness in relation to the support provided by those key individuals. The first thing to consider is the support of a program champion who can influence both upper management to gain their buy-in as well as stoking interest among the stakeholders who would either help fund the program or benefit from it. Establishing *management readiness* really focuses on communicating the impact of BI—the definition of performance measures coupled with the expectation that as opportunities are identified for improving the business, those managers are committed to making changes to processes, changing behaviors, or even making staffing decisions that are in line with strategic decision-making.

OPERATIONAL READINESS

Without management support, the program is likely to stall. But even with management support, the program still needs the resources to put the operation into production. *Operational readiness* implies that engagement has been institutionalized: budgets have been allocated, skilled staff members have been hired, the customers and stakeholders have been engaged and trained, and there is an organized governance and approval infrastructure in place.

PREPARING FOR CHANGE

So how do you prepare the organization for the kinds of changes that will result from performance measurement and reporting? If you have the foundation in place, an exercise considers the future operating model and compares it to the current state. For example, the future vision may incorporate changes in the ways that customers are engaged based on their demographic profile. But in order to make that change, the sales staff members need to incorporate demographic profiles into their sales process. Therefore, that awareness and training must become a priority and be done before handing off a newly developed sales application.

Essentially, the future state can reflect a generic approach to "problem-solving," in which the BI teams work with the business users in:

■ Understanding the business problem by examining the core business challenges, determining what is known and what is unknown, describing the desired results, and considering similar scenarios or related problems;

■ Assessment and determining feasibility by considering the unknowns and seeing whether the methods of addressing the similar business problems can be adapted to this problem, considering the effects of the solution, and determining if the changes can be deployed;

■ Planning to develop the analytical solution by performing a data requirements assessment, determining the tools and methodologies to be employed, conditions for success, and barriers to execution; and

■ Execution of the solution by engaging the team members, assigning their tasks, building the solution, and measuring improvement.

The current state can be assessed in relation to the critical aspects of preparedness for change. A simple beginning is to use a low/medium/high approach, where specific criteria can be assigned for each assessment level. For example, the absence of a program champion would be measured as "low," the presence of a champion who is deeply engaged would score a "high," and anything in between might be a "medium." Given the current state assessment, the future state can be compared to identify gaps, determine action items, and develop the roadmap. As an example, you might determine that the line of business teams are extremely siloed, with a low level of alignment with the corporate mission. The corresponding action items involve establishing awareness of how a line of business activities contribute to corporate objectives and determine where local optimizations impede enterprise success.

The complete assessment would shed light on areas of risk of achieving change. The resulting plan should detail what needs to happen, who must be involved, and how a program champion maintains management engagement. It will help in achieving the operational readiness levels including resources, funding, training, and plans for continuity. In turn, the roadmap will direct the socialization of BI and guide the marketing and communication of short- and medium-term successes within a management plan for program sustainability.

Initial Steps in Starting a Business Intelligence Program

Technicians are drawn to large-scale data-intensive projects because of the technical challenge as well as the alluring draw of "cool technology" or the opportunity to learn new skills and enhance a resume. Business people are attracted by the belief that a BI program will magically increase profitability while drastically decreasing costs. Business people are incessantly pitched the silver bullet that is going to solve all their past, current, and future business problems.

While either of these drivers may have been enough in the past to guarantee a BI budget, the poor track record of these kinds of projects coupled with increasingly focused project management and governance has forced the reduction in budget, resources, and in the worst case the ultimate elimination of BI programs. It is extremely important to understand some key success factors that will help maintain corporate investment in BI. In the next sections we will drill down into fundamental aspects of the BI program such as:

- **Championship**. Senior-level champions ensuring corporate sponsorship;
- **Level-Setting**. Establishing high-level goals and setting expectations;
- **Partnering**. Creating a partnership among the participants that provides incentives to act strategically;
- **Vision**. Asserting a strategic vision that guides design, development, and deployment;
- **Plan**. Establishing a plan that delivers intermediate value while achieving the long-term goals.

CHAMPIONSHIP AND MANAGEMENT SPONSORSHIP

There is no doubt that after reading any article, white paper, blog posting, or book on data warehousing, BI, business analytics, master data management, or customer relationship management (CRM), we might think that no single technological advance could ever have taken place without the backing of a senior business manager. And in spite of the concept being a cliché, when we consider the intricacies of integrating an analytical, strategic program into an operational environment, the roadblocks that appear are not technical but mostly personal and political, necessitating a strong personality to champion the cause within the organization.

Reading between the lines in the literature, what we can infer is that one of the reasons most frequently cited for the failure of a BI program is the *lack* of senior-level sponsorship. But what is meant by *senior-level sponsorship*? This term alludes to two different concepts: explicitly, it is indicative of the seniority of the manager(s) involved, but perhaps more importantly, it implicitly refers to ensuring a corporate financial partnership for the program.

The first concept focuses on establishing a partnership with a senior-level manager (or, better yet, managers) at a level high enough to impose governance on the program and one who is able to enforce cooperation with those entrusted with the implementation of the program. This includes defining and ensuring the organizational commitment along and across the organization structure and removing barriers to success.

The second concept focuses on the senior management's establishing a vested stake in the success of the project. Whether this involves direct profit and loss (P&L) responsibility or whether it is defined more loosely in terms of stated business expectations, having a senior manager with a personal stake in the success (and correspondingly, the prevention of failure) of the program will project a corporate commitment to project accountability. Even more important is the financial backing (in other words: budget) needed to design, acquire the componentry for, build, and deploy the necessary infrastructure as well as engage the right team with the necessary skills. Also, attributing successes in the BI program to those managers with a stake provides an additional personal incentive to make sure the project succeeds.

ESTABLISHING HIGH-LEVEL GOALS AND SETTING EXPECTATIONS

When program failure is manifested as "missed expectations," it often implies a misalignment between the developers' goals and the end users' expectations. In essence, user expectations must be set in the context of the value drivers for BI, the ability of the technologists to develop tools to meet those expectations, and the collective business users' appetites for change. Any misalignment will lead to an absence of well-defined goals, and in the absence of well-defined goals, how can we ever determine the point of success of a project?

One of the most frequent critiques of the BI industry is the general expectation that "if you build it, they will come." In other words, build the data warehouse and suddenly business clients will line up to drink from an unlimited tap of business value. But if there are no goals for achieving value, the value drivers are not refined, or if there are no measures or methods of measurement of success, what often happens is that the time to build the data warehouse exceeds the patience level of the business partners. By the time the data warehouse is completed, there is either significant difficulty in extracting the right kinds of reports from it or limited trust in the information that is extracted from it.

To properly recognize success, we must have proper metrics used to measure success. This has to be defined in terms of delivering the value that the client expects. This means that there has to be a well-defined approach to soliciting business user needs, expectations, and performance measures, and we will address that in greater detail.

PARTNERING

Performance improvement can be motivated through measurement and reporting, but the value of improving performance can only be achieved when all constituents work together. That being said, there are going to be times when different participants' perceptions of value differ, even though all participants are being asked to contribute to the program success. But people are human, and it is always going to be easier to engage individuals when they have a clear expectation of the value they will receive as a result. This concept must be applied across the organization in a way that engages all participants by effectively communicating each participant's stake in both the short-term and the long-term success of the program.

This implies that there is some incentive for everybody associated with the project to achieve the specified goals. In a number of organizations I have observed, two environments that conflict with the notion of a stake in success seem to prevail. The first is the "What have you done for me lately?" mentality, which rewards individual achievements accomplished within short-term periods. This attitude encourages tactical steps at the expense of long-term strategy and stifles strategic thinking. The second environment is the "inequitable risk/reward" mentality, where individuals who have taken on added risk and have sacrificed short-term successes in exchange for long-term strategy are overlooked when it comes to advances in compensation or position, which in turn also discourages strategic thinking.

The success partnership should be designed so that short-term successes can be engineered into a long-term strategy, where components of a BI strategy are implemented in a sequence that provides ongoing value. In turn, all participants are to be rewarded for meeting well-defined milestones and achieving specific goals within reasonable deadlines. This is in contrast to the "big bang" approach, where three years are spent building the all-encompassing environment and where all centralized governance and business value becomes secondary to delivering a complete, fully integrated enterprise data warehouse.

ESTABLISHING A VISION

A vision statement is a straightforward declaration describing how the control and exploitation of actionable knowledge will add value to the organization. Those organizations that are bound to this type of vision will best demonstrate execution of strategy to gain competitive advantage.

Vision statements are precise and are crafted specifically for each organization within each industry. For example, in the financial industry, it may be expressed in terms of recognizing that the potential for increasing value lies in the most precise and fastest analysis of financial information, followed by taking some action to exploit that advantage, such as in financial arbitrage. Another example might be the retail industry, where the value vision is expressed as using information to completely understand the customer, which in turn can lead to more effective targeted marketing, increased volume sales, reduced customer churn, and overall improved customer satisfaction.

This vision embodies an agreement between the business management and the technologists that long-term corporate information-based strategy is critical to the future of a business and that synergy and cross-fertilizing technology and business expertise will result in higher profits and lower costs for the business and in personal rewards for all participants.

DEVELOPING A PLAN

A strategy translates the overall vision into a set of tactics for execution. A blueprint provides a high-level guide to executing the strategy, and the BI roadmap will detail the stages in which those concepts are brought to fruition. A good program manager will adapt the roadmap into a program plan that details the resources, tasks, and schedule for requirements analysis, design, validation of design, development, implementation, and deployment to production.

Bridging the Gaps Between Information Technology and the Business Users

If one of the success factors in gaining the best advantage from a BI and analytics program is establishing a partnership between the business users and the information technology team, what are the barriers between these two groups, and how can they be overcome? To answer this question, we can look at how over time, the evolution of technical resources has had an interesting influence on more than the speed at which things get done.

There is what we might call a psychological effect on the way people work together (or not) based on the allocation and distribution of technical resources. This is reflected in the evolution of approaches for how technology development and support has been linked to business applications in a relatively siloed manner. In the early days of computing, all technical/business analysts shared time on huge computers housed in separate rooms; the services provided were purely operational—there were no BI applications at all.

But as technology increasingly has become both smaller and more affordable, there are corresponding changes in connecting technology to the business. For example, the era of both the minicomputer (operating as a departmental resource) and the personal computer, along with the trend of distributed computing, enabled some degree of "self-service" that led to some operational efficiencies as well as some degree of freedom. With a machine on his or her desktop, a business manager could make use of desktop productivity tools for both operational and intelligence-oriented processing; you no longer needed to be a scientific programmer carrying stacks of punch cards to use computers. There was a need for technical support, and the concept of the information technology department evolved into a technology development, support, and evaluation organization, investigating new hardware and applications.

DICHOTOMY

On the other hand, the way the information technology department has evolved has imposed an artificial boundary between those who require computer services and those who provide those services. This is mostly because the ability to build user-friendly end-user applications has broken down the barrier to entry to exploiting computers. In turn, there is a greater need for both technicians to solve problems with computer use and those who can translate a business user's problems into a collection of technical issues. And although the way that these IT personnel were compensated evolved into complicated charge-backs and accounting tricks, it was clear that the division between business and IT is essentially a budgetary one: IT is usually a cost center, as opposed to the business units, which are supposed to be profit centers. But this split imposes a deeper philosophical division between information technology providers and business users because the interaction framework is built around the IT folks asking the business folks to support the IT initiatives (i.e., with money).

This is demonstrated by considering a typical exchange between developers and business users: The implementers say, "We want to make improvements, but our budget has been cut. How can we do this with no additional spending?" The business users say, "We expected the data warehouse to be online already, but it is a year late and over budget and is still unusable!" The implementers say, "We want to get the project finished, but the requirements keep changing!" The users say, "The business environment continues to change, and what were requirements a year ago, when we first planned the project, are no longer the same." Clearly, the entities perceived as the "IT side" and the "business side" have aligned themselves in an adversarial relationship. Taking this interaction to its extreme, both sides are eventually dissatisfied, because reduced budgets lead to missed deadlines and unmet business-side expectations.

PARTNERING

Fortunately, there is a growing knowledge overlap between the IT and business sides. As the relationships between business units and IT groups grow, we find that the IT side gradually learns more and more about how the business works and that the business side has a growing understanding of the capabilities and limitations of the technology. These business people now understand more about the relationship between business applications and the hardware, software, and developer resources they require, and the technologists document and learn more about business process modeling and how those processes can be encapsulated within an operational system. This is a growing knowledge management trend that reflects the need for a deeper understanding of how to exploit data and technology to gain a competitive edge.

One aspect of this trend is the abstraction of the components of the BI process. Recurring themes such as business rule management, data governance, business metadata and data lineage, workflow analysis, classification and segmentation, and business process modeling are continually being introduced and refined within frameworks for business/IT partnerships, effectively providing a way to formalize and document the ground rules associated with the way the BI program will work, as well as a means for planning the implementation of that program.

Knowing the Different Types of Business Intelligence Users

There is increasing penetration of the results of data analytics and BI across the organization to influence decision-making at many different management levels. Understanding the reporting and analytics user community sheds light on the reliance on different types of analytic applications.

Analytic Databases and Information Consumers

An insightful Forrester[1] report in the mid 2000s suggested classifying information consumer communities associated with BI as a way of assessing business needs for reporting and analytics tools as well as qualifying suitability of BI tools to meet those needs. While their characterization focused largely on consumers interacting directly with the analytics products, we can provide an augmented classification of roles who benefit from reporting and analysis engines:

- **Power users**, who constitute a community of experienced, sophisticated analysts who want to use complex tools and techniques to analyze data and whose results will inform decision-making processes.
- **Business users**, who rely on domain-specific reporting and analyses prepared by power users, but who also rely on their own ad hoc queries and desire access to raw data for drilling down, direct interaction with analytics servers (such as OLAP tools or "mash-ups"), extraction, and then further manipulation, perhaps using desktop utility tools.
- **Casual users**, who may represent more than one area of the business, and rely on rolled-up metrics from across functions or operational areas summarized from predesigned reports presented via scorecards or dashboards.

- **Data aggregators or Information providers**, which are businesses that collect industry- or societywide data and enhance and reorganize that data as a way of providing value-added services to customers and subscribers. Some examples include database marketing services, financial and credit information services, real estate business information services, audience measurement services, market research providers, and national statistical agencies, among others.
- **Operational analytics users**, who indirectly rely on the results of analytics embedded within operational applications. Examples include call center representatives whose interactive scripts are adjusted interactively in relation to customer profiles, predicted behavioral predispositions, and real-time customer responses, web site offers and ad placement, or users of retail shelf management systems that adjust stock levels based on demand across multiple regions.
- **Extended enterprise users**, composed of external parties, customers, regulators, external business analysts, partners, suppliers, or anyone with a need for reported information for tactical decision-making.
- **IT users**, mostly involved in the development aspects of BI, and whose use of BI is more for supporting the needs of other information consumers.

Across levels of skill, management role, or even with customers outside the enterprise, it is likely that information consumers benefit from the aggregation and analysis of massive data sets. Increasingly, operational decision-making at all levels of the organization is informed via notifications and alerts through a variety of channels resulting from continuous pervasive BI and analysis, and in fact, the analysis process itself is supplemented (e.g., customer profiling, classification, and segmentation) using results computed with and distilled from collections of distinct (and increasingly massive!) data sets.

Business Intelligence Success Factors: A Deeper Dive

Having established the fundamental basics for instituting a BI and analytics program, it is worth exploring success factors at a deeper level.

STRONG, DEDICATED MANAGEMENT

It is important to have strong business management team members who can help bridge the gaps between the line of business end users and the IT team members. In particular, the management team must be able to:

- Direct the process of engaging the right business side participants;
- Direct the solicitation of business user expectations and help translate those into specific requirements;

- Guide the definition of success and the associated metrics;
- Engage team members with the right skills and ensure proper training;
- Manage the knowledge and technology acquisition process;
- Develop and manage a program plan;
- Manage program implementation; and
- Defuse any political time bombs.

SETTING APPROPRIATE EXPECTATIONS

To avoid the perception that expectations are not being met, it is important to have a process for determining, articulating, and *documenting* the appropriate expectations regarding:

- **Functionality**, referring to the types of reporting and analytics applications to be provided and the features of these applications;
- **Accessibility**, which ensures that those clients who are meant to derive value from a particular BI application are able to access the application and the data underlying the application;
- **Performance**, which refers to interactive performance, supporting mixed use capabilities, and scalability;
- **Delivery**, which refers to the timeliness and predictability of delivering functionality on a predetermined schedule;
- **Quality**, in terms of data, applications, and reporting;
- **Availability**, which can be dictated based on agreed-to service-level agreements; and
- **Business relevance**, which is of primary importance, because it relates the objectives to key business performance indicators, such as cost reduction, increased throughput or volume, and higher profits.

Very often, clients define their own expectations as a by-product of a business application or service that is to be supported by a technical solution. In these cases, the perception of success or failure is (mistakenly) related to each client's ability to perform his or her own job, which may or may not relate to the correctness of the technical solution. This is a symptom of improperly setting expectations; instead, the path to success is for the business client to articulate the business problem and then to discuss the solution process with the implementers.

Consider this example: The supplier management team for a large manufacturer wants to build a data mart to figure out how much business the company does with each of its suppliers. The team supplies its data to a data-enhancement company for the purpose of company name aggregation. Unfortunately, the enhancement company, doing what it normally does, aggregates by corporate *hierarchy*, not by company, which resolves multiple, mostly independent subsidiaries into the same grouping, which may be overkill for what the client wants. Not only does the supplier management team not get its desired results, the quality of the data sets is worsened for the uses for which they were intended. The ultimate result is that the entire project is viewed as a complete failure. Yet had the team properly articulated its result expectations to the enhancement company, it is likely that the data mart would have been properly constructed and then seen as a success.

ESTABLISHING METRICS FOR SUCCESS

The previous section explored some dimensions for setting expectations; this section talks about what is needed to determine compliance with those expectations. This boils down to the ability to identify a way to quantify compliance with an expectation and the means to measure that compliance. As an example, we can look at defining measures within these types of dimensions:

- **Functionality**, which can reflect an enumeration of expected service or product features; success can be measured by how many of those features are supported by that service or product.
- **Accessibility**, which can reflect giving the right individuals the proper access to the information they need and are entitled to see at the right times. For example, this can be manifested as a collection of access policies allowing specific information consumers to specific data marts based on defined access controls. Accessibility can be measured as a function of how many clients there are, what their access path is (e.g., software connectivity), and whether proper access has been granted.
- **Performance** can be distilled into individual performance components, such as timeliness (How quickly is information available?), ability to satisfy a mixed set of applications simultaneously, the speed of processing (How quickly are processes needed for analysis finished?), and volume/throughput (How many can I process? And at what rate?).
- **Delivery** is a function of whether what has been promised is delivered within a timely manner. Practically speaking, a program for which promises made by individuals or teams are not delivered is a program destined for failure. Even if the delivery time is not as timely as the client would like, what is more important is *predictability*; in other words, knowing when you can reliably expect a feature or access rights to be made available.
- **Quality** is very frequently talked about but seldom addressed. High quality of information in a BI program is probably the most important success factor, because if the information is of low quality, no other component of the system

can be trusted. The measurement of quality is a funny thing; when we talk about manufactured objects, we can define some expected result and then impose some range of acceptable values. For example, if we are making 1-inch-long screws, perhaps we can accept screws that are 1.002 inches long. On the other hand, because it is hard to define what is right and what is wrong for data, it is very hard to objectively define data quality metrics.

■ **Availability** is relatively easy to measure; in fact, many systems refer to both uptime and downtime as a measure of availability. We can also incorporate a measure of those scheduled hours the systems are expected to be available. There are also concepts of the expected lifetime of various components that relate to availability, such as mean time between failures (MTBF) for hardware, and such.

■ **Business relevance** is easy and hard—easy because the effects of a successful program are immediately clear, hard because whether the result is attributable to the original BI may not be clearly evident. When we look at modeling the business process and then determining the importance of the pieces of the BI program within that process, we may have a better way to track bottom-line improvement to the technical program. We will explore the concept of business process modeling in greater detail in the next chapter.

BUILDING A STRONG TEAM

Assembling the right set of smart, motivated people to take on part of the BI program is critical to success. We discuss this in more detail in the later section on Team Building.

UNDERSTANDING THE TECHNOLOGY

Anyone involved in the BI and analytics lifecycle, including the business partners, should have some understanding of the technology that comprises the BI program. There are a few reasons for this, such as:

■ **Level-setting**. Understanding the technology provides some grounding in what is possible and what is not possible.

■ **Resource planning**. Awareness of the complexity of some analytical applications will help in determining the resources needed to properly service the client base.

■ **Procurement**. Many vendors dress up simplistic applications with fancy visual interfaces as a way to hide product deficiencies. Understanding the technology will help customers evaluate different products and determine which tools are of value and which are not.

DATA ARCHITECTURE

When we build a system, we also build the representation of information within that system. This representation, which is called a *data model*, describes the different entities that exist within the system along with the relationships between those entities. But it is important to remember that it is still *just a model*, and that model, once defined and put into production, remains relatively static. On the other hand, what is being modeled is not necessarily static. This means that as things in the real world change, there must be some way to reflect those changes in the model.

A well-organized data architecture will account for this possibility. The data architecture reflects the needs and interactions of the business applications, including the entity relationships, as well as data standards, metadata, and methods for information sharing.

USING QUALITY INFORMATION

A common theme throughout this book is the importance of high-quality data to any BI program. Clearly, invalid inputs will affect the outcomes, and if the input to a decision process is flawed, the decisions will be faulty. Whether the application is an operational process or an analytical process, errors in data may cause glitches in processing streams, result in incorrect analyses, or even lead to errors in judgment when carrying out the actions prescribed by the analytical process.

Different kinds of errors can wend their way into data. Some examples include data-entry errors (e.g., someone types in a last name with a different spelling than has been entered before), data-transcription errors (e.g., the data-transformation process is flawed, creating inconsistencies in the data), or analysis errors (e.g., summarizing averages of values without considering how null values are to be treated). Integral to any BI program is a clearly defined data quality initiative and a later chapter is dedicated to exploring data quality in much finer detail.

ENTERPRISE DATA INTEGRATION

A successful BI program creates an intelligence capability that both draws on enterprise data resources and is available as a resource across the enterprise. This implies that there must be well-defined processes for integrating data from multiple sources, whether it means merging data sets aggregated and deposited at a staging area or providing the means for integrating collections of data instances as they move through articulation points in the enterprise. Extract/transform/load (ETL) processing, enterprise application integration (EAI), data virtualization, change data capture, and services-oriented architecture are all types of process approaches that contribute to a holistic approach for enterprise integration.

Benefitting from Reuse

The concept of reuse is to leverage work that has already been done and to avoid simultaneous duplicated effort. Some specific areas of reuse that can benefit your program are:

- **Reuse of data**. Replication and duplication of data sets (especially reference data) lead to inconsistencies and errors. If there are data sets that are ultimately used in multiple information flows, it is worthwhile to manage those data sets as a shared resource and likewise share in the management responsibilities. Consistent shared data sets add significant value.
- **Reuse of metadata**. As distinct data sets are integrated into a single BI repository, there are likely to be differences in the way that similar entities are represented. Consolidating the metadata representations and creating transformations from original sources into that representation will ease the data integration process.
- **Reuse of business logic**. If the same data sets are reused throughout the BI program for different aims, then it is possible that similar business rules may need to be applied to the data at different points in the information flow. Archive and manage those business rules as content, and use a methodology to make those rules actionable.
- **Reuse of business process**. If there is a human-oriented process (i.e., communications and interaction) that is successful, try to recreate the same cooperation in all aspects of the program.

Managing Scope

A by-product of poor requirements gathering is repetitive refinements in specification. Scope creep, which is the continuous addition of deliverables into an already agreed-to scope of work, extends the time to delivery of milestones. A successful manager maintains control on the scope and makes sure that additional noncritical items are relegated to a follow-on scope so as not to disturb the ability to deliver.

Scalability

Remember that as the program grows and is more successful, current client use will grow and the program will attract more clients of the different user types discussed earlier in this chapter, leading to increasingly diverse sets of uses, often run simultaneously. As the pressure on the system grows, more and larger data sets will be integrated into the repository, and the interactivity will increase. Therefore, plan your BI and analytics program so that it can be easily scaled so as to maintain performance at the agreed-to service level.

More on Building Your Team

Because BI is not a purely technical solution, the team leader must have the ability to assemble the right team that can successfully implement the selection of technical components to the BI solution as well as articulate the needs and understand the results. When selecting team members, keep the following ideas in mind:

- **Insist on business participation**. The team is not complete without the participation of the business client. The business use of information should drive the program, and as already discussed earlier, senior management sponsorship is a critical success factor.
- **Clarify roles and responsibilities**. There will always be a difference between what is described in an employee's job description and "doing what needs to be done." Team members should be willing to take on added responsibility when it is critical to program success, and they should be rewarded accordingly.
- **Create leadership possibilities**. An organizational structure can impose a hierarchy on a set of individuals, but the placement of one box on top of another set of boxes does not create a leader. Leaders arise out of opportunities to take action and responsibility for getting things done. In a strict hierarchy, fresh leadership is stifled, which only frustrates good people and leads to the turnover of critical employees. To prevent this, provide many opportunities (while, of course, mitigating risk) to let good people bubble up to their leadership role.
- **Create an ego-free culture**. Insist that any successes experienced by the business client are attributable to all team members. Employ implementation standards during development to ensure that the tasks can be executed by anyone on the team. This can lead to an environment that is *ego-free*, which means that all individual successes and contributions were highlighted and rewarded internally but not exposed externally. This can lead to a seamless result that is easily maintainable. In addition, this approach encourages a high level of conformance to internally specified standards.

  In the development of a BI program, it may be unreasonable to expect that any one team member will have *all* the skills needed for the project. But the concept of the ego-free culture implies that all team members should understand that in order for the project to be successful, all contributions are valuable.
- **Cultivate believability**. A major failure of BI is overpromising and underdelivering. This happens when project managers mindlessly accede to client requests without determining feasibility first, which raises expectations that can never be

met. Before making any promises, a project manager should discuss the tasks necessary to meet that promise and have team members project how long those tasks should take to complete. Then team members should be encouraged to commit to completing their tasks within that predicted amount of time.

■ **Maintain diversity of opinion**. A team of yes-people will not lead to a successful program; look for those people who have different opinions and are willing to voice them. Disagreement in a divisive manner is counterproductive, but encouraging team members to look for faults in solution paths and to voice disagreement early on will stimulate more robust and complete solutions.

■ **Look for diversity of technical skill**. Some of the best data-management people I have met had their original training in other areas and came to data management as a way of achieving goals in their selected profession. Their business background prepared them for looking at information modeling and use in creative ways. Yet there is also a need for personnel trained in engineering and computer science to ensure that things are being done efficiently and in accordance with best practices.

■ **Maintain focus on program objectives**. Remember that the goal is not to build the most impressive piece of technology, but to integrate the practices, software, and hardware into a system for addressing business needs. Remember the 80/20 principle: 80% of the value can be achieved with 20% of the work. Do not let your team be distracted by focusing on getting a complete solution if one is not necessary to reap most of the benefits.

Strategic Versus Tactical Planning

If BI program failures are attributable to incomplete requirements and missed expectations, then to succeed, we must strike a balance between aiming to meet the long-term desires while satisfying the clients' immediate needs in the short term.

Long-Term Goals

The long-term strategy of a BI program involves building an analytical information platform from which business value can be derived. The seamless enterprise BI environment essentially is a factory to collect information from multiple sources, prepare that data for use, aggregate it in a repository, provide analytical services, and supply the means for accessing and viewing the results of those analytical processes.

The appeal of this end state is its provision of the necessary business-oriented functions that any particular vertical area could desire. Yet the inability to deliver the entire package within a short amount of time limits the feasibility of a team's building the entire intelligence resource at one time. In fact, committing a large amount of resources to a long-term project without identifiable short-term results is the kind of risk that most senior-level managers are not likely to take.

Therefore, it is important to develop the end-state vision while keeping in mind that short-term successes are critical. And designing the implementation plan with those short-term value-adding deliverables in mind is more likely to lead to overall success than the big-bang approach.

SHORT-TERM SUCCESS

The smart approach is to look for opportunities for short-term successes that conform to the plan for reaching the end state. For example, if a business client anticipates having a data mart populated from a data warehouse, it may not be necessary to source the mart directly from a data warehouse. Instead, it may be possible to create a data mart from the required data sources that satisfies the clients' needs, and providing the mart and the associated analytical and reporting components will yield business value while not detracting from the strategic goal. Later, when the large-scale repository is available, the data mart can be reconfigured to be sourced instead from the repository. In this case, the client may see no difference in the analytical environment, so having implemented the mart first is a short-term success that fits in with the long-term goals.

Other ways to achieve short-term successes include aspects of the program that will have auxiliary benefits. For example, a data cleansing effort that improves a data set's quality will benefit the current users of that data as well as the BI clients. Funding and deploying a data quality effort will not only provide immediate value, it will also provide a set of business processes and tools that can be leveraged for future data cleansing projects.

Deciding which program components to deploy early in the plan should be directly driven by client needs. It is possible that some work may need to be done in the wrong logical order or perhaps may even need to be implemented twice. But if this must be done to satisfy the senior-level sponsor, it is important to make sure business clients are satisfied that their perceived intelligence needs are being met. And remember: Always look for an opportunity for reuse, whether it be a tool, a process, metadata, or data sets.

Summary

In building a BI program, it is important to focus on the idea that the success of the program is not always tied to whiz-bang technology. The most important factors to success are being able to partner with senior-level business sponsors, identify and articulate high-level goals and expectations, and build the right team to execute the vision. Keep these success factors in mind throughout the process:

- Maintain strong management.
- Set appropriate expectations.
- Establish metrics for conformance with those expectations.
- Understand what technology can and can't do for you.
- Create a flexible and extensible data architecture.
- Use only high-quality data.
- Reuse as much as possible.
- Deliver on your promises.

Long-term strategic compliance can be achieved through tactical short-term successes. Plan to be flexible with the long-term implementation plan if that guarantees continuation of the program. And always keep your eye on the prize!

Endnotes

1. Keith Gile, "Tech Choices: Grading BI Reporting and Analysis Solutions," Forrester Research.

Chapter 4

Developing Your Business Intelligence Roadmap

A Business Intelligence Strategy: Vision to Blueprint

While this book is not intended to be an implementation manual for all things BI, it would be incomplete as a guide book if we did not consider how business information consumers, BI managers, and developers team to articulate the long-term vision, a strategy for achieving that vision, and the practical tactics to be taken to implement that strategy. There are certainly good texts that guide the development of a BI roadmap. One that is particularly useful (and has guided the development of this chapter) is by Larissa Moss and Shaku Atre, titled *Business Intelligence Roadmap*.

This chapter is intended to guide the reader in considerations for developing the BI roadmap, but is not intended as a replacement for more comprehensive guides. For more information on additional good texts that will help guide the development of the roadmap and plan, see my posts at http://www.businessintelligence-book.com.

Review: The Business Intelligence and Analytics Spectrum

The promise of using BI and analytics for creating value often masks the complexities of translating the vision into reality. In this section we anticipate the **53** desired end state and walk backward to consider the development and maturation of the BI capabilities.

In Chapter 1, we introduced the notion that a BI capability evolves and matures over time, initially focusing on measurements intended to help in understanding the current state of the business reflected through its historical performance along a number of key performance indicators, and eventually transitioning into an environment in which predictive modeling and forecasting help optimize business decisions, strategy, and operations. This "analysis spectrum" is shown in Figure 4.1.

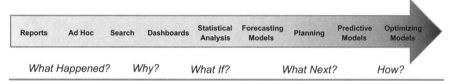

Figure 4.1 The BI analysis spectrum.

INCREMENTAL IMPROVEMENT

In the interim, the organization must retrain staff members to adjust the way they make decisions and adopt changes to the business processes in ways that best take advantage of informed decision-making. We can suggest that the evolving maturity of BI capabilities can be coupled with iterative improvements in making informed decisions across these conceptual levels of understanding:

■ **Reflection**. At this level, the business users are most concerned with the fundamentals of measurement, focusing solely on past performance. This is where the business data consumers ask "what happened" and employ standard reports that summarize historical activities, performance, and can show trends. At the same time, users with insight into the existing data assets can interact with the data by issuing ad hoc queries, and the results can provide additional insight into what has happened, leading to the next level, namely understanding why those things have happened.

■ **Understanding**. At this level, the information consumers begin to explore the root causes behind what has happened, and use tools to help frame the performance measures and at the same time provide a means for presenting summarized information while enabling drill-down to explore dependencies and correlations.

■ **Scenarios**. With some level of understanding of the potential causal issues for what has happened in the past, the decision-maker would benefit from envisioning different scenarios that could have developed had different decisions been made. This type of modeling is part of the discovery and analysis process to assess existing patterns with the analytical models that can be used to trigger specific actions to benefit the business.

- **Planning**. Two aspects of the previous levels help guide planning. The first is the use of the analyzed patterns to integrate predictive capabilities into existing business processes. The other is the use of historical analysis to guide forecasting and business planning.
- **Optimization**. At this level, the BI and analytics are fully integrated into operational and strategic processes to streamline business activities based on specific performance objectives, and to free up resources to continue to look for new innovative uses of analytics.

Each of these levels is enabled as a by-product of applying the right amount of technical capability for business process improvement. The BI roadmap should map the developing capabilities on the technical side to facilitate improvement on the process side.

MAINTAINING THE BUSINESS FOCUS

Chapter 2 focused on the value drivers for BI and analytics (actually, for any information-oriented program), and no BI blueprint or roadmap should be considered without a clear business justification. As we will consider in this chapter, clarifying that business justification is one of the first phases of the roadmap, and should be a gating factor for executing the BI program.

The Business Intelligence Roadmap: Example Phasing

A loose phasing of that transition reflects growing levels of capability and maturity in using BI concepts for business improvement, shared in Table 4.1.

The last set of phases (16–19) is really a repeatable development cycle. As your program matures and you integrate more capabilities, your user community will look for different ways in which the BI program can inform different business processes or help improve the creation of value. These may create demands for deploying the same tasks (reporting, ad hoc queries, OLAP, etc.) for different areas of the business, or it may need different analytical techniques (such as data mining and predictive modeling, forecasting models, pervasive BI) that will each require going through the requirements/design/implement/deploy stages.

Planning the Business Intelligence Plan

Needless to say, although this chapter is not intended to provide a full-scale plan for program implementation, it will be necessary to use the roadmap to map out a more

TABLE 4.1 Example Phasing for BI Program

Phase	Name	Business Objectives	Capabilities
0	Initial	Develop business justification	Assess business drivers Analyze "burning platform" issues Cost/Benefit analysis Assess risks
1	Discovery	Assess current capabilities Develop baseline measures	Process for engaging business users Clarification of key performance measures Selected methods for measurement
2	Baseline and Gap Analysis	Establish baseline measurements Specify performance targets Identify gaps Determine feasibility	Measurement methods Data collection Simple metrics
3	Plan	Infrastructure and capability evaluation Program planning	Determination of hardware, software, process infrastructure needs Program plan
4	Business Analysis	Solicit requirements Specify key performance measures and indicators Identify target scores for key performance measures and indicators	Specify business data, technical, and system requirements Key Performance Indicators (KPIs)
5	Modeling	Develop data warehouse and analytical system models	Enterprise models

6	Design, Develop, Deploy data warehouse	Create initial version of repositories for loading data for reporting and analysis	Initial version of data marts and data warehouse
7	Data quality and metadata	Assess the quality of data sources Enterprise business term glossary and definitions Business rules	Data quality assessment processes Data quality assurance processes Metadata management
8	Data integration	Extraction of data from sources Transformations in preparation for use within analytical platform	Extract/Transform/Load (ETL) or Extract/Load/Transform (ELT) processes Loading of data into data warehouse/analytical platform
9	Design: Reporting and ad hoc	Initial designs for canned reports and ad hoc queries to data warehouse	Design for standard reports and interfacing for ad hoc queries
10	Implement: Reporting and ad hoc	Development and implementation	Development and testing for BI projects
11	Deploy: Reporting and ad hoc	Publish capabilities to business users	Creation and delivery of standardized reports Drill-down
12	Design: OLAP, dashboards, and scorecards	Mature the BI capability	Design for dimensional analysis, dashboards, scorecards
13	Implement: OLAP, dashboards, and scorecards	Development and implementation	Creation and delivery of dimensional analysis, dashboards, scorecards

(Continued)

TABLE 4.1 Example Phasing for BI Program *(Continued)*

Phase	Name	Business Objectives	Capabilities
14	Deploy: OLAP, dashboards, and scorecards	Publish capabilities to business users	Enable framework for dimensional analysis Enable dashboards and scorecards Self-service BI
15	Review Business Analysis	Determine ways that the BI program is positively impacting the business Identify new opportunities for analytics that will increase corporate value	Continuous monitoring for improvements Identify opportunities for innovation
16	Design: Selected Capability	These steps are a cycle for prioritizing, selecting, designing, developing, and deploying capabilities	
17	Implement: Selected Capability		
18	Deploy: Selected Capability		Capabilities for: Alerts, notifications, integrated analytics, pervasive analytics, predictive models, optimizing models
19	Repeat (go to phase 16)		
20	Maintenance	Continued updates and improvements to existing program	

comprehensive program plan with details as to milestones and deliverables. Here are some thoughts to help guide that planning process:

- Often, companies already have standards for the application system development lifecycle, and it would be wise to "hook into" that same set of practices and benefit from the knowledge of experienced business planning professionals.
- Make sure that the results of the implementation and deployment remain connected to achieving the original business objectives. Focus on the business justification, and link progress to achieving the goals set out in that value proposition.
- Remember that the plan is not written in stone. If the projects are not yielding the expected benefits, don't be afraid to make minor, or even major changes to the plan.
- Maintain connectivity with your business sponsors and make them part of the planning process.

One last comment: Note that our example roadmap phasing did not explicitly call out the assessment and purchase of tools. Although BI tools will be a key component of your program, their acquisition in and of itself does not correspond to the deployment of the program. Rather, their acquisition should be part and parcel of the design, development, and deployment, and the intent and objectives of those phases should be the creation of the capability. If that is supported through the tools, that is great, but without adhering to the plan, the task of purchasing tools can become a distraction to achieving the desired goals.

The Business Intelligence Environment

Chapter 5

Organizations are outgrowing their strictly operational environment and are evolving their analytical capabilities, especially with the need to ensure high levels of performance for the numerous cross-functional activities. Reporting and analytics is an essential necessity in any performance-oriented organization. Concurrent with the growing recognition of the need for analytics is the maturation of an enterprise framework supporting the business intelligence (BI) needs of the user communities.

In competitive organizations, the demands of the different types of BI users go beyond a straightforward capability for reporting and delivery of canned reports and occasional notifications. What began as a collection of disjoint tools used by power users has merged into a more standardized approach to facilitate the delivery of actionable knowledge.

The BI environment incorporates a spectrum of capabilities ranging from the operational aspects including data extraction, data integration, parsing and standardization, and data cleansing and validation, all the way to the analytical parts including data warehouse platforms, analytics tools, OLAP cubes, data mining, presentation schemes, and visualization methods for creating scorecards, dashboards, and other types of visualizations, graphical presentations, and mash-ups.

And because BI and analytics are increasingly being directly integrated into operational environments to address the decision-making needs of different user communities within and outside the enterprise, there is a pervasive need for the ability to exploit huge amounts of data collected, shared, and consolidated from many different sources with results fed to different types of consumers within real-time constraints.

The processes facilitating the BI and analytics program center on an enterprise feedback loop that funnels data associated with operations into various platforms in which the data sets are transformed, consolidated, reorganized, aggregated, and then presented to decision-makers. The resulting decisions are intended to identify opportunities for creating new value, which, in the best scenarios, are communicated back to the operational process owners to implement and measure.

A plan for a BI program encompasses the management of the people, process, and the technology for reporting and analytics. Assembling that plan requires at least a high-level understanding of those technical components, and without that fundamental grounding it is unlikely that your project will succeed. In this chapter we provide the manager with a working vocabulary envisioned through a high-level view of a reference BI architecture. Armed with this knowledge, team leaders will be aware of the scope of the requirements, design, and implementation of the different technology aspects, and help in identifying potential knowledge gaps before the projects begin.

Keep in mind that the technology requirements are driven by the business requirements. Before engaging vendors and reviewing their products remember that the actual architecture will be guided by the business needs identified in relation to achieving the specified organizational objectives. In other words, the technology choices are influenced as a result of

- Assessing and understanding the business requirements;
- Documenting the user types and the kinds of decision support each needs;
- The implied data requirements from a data domain perspective;
- The types of analytical applications potentially needed to support those requirements;
- The subject areas around which those analytical areas revolve and a metadata framework for a unified structural and semantic representation for each of those subject areas;
- Identification of candidate data sources; and
- Methods and approaches for data integration.

All of these must be considered before a framework for addressing the business expectations can be defined as requirements and used to guide the design of a target BI architecture.

Aspects of a Business Intelligence and Analytics Platform and Strategy

Often the initiation of a BI program is expected to coincide with the acquisition of "BI tools," with the expectation that installing the tools immediately delivers actionable insight. But a business analytics strategy goes way beyond the selection of a reporting and query tool set or an executive dashboard. A strategic approach focuses on understanding the business user community's needs for reporting and analysis, instituting fundamental processes for requirements analysis and design, engineering, deploying, and testing a full range of tools, and providing continuous service and maintenance to continue to bring actionable knowledge to the right individuals at the proper times. There is a wide range of capabilities that must work well together, including assessment, requirements, capture of requirements, metadata, modeling, data warehousing, data integration, virtualization, high performance platforms, data quality, delivery, interaction, reporting, analytics (data mining/text data processing), and visualization.

Essentially, the intent of the strategy is to enable a complete end-to-end business reporting and analytics capability that can scale to deliver valuable benefits to an ever-growing, yet broad range of communities of BI consumers. This capability must be delivered through a variety of channels, including traditional reports, ad hoc analysis, via the Web, or direct to mobile devices. A pragmatic view of the business analytics strategy melds the needs of the different types of business information consumers with the procedural and technical mechanics to extract, transform, organize, and deliver actionable knowledge. These key components of the business analytics strategy provide the "wire frame" for layering the tools, techniques, and expertise for reporting and analysis.

FUNDAMENTALS AND REQUIREMENTS

Creating measurable value in relation to what have been identified as the organization's key performance indicators may be the ultimate intent, but that implies that the practical aspects of collecting the source information and calculating the scores for these measures are linked to specific business user expectations and requirements. The requirements solicitation and analysis process itself creates a need for tools supporting the exploratory and documentary aspects of BI and analytics. These types of tools must help the analysts in understanding the business performance objectives and key value drivers for the organization and allow for documenting business expectations for reporting and analysis and for the discovery and analysis of existing business applications and their corresponding data sources to assess suitability to address business needs.

BUSINESS INTELLIGENCE ARCHITECTURE AND DESIGN

Once the key expectations have been documented and suitable data sets have been identified, the BI professionals will need to review the collected expectations and synthesize specific requirements based on the types of queries, reporting, and analyses to be performed. This also means that there is a need to design data models within a data warehouse as well as the corresponding services to stream data into the analytical platforms where the data warehouse and data marts reside. In addition, the BI architecture will incorporate designs for the platforms to enable analysis, as well as application design, testing, and the necessary project management.

DATA PREPARATION

Having identified the sources of data and developed the target data models within the data warehouse, the next component addresses the streaming of information from the originating sources into the analytical platform. This incorporates all aspects of preparing data for integration into a platform for reporting and analysis, including data extraction, data quality (including parsing, standardization, matching, and data cleansing), data transformation, as well as other integration and preparation techniques such as data virtualization, change data capture, and data warehouse loading.

DATA INTEGRATION

The original terms used for data integration were Extraction, Transformation, and Loading, or ETL. But these days data integration encompasses much more than these aspects of moving data from the sources to the targets. It involves all aspects of data sharing, which can lever the traditional ETL or rely on alternate approaches for accumulating the data from the originating sources that will be used to populate the main enterprise data repository and the facilitation of the delivery of information to the target consumers.

For example, a company might want to build a data warehouse that will support customer analytics. That might imply a data warehouse that is populated with customer data pulled from a master data repository, lead-generation and prospect information, transaction histories, customer service histories, externally sourced credit data, acquired product data, web activity data, along with external demographic and psychographic data enhancements. Most of this data will come from different sources.

BUSINESS INTELLIGENCE PLATFORMS

One focal point of the scalable end-to-end BI platform involves the computational platforms used as the basis for BI reporting and analysis, which typically is referred to as a data warehouse. There are different philosophies regarding the nature of the data warehouse, mostly focusing on the difference between a monolithic approach and a collection of smaller subject-area repositories. Either way, the data warehouse must be able to satisfy the range of mixed analytics uses as well as address the needs of the different user communities.

ANALYSIS

The "intelligence" in business intelligence comes from a combination of ways of aggregating, summarizing, organizing, and analyzing data, with the results presented to the knowledge consumers. The analysis component incorporates a range of techniques, including standard reporting, responding to ad hoc queries, as well as multidimensional analysis, data mining, predictive modeling and analytics, text analytics, and social media analysis, among others.

DELIVERY AND PRESENTATION

Lastly, an organizational BI and analytics strategy enables the delivery and presentation of analytical results to the different types of users. This component of the framework provides the means for developing and delivering reports, responding to ad hoc queries, as well as interactive delivery and presentation of dashboards, scorecards, key performance indicators, and delivery to a diverse set of web-based, mobile, and handheld platforms.

The Organizational Business Intelligence Framework

To support any BI and analytics strategy, there is a need for a combination of the policies, processes, technologies, and skills to accomplish the reporting and analysis objectives. This incorporates the procedural approaches to soliciting requirements, developing models, and developing business analytics applications with the supplemental tools, employed by skills engineers applying techniques to use those tools. Figure 5.1 provides a conceptual view of the end-to-end strategy, overlaid with the types of tools used to make the processes effective.

Ultimately these component areas of the BI and analytics strategy can be mapped to specific tools and technologies that compose an organizational solution. Here we

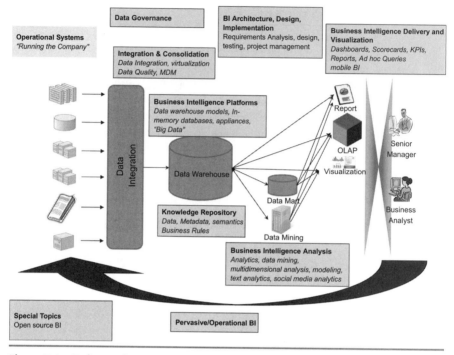

Figure 5.1 End-to-end strategy.

provide an introduction to many of these component areas. Most of these will be covered in greater detail in other areas of this book.

Business Process Modeling and Analytic Needs Assessment

Business process modeling engages both the business people and the technologists to review the task flows of both operational and analytical business activities. Business process modeling and information flow modeling together expose what information a business needs and how that information moves from its sources to its destination.

For reporting and analysis purposes, business process modeling goes hand-in-hand with analytic needs assessment, mostly to ensure that the analysts understand how the results of any business area contribute to organizational success, the activities that compose that business area, and that a coherent and meaningful set of analyses or key performance measures can be associated with each business area.

Metadata Management

The organic development of application systems over time has created an environment of disparate representations of source data, which complicates the process of merging and consolidation when data sets are brought into the data warehouse. In fact, we might say that one of the biggest challenges associated with transforming disparate data sources into a coherent view for analysis is the variation in originating data formats, structures, types, and importantly, meanings.

These concepts, referred to collectively as "metadata," provide the details about what is intended through the use of particular data element concepts, conceptual data domains, and the ways these are deployed across the organizations. A BI and analytics framework must employ a metadata management environment that can support the discovery and documentation of existing data sets and their corresponding data attributes, managing a catalog of business terms and corresponding definitions and data domains, assessment of suitability for use in BI applications, and for capturing and documenting knowledge worker expectations for reporting and analysis.

DATA MODELING

Variations in original source table and file structures also complicate the data consolidation process. On the other hand, having common representations of common data domains for consumers of the business analyses improves consistency and coherence. This suggests a need for developing common data models for integration, analysis, and for presentation. Data modeling tools are used in capturing existing source data models, molding suitable representations of domains and activities to be analyzed, as well as facilitating reports and responding to analyses and queries.

DATA PROFILING

Data profiling refers to a number of processes used to discover metadata, evaluate the statistical characteristics of data sets, validate data against defined business rules, and document relationships between columns within a data set. Data profiling tools are used as part of the data discovery and assessment processes to identify candidate data sources suitable for analysis, as well as instituting the data quality controls during the data integration and consolidation processes.

DATA QUALITY

Data quality tools are used to validate data during the data extraction and transformation phases based on rules related to client data expectations. These expectations are also used as the basis for cleansing and information compliance. Because of the potential data inconsistencies and missing data, source data sets are subjected to parsing, standardization, matching, correction, cleansing, and enhancement in preparation for analysis.

Business Rules

We might say that any operational or analytical process that is involved in running or improving a business is driven by a set of business rules. Whether these rules are dictated by external bodies (such as a regulatory board), by internal directives (such as an executive process leadership group), or by the way that business is done within an industry, there is a method to separate the rules that drive a process from the process itself. Business rules expose the logical abstraction of a business process, and the collection of a process's business rules would be considered to be a large part of its metadata.

Database Management System

Whether it is used as a temporary holding place for staging data or as the database platform in which the data warehouse data is stored, the BI environment relies on the use of a database management system (DBMS) for information management. Even as data is stored in a format that often best suits analytical processing (one form, called a star schema, will be described in greater detail in Chapter 8), the linkage between the tables is enabled through a relational database framework. Separate analytical servers may manage their own copies of data in a dimensional database that is separate from the data warehouse.

Data Integration

Data transformation and integration refer to the process of modifying data to conform to the target formats or applying transformation to enable the combination of data sets, as a prelude to the actual integration and binding of those data sets into a form suitable for loading into a data warehouse. Data integration tools are critical to moving data from the original sources into the platforms for analysis and reporting. Data integration goes beyond extracting data sets and transforming them in preparation for loading into a target system. Data integration also incorporates methods for data sharing and publication, as well as the data virtualization that abstract access through a virtual layer as well as change data capture and replication that increase data coherence and consistency while reducing the time and effort for moving data from the original sources to the target systems.

Analytical Platforms

To offload the analysis from the original transactional systems (and thereby reduce impact on operations), analysis and reporting are driven off an analytical platform specifically designed for business analytics. With growing data volumes and business analytics demand, the analytical platform is intended to provide a high performance, scalable platform to satisfy the reporting and analysis demands of the variety of business users.

Although there are evolving approaches to facilitating a unified view of data for analytical purposes, the most frequently used approach for enabling the typical reporting and analysis done in a nascent BI program is a centralized enterprise data repository. We have used the term *data warehousing*, which is commonly used to describe this topic. A *data warehouse* is a centralized, nonvolatile repository of enterprise information, gathered and integrated from multiple sources and placed in a data model that is suitable for the analytical process. In this book we discuss representative schemas and structures used within a basic data warehouse data model, look at the difference between that model and the entity-relationship model, as well as the corresponding use of metadata and reference data.

There are different logical system platforms used in a BI program, each corresponding to different aspects of provisioning information from source to ultimate destination. Some of those systems are:

- **Operational data stores**, which are "holding areas" for data flowing from operational systems in preparation for inclusion in a data warehouse.
- **Staging areas**, which provide a target area where data from the different sources are collected and integrated in preparation for loading into the data warehouse.
- **The data warehouse** itself, providing a centralized nonvolatile data repository.
- **Analytical environments**, consisting of data marts, which are subject-oriented subsets of the data warehouse (and which source data from the data warehouse), or analytical systems where statistical and probabilistic methods are used for different types of analytics. These are often coupled with the analytical interfaces and tools that provide the interface to the user.

Although it is likely that there is only one staging area and warehouse, there may be many instances of the analytical systems, each possibly requiring its own physical system.

"CANNED" REPORTING

The needs of many business analytics consumers are often met with straightforward presentations of predefined, or what can be called "canned" reports. These standard reports are meant to convey the status of the business in operation, such as P&L reports, budget versus actual spending, expense reports, and production reports. Tools for configuring and producing these predefined reports provide the first wave of delivery techniques for analytical results.

A query and reporting tool is a visual interface that allows the data client to formulate the queries required for a particular business report and then to assemble the report presentation. The tool will mask out the technical details of the data access and configuration and can be used to manage and reuse canned queries or sequences of ad hoc queries.

DIMENSIONAL ANALYSIS

More interactive users might want to "slice and dice" their data sets, and online analytical processing (OLAP) is both a process of viewing comparative metrics via a multidimensional analysis of data and the infrastructure to support that process. OLAP can support aggregation of cumulative data (e.g., sums, averages, minimums, maximums) or numeric data (such as sales, number of employees, number of products produced, inventories) presented in a way that allows for interactive "drill-down," or successive detail analysis and exposition. OLAP is both a process and representative of infrastructure, and is the focus of further discussion in later chapters. The OLAP platform exposes the data to these interactive business analysts, and allows greater freedom in the search for actionable knowledge.

AD HOC/SELF-SERVICE

For more sophisticated users, there may be an interest in more details about particular reports. In these cases, the users can perform structured queries, which provide greater details about specific routine queries such as sales per region, perhaps aggregated at a finer level of precision, or limited to a particular area. When predefined reports are not sufficient, more savvy business users might have specific questions that can be answered using self-service access and ad hoc reporting tools. Reports accessed via these methods can be parameterized to allow different clients to modify aspects of the queries for their own personalized use. Using these access methods, the users can narrow down the answers to specific questions as they arise:

- **Query and report management** from the content-based side (i.e., being able to create the queries for reports and manage those queries so that they can either be exploited in raw form or exported to individuals for customization).
- **Ad hoc query systems**, which allow the client to formulate his or her own queries directly into the data. Some systems will provide query builders to help those unfamiliar with the query language syntax to assemble proper ad hoc queries.
- **Exception-based reporting**, which alerts individuals to events that have taken place within the environment.

SEARCH

An organization's data asset may expand beyond limited sets of structured data, and the ability to access information through semantic *search* allows the business user to combine data captured in a data warehouse for analysis with relevant business information derived from additional structured and unstructured sources.

TEXT ANALYSIS

Data organized within a formal representation that conforms to defined types and structures is called *structured* data; information that is incorporated into a document (or framework) that has some basic structure and taxonomy (such as certain kinds of web pages, wedding notices, catalog descriptions) are said to be *semistructured*, in that they exhibit some structure that is looser than the standard <attribute, value> pairing of data within a database table. Free-form text is said to be *unstructured* data.

It is relatively easy to look at structured data and figure out what to do with it, because effort has already been invested in binding values to named column values within a record. It is more difficult to make sense out of less structured data, and we rely on more complicated text analysis tools to scan through that kind of information to extract any usefulness. The most recognizable form of text analysis tool is an indexing application that then allows for indexed searching, such as those web sites that provide search capability through other web sites.

More complex text analysis tools are used to try to extract information from unstructured data. Entity identification, identity resolution, concept analysis, meta-tagging, and semantic analysis are all processes that are applied to transform the data embedded within the text into something that is meaningful. For example, a recruiter might fancy a system that can transform a candidate's resume into a structured representation of that candidate's skills and training, with some value judgment of that candidate's skill level with each skill area. Because resumes are semistructured, this kind of text miner or analyzer would need to understand the structure of a resume as well as the key words that are of relevance in the business context. The same types of analyses are being applied to social media text, web content, as well as transcripts of audio from videos, podcasts, telephone conversations, and other sources.

PREDICTIVE ANALYTICS

Predictive analytics use statistical analysis as well as data mining techniques such as clustering, classification and segmentation, and pattern detection. Predictive analytics processes are rapidly becoming a necessary business analytics component. Developing predictive models to be used to identify opportunities for increased value is a major part of any business analytics tool stack.

DASHBOARDS AND OTHER VISUALIZATION TECHNIQUES

Information packaging and delivery provides for assembling reports and documents in the best format for the business client and the means for delivering all the information packages to their destinations in a timely manner. An example might be capturing the results of a financial analysis through a series of data mart queries, but then assembling the report in spreadsheet form that can be automatically delivered to a business client's desktop.

Senior executives often refer to *dashboards* and *scorecards* to provide a high-level review of key performance indicator scores. When the indicators suggest issues or opportunities, interactive components allow the executive or manager to drill through the metrics to focus on the source of the opportunity. In turn, alternate aspects of the business analytics strategy can be invoked to suggest alternative actions to take and to continuously monitor the results of taken actions.

The term *visualization* can refer to the different ways that information can be represented for the purposes of quick analysis. Visualization can refer to the ability to create two- and three-dimensional views of numeric data, which can ease the process of looking for unusual data or outliers within a data set, or perhaps summarize a business event or situation that is difficult to express in a text report.

Visualization can also refer to more creative ways of exploring information, such as connectivity relationships between entities, widgets (i.e., components) for building dashboards, displaying attribute intensity (such as how "hot" a product is based on the acceleration of demand in particular regions), and geographical plotting. Visualization tools often accompany other analysis end-user tools, such as OLAP environments.

SYSTEM/NETWORK MANAGEMENT

As in any multitiered hardware and software architecture, the more mundane aspects of network and system management are not to be ignored. Typically, your data consumers will expect the BI team to guarantee certain levels of service, with respect to content delivery as well as timeliness of data warehouse population, propagation of data to the data marts and OLAP servers, and especially system response times and the delivery of reports. After the process has been refined, these service levels may depend on operating a healthy system, which in turn requires staff and tools for system and network management.

The system administration effort incorporates the following topics:

■ **Performance management**, which evaluates system performance and highlights bottlenecks within the environment;

- **Capacity planning**, which is the task of determining how to size the components within the environment;
- **Backup and recovery management**, for backing up data resources and restoring the data after a data loss;
- **Configuration management**, for mapping and designing the network and system layout, managing changes throughout the systems (such as upgrading client software at a large number of client desktop machines), and versioning (such as managing multiple generations of metadata or system configurations);
- **Continual monitoring**, which incorporates tools to keep track of how the system is performing and to generate alerts when performance or correctness issues arise.

DATA SECURITY

Many of your data clients will not be physically located at the site of the data warehouse or even in the same building. Also, there may be sensitive data that is now to be seen by all data consumers. Last, even data that is visible to all internal clients should not be readable by malicious people external to the organization. There is a requirement to integrate a security framework as part of the BI architecture.

A security framework incorporates:

- Hardware and software firewalls for managing network traffic;
- Encryption of data at any point that data is "in the clear," or moving between systems such as data integration, consolidation, or as reports or notifications;
- Intrusion protection, to prevent outsiders from breaking into the system; these applications may include rule-based and behavior-based monitoring to look for suspicious network behavior;
- Policies for managing or restricting client access to specific data sets within the RDBMS, whether on the table, column, or row level; and
- Policies for controlling access to data and security for analytical and interface tools.

Services and System Evolution

It is probable that the expertise required to assemble and run the BI program is not available within your organization. It is also probable that many stages of building the BI infrastructure require expertise no longer needed once the system has been put into production. For these and assorted other reasons, it is probable that you will need to augment your staff with external service providers to help move the BI program along. In this section we look at some of the services external suppliers can provide.

ARCHITECTURE AND INTEGRATION

When assembling a data warehouse and BI architecture, it may be beneficial to bring in consultants who have worked on previous successful BI projects to help architect the overall solution. Frequently the concept of "not invented here" (NIH) cannot only slow down the construction of the environment but also lead to its demise. Remember that the ultimate client is the business partner and that making that business partner satisfied with the program is the ultimate project goal. If that means hiring external consultants to help make it happen—do it!

In terms of data integration services, the numerous data integration and ETL software providers are likely to have supplied software to many similar organizations building similar systems. They may also offer consultative help in assembling the data integration process and making sure that it works.

At the end of the spectrum are service providers willing to import your data and your integration parameters, perform the integration, and then return the reformatted data to you. This may be a viable option when the provider has numerous tools and hardware at its disposal, for which you can eliminate your company's capital investment requirements.

DATA GOVERNANCE

Most transactional or operational business applications use data as a means to accomplish immediate needs, but as more data sets are funneled into a data warehouse and are repurposed for analysis, the needs and expectations for quality, availability, and accessibility change dramatically. However, those in control of the origination of these data sets may not be aware of the importance of observing the collected requirements of all downstream consumers.

In order to ensure that all data needs are met, a data governance program can be instituted to help oversee all aspects of the data life cycle. Creating an organization of data governors and data stewards helps to ensure that data policies are defined, proposed, agreed to, disseminated, and enforced. This helps in aligning expectations across the enterprise, reducing inconsistency, and eliminating costly reconciliations and recalculations. Often organizations will engage external expertise in defining and guiding the deployment of a data governance program.

MIGRATION

Some organizations are interested in instituting a BI program, but their data resources are not in a state that can be properly integrated into a BI environment, either because their environment is in disarray or because their information is embedded in proprietary legacy systems from which it is hard to extract. As a preface to building a BI program, and in conjunction with a business process improvement program, it is useful to migrate older systems into more modern systems that are more amenable to data extraction and manipulation. Because this system or data migration is a one-time deal, bringing in a service provider to assist in the migration process is a reasonable choice.

ANALYTICAL SERVICE PROVIDERS

If the cost of building the infrastructure is too much for your organization, though you still want to exploit a BI environment, then the answer might be an analytical service provider. This is a company that can provide any or all the components of the BI process, ranging from data cleansing and integration services all the way to completely hosted data warehouse and analytical solutions.

TRAINING

There are organizations dedicated to providing training and education in the BI and data warehousing areas. It is worthwhile to make sure that your staff members are properly trained and that the organizations doing the training are recognized as providing the best knowledge when it comes to the techniques, design, and strategies to build successful BI programs. Training should focus on all aspects of the BI program, including data warehouse architecture, data integration, data marts, operational data stores, as well as the tools that are used, such as data extraction and transformation, OLAP systems, and front-end data consumer analysis tools.

STRATEGIC MANAGEMENT

Last, sometimes neither the technical staff nor the business clients are completely aware of the capabilities that exist within the marketplace for providing business analytics. Again, it may be beneficial to engage external consultants familiar with your industry and with the analytical applications that have been built to support your industry.

Management Issues

The most critical management issue to be aware of at this point is that although the conceptual structure of a BI program is relatively straightforward, there are a lot of pieces that need to properly fall into place for the program to be successful. Realize that neither you nor those on your staff can possibly be experts in all the areas necessary to successfully build the program. Also, any time implementation starts to be driven by technology (i.e., "what's cool") rather than by business client needs is a serious red flag signaling that clients' needs are not being addressed at the necessary level. Make sure that the business partners are incorporated into the high-level architecture process as a way of vetting that design for their specific needs.

Additional Considerations

The BI process is a combination of infrastructure and methodology. In this chapter we have tried to enumerate the high-level overview of both infrastructure and process. In the coming chapters we will peel away some layers of the onion to provide insight into those areas that require the most detailed management focus and understanding. But don't let this detract from the importance of the infrastructure details. Use this as an opportunity to explore those other books that treat it in much greater detail.

Business Processes and Information Flow

Business applications exist for *running* the business, while business intelligence (BI) applications report performance measures reflecting how well the business is run. There should be a logical sequence to application development that begins with an assessment of the scope of a particular desired outcome, usually related to an existing (or developing) process employed in operating the business. The result of executing an application should be consistent with the expected results of the business process. For example, within an accounting and finance function, an invoicing application is intended to review customer accounts, identify those accounts for which there are outstanding balances to be paid, generating statements, and sending those statements to the right set of customers. Other side effects may include registering accounting details and the calculation of a monthly usage report, but overall the application is meant to create bills.

Clearly, though, operational and analytical applications share the same information about customers, products, accounts, vendors, staff, and such, so we might expect that the obvious sources of information for the BI applications are the existing transactional or operational systems. And if those applications implement the business processes, it should be simple to use those systems as data sources.

Unfortunately in practice, over time these applications are modified, merged, and expanded, and the high-level mapping of business process to implementation yields to dependence on implementation details. Historical decisions impose artificial constraints on the system.

The approaches used for algorithm and system design map business processes to application control, but often impose constraints on the way that information flows through the processing. And this control structure does not always reflect the true dependencies inherent within the original application, because, for instance, we may have decided to break up a single subprocess into two stages that could truly have been executed in parallel, but an implementation decision may force one stage to precede another.

Over time, as the external perceptions of business processes change, and as the system evolves, technical employee turnover leads to a loss of knowledge about how any application really models the original business problem. Interim decisions have imposed a strict flow of processing control, which may no longer reflect the true data dependence of the application. So when they attempt to dissect the way information is being used within the system, most analysts might throw up their hands in frustration.

As a case in point, I remember a particularly difficult analysis project meant to identify performance optimization opportunities within a processing environment in which 40,000 programs were being run. Our goal was to look for ways to streamline the processing by finding programs that could be run in parallel. In theory it should have been simple to figure this out, because the environment in which these programs were run required manual scheduling. Yet the imposed execution schedule did not reflect the true control and data dependencies among the programs; instead, the schedule was based on the historical clock times at which the critical programs had finished! In the absence of a proper business model describing the control and data flow, this proved to be an exercise in futility.

This chapter provides a high-level glimpse into the intricacy of business process modeling, corresponding issues associated with information flow and data dependencies, and how increasing needs for sharing information demand a renewed focus on how an enterprise information architecture can satisfy transactional, operational, and analytical information needs of the organization.

Analytical Information Needs and Information Flows

A good way to motivate the discussion of business process mapping and information flows is looking at a specific example, such as analyzing customer activities for the purposes of creating customer profiles. Let's say you have been tasked with building a data mart for the purpose of analyzing a customer value portfolio based on all customer interactions, ranging from telephone inquiries to purchases, returns, customer service calls, payment history, and so on. This implies a number of information needs.

First, you must determine what information will be required to do this analysis, and then determine where the data sets will be sourced, as well as how the information is to be extracted, transformed in preparation for integration into the analytical platform, and how that information is to be organized for analysis. Next, you must be able to consider rapid methods for integrating new data sets when it is determined that they are to be included in the analytical environment. Alternatively, you must be able to manage the provision of results (whether that is simple reports or more complex presentation of actionable knowledge) to the business analysts, each of which may be logically or physically situated in a different location.

It would be difficult, if not impossible, to build an analytical system without having a clear understanding of which data sets are potential inputs, what internal models are to be used for representation, where the data sets come from, how those data sets need to be manipulated before they can be imported into a data warehouse, what information is to be provisioned through different subject or content data marts, and what kinds of applications are using that data. More importantly, after the system is built it is critical to have a blueprint of the way that information flows into and out of the system to provide a tracking mechanism to back up any conclusions that are drawn through data analysis. To get a handle on how to manage this environment, it would be useful to have a high-level model of the processes associated with populating and using an analytical environment.

THE VALUE OF MODELING INFORMATION FLOW

Even when considering the creation of an analytical environment, there is value in understanding the ins and outs of the transactional and operational business processes and their corresponding application and information flows. The results of a BI activity are not limited to a company's interaction with customers; those analyses can generate actionable knowledge as a result of manipulating data sets accumulated from a large collection of data producers, such as internal (i.e., within the organization) and external (i.e., cross-company) business applications. As an example, consider a supply-chain interaction between your company and a collection of product suppliers. There is embedded business knowledge that can be derived from examining all details of those interactions, including measuring vendor sensitivity to your requests, response time, methods of delivery, compliance with contractual agreements, and conformance to just-in-time delivery issues. To extract this intelligence we must understand how we have implemented our business applications and determine what data we need to collect and where that information needs to be collected. The information flow model will assist in this determination.

PROCESS DESIGN VERSUS APPLICATION IMPLEMENTATION

Traditionally, implementers are trained in algorithm design to break down each application into a collection of discrete processing stages that can be essentially implemented in isolation. When all the stages are finished, they are combined to form the complete application. But this process of discretizing the construction of applications leads to an assembly line model of information processing in the way that data and partial results are forwarded from one processing stage to another. These processes take data (e.g., a transaction stream or extracted records from multiple data sets) as input and provide some product as output. That can be a physical product (such as invoices to be sent out to customers), a side effect (such as the settlement of a sequence of transactions), or an information product (such as a BI report).

To remedy the eventual effects of this development process, an important part of the methodology of designing and implementing a business application is modeling the business process as a way of guiding the algorithmic implementation. In fact, building this model is the first step in the process of exploiting information. This business process modeling incorporates descriptions of the business objects that interact within the system as well as the interactions between users and those business objects. The same concept holds true for analytical and intelligence applications, where the eventual product is described in terms of analytical use and benefit.

BENEFITS OF THE BUSINESS PROCESS MODEL

There are some major benefits for building this model, such as:

- Understanding an information flow provides logical documentation for the business process;
- The review may uncover additional opportunities for adding value through different kinds of analytical processing;
- Business modeling process helps in understanding business consumer data use; and
- Business modeling helps in communicating user requirements to the implementation team.

When a formal framework is used to describe a process, not only does it ease the translation of user needs into system requirements, it also provides the manager with a high-level view of how control migrates throughout the system and how information flows through the business, both of which in turn help guide the dissection of the problem into implementable components.

More generally, an information flow, as embodied as part of a business process model, provides the following benefits:

- **Development road map**. Identifying how information is used and diffused helps direct the development of interfacing between the discretized execution components as well as tracking development against the original requirements.
- **Operational road map**. When the application is in production, the model provides a description of how any analytical data sets are populated as well as a launch point for isolating problems in operation. It can also be used to track and isolate data quality problems, map workflow and control back to information use, and expose opportunities for optimization.
- **Management control**. This model provides a way to see how information propagates across the organization, to identify gaps in information use (or reuse), and to expose the processes involved in information integration.
- **Consideration of return on investment**. This allows the manager to track the use of information, the amount of value-adding processing required, and the amount of error prevention and correction required to add value and to relate the eventual business value back to the costs associated with generating that business value.

Information Processing and Information Flow

The critical dependencies between successful business processes and the use of information effectively demonstrate the need to understand how information flows through processes and how information is used to support those processes. Mapping data lineage across the process will shed light on where decision steps can be improved by actionable knowledge. In this section we look at a number of different kinds of processing paradigms and how they reflect the application's implementation of the business activities.

TRANSACTION PROCESSING

Operations in a transaction processing system are interactions between a user and a computer system where there is the perception of an immediate response from the system to the user's requests. A commonly encountered example of transaction processing is the use of an automated teller machine (ATM), as shown in Figure 6.1.

Although there is an appearance of a monolithic system that responds to user requests, behind the scenes each interaction may involve a large number of interdependent systems. The concept of a transaction actually incorporates this reality: A transaction is really a set of operations grouped together as a unit of work, where no

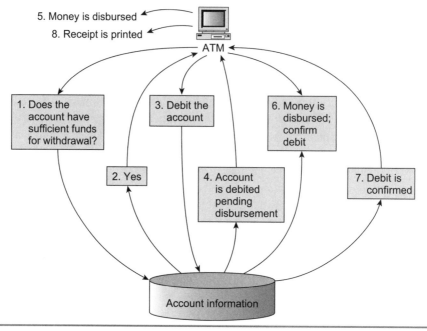

Figure 6.1 A transaction-based information flow.

individual operation takes its long-term effect unless all the operations can take effect. So, using the ATM example, before the bank allows the ATM to disburse cash, the user's account balance must be queried to see if there are sufficient funds, the ATM must be checked to see if it has enough cash to satisfy the request, the user's account must then be debited, and the cash can be disbursed. Yet if the result of any of these subsidiary operations indicates that servicing the request is infeasible, all the operations must be rolled back—you wouldn't want the bank to debit your account without giving you the cash, nor would the bank want the cash to be disbursed without debiting your account. In this case the information flow follows the thread of control as it passes through the individual interaction associated with each transaction.

Operational Processing

We will use the term *operational processing* to refer to a system that makes use of computers to control a process. These controlled processes can be related to automated activities or might even be used to guide workflows such as opening a bank account, picking and packaging materials for shipment, or performing diagnostic tests for your car.

As an example, an automated manufacturing line may have multiple machine components, each requiring system control instructions based on its internal operational requirements as well as depending on information inputs from other interconnected machine components within the entire system. For example, a potato chip manufacturing process contains a series of machines, such as a washer, a slicer, a fryer, a sorter, a flavor enhancer, and a packaging machine, each of which helps transform a potato into a collection of potato chips.

In this example, there is a lot of information required at multiple processing locations throughout the system to guarantee continuous, managed control of the system. Data about the individual interactions between sequential stages as well as systemic data need to be propagated to multiple controllers. To continue our potato chip factory example, each processing stage requires information about the flow of (unfinished) product from the previous stages. In addition, certain events will trigger auxiliary control operations (e.g., the seasoning hopper volume falls below the required amount, triggering an alert and a pause in the assembly line). And global events can also trigger actions (e.g., the cooking temperature exceeds a safe limit, triggering a complete line shutdown).

Operational process information flows are likely to connect heavy sequential operational processing augmented by lightweight interconnections for sharing information.

BATCH PROCESSING

In contrast with transaction processing, batch processing takes collections of sequences of similar operations that are to be executed in *batches* (hence the name). Although both transaction processing and batch processing execute a series of operations, batch processing differs from transaction processing in terms of information flow in the granularity of application of each processing stage. A batch processing application is more likely to apply each processing stage to a set of data instances as a whole and then push the result to the next processing stage.

As an example, a company might accumulate transaction-based sales orders during the day but process those orders and prepare order fulfillment as a batch process at night. The fulfillment processing aggregates order line items by customer, determines packaging requirements, generates pick lists that instruct the warehouse workers what items are to be selected for each shipment, generates shipping labels with appropriate shipping vendor data, updates inventory totals, and generates orders to restock inventory, among other operations.

Batch processing information flows typically convey heavy data payloads between multiple processing stages, each of which performs a single component of the overall unit of work for the data collection.

Analytical processing involves the interaction between analysts and collections of aggregated data that may have been reformulated into alternate representational forms as a means for improved analytical performance. In this case, the information flow model most likely will take on two aspects: the flow of information into the analytical processing environment from its suppliers and the flow of information from the analytical processing system to its users. The first flow is likely to be more of an operational flow, in which data sets may be extracted and moved in large chunks to a staging area where those data sets move through different processing stages. And despite the BI aspect of the users' interactions, the information flow between the data mart clients may resemble a transactional information flow, with multiple analysts executing sequences of queries, although here they are less likely to be true transactions.

The Information Flow Model

While business process models are intended to capture the details of the tasks and interactions with a process, it is useful to augment the business process model with the corresponding information flow. This will expose how both information and control are shared and propagated through the business application. It is useful to have a method for describing the way data propagates through a system, and this section describes some aspects of a high-level information flow model.

An information flow model distinguishes the discrete processing stages within the process, describes how information flows through that system, characterizes the kinds of data items that flow through the process, and captures the type or method of data access. This model is valuable because it provides a basis for distinguishing between data dependencies, control dependencies, and artificially imposed implementation dependencies, which in turn can lead toward flow optimization, identification of bottlenecks, finding locations for insertion of data validation monitors, inserting data collection points for later analysis, and opportunities for increased business analysis points.

INFORMATION FLOW: PROCESSING STAGES

In an information flow model, we distinguish discrete processing stages. Although the following list is by no means complete, we can characterize each information flow stage as one of these classes.

- **Supply**, representing external data suppliers provide
- **Acquisition**, representing the point at which existing data instances are acquired

- **Transformation**, representing the point where a data instance is modified to conform to another processing stage's expected representative format
- **Creation**, the point at which new data instances are created
- **Process**, representing points at which system state is modified as a result of input data
- **Store**, in which a data instance is stored in a persistent system
- **Packaging**, in which data is collated, aggregated, and/or summarized
- **Switch/route**, where a set of rules is used to determine where and how to route data instances
- **Decision point**, which is a point at which a data consumer (real or automated) is solicited for a decision
- **Deliver**, the delivery point for data that is meant to be consumed
- **Consume**, the presentation point for information presented by the system

INFORMATION FLOW: DIRECTED CHANNELS

Data moves between stages through *directed information channels*. A directed information channel is a pipeline indicating the flow of information from one processing stage to another, indicating the direction in which data flows. Our model is represented by the combination of the processing stages connected by directed information channels. Once we have constructed the flow model, we assign names to each of the stages and the channels.

DATA PAYLOAD CHARACTERISTICS

The last aspect of an information flow model is the description of the data items that are propagated between any pair of processing stages. The characteristics include the description of the information structure (i.e., columnar attribution), the size of the data instances, and the cardinality of the data set (i.e., the number of records communicated). More sophisticated models may be attributed with business rules governing aspects such as directional flow, validation, and enhancement as well as processing directives.

Practical Use

This section provides a few examples where value can be derived from modeling business process and information flow.

INFORMATION VALUATION

Previous chapters have dealt with the concept of deriving value from the use of information. A business process model can help guide the determination of metrics used for measuring value improvements in relation to data use, as well as identifying the locations for the insertion of monitors to collect those measurements. For example, if we want to measure how much a certain data set is used, we may want to tag the data at its insertion point into the information flow and to insert monitors at delivery points to check for the tagged item to tally usage statistics.

ROOT CAUSE ANALYSIS

One example of the use of an information flow model is in identifying the procedural root cause of a recognized problem. The effects of a process failure might manifest themselves at different stages within an information flow, perhaps at different data consumption stages. But what appears to be multiple problems may all be related to a single point of failure from earlier in the processing. By identifying a set of information expectations and creating validation rules that can be imposed at the entry and exit from each processing stage, we can trace back through the information flow model to the stage at which the issue first appeared. At that point we can follow forward through the information flow to find all processing stages that might be affected by this problem. Fixing the problem at the source will have a beneficial effect across the board, because all subsequent manifestations should be eliminated.

OPERATIONAL PERFORMANCE IMPROVEMENT

Another use of an information flow model is to gauge both the strict control and data dependencies within the system, and the performance behavior for transferring data between processing stages as well as processing at each stage. An information flow model will show the true dependencies, which can then expose opportunities for exploiting task parallelism at the processing stage level. In other words, if there are two processing stages that are control independent (i.e., neither stage requires the completion of the other in order for it to begin) and data independent (i.e., neither stage's input is directly or indirectly derived from the other), then those two stages can be executed at the same time.

Large data set transfers also form bottlenecks, as do computationally intensive processing stages. If there are no data dependencies associated with the data flow or associated with each processing stage, then the business and information flow model can be used to explore opportunities for exploiting data parallelism. For example, if there is a large data transfer between two processing stages, it may be of value to break up the transferred data set into chunks that can each be transferred over multiple physical input/output (I/O) channels.

Modeling Frameworks

Conceptual business process and information flow modeling can be actualized in different ways. In this section we'll explore some formal frameworks used for information and activity modeling, although these are just a sampling of the many frameworks available.

INTEGRATED DEFINITION LANGUAGE

One early set of approaches to process modeling looked at a relatively high level abstraction for modeling activities. Integrated Definition language (IDEF) is a modeling language designed to describe functional processing and information flows. It comprises two descriptive standards: IDEF0, which is used to describe activity models, and IDEF1X for describing data models. Although IDEF was mostly used for system requirement analysis and workflow modeling, the IDEF language can be used for modeling information flow.

The basic IDEF0 activity modeling object in an IDEF model is referred to as an ICOM, an acronym for "input, control, output, and mechanism." For modeling information flow, each ICOM object would represent a processing stage, with the input(s) and output(s) representing information channels and the control and mechanism describing the gating factors controlling the activity as well as the activity that takes place within the processing stage. The data that is being propagated along the inputs and outputs within the model is characterized using IDEF1X; each IDEF1X object describes an entity being modeled as well as relationships to other entities.

A complete system model, which embeds the information flow, is constructed as the outputs of one ICOM are connected to the inputs to other ICOMs. This sequential ordering of ICOMs exposes the operational dependencies inherent in the process and highlights the data dependencies. In addition, we can represent a processing stage at a high level and then decompose that stage into multiple ICOMS at a lower level, providing a hierarchical view through which the system may be drilled down.

USE CASE MODELING

Use case analysis, a process described by Ivar Jacobson in his book, *Object-Oriented Software Engineering*, was designed to understand the nature of interaction between users of a system and the internal requirements of that system. A use case model specifies the function of a system and describes what the system should offer from the user's perspective, using three components:

- **Actors**, representing the roles that users play;
- **Use cases**, representing what the users do with the system; and
- **Triggers**, representing events that initiate use cases.

Whereas a use case describes a specific way of using the system by performing part of the function, a use case also represents a course of events that takes place when an actor interacts with the system. In the use case model, a trigger (which may occur as a result of an input data structure or an actor requesting an action, such as a report, but providing no input data, time, or some internal database or system event) is an event that initiates a use case. The collection of use cases constitutes a specification of the system. Embedded in the use case model is the conceptual business process model, although because the model is meant to help drive the requirements gathering for implementation, it may not be sufficient to represent the actual information flow model we discussed earlier.

UNIFIED MODELING LANGUAGE

As a successor to use cases, the Unified Modeling Language (UML) was developed as part of the Object Management Group's (OMG's) model-driven architecture. UML is a very rich descriptive framework that allows analysts to describe many aspects of system architecture. UML integrates some of the best notions of previous formalisms, including use cases.

UML can be used to develop business process and information flow models, especially because it has a facility for describing system behavior. In particular, state machines and activity graphs can be used to model process stage interaction. In a *state machine*, each state represents a situation where some condition is true. When a condition changes, the system is represented by another state; this behavior is modeled as a transition from one state to another within the state machine, which ultimately summarizes the entire system behavior as transitions between multiple states within the system.

An *activity graph* is a special kind of state machine that models a computational process in terms of how control flow and object flow affect transitions between states. It is the activity graph that could be best used for modeling information flow.

BUSINESS PROCESS MODEL AND NOTATION (BPMN)

For readers interested in a more comprehensive methodology for modeling business process flows, there is the Business Process Model and Notation, or BPMN, which provides a rich and generally broad graphical notation for modeling and representing business processes. The notation is intended for describing many aspects of the business architecture, corresponding system architectures, and for sharing that information in a way that is intuitive to business users but also maps to execution languages that can guide system architecture design and development. The Object Management Group (OMG) currently maintains BPMN.

As a framework that has evolved from a variety of concepts for business process modeling, BPMN encompasses a number of formalisms to help business analysts define and then refine business processes and help the data architects and system designers translate those concepts into an implementation. BPMN is intended to capture aspects of organizational structure, functional interactions, and data models, and for our purposes, it can be used to show how information flows among different functions and how different data artifacts are associated with business activities.

BPMN's basic categories of elements include items that are used to create simple process diagrams, including:

- Flow objects (events, activities, gateways);
- Connecting objects (for process sequence flow, message flow, and association);
- Artifacts (data objects, groups, and annotation); and
- Swim lanes.

For additional details, consult the OMG's BPMN web site at www.bpmn.org.

Management Issues

Probably the most critical management issue associated with business process and information flow modeling is the disconnect between the representation of the model and the actual implementation. Even with BPMN as an emerging standard, one critical issue is that despite the availability of tools for developing models using any of the different modeling notations, the output of these tools most likely will not be in a form that can either be integrated with legacy systems or future systems without a lot of external effort. In addition, even if these tools are used to generate code for actual use, there is little support for what could be referred to as the *roundtrip*, where generated code is modified or retooled for some reason but where that modification cannot be recaptured in the original modeling framework.

These issues imply that without a lot of investment in software infrastructure and management, the utility of a business process flow model is limited to management purposes, and positive input must be made by the savvy manager to relate application development and operation back to the model. This means that there must be frequent synchronization between the documented model and the actual system itself.

Another issue is the sheer size of these modeling frameworks. Because of the attempt at converging on one modeling framework, attempts at standards include so much material that it is unlikely that you would ever be proficient in all aspects of the modeling language, which adds to the risk of using any particular choice. Also, the learning curve for these modeling languages may be quite steep, requiring an investment of time and money in training staff.

Deeper Dives

The modeling of how information flows through the different implemented business processes in an organization can provide detailed information about how the business is run. In turn, this information can be captured as virtual metadata that can be fed into later analytical contexts. This flow of information can help in the determination of what data sets are to be incorporated into the enterprise data warehouse that will eventually feed the analytical applications. It also identifies the best locations within the information flow from which the data should be extracted.

The use of development tools to augment the documentation of information flow (and general workflow) is a good idea, although it is preferable to use tools that do not rely on proprietary formats and that can export their representations to other knowledge management tools. This book's bibliography contains some references that are useful in learning more about business processes and information flow.

Data Requirements Analysis

Introduction

When the key stakeholders in the organization have agreed to pursue a business intelligence (BI), reporting, and analytics strategy, it is difficult to resist the urge to immediately begin evaluating tools for the purposes of acquisition and deployment. The process of acquiring BI tools acquisition is well-defined, with clearly-defined goals, tasks, and measurable outcomes. The problem, though, is that while a successful acquisition process gives the appearance of progress, when you are done, all you have is a set of tools. Without the data to analyze, your reporting and analysis still has to wait.

So how do you determine what data sets are going to be subjected to analysis? Since the BI methodology advocated in this book concentrates on the business expectations for results, our motivation for determining the data requirements should be based on the analyses to be performed. Performance measures will be calculated using the information that reflects the way the business is being run. These data sets are typically those used to capture the operational/transactional aspects of the different business processes. While some organizations already use these data sets to establish baseline measures of performance, there may be additional inputs and influencers that impact the ability to get visibility into opportunities for improvement, such as geographic data, demographic data, as well as a multitude of additional data sets (draw from internal data sources as well as external data sources) as well as other data feeds and streams that may add value.

Identifying the data requirements for your business analytics needs will guide the BI process beyond the selection of end-user tools. Since data acquisition, transformation, alignment, and delivery all factor into the ability to provide actionable knowledge, we must recognize that data selection, acquisition, and integration are as important (if not more important) as acquiring tools in developing the business analytics capability. In this chapter we will consider the business uses of information to frame the process for engaging the downstream data consumers and solicit their input. Their needs for measures to help improve performance will guide the definition of data requirements as well as specify the suitability criteria for selection of data sources.

Business Uses of Information

As we have discussed in Chapter 3, there is a wide variety and number of consumers of BI and analytics across the organization. Some of these consumers are more casual than others when it comes to reporting and analytics, but one common theme among the different types is the use of the information to inform and influence decision-making. In essence, the motivating factors for employing reporting and analytics are to empower users at all levels of decision-making across the management hierarchy:

■ Strategic use for informing decisions associated with corporate mission and vision, setting corporate business objectives, monitoring organizational "macro" behavior, and business decisions affecting the achievement of corporate objectives;
■ Tactical use driving decisions associated with operations such as supplier management, logistics, inventory, customer service, marketing and sales;
■ Team-level use, influencing decisions driving collaboration, efficiency, and optimization across the working environment; and
■ Individual use, such as results that feed real-time operational activities such as delivery routing, call center interactive scripts, or web site offer placement.

The structure, level of aggregation, and delivery of this information is relevant to the needs of the target users, and some examples, provided in Table 7.1, include:

TABLE 7.1 Sample Business Analyses and Their Methods of Delivery

Level of Data Aggregation	Users	Delivery
Rolled-up summaries	Executive staff	Dashboards or scorecards
Aggregated management data	Mid-level and senior managers	Summary stats, alerts, queries, and scorecards
Structured analytic data	Special purpose—marketing, business process analysis	Data mining, OLAP, analytics, etc.
Detailed operational data	Front line employees	Alerts, KPIs, queries, drill-down (on demand)
Aggregate values	Individual contributors	Alerts, messaging

- Queries and reports support operational managers and decision requirements;
- Scorecards support management at various levels and usually support measurement and tracking of local objectives;
- Dashboards normally target senior management and provide a mechanism for tracking performance against key indicators.

Metrics: Facts, Qualifiers, and Models

Performance monitoring and improvement both rely on measuring and reporting the scores for metrics used to quantify the effectiveness of particular processes and the value of their outcomes. Although metrics scores are used in different ways based on the business processes being monitored, there are certain characteristics that are common to the concept of a metric. At the most basic level, a metric represents a quantification of a single score to answer a specific business question, and the base level metric, in many cases, can be a simple aggregate value such as a count or an average. In turn, individual metrics can be grouped together into higher-level scores computed as functions of the individual component measurements.

Every metric is intended to contribute in answering business questions. A prerequisite to defining data warehouse models or building a reporting system is engaging the business users to help in identifying, clarifying, and documenting specific business data needs for the system. This requires interviewing key system stakeholders and customers to clarify business processes and needs as a prelude to synthesizing the requirements for the system model. This incorporates reviewing, analyzing, and integrating system information and stakeholder interview data to create key artifacts such as a fact/qualifier matrix that will drive the definition of the model, the determination of data sources to populate the model, and the processes for presenting metric information back to the business users.

The Fact/Qualifier Matrix

Without loss of generalization, let's initially consider the base level metric and enumerate key attributes that are relevant for capturing the performance measures critical for answering the business questions in a fact/qualifier matrix. A fact/qualifier matrix is a standard data warehouse development tool designed to organize specific business information needs into a format that aids in developing relational and multidimensional data structures. Facts represent specific business questions or discrete items of information that are tracked or managed, and are generally items that can be counted or measured such as quantity or volume. Qualifiers represent conditions or dimensions that are used to filter or organize your facts. Qualifiers include items such as time or geographic area.

In a fact/qualifier matrix, all business facts are listed down the left-hand column and all possible qualifier dimensions are listed across the columns. An entry at any intersection identifies the qualifying dimensions used to filter, organize, or aggregate the associated fact data.

As an example, business questions like "How many widgets have been shipped by size by warehouse each week by color?" and "What are the total sales for widgets by size each week for each salesperson by region?" provide insight into the progress of a metadata registration process as part of a performance management activity. The fact/qualifier matrix will specify the business facts that are expected to be measured—in this case, "the number of widgets shipped" and "total sales of widgets shipped," and the specific dimensional qualifiers are "size," "color," "week," "warehouse," "salesperson," and "region" (Table 7.2). Subsequent iterations of the analysis process may derive greater precision for some of these

TABLE 7.2 Example Fact/Qualifier Matrix

	Facts	
	Number of Widgets	Total Sales
Qualifiers		
Size	X	X
Warehouse	X	
Color	X	
Week	X	X
Salesperson		X
Region		X

qualifiers, such as breaking out the week qualifier into time frames with different levels of granularity (such as daily, hourly, yearly, etc.).

Documentation for the facts and their qualifiers may already exist, but restructuring those requirements within a fact/qualifier matrix provides some benefits:

- It provides a logical structure for capturing business user requirements.
- It provides a standardized way to present the requirements back to the business users for validation.
- It enables the analyst to review the collected business requirements and determine if there are any overlapping facts or common dimensional qualifiers.
- It guides the analysts in identifying the data sources that can be used to populate the metrics data model.

THE METRICS MODEL

The fact/qualifier matrix provides guidance for developing how the metrics are used, combined, or rolled up to provide summarization and drill-through. For example, each presented score can either be a base metric score, consisting of a single quantification of a requested qualified fact, or a qualified score computed as a function of the weighted scores associated with other metrics. These scores are often accompanied by other relevant metadata such as units of measure, classification, and evaluation criteria (or thresholds) for reporting satisfaction of business user expectations.

To continue our example, the business user might be interested in more than just knowing the number of widgets shipped. Instead, that manager might want to ensure that each warehouse is shipping a minimum level of 20 units of each size and color of widget every week, and anticipating shipping more than 30 units of each size of widget each week. In this case, the metric is the count (broken out along the defined dimensions), and the evaluation criteria might be specified in terms of a three-tiered scoring:

- Green if the number is greater than or equal to 30;
- Yellow if the number is greater than or equal to 20 and less than 30; and
- Red if the number is less than 20.

Metrics defined at a higher aggregate level will compose the results of the incorporated metric scores. In our example, the cumulative score for all the warehouses for each widget size shipped is the sum of the number of widget units shipped for each size, divided by the number of warehouses. In other words, the cumulative average reflects the higher level of performance, and we can use the same thresholds for scoring as at the lower level.

Since metrics and scores associated with compound metrics are to be reported to the end-client, the designer must enable the definition of "buckets" or categories for the alignment of metric scores into the right collection. For example, we might group the logistics performance metrics together into one category, product-oriented performance metrics (such as color and size) into another category, and the sales metrics into another. This effectively defines a taxonomy structure for metrics. However, we must be aware that some metrics may be suitable to support more than one hierarchy, so the model's means for categorization must not restrict the inclusion of a metric into a single logical bucket.

The metrics model must be able to support the capture of both the base-level metrics (pure counts) and the more complex compound metrics composed of lower levels. This suggests a model that supports a hierarchy that captures the parent-child relationship as well as the categories associated with the eventual reporting scheme. Doing so enables the end-client to review the top-level report, but also enables the drill-through capability that allows the analyst to seek out root causes exposed through the reporting. As long as the model captures the score for each metric as well as the evaluation criteria within each hierarchy, the analyst can drill down through the hierarchy levels to determine where the specific measures indicate an opportunity for operational improvement or for instituting alternate policies to improve performance.

What is Data Requirements Analysis?

Determining the requirements for data sets used to source a reporting and analytics program uses a top-down approach that emphasizes business-driven needs. This approach not only establishes boundaries around the types of data concepts necessary to satisfy the users' expectations, it scopes the discussions so that the interview and requirements solicitation steps are conducted in a way that ensures relevance of the identified requirements while keeping a continual eye out to ensure feasibility of execution.

The process incorporates data discovery and assessment in the context of explicitly qualified business data consumer needs. Having identified the data requirements, candidate data sources are determined, their quality can be assessed, and their usability can be evaluated using criteria such as those discussed later in this chapter. The data requirements analysis process consists of these phases:

- Identify the business contexts.
- Conduct stakeholder interviews.
- Synthesize expectations and requirements.
- Develop source-to-target mappings.

IDENTIFY THE BUSINESS CONTEXT

The business contexts associated with data reuse, creation of performance measures, and consumption of analytical results scope the discussion of what data sets will

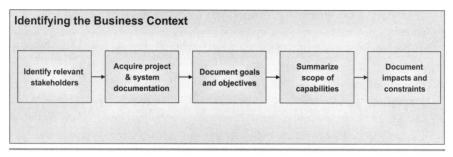

Figure 7.1   Identifying the business context.

contribute to the reporting and analytics framework. Conferring with enterprise architects to understand where system boundaries intersect with lines of business will provide a good starting point for determining how (and under what circumstances) data sets are used.

Figure 7.1 shows the steps in this process:

1. **Identify relevant business data consumers**. These stakeholders may be identified through a review of existing system documentation or may be identified through discussions with business analysts, enterprise analysts, and enterprise architects. As suggested by the wide range of different kinds of BI users, the pool of relevant stakeholders may include business program sponsors, business application owners, business process managers, senior management, information consumers, system owners, as well as front-line staff members who are the beneficiaries of reporting and analytics.

2. **Acquire documentation**. The BI analyst must become familiar with overall goals and objectives of the target information platforms to provide context for determining types of data sources and assessing whether the specific information within those data sets can meet defined requirements. To do this, it is necessary to review existing artifacts that provide details about the consuming systems, requiring a review of project charters, project scoping documents, requirements, design, and testing documentation. At this stage, the analysts should accumulate any available documentation artifacts that can help in determining downstream use of aggregated reports and such.

3. **Document goals and objectives**. Determining existing performance measures and success criteria provide a baseline representation of high-level system requirements for summarization and categorization. Conceptual data models may exist that can provide further clarification and guidance regarding the functional and operational expectations of the collection of target systems.

4. **Summarize scope of capabilities**. Document the presumed functionality and capabilities of the systems feeding the BI function, as well as providing details

of functional requirements and target user profiles. When combined with other context knowledge, you can create a business context diagram or document that summarizes and illustrates the key data flows, functions, and capabilities of the downstream information consumers.

5. **Document impacts and constraints**. Constraints are conditions that affect or prevent the implementation of system functionality, while impacts are potential changes to characteristics of the environment in order to accommodate the implementation of system functionality. Identifying and understanding all relevant impacts and constraints to the target systems is critical, because the impacts and constraints often define, limit, and frame the data controls and rules that will be managed as part of the data quality environment. Not only that, source to target mappings may be impacted by constraints or dependencies associated with the selection of candidate data sources.

This process allows the data analysts to capture the expectations for the high-level functions of downstream systems, and how organizational data is expected to meet those systems' needs. They will also document any identified impacts or constraints of the targeted systems, such as legacy system dependencies, security and protection policies, definitions of key reference domains used that might populate hierarchies within identified dimensions, global reference tables, existing standards and definitions, and data retention policies. This process will also provide a preliminary view of global reference data requirements that may impact source data element selection and transformation rules. Lastly, this process can help identify characterizations of dimensionality that already exist in the organization associated with time, geography, precision of transactions and other events, as well as availability of potential data sources, frequency of updates, and approaches for data extractions and transformations.

CONDUCT INFORMATION CONSUMER INTERVIEWS

Reviewing documentation provides a snapshot of what is perceived to be true about available data sets within (and sometimes outside of) the enterprise, and more information can be accumulated from the business users who will be the customers for reporting and analytics. This task is to conduct conversations with the key information consumers and decision-makers and solicit their input for what types of metrics they seek to report, and how those metrics can be articulated as specific measures that can be calculated using available data concepts.

Figure 7.2 shows how the process consists of these five steps:

1. **Identify candidates and review roles**. Review the general roles and responsibilities of the interview candidates to guide and focus the interview questions within their specific business process (and associated application) contexts.

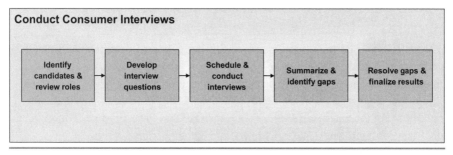

Figure 7.2 Engage the stakeholders and consumers.

2. **Develop interview questions**. The next step in interview preparation is to create a set of questions designed to elicit the business information requirements. The formulation of questions can be driven by the context information collected during the initial phase of the process. There are two broad categories of questions—directed questions, which are specific and aimed at gathering details about the functions and processes within a department or area, and open-ended questions, which are less specific and often lead to dialogue and conversation. They are more focused on trying to understand the information requirements for operational management and decision making.

3. **Schedule and conduct interviews**. Interviews with executive champions and stakeholders should be scheduled earlier, since their time is difficult to secure. Information obtained during executive interviews provides additional clarity regarding overall corporate goals and objectives and may result in refinement of subsequent interviews. Interviews should be scheduled at a location where the participants will not be interrupted.

4. **Summarize and identify gaps**. Review and organize the notes from the interviews, including the attendees list, general notes, and answers to the specific questions. By considering the business definitions that were clarified related to various aspects of the business (especially in relation to known reference data dimensions such as time, geography, regulatory, etc.), we continue to formulate a fuller determination of system constraints and data dependencies.

5. **Resolve gaps and finalize results**. Completion of the initial interview summaries will identify additional questions or clarifications required from the interview candidates. At that point the data quality practitioner can cycle back with the interviewee to resolve outstanding issues.

Once any outstanding questions have been answered, the interview results can be combined with the business context information to enable the data quality analyst to define specific steps and processes for the request for and documentation of business information requirements.

SYNTHESIZE REQUIREMENTS

The notes from the interviews coupled with the collected documents provides the pallet from which the results can be synthesized to shed light on the necessary metadata concepts and data expectations in relation to existing business process flows. The analysts will review the expected use of business information (largely in the context of the business questions to be answered) to identify named data concepts and types of aggregates, and associated data element characteristics.

Synthesizing requirements, shown in Figure 7.3, is a sequence of steps:

1. **Document information workflow.** Create an information flow model that depicts the sequence, hierarchy, and timing of process activities. The goal is to use this workflow to review data touch points and corresponding structures and semantics to ensure that the data items are consistent for consolidation, aggregation, and subsequent reporting.
2. **Identify required data elements.** Reviewing the business questions will help segregate the required (or commonly used) data concepts ("party," "product," "agreement," etc.) from the characterizations or aggregation categories ("grouped by geographic region"). This drives the determination of required reference data and potential master data items.
3. **Specify required facts.** As described earlier in this chapter, the facts represent specific pieces of business information that are to be tracked, managed, used, shared, or forwarded to a reporting and analytics facility in which they are subjected to measurement and aggregation as part of performance metrics. In addition, we must document data characteristics that represent qualifiers or dimensions that are used to filter or organize your facts (such as time or location). The metadata for these data concepts and facts will be captured within a metadata repository for further analysis and resolution.
4. **Harmonize data element semantics.** Use a metadata glossary to capture the business terms associated with the business work flows. Reference metadata can be organized and classified hierarchically to support the composition of

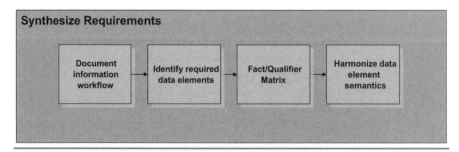

Figure 7.3 Synthesizing requirements.

any aggregated or analyzed data concepts. Glossaries may be used to consolidate and harmonize the core set of terms across the enterprise. When possible, use existing metadata repositories to capture the approved organization definition.

Some issues can be avoided as part of the harmonization process by formulating agreed-to definitions for commonly used terms. This is particularly true when aggregations are applied to counts of objects that may share the same name, but don't really share the same meaning. Harmonization will help eliminate inconsistencies in reporting, analyses, and operational activities, and increase the level of trust in resulting reports and analyses.

DEVELOP SOURCE-TO-TARGET MAPPING

The objective of this process is to both identify the data elements in source data systems that are potentially incorporated into analytical processing and understand any requirements for transformations or alignments to be performed. These modifications may be needed to retain semantic alignment when data sets are merged from multiple sources. At the same time, the analysts must determine the level of atomic data needed for drill-down to satisfy downstream user needs for more precise investigation or analysis.

These transformations will specify how upstream data elements are modified for downstream consumption, as well as business rules applied as part of the information flow. This process will also help link source data elements to shared reference metadata that can be standardized for analysis and for presentation purposes.

Figure 7.4 shows the sequence of these steps:

1. **Propose target models for extraction and sharing**. Evaluate the catalog of identified data elements and look for those that are frequently created, referenced, or modified. By considering both the conceptual and the logical structures of these data elements and their enclosing data sets, the analyst can identify

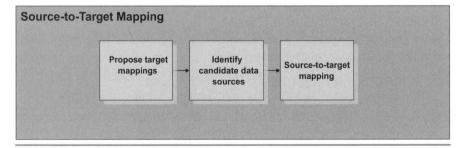

Figure 7.4   Source-to-target mapping.

potential differences and anomalies inherent in the metadata, and then resolve any critical anomalies across data element sizes, types, or formats. These will form the core of a data sharing model, which represents the data elements to be taken from the sources, potentially transformed, validated, and then provided to the consuming applications. These models may evolve into a unified view for virtualized data services in a data federation environment.

2. **Identify candidate data sources**. Consult the data management teams to review the candidate data sources containing the identified data elements, and review the collection of facts needed by the reporting and analysis applications. For each fact, determine if it corresponds to a defined data concept or data element, if it exists in any data sets in the organization, if it is a computed value (and if so, what are the data elements that are used to compute that value), and then document each potential data source.

3. **Develop source-to-target mappings**. Since this analysis should provide enough input to specify which candidate data sources can be extracted, the next step is to consider how that data is to be transformed into a common representation that is then normalized in preparation for consolidation. The consolidation processes collect the sets of objects and prepare them for populating the consuming applications. During this step, the analysts enumerate which source data elements contribute to target data elements, specify the transformations to be applied, and note where it relies on standardizations and normalizations revealed during earlier stages of the process.

Assessing Suitability

If we have executed these processes properly, we should essentially have a catalog of source data sets from which to select, access, extract, and transform data for our BI environment. However, not all data sets are created equally. Or rather, not all data values are created with the same level of oversight, validity, and ultimately, usability. Meeting downstream consumer requirements must also factor in a characterization of the data sets' usability to inform the decision-makers about the suitability and reliability.

Here are some concepts to keep in mind when identifying data requirements and assessing suitability of data sources:

- **Measured variables**. Providing performance reports and scorecards or dashboards with specific performance measures implies the collection of information needed for the computation of reported variables; enumerating those calculated variables is the first task, as the dependencies will be tracked backward to identify which data sources can satisfy the needs of the downstream consumers. Consider

whether the selected data sources can adequately compose the calculations necessary to deliver the expected rolled-up reported variables.

- **Qualifiers and hierarchies**. Having already identified the variables to be
scrutinized, the next step is to determine whether the available data sets can
provision the different ways that key facts could be sliced and diced. For
example, if we'd like to monitor customer complaints as our main measured variable, there might be an interest in understanding customer complaints by time
period, by geographic location, by customer type, by customer income, and so
on. This means not only ensuring that criteria are differentiated from each other,
but also that any relationships and hierarchies within each qualification facet can
be provided. For example, geographical regions can be mapped at a high level of
precision ("ZIP+4") or low-level precision ("continent"), and can be inclusive
or nested (for example, you can drill through country to state to county to town-
ship to ZIP area to ZIP+4).

- **Business process dependencies**. It is critical to be aware of the business
processes that create or update the dependent variables and know where those
dependent variables are stored and managed. Since identifying the business
processes that touch the dependent variables is useful in identifying candidate
source systems, it is important to maintain awareness of any changes to the
processes that might modify the structure or semantics of those variables that
might impact the analytical environment.

- **Data accessibility and availability**. Just because dependent variables are
managed within siloed business applications, the data instances themselves are
not always available for use. You must not only find the candidate data sources,
but also determine any limitations on their availability and accessibility, and this
is a measure of feasibility of use for analytical purposes. For example, the data
sets may be classified as "protected personal information," in which case there
may be a need for additional security techniques to be applied to ensure that
private data is not inadvertently exposed, those seeing the data have the appropriate access rights, and that in the event of an exposure, the right encryption
is applied to reduce data usability.

- **Computations**. Knowing the desired measures also drives the determination of
ways those measures are calculated, and this poses a number of questions about
capability, precision, and redundancy of those calculations, such as:
  - What are the inputs for the calculation?
  - How many inputs are needed?
  - Are there direct calculations or are there aggregations or reductions (sum as
  averages or sums) involved?
  - What are the further dependent variables? For example "total corporate sales"
  may be accumulated from the totals for each area of the business, each of
  which in turn related to specific product family sales.

Not only does this require understanding how the measures are rolled up and computed, it also exposes the chain of dependent variables looking back through the information production flow.

Summary

This provides a good starting point in the data requirements analysis process that can facilitate the data selection process. By the end of these exercises (which may require multiple iterations), you may be able to identify source applications whose data subsystems contain instances that are suitable for integration into a business analytics environment. Yet there are still other considerations: just because the data sets are available and accessible does not mean they can satisfy the analytics consumers' needs, especially if the data sets are not of a high enough level of quality. It is therefore also critically important to assess the data quality expectations and apply a validation process to determine if the quality levels of candidate data sources can meet the collected downstream user needs, and this will be covered in subsequent chapters.

Data Warehouses and the Technical Business Intelligence Architecture

Introduction

Production application systems are designed to execute business transactions or manage operational systems, but are not designed to support reporting and ad hoc queries, and certainly are not engineered to support the kinds of analytical applications that most organizations now seek to deploy. And even with new developments in performance-oriented database systems and analytical appliances, the hub of the business intelligence (BI) environment remains the data warehouse.

A data warehouse is a centralized repository of data that has been compiled from a number of disparate data sources and is in turn used to power the analytical processing from which business value is derived. For the savvy manager to get the high-level view of the data warehouse, he or she must first be aware of the differences between traditional entity-relationship models and dimensional modeling, which is more suitable to the data warehouse environment.

The importance of data modeling in an analytical context, coupled with managing the metadata associated with that data, has evolved as a critical component to the BI environment. In this chapter we will look at data modeling and online analytical processing, which both incorporate ways to represent information for the purposes of reporting and analytics.

There is a significant difference between the traditional use of databases for business purposes and the use of databases for analytical purposes. The traditional use centers on transaction processing as the means by which a business's set of operations is modeled. The processes that surround the translation of a business operation into an operational system concentrate on two ideas: (1) Business requirements reflect interactions and relationships between modeled entities; (2) each discernable business activity can be described as a sequence of transactions grouped together as a single virtual operation to capture the effects of that activity in the model.

The evolution of relational database systems to accommodate the transactional flavor of the entity-relationship model was driven by the need to streamline this kind of business activity. On the other hand, the representation of information in this framework is not suitable for analytical purposes. First of all, the data model is optimized for the transaction process, but analytical performance would severely suffer, and second, the contortions through which database analysts put their models result in a data layout that is likely to be confusing to a business analyst.

To this end, the BI community has developed a different kind of data model that more efficiently represents data that is to drive analytic applications and decision support, called a *dimensional model.* By creating a centralized data repository using this kind of data model and aggregating data sets from all areas of the corporate enterprise in this repository, a data warehouse can be created that can then supply data to the individual analytic applications.

It would be difficult to initiate a BI program without envisioning an environment for reporting and analysis. And given the fact that the data that will ultimately feed those reports will emanate from many different and variant sources across as well as outside the enterprise, until the program (and more importantly, the data integration infrastructure) has reached a level of maturity, there will be a need for the ability to separate and formulate data for analysis, whether through the construction of a data warehouse or through individual data marts.

Data Modeling and Analytics

Practically all modern business applications that employ a data subsystem represent their data sets using data models. A data model is a discrete structured data representation of a real-world set of entities related to one another. Each entity (most often represented using a *table*) carries a set of characteristic attributes (described as *data elements*). Yet over time, our understanding of the ways that real-world objects and events are captured within a structured representation must adapt to the context in which the data sets are used and the ways the information satisfies the needs of the business processes.

Transaction processing systems need to have visibility into all aspects of a limited number of data instances at a time (such as a single *customer* buying a particular *product*). Analytical systems may need to support rapid aggregation to quickly respond to ad hoc queries relating to many data instances (such as "how many customers bought this specific product?"). In other words, there is bound to be a significant difference between how we use data in an operational/tactical manner (i.e., to "run the business") and the ways we use data in a strategic manner (i.e., to "improve the business").

The traditional modeling technique for operational systems revolves around the entity-relationship model. Unfortunately, reporting and analytical applications are generally less well-suited to utilizing data structured in the entity-relational form (although there are emerging environments that make this less true). The alternative is to restructure transaction or event data using what is called "dimensional modeling" that is better organized to provide rapid responses to different types of queries and analyses.

TRANSACTION PROCESSING AND DATA MODELING

It is valuable to consider the history of database modeling to understand the drivers for cresting a segregated system and data environment used for analytical purposes. Early application systems focused solely on execution of the specific transactions.

All the aspects of a data object or transaction (such as a bank account or a store purchase) would have been likely stored in a single entry in a data file, with all the aspects of the data instance embedded within a single row in that file. Eventually, those files evolved into database tables, and each row became known as a record. To illustrate the simplicity of that model, a sales record might capture the buyer's name, address, the time of the transaction, and then a list (perhaps separated by commas) of the items and quantities of each product that was purchased (see Figure 8.1).

In terms of running the business, this may have been sufficient, but it was difficult to manage. The transactions did not execute in real time, but rather were collected up and run in batch at a particular time of day. Reporting on these transactions was more of a challenge. Application code was written to handle any data manipulation necessary to extract any kind of information from these systems. Additionally, because the buyer information was collected for each transaction, there was a significant amount of repeated and redundant data being unnecessarily stored, with the possibility of many errors creeping into the system.

In the early 1980s, a number of practitioners and researchers (most notably, E. F. Codd and Chris Date) explored the concept of a relational database, in which the way that information was modeled was viewed in the context of representing

Name	AccountNum	Address	City	State	Order
David Loshin	018776	123 Main Street	Springfield Heights	NY	1 sprocket 10-X12, 3 widgets 10-Y39, 1 Vertical Wedge 11-8773, 2 Monc. 12-Y6554
James Banding	021745	84 Causington Way	Springfield	NY	4 5/8 widgets 10-Y33, 1 Horizontal Splunge 11-H6473, 1 cantiv. 19-K754, 2 sprocket 10-X12
SprockCorp	014145	10244 Washington Hwy	Springfield	NY	42 sprocket 10-X12, 42 sprocket holder 10-X12a
Shelbyville Engineering, Inc.	013189	1477 Shelbyville Tpk.	Shelbyville	NY	13 7/8 widgets 10-Y34, 1 Diag. Corker 17-D1273, 11 cantiv. 19-K754, 2 sprocket holder 10-X12a
Roger Simmons	016290	1022 Elm St.	Springfield Hghts	NY	12 Widget chains 10-Y72, 4 3/4 glod. 17-G511, 10 widget 10-Y39

ooo

Dave Lotion	018777	123 Main Street	Springfield Hghts	NY	2 sprocket 10-X12, 1 widget 10-Y39, 5 Vertical Wedge 11-8773, 2 3/4 glod. 17-G511

Figure 8.1   A simple sales record format.

entities within separate tables and relating those entities within a business process context between tables using some form of cross-table linkage. In our (simplified) relational view of our sales database, we would have broken up our table into a customer table, a product table, a sales table, and a sales detail table, where each record in the sales table would represent a purchase transaction by a related customer and each item and quantity purchased would be in a related record in the sales detail (see Figure 8.2).

Using an entity-relationship modeling approach simplifies the development of transaction processing applications. Corresponding business processes can easily map to a sequence of operations to be executed on a collection of related tables, and then grouped together as a single unit of work. The result of executing the group of

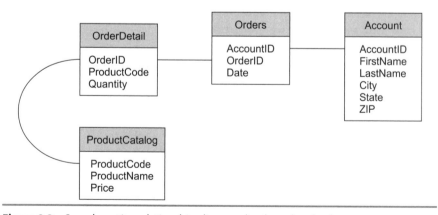

Figure 8.2   Sample entity-relationship diagram for the sales database.

operations is to reflect the effects of the business transaction inside the data model. Another essential goal of the relational model is the identification and elimination of redundancy within a database. This process, called *normalization*, analyzes tables to find instances of replicated data within one table (such as the names and addresses in our old sales table) that can be extracted into a separate table that can be linked relationally through a foreign key.

Although the entity-relationship model significantly helps in the design of operational systems, the diffraction of the information into the relational entities is, to some extent, confusing (consider the hallway-length entity-relationship diagrams that decorate the Database Administration [DBA] department's walls). In addition, the kinds of analytical extractions that are useful for BI applications are constrained by the representation of data in the pure relational model, turning what we might think would be an intuitive extraction into a set of poorly performing queries.

DIMENSIONAL MODELS

The challenge in using the standard entity-relationship model for reporting and analysis lies in the interconnectedness of the entities and the corresponding complexity in accumulating the information necessary for hierarchical aggregations. The alternative dimensional modeling technique captures the basic unit of representation as a single multikeyed entry in a slender *fact* table, with each key exploiting the relational model to refer to the different *dimensions* associated with those facts.

A maintained table of facts, each of which is related to a set of dimensions, is a much more efficient representation for data in a data warehouse and allows for information to be represented in a way that is more suitable to high-performance access. This is due to the ability to efficiently create aggregations and extractions of data specific to particular dimensional constraints quickly while being able to aggregate information.

The representation of a dimensional model is straightforward in that each row in the fact table represents a unique observable transaction or event within a specific business context. For example, a sales transaction would be represented as a specific fact record capturing all details of the event:

Time	Customer	Quantity	Item	Clerk	Unit Price	Total	Promotion	Location

This representation captures both entity data and quantifiable data. The entity data items, such as *customer* or *location* are not the actual values but instead are references (or foreign keys) to the dimension tables. The quantifiable items (such as *quantity* or *unit price*) are specific pieces of information relevant to the fact and are captured in the fact record. This data is typically numeric so that it is amenable to aggregate functions (sum, max, min, etc.). Each fact represents the total quantity of a product sold to a specific customer at a particular point-of-sales location at a particular point in time. A rough visualization of this sales fact table model is shown in Figure 8.3.

This model contains six dimensions: Time, Customer, Item, Promotion, Location, and Clerk. When you look at the picture of the model in Figure 8.3, you can see that the relationships between the fact table and the dimensions resemble a star, which is why this model layout is referred to as a *star schema*.

This model easily adapts to support aggregation by essentially sorting and accumulating within the set of dimensions under investigation. So for example, to derive information about the sales of any particular item by sales location, you would sort the fact table records by sales location and then by product. At that point you could group the total counts and amounts by product within each sales location. With the right set of indexes introduced, reporting these aggregates is simply done using SQL queries.

The fact table is related to dimensions in a star schema. Each entry in a dimension represents a description of the individual entities within that dimension. For

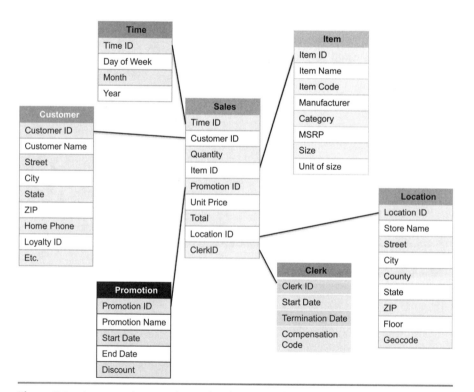

Figure 8.3 An example star schema for dimensional analysis.

example, in our sales example, the item dimension contains information associated with each item that could be sold, with descriptions that describe the attributes and characteristics of the item, such as item category, description, manufacturer, SKU number, size, unit of measure, package type, and package size, among a myriad of other relevant pieces of reference information.

USING THE DIMENSIONAL MODEL FOR BUSINESS INTELLIGENCE

This dimensional model has become the *de facto* standard for representing and managing data in a data warehouse, for a number of reasons, such as:

- **Simplicity**. There is a certain elegance in the predictability of the model, since it simplifies the process of satisfying requests for reporting via the variety of knowledge delivery and reporting tools. In fact, there is a generic process for extracting information that relies on the star schema: Create a join between the fact table and the desired dimensions and then group by dimension. By virtue of the key relationship between the fact table and the dimensions, this join is basically a single pass through the fact table.
- **Lack of bias**. Even with multiple dimensions, there is no inherent bias lent to any individual dimension. This means that as data consumers change their activity or behavior associated with the kinds of analyses or reports they desire, no specific action need be taken to rebalance the data to improve performance. In other words, the performance characteristics are not related to the data layout.
- **Extensibility**. Because the dimensional model is easily modified, changes to the model can be handled gracefully without disrupting the operation of the data warehouse. For example, adding new values to a dimension (such as adding a new customer or a new item) involves simply adding new rows to that dimension. This can be aligned with a master data registry or repository; each enables greater consistency across systems. Adding a new dimension is done by creating the new dimension table and modifying the key values in the fact table to incorporate the references back to the new dimension. Adding new attributes to dimension values is done by altering the tables and adding the new attribute values.

Dimensional modeling is not limited to customer and sales data. The same approach can be taken to model any collection of transactions or events, such as transportation and logistics, telecommunications transactions (call detail data), insurance claims, web log transactions, social media postings, nonprofit donations, medical encounter data, and so on.

There are variations on the star schema that involve breaking out additional dimension information associated with a preexisting dimension, and this allows for additional hierarchical grouping. An example would be customer categories that are applied at the highest level and then having the different customers enumerated within dimensions of that dimension. In either event, the general star schema is a powerful representational abstraction that is ubiquitous in building models for capturing data to supplement reporting and analytics.

The Data Warehouse

We have used the term "data warehouse" as a catch-all phrase describing the location from which our reporting and analytics will be served. Basically, a data warehouse is the primary source of information that feeds the analytical processing within an organization. In Chapter 2 we discussed a number of different analytic applications that are driven by business needs, yet most, if not all of these applications are driven by the data that has been migrated into a data warehouse.

There are conflicting ideas about the formal definition of a data warehouse, but there is general consensus on some fundamental aspects.

- A data warehouse is a centralized repository of information.
- A data warehouse is organized around the relevant subject areas important to the organization.
- A data warehouse provides a platform for different consumers (both human and automated) to submit queries about enterprise information.
- A data warehouse is used for analysis and not for transaction processing.
- The data in a data warehouse is nonvolatile.
- A data warehouse is the target location for integrating data from multiple sources, both internal and external to an enterprise.

A data warehouse is usually constructed using a dimensional model. Information is loaded into the data warehouse after a number of preprocessing steps. Initially, as we discussed in the previous chapter, the BI consumers will have been engaged to provide their requirements, after which the candidate data sources will have been selected. The quality of those data sets can be assessed through data profiling. At the same time, the data analysts and modelers will design and build the dimensional models for the analytical platform.

Once the candidate sources have been selected, the data is extracted, cleansed, potentially transformed, and then prepared to be loaded into the warehouse model. This may incorporate business rules as well. That data is subsequently reformulated into dimensional form and loaded into the target warehouse. These processes compose what is referred to as the data warehouse's *back end*.

Once the data is in the warehouse, it may be used for any of the reporting and analysis purposes we will explore in subsequent chapters. Certain tools may draw their input directly from the data warehouse or from data marts that are extracted for specific purposes. The data warehouse can also act as a data source for algorithmic analytics performed on specialty analytical frameworks, as well as provide an "anchor point" for collecting and storing additional analytical results from these algorithms.

Analytical Platforms

At the beginning of your BI and analytics program, the creation of a data warehouse to address well-defined reports and some ad hoc querying may be sufficient as a starting point. But as the data warehouse absorbs more (and bigger) data sets, the scope of business performance analysis expands, and the needs of new consumers increase, a maturing BI program will require more specialized types of platforms for analysis. Some examples are discussed in this section.

DATA MARTS

A data mart is a subject-oriented data repository, similar in structure to the enterprise data warehouse, but it holds the data necessary for the decision support and BI needs of a specific department or group within the organization. A data mart could be constructed solely for the analytical purposes of the specific group or could be derived from an existing data warehouse. Data marts are also built using the star join structure.

There are differences between a data mart and a data warehouse, mostly due to the different natures of the desired results. There is a school of thought that believes that data warehouses are meant for more loosely structured, exploratory analysis, whereas data marts are for more formalized reporting and for directed drill-down. Because data marts are centered on the specific goals and decision support needs of a specific department within the company, the amount of data is much smaller, but the concentration is focused on data relevant to that department's operation. This implies that different departments with different analytical or reporting needs may need different kinds of data mart structure (which may account for the diverse set of data mart products on the market).

OLAP AND CUBES

Online analytical processing is different from the typical operational or transaction processing systems. There are many proposed definitions of OLAP, most of which describe what OLAP is used for. The most frequently used terms are "multidimensional" and "slice-and-dice." Online analytical processing tools provide a means for presenting data sourced from a data warehouse or data mart in a way that allows the data consumer to view comparative metrics across multiple dimensions. In addition, these metrics are summarized in a way that allows the data consumer to *drill down* (which means to expose greater detail) on any particular aspect of the set of facts.

The data to be analyzed in an OLAP environment are arranged in a way that enables visibility along any of the dimensions. Usually this is described as a *cube*, although the organization is intended to allow the analyst to fix some set of dimensions and then see aggregates associated with the other dimensional hierarchies. Let's resume our sales analysis from earlier in this chapter, and consider a sales fact table that records every sales transaction, including date, time, location, customer, item, quantity, price per product, sales clerk, sales promotion, and total sales. We might configure an OLAP cube with these dimensions:

- Customer
- Sales Location
- Product
- Time
- Clerk
- Sales Promotion

Within each of these dimensions is a hierarchical structure, such as time periods (hour, day, week, month, quarter, year), sales locations (point of sale, store, city, county, state, region), and item categories (including specialized products such as shampoo, which is contained within the hair-care product class, which is contained within the beauty aids product class). The OLAP environment provides an aggregate view of data variables across the dimensions across each dimension's hierarchy. This might mean an aggregate function applied to any individual column across all the data related to each dimension (such as "total dollar sales by time period by sales location" or "average price by region by customer class"). For example, the data analyst can explore the total sales of beauty aid products within the Western region and then drill down across another dimension, such as the product dimension (total sales of hair-care products within the Western region) or the region dimension (total sales of beauty aids in California).

Because of the cube structure, there is an ability to rotate the perception of the data to provide different views into the data using alternate base dimensions. This conceptual ability to pivot or rotate the data provides the "slice" part; the ability to drill down on any particular aggregation provides the "dice" part.

The value of an OLAP tool is derived from the ability to quickly analyze the data from multiple points of view, and so OLAP tools are designed to precalculate the aggregations and store them directly in the OLAP databases. Although this design enables fast access, it means that there must be a significant amount of preparation of the data for the OLAP presentation as well as a potentially large storage space, because the number of cells within the cube is determined by both the number of dimensions and the size of each dimension.

For example, an OLAP cube with two dimensions, customer (1000 values) and sales locations (100 entries), would need 100,000 cells. Add a third dimension, product (with 200 entries), and you suddenly need 20 million cells. Add that fourth dimension, time (52 weeks), and your space requirement jumps to 1.04 trillion! Not only that, computational requirements grow in this same manner, because those aggregations need to be calculated and stored. No wonder many vendors rely on parallel machine architectures to support the OLAP data environment.

PREDICTIVE ANALYTICS ENGINES

As opposed to canned reporting, responding to ad hoc queries, or supporting dimensional analysis, there are alternative types of analytics that are not database-centric but are algorithmic in nature. These analyses may use data from a data warehouse, but may extract that data into a separate processing "engine" specifically dedicated to executing these algorithms. For example, many data mining techniques are performed on specialty systems. We will look at some of these algorithmic approaches in later chapters, especially in relation to analysis of massive data sets.

Operational Data Stores

Data warehouses are perceived to contain large amounts of historical information, potentially loaded at one time or in relatively large chunks in periodic intervals. The periodic nature of the data warehouse in comparison to the transactional and operational systems led to a situation in which the data in the warehouse could be out of sync with the other systems, and be less useful when it came to providing actionable knowledge in relation to real-time activity.

Yet because of the expectation for real-time access to up-to-date data, an alternate environment has been developed to provide more direct access to data from transaction processing systems called an *operational data store* (ODS). The ODS is similar to the data warehouse in data model and architecture, but differs in a number of ways. In many environments, the ODS focuses solely on a particular subject ("customer service data") or process, and data is trickle-fed from multiple sources to retain synchrony between the ODS and multiple source systems.

The ODS can be used for operational querying (such as accessing customer data to inquire about credit worthiness) without interrupting production transaction processing systems. Because of the trickle feeds, an ODS is going to be more volatile than a data warehouse, but it will be more up to date. The ODS is also often used to collect information about a business process (such as customer service or vendor performance) for particular subject areas, and then becomes a primary source for subject area reporting. The ODS is frequently used as a staging area for data that propagates through to the data warehouse.

Management

We have already stressed that the development of a reporting and analytics environment is more than just installing and implementing software. Often, the excitement and buzz surrounding BI and data warehousing raises expectations that often are not met, leading to disappointment, and often project failure. Therefore, understanding some additional aspects of BI and the data warehousing architecture can help the program manager avoid inflated expectations.

THE RELIGION OF DATA WAREHOUSING

There are basically two different schools of thought about how to build a data warehouse and a BI program, and for some reason there seems to be an almost religious adherence by practitioners of these different schools. One approach believes that a data warehouse is essentially the union of a number of data marts and that a warehouse can evolve over time from individual data marts. The other approach focuses on defining the centralized repository first, which then is used for sourcing the individual data marts.

The first approach provides the ability to deliver some value on a regular basis, whereas the second approach is more of a delayed big bang from which value can be achieved quickly after the initial implementation. In reality, there are advantages to both approaches, and perhaps there is some common ground that might apply to both approaches, in an iterative sense, to achieve intermediate results while conforming to the concept of an information factory driven by an enterprise warehouse.

THE TECHNOLOGY TRAP AND THE STRATEGIC PLAN

One major plague of the data warehouse industry is that it is very easy to lose sight of the ultimate goal, which is to provide an environment from which business data clients can analyze and explore data that can help to improve their business. I have sat in interminable meetings associated with a particular project where data warehouse and metadata management architectures were discussed for hours on end without a single mention of why one choice was better than another for the ultimate business clients. Needless to say, not only was that project cancelled, but also within a year almost none of the meeting participants still worked at that company.

Planning must incorporate a long-term perspective, especially when the plans are developed long before the tasks in the plan can be started. In some organizations, technology development roadmaps and capital acquisition budgets for both hardware and software are planned way in advance of the initiation of the budgeted projects, with the somewhat fuzzy approach to setting milestones based on knowledge of the current state of the environment and current technology trends.

Organizations that are not exposed to new methods, techniques, and tools are doing themselves a disservice, and adopting new ideas and methodologies can help a company gain competitive advantage. This means that managers must plan to accommodate the use of technology but keep it targeted to align with the business objectives.

Incorporate the introduction of new (and potentially disruptive) technologies in a way that is seen to contribute to existing objectives or can be envisioned to address future business objectives. Allow for innovation as long as there is potential business value and provide clear measures and methods for assessing that value. Identify the successful techniques and make sure that you have a process for integrating best practices for new technologies into the corporate framework and enterprise architecture.

WORKING WITH VENDORS

There are many vendors producing canned solutions and products under the guise of data warehouse, data mart, metadata repositories, and OLAP environments. Many of these are good products and can provide significant value to the process. However, each organization is different, and many vendor products require significant adaptation of adjustment before the product provides the anticipated value. There are many examples of high-cost software products that are too complicated for the customer to use without additional investment in training and consulting, and these ultimately end up as "shelfware."

One reason this occurs is the jump to purchase tools long before there is an awareness of what the tools are being used for. However, following the guidance in this book may help to alleviate this issue, especially if the requirements and needs are solicited and conceptual models developed before the tools procurement begins.

Do You Really Need a Data Warehouse?

Recent developments in high-performance data management systems incorporate ideas such as optimized data layouts and in-memory data management that reduce much of the overhead and latency traditionally driving the creation of a data warehouse. Software vendors seek to take advantage of new methods for homogenizing access to heterogeneous systems. The result is the ability to create analytical platforms that are not modeled in the traditional data warehouse style, but instead mimic more familiar frameworks such as desktop spreadsheets. Cloud environments allow you to load data into a virtual warehouse with managed access directly to the data sets. Software as a Service (SaaS) techniques synchronize analytical engines (especially for predictive analysis) with existing enterprise (and often, desktop) tools to allow seamless analytics to be delivered to your user community. So this leads to the question, do you really need to have a data warehouse (and of course, the accompanying infrastructure) to enable BI, reporting, and analysis?

The answer depends on the level of maturity your organization exhibits when it comes to the use of actionable knowledge. On one level, if all the technical capabilities of the data warehouse can be served by alternate means, then you might consider the effort to build the warehouse superfluous. On the other hand, organizations that are evolving this capability may not be well-trained in the usability of analytical platforms, and the exercise in assessing the requirements, developing the models, extracting data from sources, and populating the warehouse can provide a learning experience for staff members to gain a level of expertise in transitioning the thought processes from function-based application development to horizontal considerations of enterprise performance.

Summary

The centerpiece of the BI environment is the data warehouse, which is a repository of data aggregated from different sources and reconfigured for analytical efficiency. Data marts are more concentrated departmental repositories that are designed for goal-directed analysis and that can be used to populate OLAP databases. Online analytical processing tools enable the data analyst to view comparative aggregated metrics across multiple dimensions while allowing for further exploration by drilling down a dimensional hierarchy.

Metadata

What is Metadata?

In the earlier days of data warehousing and business intelligence (BI), the concept of metadata was often described using the phrase "data about the data"—a somewhat nonenlightening description, teetering on the edge of being a circular definition. Not only that, while the practice area of metadata management is typically embraced by corporate stakeholders at first, the challenges of defining, planning, and executing a metadata strategy coupled with the complexities of the tools and supporting techniques for metadata management can stall a metadata initiative, and can lead to its incremental compartmentalization and eventual marginalization into oblivion.

Yet the seeming marginalization and potential abandonment of the metadata tools should not be taken as an indictment of the practice. Metadata management can be particularly valuable for specific functional areas such as data warehousing and BI. In fact, we could not populate a data warehouse without knowledge of both source and target metadata. However, there is a nascent awareness that understanding metadata and harnessing a metadata environment within the context of the right level of data governance can provide significant value as the perceptions of data reuse and

119

repurposing change in reaction to (or in alignment with) new demands for data management and business analytics.

The past decade has seen a number of metadata technologies designed, developed, and ultimately integrated into much more comprehensive enterprise information management programs. But why has the practice been subject to such troubles? Before we explore the answer to that question, it is worth providing a bit of an overview of what can be lumped under the rubric of metadata. At that point we can consider some of the issues and challenges with actualizing the value of enterprise metadata management.

The Origin and Utility of Metadata

We can think about metadata as a catalog of the intellectual capital surrounding the creation, management, and use of a data set. That can range from simple observations about the number of columns in a database table to complex descriptions about the way that data flowed from multiple sources into the target database or how unstructured data input streams are absorbed into a big data analytical platform. From relatively humble beginnings as the data dictionary associated with mainframe database tables, the concept of metadata has evolved over time, and has certainly become a key factor and component supporting a BI program.

Metadata has evolved out of the data dictionary in relation to the increase in information sharing. Data warehousing and BI are two facets of a framework for information sharing. Aggregating data from multiple sources into a target data warehouse model is the "provisioning" side; accessing data from the warehouse and delivering it in a usable form through BI presentation and visualization tools is the other. In essence, for the purposes of BI and data warehousing, metadata is a sharable master key to all the information that is feeding the business analytics, from the extraction and population of the central repository to the provisioning of data out of the warehouse and onto the screens of the business clients.

Metadata management is probably one of the most critical tasks associated with a successful BI program, for a number of reasons, including these:

- Metadata encapsulates the conceptual, logical, and physical information required to transform disparate data sets into a coherent set of models for analysis.
- Metadata captures the structure of the data that is being used for data warehousing and BI.
- The recording of operational metadata provides a road map for deriving an information audit trail.
- Metadata management processes provide a way to segregate the different meanings associated with source data and provide methods for the analyst

to ensure coherence once data has been made available for reporting and analytics.

■ We can capture differences associated with how data is manipulated over time (as well as the corresponding business rules), which is critical with data warehouses whose historical data spans large periods of time.

■ Metadata provides the means for tracing the evolution of information as a way to validate and verify results derived from an analytical process.

Types of Metadata

From an organizational standpoint, we can consider different categories of metadata. The more familiar, foundational aspects of metadata have to do with structure or use, while the analytical and reporting needs are more reliant on the business types of metadata, as shown in Table 9.1.

The next sections provide some additional drill-down into the different types of metadata, but it would be outrageous to claim that it is all-inclusive. It is up to the system designers and implementers to determine what information about data is required. It is also important to maintain metadata for all the different data sets that are relevant to the BI processes, which spans the sets of data that source a data

TABLE 9.1 Types of Metadata

Type	Description
Structural	A technical type of metadata composed of what is traditionally considered the aspects of form and format, such as table names, number of columns, and size and type of data elements.
Technical	A technical type of metadata encompassing the information necessary for application development and execution.
Reference	A technical type of metadata representing the shared sets of reference tables and associated units of measures, enumerations, and mappings.
Operational	A technical type of metadata mostly consisting of logged operational reporting and statistics.
Information Architecture	A hybrid type of metadata including conceptual data models, logical data models, master data entity descriptions.
Analytical	A business type of metadata related to the packaging and delivery of reports and analyses, including report names, nonpersistent columns for reporting, or types of predictive models.
Semantic	A business type of metadata composing a business term glossary cataloging business terms, mappings to data element concepts, or tags for linking term use to concepts within semantic hierarchies.

warehouse, including legacy or mainframe systems, externally supplied data, vendor application data (such as the data stored in proprietary enterprise resource planning [ERP] systems), the data representation at the preprocessing staging area, the data warehouse, any data marts, and all business analytics applications.

On the other hand, comprehensive metadata implementations are rare. Realize that despite the length of this list, there are few organizations that capture all of this metadata. In addition, even those organizations that do capture a lot of metadata still have ample opportunity to make use of it.

STRUCTURAL METADATA

Structural metadata comprises most of what is traditionally considered metadata that is organized as the data dictionary, and is derivable from database catalogs. This type of metadata can include:

- **Data element information**, like data element names, types, lengths, definitions, and other usage information;
- **Table information**, including table names; the description of what is modeled by each table; the database in which the table is stored; the physical location, size, and growth rate of the table; the data sources that feed each table; update histories (including the date of last update and of last refresh); the results of the last update; candidate keys; foreign keys; the degrees of the foreign key cardinality (e.g., 1:1 versus 1: many); referential integrity constraints; functional dependencies; and indexes;
- **Record structure information**, which describes the structure of the record; over-all record size; whether the record is a variable or static length; all column names, types, descriptions, and sizes; source of values that populate each column; whether a column is an automatically generated unique key; null status; domain restrictions; and validity constraints.

TECHNICAL METADATA

Technical metadata encompasses the information necessary for application development and execution, including:

- **Connectivity metadata**, which describes the ways that data consumers interact with the database system, including the names used to establish connections, database names, data source names, whether connections can be shared, and the connection timeout;
- **Index metadata**, which describes what indexes exist, on which tables those indexes are made, the columns that are used to perform the indexing, whether nulls are allowed, and whether the index is automatically or manually updated.

REFERENCE METADATA

Reference metadata spans the collections of conceptual data domains (which contain a collection of the value *concepts* within a reference data set), value domains (which contain enumerations of specific values that belong together), functions representing domain value sets, value ranges, mappings between conceptual domain values to those represented by specific value domains, and correspondence mappings between data domains. Reference metadata can also include the likely values for certain types of business rules such as reasonableness and validity tests.

OPERATIONAL METADATA

Operational metadata is made up of the operational reporting and statistics such as access logs, timestamps, transaction counts and volumes, or system performance and response time, as well as:

- **Physical features metadata**, such as the size of tables, the number of records in each table, and the maximum and minimum record sizes if the records are of variable length;
- **Record manipulation metadata**, which includes record creation time, time of last update, the last person to modify the record, and the results of the last modification;
- **Management metadata**, such as the history of a data table or database, stewardship information, and responsibility matrices;
- **Data practitioners**, which enumerates the staff members who work with data, their contact information (e.g., telephone number, e-mail address), and the objects they access;
- **Security and access metadata**, which identifies the owner of the data, the ownership paradigm, who may access the data and with which permissions (e.g., readonly versus modify).

INFORMATION ARCHITECTURE

The information architecture incorporates the modeling aspects of the data and the way the data sets are used, including:

- **Modeling metadata**, which includes the conceptual data models, logical data models, master data entity descriptions, linkage of data element concepts and data element instances within conceptual and logical models, entity-relationship diagrams, lineage mappings, and information dependencies across business processes;

- **Transformation metadata**, which describes the data sources that feed into the data warehouse, the ultimate data destination, and, for each destination data value, the set of transformations used to materialize the datum and a description of the transformation;
- **Process metadata**, which describes the information flow and sequence of extraction and transformation processing, including data profiling, data cleansing, standardization, and integration;
- **Supplied data metadata**, which, for all supplied data sets, gives the name of the data set, the name of the supplier, the names of individuals responsible for data delivery, the delivery mechanism (including time, location, and method), the expected size of the supplied data, the data sets that are sourced using each supplied data set, and any transformations to be applied upon receiving the data;
- **Data warehouse metadata**, which captures entity-relationship diagrams associated with the data warehouse, dimensional layouts and star join structures, logical data models, and physical data models.

ANALYTICAL METADATA

Analytical metadata describes the types of analyses that are performed, variable names and meanings for presented information, dimensions used in dimensional modeling, hierarchies for categorization, value ranges for quantization of value ranges, profiling characteristics, more reference data, units of measure, along with presentation and delivery criteria and characteristics.

SEMANTIC METADATA

Semantic metadata encompasses the aspects of the metadata necessary for aligning meanings, including the establishment of a business term glossary cataloging business terms, their definitions, mappings to data element concepts, tags for linking term use to concepts within semantic hierarchies, and business process models, among other aspects of information meaning. The concept of semantic metadata is particularly important for BI, and aspects of this area of practice warrant more detailed consideration, as we will see later.

BUSINESS METADATA

Business metadata is layered on top of these different types of metadata to enable business processes and business analytics to make sense, and effectively merges the technical metadata with:

- Metadata that describes the structure of data as perceived by business clients;
- Descriptions of the methods for accessing data for client analytical applications;
- Business meanings for tables and their attributes;
- Data ownership characteristics and responsibilities;
- Data domains and mappings between those domains, for validation;
- Aggregation and summarization directives;
- Reporting directives;
- Security and access policies;
- Business rules that describe constraints or directives associated with data within a record or between records as joined through a join condition.

Semantic Metadata Processes for Business Analytics

When building a business analytics program, there is no doubt that the standard types of metadata for the physical design and implementation of a data warehouse and corresponding BI delivery methods and tools are required. For example, it would be impossible to engineer the data integration and transformations needed to migrate data out of the source systems and into an operational data store or a data warehouse without knowledge of the structures of the sources and the target models. Similarly, without understanding the reference metadata (particularly the data types and units of measure!), the delivered reports might be difficult to understand, if not undecipherable altogether.

But even presuming the soundness of the management of the technical, structural, and operational metadata, the absence of conceptual data available for shared information will often lead to reinterpretation of the data sets' meanings. The availability of the business metadata, particularly semantic metadata is somewhat of a panacea, and that means there must be some well-defined processes in place for soliciting, capturing, and managing that semantic information. Some key processes will focus on a particular set of areas of concentration, as we explore here.

MANAGEMENT OF NONPERSISTENT DATA ELEMENTS

We often will assume that the business terms, data element concepts, and entity concepts that are managed within a metadata framework are associated with persistent data sets, either operational or transactional systems or with data sitting in a data mart or warehouse. It turns out that numerous data elements are used but not stored in a persistent database.

The simplest examples are those associated with the presentation of generated reports and other graphical representations such as column headers or labels on charts. Another example is interim calculations or aggregations that are used in preparing values for presentation. These data elements all have metadata characteristics—size, data type, associated data value domains, mappings to business terms—and there is value in managing that metadata along with metadata for persistent items.

BUSINESS TERM GLOSSARY

The most opportune place to start is establishing a business term glossary, which is a catalog of the terms and phrases used across the different business processes within (as well as relevant external interfaces to) the enterprise. It would not be a surprise to learn that in most organizations, the same or similar words and phrases are used (both in documentation and in conversation) based on corporate lore or personal experience, but many of these terms are never officially defined or documented. When the same terms are used as column headings or data element names in different source systems, there is a tendency to presume that they mean the same things, yet just as often as not there are slight (or sometimes big) variations in the context and consequently in the definition of the term.

Establishing a business term glossary is a way to identify where the same terms are used with different meanings and facilitating processes for harmonizing the definitions or differentiating them. The metadata process involves reviewing documentation and business applications (their guidelines as well as the program code), and interviewing staff members to identify business terms that are either used by more than one party, or are presumed to have a meaning that is undocumented. Once the terms have been logged, the analysts can review the definitions and determine whether they can be resolved or whether they actually represent more than one concept, each of which requires qualification.

MANAGING SYNONYMS

The more unstructured and externally streamed data consumed by the analytical platforms, the greater the potential for synonyms, which are sets of different words or terms that share the same meaning. The synonym challenge is the opposite problem than the one posed by variation in definitions for the same term. For example, the words "car," "auto," and "automobile" in most situations will share the same meaning, and therefore can be considered synonyms.

This process becomes more challenging when the collections of terms are synonyms in one usage scenario but not in another. To continue the example, in some cases the words "truck," "SUV," and "minivan" might be considered synonyms for automobile, but in other cases, each of those terms has its own distinct meaning.

Developing the Business Concept Registry

We can take the idea of a business term glossary one step further by combining it with the management of synonyms to create a business concept registry that captures the ways that the different business terms are integrated into business concepts. For example, we can define the business term "customer," but augment that description with the enumeration of the business terms and concepts that are used to characterize a representation of a customer.

This can be quite complex, especially in siloed organizations with many implementations. Yet the outcome of the process is the identification of the key concepts that are ultimately relevant to both running the business (absorbed as a result of assessing the existing uses) and to improving the business, as the common concepts with agreed-to definitions can form the basis of a canonical data model supporting business reporting and analytics.

Mappings from Concept to Use

If one goal of a BI program is to accumulate data from the different areas of the business for reporting and analysis, the designers' and developers' understanding of the distribution of content in the source systems must be comprehensive enough to pinpoint the lineage of information as it flowed into the data warehouse and then out through the reports or analytical presentations. That suggests going beyond the structural inventory of data elements, but encompassing the business term glossary and mapping those terms to their uses in the different systems across the organizations.

For example, once you can specify a business term "customer" and establish a common meaning, it would be necessary to identify which business processes, applications, tables, and data elements are related to the business concept "customer." Your metadata inventory can be adapted for this purpose by instituting a process for mapping the common concepts to their systemic instantiations.

Semantic Hierarchy Management

The next level of business metadata complexity centers on the organization of business concepts within the contexts of their use. We can return to the automobile example from before: "car" and "auto" may be defined as equivalent terms, but the particular class of car ("SUV," "minivan," or "truck") might be categorized as subsidiary to "car" in a conceptual hierarchy.

The hierarchical relationship implies inheritance—the child in the hierarchy shares the characteristics of the parent in the hierarchy. That basically means that any SUV is also a car (although not the other way around), and like a car it will have brakes and a rear-view mirror. On the other hand, the descendants in the hierarchy may have characteristics that are neither shared with the parent nor with other siblings. The hierarchy is expandable (you could have a "4WD SUV" and a "2WD SUV" subsidiary to an "SUV"). It is also not limited to a single-parent relationship—you could have a hybrid SUV that inherits from both hybrid cars and SUVs.

The hierarchies lay out the aggregation points along the dimensions. Continuing the example, an auto manufacturer might count the total number of cars sold, but also might want that broken down by the different subsidiary categories in the hierarchy.

CONSIDERATIONS: ENTITY CONCEPTS AND MASTER DIMENSIONS

All of these metadata ideas converge when lining the information in the analytical environment up with that of the other data sources across the organization, especially when it comes to key master concepts that are relevant for transactional, operational, and analytical applications. The master entity concepts (such as "product") are associated with master dimensions (such as the automobile hierarchy), but the value is the semantic alignment that allows the business analyst reading the report to be confident that the count of sold SUVs is consistent with the operational reporting coming out of the sales system. These aspects of semantic metadata enable that level of confidence.

Further Considerations

As you might tell, the more we think about metadata, the more complex and (yet at the same time) valuable metadata can be. There are some straightforward business benefits for metadata, and these are worth a short review as well. For example, consolidation of customer data sets as a result of corporate mergers or acquisition require knowledge of both organization's data representations and rules for linkage, merging, and consolidation.

As another example, data integration for data warehousing is impossible without knowledge of the metadata associated with the data sources used to populate the warehouse. In order to organize data for analytical purposes, it will need to be extracted from the original source (source metadata), transformed into a representation that is consistent with the warehouse (target metadata) in a way that does not lose information due to differences in format and precision (structure metadata) and is aligned in a meaningful way (semantic metadata).

Perhaps one of the emerging uses of metadata is associated with big data and the need to consume and absorb large volumes of a variety of data sources with limited degree of structure. The need to scan unstructured data streams and extract meaning from those streams depends on mechanisms for parsing the data (structural metadata), recognizing relevant patterns (structural metadata), and making sense of them (semantic metadata). Text analytics is acutely related to semantics and business rules, so it would be virtually impossible to do without metadata.

So what has been the impediment to making use of metadata environments? In those scenarios where metadata is crucial to the project (such as data integration for data warehousing), there is no doubt that the project will demand the use of a metadata tool. The same can be said about mergers/acquisitions, or the other use cases we have discussed. The issue occurs *after* the project is done. Once we have finished the consolidation of data from the acquired company, there is still some level of effort and investment associated with *maintaining* the metadata repository—staff time, hardware, software, and so on. But after the projects are done, the specific need diminishes as well, leading to a corresponding diminution in the investment in metadata maintenance.

Other challenges persist as well. One major challenge is that documenting metadata may be (in most cases) simplistic, but that doesn't mean it isn't hard work. Sit back for a moment and consider how many databases, tables, data elements, and reference data sets there are in your organization. And assume that documenting each data element takes on the average 30 minutes. In a reasonably sized company, there are at least on the order of 5,000–10,000 data elements. The math is easy: 10,000 data elements * ½ hour per element = 5000 staff hours, or 2½ staff years (assuming no breaks ;-). Actually, most organizations have way more than that, once you start to include spreadsheets and desktop databases, so the number may continue to increase. So there is a lot of work to do, but once the work is done, who is actually using it? Maintenance, updates, and new systems add to the confusion.

Last, many metadata implementations are spearheaded as technical initiatives, yet their potential value has to revolve around the areas of the business, especially for processes that cross business function boundaries. This implies yet another success factor: the need for data governance policies that encapsulate both the authority for oversight of the metadata program as well as the processes and procedures for engaging business data consumers, soliciting their input regarding definitions and semantics, documenting data standards, managing the approval workflow processes, tracking lineage—basically any aspect of metadata creation or use must be associated with data policies.

So it is interesting to use 20/20 hindsight to assess the success or failure characteristics of metadata projects so that we can learn from history and not make the same mistakes. Because as more and bigger data sets are increasingly reused and repurposed for more cross-functional and extra-enterprise activities, it is clear that metadata is going to be a critical component of any enterprise architecture.

Using Metadata Tools

Metadata is data, which means that it can be modeled and managed the same way other data is managed. As the primary source of knowledge about the inner workings of the BI environment, it is important to build and maintain a metadata management tool or repository that is available to all knowledge workers involved in the BI program.

Most metadata tools have been pretty good at managing the foundational aspects, although in isolation, much of this data is managed within database catalogs or can be handled using desktop tools like spreadsheets or documents. As we have seen, there are numerous other types of metadata that are much more interesting and valuable because they convey information about the utility of the data as well as facilitating methods for reusing or repurposing information in different ways, and the existing tools still require some degree or maturation to reach the point where they can satisfy the collected needs of the organization.

Whether the metadata repository is physically centralized or distributed across multiple systems and however it is accessed, it is important to provide a mechanism for publishing metadata. The existence of disparate data systems that contribute information to the BI environment complicates this process, because each system may have its own methods for managing its own metadata. Yet ultimately the metadata analysts will need to formalize practices and procedures for soliciting information from the different system owners and consolidating that knowledge within the capabilities of existing frameworks.

Chapter 10

Data Profiling

We have considered the structure and models for data warehouse data, as well as the metadata that facilitates the use of that data. In fact, most of the book so far has basically centered on planning and infrastructure—what goes into the project before you actually start. At this point, we will finally begin to examine the data sets themselves, using a technique called *data profiling*, and get an understanding as to their usability. And often, despite what you believe to be represented within those source data sets, you may be surprised to find out that some data sets do not really represent what you think they do.

Data profiling is a process of analyzing raw data for the purpose of characterizing the information embedded within a data set. Data profiling consists of different statistical and analytical algorithms that provide insight into the content of data sets, and qualitative characteristics of those values. One goal of profiling data is to discover metadata when it is not available and to validate metadata when it is available. Data profiling incorporates column analysis, data type determination, cross-table analyses, and exploration and discovery of relationships and dependencies across columns. The result is a constructive process of information inference to

131

prepare a data set for later integration. This chapter discusses these issues and describes the data profiling processes.

Establishing Usability of Candidate Data Sources

No business intelligence (BI) and analytics program can be built without information. That information will originate in data sets coming from many different sources and providers. Few of these providers will have a stake in the success of the outcome of your BI program. It is therefore not surprising that there is an oft-quoted (although difficult to source!) statistic claiming that 70% of the effort associated with a data warehousing or data mining project is spent on data preparation. A large part of this effort involves trying to harmonize data sets from disparate sources into a single repository. To this end, those responsible for accessing, extracting, and preparing data for loading into an analytical platform must understand the particulars about the data in the source systems prior to its extraction and integration. This involves more than trusting the supplied documentation, data dictionaries, or printouts of data models.

Anyone who has gone through the drill of preparing data for analytic processing understands this. The data that we are given is seldom in a pristine form, with some data sets having do details at all. Different data sets may be more or less usable in their original states, and the value of that data may differ based on how much effort needs to be invested to ensure that the data can be consistently integrated into the data warehouse. When faced with an integration process incorporating disparate data sets of dubious quality, data profiling is the first step toward adding value to that data. Data profiling automates the initial processes of what we might call *inferred metadata resolution:* discovering what the data items really look like and providing a characterization of that data for the next steps of integration.

Preliminary data profiling prior to data integration provides a reasonable characterization of the metadata associated with a data set, which can help reduce the amount of effort required for integration. The information collected via profiling will help to automate the preparation of data for integration into a data warehouse, which then yields a significant reduction in the cost of building that data warehouse. In Jack Olson's book, *Data Quality, The Accuracy Dimension*, it is noted that a Standish Group report, "performing data profiling at the beginning of a project can reduce the total project cost by 35%." If this is true, it suggests that for many data warehousing projects, the cost of a data profiling tool is dwarfed by the potential cost savings.

Data Profiling Activities

Data profiling is a hierarchical process that attempts to build an assessment of the metadata associated with a collection of data sets. The bottom level of the hierarchy characterizes the values associated with individual attributes. At the next level, the assessment looks at relationships between multiple columns within a single table. At the highest level, the profile describes relationships that exist between data attributes across different tables.

The complexity of the computation for these assessments grows at each level of the hierarchy. The attribute-level analysis is the least burdensome, whereas cross-column analysis can actually be costly in terms of computational resources. This provides one aspect of evaluation of data profiling tools: performance.

Another important evaluation criterion is ease of use of the results. Because there is so much information that can be inferred from the data values that make up a data set, it is easy to get lost in reams of statistics and enumerations. Remember the goal of reducing the effort required to integrate data, and keep this in mind when reviewing a profile assessment.

One other item to keep in mind while profiling data is that the most significant value is derived from discovering business knowledge that has been embedded in the data itself. Old-fashioned (and currently frowned-upon) database administration (DBA) tricks, such as overloading data attributes (in lieu of adding new columns to production databases) with encoded information, carry embedded business knowledge that can be shaken out and lost during an automated data cleansing process. As an example, in one of my client's employee identifier fields, most of the values were all digits, but a large number of records had a value that was all digits except for the character "I" appended to the end of the number. Appearances of asterisks as the last character in a name field and combination codes in a single column (i.e., a single string that comprises three distinct coded values, such as "89-NY/USA") are other kinds of examples of business knowledge embedded in the data.

The existence of a reason for a rule shows one of the subtle differences between a data quality rule and a business rule. Declaring that all values assigned to a field in a database record must conform to a pattern gives us a way to validate data within a record but gives us no insight into why the value must be in that form. When we associate meaning with a data quality rule, we suddenly have a context that allows us to understand why values must conform to that format and what deviations from that format mean.

Data Model Inference

When presented with a set of data tables of questionable origin (or sometimes even with a pedigreed data set), a data consumer may want to verify or discover the data model that is embedded within that set. This is a hierarchical process that first focuses on exposing information about the individual columns within each table, then looks at any relationships that can be derived between columns within a single table, and then resolves relationships between different tables to generate a proposed data model for a data set. We look at some of the more complicated details in the upcoming sections on Attribute Analysis and Relationship Analysis, but here we'll look at some high-level ideas regarding type inferencing and relational model inferencing.

SIMPLE TYPE INFERENCE

When we structure information within a logical framework, we impose some semantic support beams that both provide guidance to the application programmer as to how to deal with manipulating data and clue the information consumer into what kinds of data values are expected. A column's data type provides this guidance by constraining the kinds of values that should appear within that column. For example, if we have a column called "sales_quantity," we might expect the values populating this column to be in whole units (e.g., we don't sell fractions of a shirt), and therefore all the values in that field should be integers. All structured data sets are typically described using some kind of data typing system.

Yet when a data set is first introduced into a data environment, even if the set is accompanied by a corresponding data definition, the analyst may choose to verify the corresponding types through the profiling process. This is done through simple type inference, which is a process of resolving the view of each column's data type to its most closely matched system data type.

Every structured data set conforms to some data type assignment, so we can always assume that there is some data type definition assigned to each column, even if that type is an extremely broad type, such as "variable-length character string," and assign its maximum length to the length of the longest character string within the column. Data type inference is an iterative analysis of a value set to refine the perceived data type. For example, a column that contains strings consisting solely of digits could have its type refined from a *varchar* type to a proposed *integer* type. A column where all values strings are 10 characters or less could be resolved to varchar(10).

Simple type inference centers only on assigning system data types (such as integer, decimal, date) to columns. This can be distinguished from the more valuable abstract type inferencing, which is more complicated.

TABLE MODEL INFERENCE AND RELATIONAL MODEL INFERENCE

Given a collection of data tables, an important piece of information is whether and how any of the tables are related in a data model. There are two approaches to resolving a relational model from a collection of data tables. The first is a brute-force approach that uses the results of overlap analysis to determine whether any pair of columns exhibits a key relationship. The second approach is more of a semantic approach that evaluates column names to see if there is any implied relation. For example, two tables from the same data set may each have a column called "party_addr_id," which might lead us to conjecture that these columns refer to the same object identifier.

Attribute Analysis

Attribute analysis is a process of looking at all the values populating a particular column as a way to characterize that set of values. Attribute analysis is the first step in profiling because it yields a significant amount of metadata relating to the data set. The result of any of these analyses provides greater insight into the business logic that is applied (either on purpose or as a by-product of some other constraints) to each column. The end product should be a list of questions about each column that can be used to determine data quality or validation constraints or even information from which some BI can be inferred.

Typically this evaluation revolves around the following aspects of a data set:

- **Range analysis**, which is used to determine if the values fit within a well-defined range;
- **Sparseness**, which evaluates the percentage of the elements populated;
- **Format evaluation**, which tries to resolve unrecognized data into defined formats;
- **Cardinality and uniqueness**, which analyzes the number of distinct values assigned to the attribute and indicates whether the values assigned to the attribute are unique;
- **Frequency distribution**, which shows the relative frequency of the assignment of distinct values;
- **Value absence**, which identifies the appearance and number of occurrences of null values;
- **Abstract type recognition**, which refines the semantic data type association with a specific attribute;
- **Overloading**, which attempts to determine if an attribute is being used for multiple purposes.

The frequency analysis also provides summarization/aggregate values that can be used to characterize the data set, including:

- **Minimum value**, based on the ordering properties of the data set;
- **Maximum value**, also based on the ordering properties of the data set;
- **Mean**, providing the average value (for numeric data);

- **Median,** providing the middle value (if this can be defined);
- **Standard deviation**, (relevant only for numeric values).

Profiling data attributes (or columns) also sheds light on details of descriptive characteristics, feeding these types of analyses:

- **Type determination,** which characterizes data type and size;
- **Abstract type recognition**, which refines the semantic data type association with a specific attribute, often depending on pattern analysis;
- **Overloading**, which attempts to determine if an attribute is being used for multiple purposes; and
- **Format evaluation**, which tries to resolve unrecognized data into defined formats.

RANGE ANALYSIS

Relating a value set to a simple type already restricts the set of values that a column can take; most data types still allow for an infinite number of possible choices. During range analysis a set of values is tested to see if the values fall within a well-defined range. If so, depending on the data type, some inferences may be made. For example, if the data type is a date, the range may signify some time period for which the corresponding data is relevant. Another example might distinguish a small range of integer values that correspond to some enumerated encoding (i.e., a hook into some other reference data set).

More complex range analysis algorithms may be able to identify nonintersecting ranges within a data set as well. Consider an integer column that contains values between 0 and 9 as well as the value 99 as an error code condition. A naïve range analyzer might propose 0 through 99 as this attribute range, whereas the more sophisticated analyzer could bisect the values into two ranges, 0 through 9 and the single-valued range of 99. The more refined the distinct extant value ranges are, the easier it is for the business analyst or domain expert to recognize a meaning in those ranges, which then can be documented as attribute metadata.

Range analysis can be used in an intelligence application to explore minimum and maximum values of interest, perhaps related to customer activity and monthly sales or to prices customers are being charged for the same products at different retail locations. Another example might look for evidence of insurance fraud based on the existence of a wide range of practitioner charges for the same procedure.

SPARSENESS

The degree of sparseness may indicate some business meaning regarding the importance of that attribute. Depending on the value set, it probably means one of two things. Either the attribute is extremely important and needs to be available so that in the rare cases there is a need for the value, it can be populated, or the attribute is effectively meaningless because so few records have a value for it. Of course, this is most likely determined by the data analyst reviewing the profile reports.

FORMAT EVALUATION

It is useful to look for the existence of patterns that might characterize the values assigned to a column. For example, if we determine that each value has 10 characters, where the first character is always "A" and the remainder are digits, we are thereby presented with a syntax rule that can be asserted as a domain definition. We can use the discovered definition as a validation rule, which we would then add to a metadata repository documenting value domains described using patterns. Simple examples of rule-based data domains include telephone numbers, zip codes, and social security numbers. What is interesting is that frequently the pattern rules that define domains have deeper business significance.

As a more detailed example, consider a customer accounts database containing a data field called ACCOUNT_NUMBER, which always turned out to be composed of a two-character prefix followed by a nine-digit number. There was existing code that automatically generated a new account number when a new customer was added. It turned out that embedded in the data and the code were rules indicating how an account number was generated. Evidently, the two-character code represented a sales region, determined by the customer's address, whereas the numeric value was assigned as an increasing number per customer in each sales region. Because this attribute's value carried multiple pieces of information, it was a classic example of an overloaded attribute. The discovery of a pattern pointed to a more complicated business rule, which also paved the way for the cleaving of the overloaded information into two separate data attributes.

One method for pattern analysis is through the superimposition of small, discrete semantic properties to each symbol in a string, slowly building up more interesting patterns as more symbol components have their meanings assigned. Consider the following symbol classifications.

- Letter
- Digit
- Punctuation
- White space

Symbol pattern assignment is the first pass at pattern analysis (Figure 10.1). In each string, we assign one of the foregoing classifications to each character appearing in a data value. When all the characters in a string have been classified, the string will have an associated pattern string as well. For each value string, we prepare

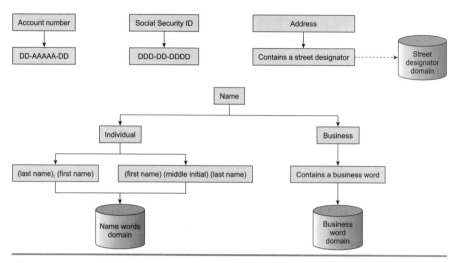

Figure 10.1 Examples of pattern analysis.

and record its pattern string. When all value strings have been analyzed, there is a column of associated pattern strings ready to be collated and counted.

At this point, there are two tasks to be accomplished. The first is to look for recurring patterns within the set of generated pattern strings; the second is to check the generated pattern strings against the known sets of patterns. Either way, the goal is to present candidate patterns representing rule-based domains to the user.

If no candidates reveal themselves through simple symbol pattern assignment, then there may be additional embedded information in the patterns themselves that should be investigated. Our next method for pattern analysis takes a more macro view of the data by categorizing strings instead of symbols. At this point, all strings can be classified as:

- Alphabetic
- Alphanumeric
- Numeric
- First name
- Last name
- Business word
- Address words
- One of any other categorized word class

In each attribute value, we now assign to each white space–separated string one of the word categories, forming a new pattern string. After all the strings have had patterns assigned, again, these patterns can be collated and counted, and we check both for recurring patterns and for matches to previously known patterns.

In either the symbol or whole word analysis, if we find common patterns that have not yet been registered, it is possible that we have discovered a new pattern, which then should be documented. At this point, it is worthwhile to perform a little detective work to see if there is some implicit business rule embedded in this pattern. It may turn out that there is some historical reason for the pattern, which may reflect some business condition that currently exists and must be maintained or one that existed at some point but is no longer valid, thereby allowing the rule to be changed.

CARDINALITY AND UNIQUENESS

The *cardinality* of a value set is the number of distinct values that exists within a column. Cardinality is interesting because it relates to different aspects of the correctness of the value set and because of how it exposes business knowledge. For example, in some contexts there is an expected cardinality, such as a SEX field, where only "M" and "F" might be anticipated. In one of my client's data tables, we found a SEX field with three values: "M," "F," and "U." The "M" and "F" were expected, and it turned out that the "U" indicated that the person's sex was unknown.

In other contexts, the cardinality of a value set should equal the number of records contributing to that data set. An example of this is an expected key field: If the cardinality is less than the number of records, there is at least one duplicate value, which in turn indicates that that field does not contain a true key. Alternatively, cardinality analysis can be used to find columns whose values are unique, from which candidate keys can be inferred.

FREQUENCY DISTRIBUTION

The frequency distribution of values yields the number of times each of the distinct values appears in a value set. This gives the data consumer some insight into whether certain values have more significance than others based on a high (or low) frequency, and it highlights potential nonconforming values that appear as outliers in the distribution report.

Frequency distribution is also useful when looking for variations from the norm that might indicate something suspicious. Consider a column whose values should be randomly distributed; if a frequency analysis showcases a handful of values whose frequency is unusually high, this might trigger some deeper investigation to determine whether those values are correct or whether they indicate some kind of fraudulent behavior.

VALUE ABSENCE

There are actually two problems associated with the absence of values that can be explored through data profiling. The first involves looking for values that are not there, and the second is to look for nonvalues that are there.

The first issue, truly missing values (which in modern relational database systems are represented using a true system null), are of significance because the data analyst may be interested in determining whether these values really should be null, under what circumstances they should be null, or perhaps why the value is missing. Of further interest may be attempting to figure out a way to fill in the missing value.

The second issue refers to those cases where some distinct value (or, more likely, values) represents one or more kinds of nulls. As we discuss in greater detail, there are different reasons why we might want to use different explicit strings as representations of correspondingly different kinds of nulls. There is a distinction between a value that is missing because the data entry analyst did not know the value and leaving the attribute null because there really is no value. Making this distinction explicit can cause problems when trying to perform further analysis. The problem is even more acute when there is no standardization of the explicit nulls.

To illustrate this, look at any database that carries an attribute for Social Security number and see how many values look like "000-00-0000" and how many like "999-99-9999." Either of these values is likely intended to convey some kind of missing value, probably the result of a business process that requires filling in a value (even if there is no valid one). But without additional information, it might be premature to claim that they have identical meanings or that they are both the same as the system null.

ABSTRACT TYPE ANALYSIS

An abstract type is a more semantically descriptive qualification of a type definition that conveys business meaning. For example, "people names," "telephone numbers," and "ZIP codes" are all abstract data types that qualify as character strings. The difference between type recognition, as discussed earlier, and abstract type analysis is the degree of complexity involved. Abstract data types are by definition more complicated, because the business meaning is captured through some set of assertions that constrain the set of values belonging to that type.

Typically abstract data types are represented by some kind of semantic definition, including:

- **Constructive assertion** (e.g., all product codes consist of two uppercase characters followed by a hyphen followed by a six-digit number, whose leftmost digit represents the factory at which the product is manufactured);

- **Value enumeration** (e.g., the set of USPS state codes via an enumeration of the valid two uppercase character values);
- **Pattern conformance** (e.g., the string matches one or more of a set of defined patterns similar to those inferred via the approach described in the earlier section about Format Evaluation).

The goal of abstract type analysis is to propose an abstract data type for a specific column based on a suggestive statistical conformance to one defined abstract type. For example, once a column has been identified as a varchar(30) data type, all the values can be tested to determine if they represent, say, a telephone number (by matching each to telephone number patterns) or colors of the rainbow (by checking for enumerated domain membership). If an overwhelming number of values match to a known type, this not only provides more business knowledge about the data model, but also provides insight into distinguishing those values that do not conform to the discovered type.

OVERLOADING ANALYSIS

Presuming that we have already identified some value sets that represent reference data domains with business value, we can attempt to resolve domain membership by checking the values in an attribute against those known enumerated domains. Yet it is possible that as an attribute's data values are checked against known domains the profiling process will see significant matches against more than one domain. This might indicate that two attributes' worth of information is in one column, where the same column is being used to represent more than one actual attribute (Figure 10.2).

Alternatively, the use of more than one domain by a single attribute might indicate that more complex business rules are in effect, such as the existence of a *split attribute,* which is characterized by the use of different domains based on other data quality or business rules. As a simple example, consider a banking application that registers customer account activity. When a customer makes a deposit, a credit is made to the customer's account in the form of a positive amount of money; when the customer withdraws money, a debit is made to the account in the form of a negative amount of money. In this case, the same column is used, but in fact there are two domains used for this attribute—positive decimal values (when the action is a credit) and negative decimal values (when the action is a debit).

Overloading can appear in other ways as well, such as the compaction of multiple pieces of data into a single character string. Sometimes this is intentional, such as the example we saw earlier where a product code carried sales region information, or perhaps less so, such as the example we saw in the section about Data Profiling Activities.

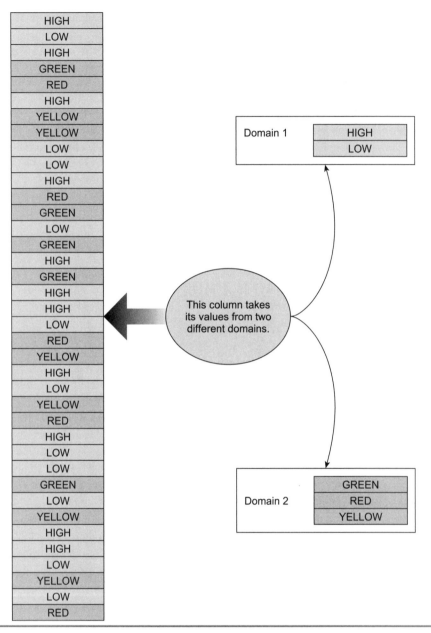

Figure 10.2 Example of an overloaded attribute.

Relationship Analysis

Cross-column or *relationship analysis* focuses on establishing relationships between sets of data. The goal of these processing stages is to identify relationships between value sets and known reference data, to identify dependencies between columns (either in the same table or across different tables), and to identify key relationships between columns across multiple tables.

DOMAIN ANALYSIS

Domain analysis covers two tasks: identifying data domains and identifying references to data domains. We have already discussed one virtual process of domain identification in the earlier section about Format Evaluation; discovered format specifications can represent data domains. Enumerated domains may be inferred and proposed from a value set when:

- The number of values is relatively small as compared to the context in which it is used (i.e., the number of possible values that an attribute might take is limited to a small set).
- The values are what we could call *intuitively distributed.* This means that the distribution, although not always even, will take on characteristics specific to the context. In some cases there is a relatively even distribution; in other cases there may be more weighting given to a small subset of those values.
- Other domains exist that may be derived from this domain.
- The domain is used in more than one table.
- The attribute that uses the value from the domain is rarely null.

Unfortunately, these are more guidelines than rules, because exceptions can be found for each characteristic. The brute-force method for identifying enumerated domains is to look at all possible value sets. We begin by presuming that each column in every table potentially draws its values from a defined domain. For every table, we walk through each column and select all the distinct values. This set is now a candidate domain, and we then apply heuristics to decide whether to call this set a domain. It turns out that sometimes we can make some kind of determination early in the analysis, and sometimes we have to wait until more knowledge has been gained.

Presuming that we have already started to build the domain inventory, we can see whether other data attributes make use of the same domain by analyzing how well the set of values used to populate one attribute matches the values of a known domain. The value-matching process for a specific attribute can be described using the following steps.

1. The attribute's distinct values are collected and counted.
2. The set of unique values is matched against each domain. Fast matching techniques are used for scalability.
3. For each domain, we compute three ratio values. The *agreement* is calculated as the ratio of distinct attribute values that are present in a domain to the total number of distinct values in the attribute. The *overlap* is calculated as the number of domain member values that do not appear in the attribute divided by the number of domain values. Last, we compute the *disagreement* as the number of values that appear in the attribute but are not members of the domain.
4. The domains are sorted by their agreement percentages. The highest agreement percentages are presented as likely identified domains.

When we compare an attributes value set to a known domain, there are four cases.

1. All the values used in the attribute are members of the known domain, and all the values in the domain are used in the attribute (agreement = 100%, overlap = 0%, disagreement = 0%). In this case, it is safe to say that the attribute takes its values from the known data domain.
2. All the values in the attribute are members of the known domain, but there are domain members that are not used in the attribute (agreement = 100%, overlap > 0%, disagreement = 0%). In this case, it is also likely that the attribute takes its values from the domain, but this may also indicate the attribute's use of a subdomain, which should be explored.
3. Some of the attribute values are members of the known domain, but some of the values used in the attribute are not members of the known domain (agreement < 100%, disagreement > 0%). In this case, there are two possibilities: (a) There is no real agreement between the attribute's values and the domain, in which case the search for a match should continue, and (b) The known domain may actually be a subdomain of a much larger set of values, which should be explored. The decision will probably depend on the percentages computed.
4. None of the values used in the attribute are taken from the known domain (agreement = 0%, overlap = 100%, disagreement = 100%). In this case it is probably safe to say that the attribute does not take its values from the domain.

FUNCTIONAL DEPENDENCY

A functional dependency between two columns, X and Y, means that for any two records $R1$ and $R2$ in the table, if field X of record $R1$ contains value x and field X of record $R2$ contains the same value x, then if field Y of record $R1$ contains the value y, then field Y of record $R2$ must contain the value y. We can say that attribute Y is determined by attribute X. Functional dependencies may exist between multiple source columns. In other words, we can indicate that one set of attributes determines a target set of attributes.

A functional dependency establishes a relationship between two sets of attributes. If the relationship is causal (i.e., the dependent attribute's value is filled in as a function of the defining attributes), that is an interesting piece of business knowledge that can be added to the growing knowledge base. A simple example is a "total_amount_charged" field that is computed by multiplying the "qty_ordered" field by the "price" field.

If the relationship is not causal, then that piece of knowledge can be used to infer information about normalization of the data. If a pair of data attribute values is consistently bound together, then those two columns can be extracted from the targeted table and the instance pairs inserted uniquely into a new table and assigned a reference identifier. The dependent attribute pairs (that had been removed) can then be replaced by a reference to the newly created corresponding table entry.

KEY RELATIONSHIPS

A table *key* is a set of attributes that can be used to uniquely identify any individual record within the table. For example, people databases might use a Social Security number as a key (although this is ill-advised, considering that many people do not have a Social Security number), because (presumably) no two people share the same one. If we have one table that contains a specified key field, other tables may be structured with references to the first table's key as a way of connecting pairs of records drawn from both tables. When one table's key is used as a reference to another table, that key is called a *foreign key*.

Modern relational databases enforce a constraint known as *referential integrity*, which states that if an attribute's value is used in table A as a foreign key to table B, then that key value must exist in one record in table B. There are two aspects to profiling key relationships: identifying that a key relationship exists, and identifying what are called *orphans* in a violated referential integrity situation.

A foreign key relationship exists between (table A, column x) and (table B, column y) if all the values in (table A, column x) overlap completely with the values in (table B, column y) and the values in (table B, column y) are unique. A data profiling application should be able to apply this assertion algorithmically to find foreign key relationships.

Orphans are foreign key values that do not appear in records in the targeted table. An example might be a reference in a catalog to a product that is no longer being made or sold by the company. The referential integrity constraint asserts that if the product is referenced in the catalog, it must exist in the active products database. If the data profiling tool is told that a foreign key relationship exists, it is simple to check for orphans. Even if the profiling tool has no prior knowledge about foreign keys, it is possible to loosen the rules for identifying the foreign key relationship to find *near-foreign keys* where there are some values that would be orphans if the relationship did really exist. As in other cases, the tool can only propose these discoveries as rules, and it is up to the analyst to determine the value in the proposal.

Management Issues

When data profiling tools were first introduced, their relatively high cost was prohibitive for many implementations. However, at this point, data profiling is essentially a commodity; most data warehousing, data quality, or data integration vendors bundle profiling within their offerings, and there are a number of open source data profiling tools available as well. Some things to be aware of, though, include system performance and scope of the results.

First off, some of the algorithms used in data profiling are actually quite computationally intensive, and it is not unusual for some of the analysis to require both large amounts of computational resources (memory, disk space) and time to successfully complete. Second, because the computations are summaries of frequency analysis and counts, the results presented tend to be almost endless, with long lists of values, each of which may have appeared only once in a column. For small tables this is not really an issue. But if you start looking at large tables (greater than 1 million records, which today is really not unusual), the output can be more than overwhelming. The savvy manager needs to be aware that some expertise is required in absorbing the results of a data profiling application and know how best to use the application.

Summary

Data profiling adds significant value to the BI program when it can be used to effectively provide the archeological or forensic evidence of why specific data is the way it is. Data profiling is also useful in exposing business rules that are embedded in data, and it can help preserve information that may be scrubbed out during the data integration stages. In addition, profiling is actually directly useful in a number of BI applications, such as fraud detection, when the data analyst is familiar with the kinds of results to look for.

Business Rules

Every industry is subject to externally defined guidelines, whether they derive from laws, industry standards, or just best practices. Yet despite the assumption that all competitors are likely to respond to any event or situation in similar ways, numerous businesses are still able to enter and compete within the same industry, with different levels of success. For example, commodity insurance companies (such as those selling automobile or home insurance) essentially sell the same or similar types of products. Each of the companies is subject to the same industry-imposed rules (e.g., standardization of information exchange) and government-imposed rules (e.g., government-imposed fees, taxes, regulations).

But clearly, some insurance companies are much more successful than others. This is probably due to the fact that each organization within an industry would be expected to have its own set of internal guidelines, policies, and directives that shape both the tactical (i.e., operational) and strategic decision-making processes.

In the past, success has been attributed to good management techniques, efficiency in running the business, and the ability to quickly recognize and capitalize on emerging opportunities. This last point implies the ability to recognize standard business operation as well as the ability to distinguish between normal operations, deviation from normal operations, and when deviation presents a profit opportunity. As the amounts of data pile up, though, the ability to absorb and, more importantly, react to opportunities exposed through data analysis decreases. Therefore, if we can articulate business behavior in a way that not only eases normal operations but also helps expose opportunities, then we can enhance our ability to succeed.

The challenge with articulating business behavior is twofold. First, most organizations do not have well-defined frameworks for capturing, documenting, and executing business behavior. Second, even with a framework, the disciplines necessary are often immature. Even so, we are interested in the technologies associated with success, and we can paraphrase the previous paragraph by saying that business operation and behavior is driven by a set of rules, laws, regulations, guidelines, and policies.

In turn, the ways that a company executes within those defined boundaries can affect that company's degree of success. From the business intelligence (BI) perspective, we might say that all business processes are governed by a set of *business rules*. More to the point, the culmination of the decision-making processes driven by the myriad queries and reports generated within any organization not only are impacted by inherent or embedded business rules, the application of business rules to data is pervasive across all aspects of applications and processes as the data sets are shared across multiple information flows.

In this chapter, the focus is on abstracting the *operation* of a business process from the *rules that govern* that process. In other words, we can differentiate between the rules that drive a process and the generic machinery that implements those rules and, consequently, that process. We refer to the separation of business logic from logic implementation as the *business rules approach*. The simplest way to describe a business rules system is as a well-described set of environment states, a collection of environment variables, a set of formally defined rules that reflect business policies, preferences, guidelines, and such, indicating how the environment is affected, and a mechanism for operationalizing those rules. In a business rules system, all knowledge about a business process is abstracted and is separated from the explicit implementation of that process. In this chapter, we will explore the use of business rules and how the use of business rules influences the development and deployment of BI applications.

The Value Proposition of Business Rules

The concept of "business rules" is widely acknowledge yet not well understood, especially when you consider how many different ways that business rules come into being, and are managed, documented, implemented, and verified. Sometimes a business rule is applied by an expert based on his or her experience and knowledge.

Sometimes the business rule is integrated into a database table structure, while at other times a business rule is embedded in application program code.

Unfortunately, there are often gaps between the knowledge and experience employed by a subject matter expert and what is assumed to be known by a database administrator or a software developer.

When it comes to a holistic understanding of varying business dependencies and controls, not only are most individuals unknowledgeable about the business details, they are also lax in documenting their implementations. Other risks to managing corporate knowledge include high employee turnover, much business logic embedded in application software, techniques for system development that bypass good documentation, and the absence of system maintenance that allows both code and documentation to quickly grow stale or, worse yet, become completely invalid.

Fortunately, therein lies an opportunity to capture business logic and turn it into a company asset. The area of business rules is a maturing evolving technology that derives its value specifically from the separation of business logic from applications that implement the logic. A business rules system is designed to capture the knowledge of all the assertions, constraints, guidelines, policies, regulations, and such that drive a business process and manage that knowledge as a corporate asset. What follows are some of the major advantages of implementing business processes using a business rules system.

ENCAPSULATION OF SUCCESSFUL BUSINESS LOGIC

Presuming that we have successfully isolated the right queries or program logic used to identify a business opportunity as part of our BI program, it is worthwhile to attempt to automate that logic to free analyst resources for exploring new opportunities. For example, if our BI process has exposed a sequence of events that take place before a customer closes a bank account, it would be worthwhile to embed the knowledge of that sequence in an operational framework that can identify the sequence at an early stage and alert the proper agent within that workflow to contact the customer before the undesired event takes place. Implementing this *sequence watch* as part of a business rules system is much more efficient than having individuals continually querying a system looking for that specific transaction sequence.

COMPONENTIZED DEVELOPMENT

Large business processes can be decomposed into smaller subprocesses, each of which can be addressed using a set of business rules. Therefore, a team can implement a series of reports, alerts, or notifications as part of a BI system that relies on business rules by selecting individual components of the BI process and incrementally developing and deploying a rule set for each component process.

SPEED OF IMPLEMENTATION

In the past, traditional business system development relied on multiperson coordination and communication that spans the gap between the business clients, data modelers, and applications programmers, filtered through a sequence of business liaisons and technical managers. The technical endpoints of this communication chain (the modelers and the programmers) are unlikely to understand much of the modeled business process, while the business clients often do not properly parse what the technical contacts are saying. This communications chain can resemble the children's game of "telephone," where the message is incrementally eroded as it passes from the source to its intended target. The result: a flawed implementation requiring additional resources to coordinate and execute these communications, followed by the need to recommunicate, redesign, and reimplement until the developed application actually somewhat delivers the desired objectives.

This iterative development cycle not only delays the delivery of what was originally intended by the BI program, it creates new bottlenecks for every subsequent project. Instead of spending time translating a business requirement into a specific hard-coded implementation, that time can be used in properly understanding and documenting the business rules to be implemented, which in turn separates the implementation of complex business logic from nonexperts. This narrows the time needed to complete an application. In addition, given the set of business rule inputs and expected outputs, many possible states of the system can be enumerated based on the rules set, and test cases can be automatically generated, subsequently reducing the time needed to test.

EASE OF MODIFICATION AND RAPID RESPONSE TO CHANGE

By extracting a process's business logic from its implementation, there is a natural mapping of business policy to the dependencies within the different systems. That means that when the business environment changes it is easier to update the rule base (instead of digging through undocumented code) to speed up policy implementation. Because a business rules system is built as a collection of rules, the system is easily changed by adding, removing, or modifying a single rule at a time. Changes to the rule base, as long as they do not create inconsistencies, can be integrated quickly into execution. Changes in policies, laws, and regulations effect changes in business processes, and rules systems make it easy to isolate those rules relevant to a specific process and adapt them to a changing environment, and because the application integration mechanics are handled by a runtime-based rules engine, the amount of coding is decreased. In addition, managing business rules as content makes business process reengineering easier. Having all the policies situated in one location enables analysts to understand what the application under investigation was meant to do.

REUSE

Employing business rules is another scenario where we can apply the idea of reuse. In any large environment, there are many situations where the same business rules affect more than one area of operations. Frequently the same business logic must be applied in different operational environments or departments. When different departments implement their own sets of business rules, each department will probably have implemented those rules in a different way, leading to dichotomies in understanding (at best) and to enterprisewide inconsistencies or even contradictions, at worst.

The idea that each group relies on similar business logic allows us to try to capture similarly defined rules and reference data throughout the enterprise into a coordinated, centralized repository. We can start out by aggregating the metadata that will support the development of second-order business logic that reflects the higher-level business rules. Once the repository of rules is created, the actual processing and execution of these rules can be replicated and distributed across multiple servers located across an enterprise network. This is increasingly more feasible within the context of services-oriented architectures, in which the underlying rules are encapsulated within homogenized sets of services that can be invoked by many different client applications. Therefore, a business rules system exposes an opportunity for enterprisewide reuse through an organizationally shared business rule repository.

PERSISTENCE OF ENCAPSULATION OF BUSINESS KNOWLEDGE

An expanding rule base is the basis for documenting and archiving the blueprints of its intellectual expertise, leading to a persistent knowledge base. The first benefit of this is that business processes that have been archived as rule sets can survive the departure of those subject matter experts (SMEs) that manage the process. This is in contrast to the past, when system knowledge was almost always embedded within the minds of individuals, although that knowledge could be considered corporate intellectual capital. Although the use of business rules cannot remove this knowledge from an individual's mind, it can encapsulate that knowledge as content that can be managed by the company, in a format that allows an easy transition during personnel turnover. The second benefit is reaped when business knowledge expressed in a format can be analyzed automatically, yielding an opportunity to infer additional BI embedded within the set of rules.

ENHANCED CAPABILITY THROUGH THE DECLARATIVE MODEL

Rules engines operate in stages: Evaluate the environment, check for triggered conditions, and execute corresponding actions. Only those rules that are affected by inputs or triggers at each execution stage are going to be executed. In procedural languages, rule sequence execution is predetermined by the programmer. This not only forces many "rules" (as embedded in "if-then" statements) to be unnecessarily executed, it opens up the possibility for incorrect execution if the nesting of rules is not appropriate.

The Business Rules Approach

The intent of the business rules approach is the ability to encapsulate and then reuse the business logic for the purpose of identifying or highlighting entities or events within a system. Capturing and formally managing this business logic allows you to automate the repetitive operations that have been properly vetted in terms of business value so that analyst resources can be engaged in discovering new opportunities for improvement or adding value. A business rules approach integrates the following:

- **Technology**, which includes the actual machinery that represents the different operational states of the business environment as well as the mechanics for describing and implementing the rules. This involves evaluating and selecting componentry and tools to use business rules and coordinating the integration with other aspects of the system.
- **Workflow**, which includes exploring the different entities involved in the business process, whether human or automated; the business scenarios in which these entities interact; and how these entities interact. The analysis for this involves describing the scenario, enumerating the entities, looking at the different business events that can take place within the environment, and evaluating how each entity reacts to each business event. In our vocabulary, the workflow aspect describes the changes in state that take place when a data input appears and a rule is applied.
- **Information**, which concerns the actual data that is used within the business process. Evaluating the data requirements of the business process eventually drives the parameters for using business rules as part of a BI program.
- **Rules**, which define the analysis of the assertional system that describes the interactions between the entities within the system. These also incorporate the description of what events trigger which responses and how those interactions relate to the business process.

The Definition of a Business Rule

According to the Business Rule Group (an independent organization composed of practitioners in the field of systems and business analysis methodology, focusing on the nature and structure of business rules and the relationship of rules to systems' architectures), a business rule is a directive intended to command and influence or guide business behavior, in support of business policy that is formulated in response to an opportunity or threat. From the information system perspective, a business rule is a statement that defines or constrains some aspect of the business. It is intended to assert business structure or to control or influence the behavior of the business.[1]

From a practical standpoint, a business rule either asserts a declarative statement about the state of a business process or provides a directive describing changes to the state of a business process. More simply, a business rule dictates what happens when a sequence of inputs is applied to one or more well-described scenarios.

There is strategic value to an organization that can consolidate its business rules and automate the implementation of those rules. Consolidation of business rules captures and controls strategic knowledge; in executable systems, this knowledge is most frequently incorporated into program logic, which is hard to both access and control. Capturing and controlling the embedded knowledge requires that it be moved from the opaque representation of the computer program and restated abstractly using a formal definition framework. But despite the potential benefits of using a business rules system, there are still some hurdles to overcome regarding the semantics and specification of rules.

RULE BASICS

Using automated business rules requires an understanding of the types of rules and the ways they can be specified. In business systems, rules form the programmed representation of business policies and practices. Here are some examples.

- Any purchase in which the total cost exceeds the purchaser's preapproved credit limit requires manual review and approval.
- A customer's total of ATM withdrawals today must be less than or equal to $500.
- If a reservation cannot be found for this customer, attempt to place the customer at another local hotel.
- A patient's personal information must not be exposed to unauthorized parties.

A rule is a statement that asserts some truth about the system, along with an implication for actions to be performed, depending on the assertion's truth value. For example, for the rule regarding the dollar limit for ATM withdrawals, if the total amount requested exceeds the limit, then the request is denied.

In fact, each of the examples reflect this characteristic, and that suggests that any of those rules can be restated in a simple yet formal representation. For convenience we will make use of the "condition followed by action" form. Actions may consist of modifying the environment (which then may turn on other conditions or assertion violations) or restricting some modification to the environment, such as disallowing a transaction. Conditions are evaluated when some trigger event occurs; when a condition is evaluated, followed by taking some action, we say that rule has been *fired*. For simplicity, we can describe different classes of business rules, and we will look at six kinds of rules, along with some examples.

DEFINITIONS AND SPECIFICATIONS

In any system of rules, there must be a well-defined, agreed-upon vocabulary for rule specification; we can then enumerate the participants within the system along with the descriptive nouns and verbs that are used in describing the business process. For example, in a telecommunications application, we might define the different kinds of customers (e.g., business versus residential), the billing plans, and the different services and products that may be provided. This encapsulates a lot of the terminology that requires SMEs, and it also provides the first cut at accumulating business knowledge from the implementation of a business process. For example, when we begin to identify and name data domains, such as "United States Postal Service state abbreviations" or "International currency codes," we begin to assign some business meaning to sets of data whose previous identity revolved solely around its strict type structure.

ASSERTIONS

Assertions are statements about entities within the system that express sensible observations about the business. Assertions describe relationships between entities and activities within the framework. Together, the definitions and assertions drive the construction of the logical data model within which the business rules operate. Assertions incorporate business knowledge, connecting noun terms with verb phrases to describe facts about the system, such as:

- An account holder may make a deposit into an account.
- Any order must reference a product code and a quantity.
- Delivery may be executed via air, rail, or truck.
- A stock option must have an underlier, expiration date, and strike price.

CONSTRAINTS

Constraints express unconditional conformance to a business statement; compared to a constraint, a data instance either conforms to that constraint or violates it. An event that violates a constraint will be rejected by the system, and therefore by definition no action can be taken that will violate a constraint. As a corollary, this implies a set of triggers and actions to indicate a violation in conformance. Here are some examples of constraints.

- A customer cannot order less than three items.
- A customer's debit total cannot exceed his account balance.

- No payment will be issued for any invoice missing a PO number.
- The kiln temperature must not exceed 2000°F.

GUIDELINES

A guideline expresses a desire about the state of the system or a warning about a potential change in the system. A violation of a guideline may indicate a change in the business process that requires attention. Here are some examples.

- If the total amount of all monthly loan payments exceeds 35% of an individual's monthly gross income, the loan request is subject to senior-level review.
- The payment is due within 10 days of receiving the invoice.
- The transaction should clear within the same 24-hour period in which it was initiated.
- If the customer has not initiated a transaction within the past 60 days, the account may be in danger of closure.

When guidelines are violated, the system is still in a valid state but may be progressing to an undesirable state in which some action is needed to prevent the system from reaching that state. Because violations of constraints do not constitute a system violation, events that violate a guideline are not rejected, but a notification should be generated to indicate the violation. Guidelines fit nicely into the BI program because we may represent trends or predictability in this format, and they may feed into direct reports or notifications to specific parties.

ACTIONS

An action is any operation that changes the system state, typically as a result of the violation of some constraint or guideline. Some examples of actions include:

- Computations involving the determination of the value to assign to a named variable based on system state;
- Initiating communication, such as packaging up a message and sending it to a specific user, or turning on a siren;
- Initiating a workflow or a sequence of actions.

TRIGGERS

A trigger specifies a collection of conditions and the initiation of an action contingent upon the conditions' value. Triggers may combine constraints or guidelines with actions. For example:

- If the patient's temperature exceeds 104°F, alert a doctor.
- If a customer's shopping cart total exceeds her credit limit, notify the customer and restore the contents of the shopping cart to a state where the limit is not exceeded.

- If the transaction is not completed within 60 seconds, remove the transaction from the queue, increase its priority, and resubmit.

INFERENCE

An inference specifies a collection of conditions establishing a fact that becomes true as a by-product of changes within the states of the system. An inference is essentially a new piece of information derived from the system state; when an inference rule is executed, that new piece of information must be integrated into the system state. Therefore, the application of an inference rule may result in the initiation of new transactions to log the new data within the logical rule model. For example:

- If the customer is delinquent in payment three times, increase the customer's default risk.
- If the number of long-distance minutes used by the customer exceeds 500 four months in a row, the customer is a "high-volume" user.

Business Rule Systems

A business rules system encapsulates sets of environment states, environment variables, and formally defined rules that reflect business policies, preferences, guidelines, triggers, and so on, and how the environment is affected based on those rules. All knowledge about a business process is abstracted and is separated from the explicit implementation of that process; in operation, rules are coupled with a generic rules engine to form an application to implement the business process. A business rules system incorporates the following components.

- A **rule definition framework** that should present a methodology and environment for defining (and managing) a set of rules that are relevant to a particular business process.
- A **persistent rule base** that enables the storing, browsing, editing, and forwarding of defined rule sets throughout the rules system. Expect to have some globally shared repository and a publish/subscribe interface.
- A **rules engine** that can read a set of rules, connect to the requisite data sources and targets, and manage the state of the rules environment.
- An **execution framework** in which the rules engine will execute, whether it refers to a message stream, a database system, a workflow environment, or the like.

We can think of a business rules system as an abstract machine with a finite number of system "states," each of which represents some aspect of a business process (see Figure 11.1). Events and data act as triggers to change a state within the system, and business rules essentially describe the current state of the system, events or data elements that trigger state transitions, and the new state of the system. This system should include all state changes related to each input, as a matter of completeness. Because rules are declarative (i.e., they describe the system) instead of procedural (i.e., a description of a sequence of operations), at any point a number of rules may be applied without any predeclared constraint as to order of execution, thereby injecting a possibility of nondeterministic behavior.

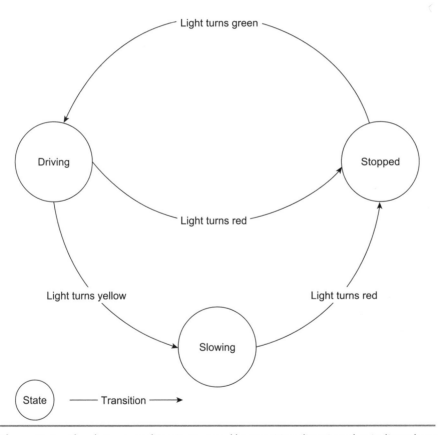

Figure 11.1   The abstract machine is governed by transition directives that indicate how the system changes state based on different inputs and events.

For example, a traffic light can be described as a simple business rules system implementing a travel safety policy. A traffic light "system" managing street crossing may exist in one of three states:

1. Green
2. Yellow
3. Red

Consider the use case of an individual driving down the street. When the system is in state 1, the light is green and the traveler may cross the intersection. If the light changes to yellow, the system moves into state 2 and any travelers who have not yet approached the intersection should slow down in preparation for the transition to state 3. When the light changes to red, the system is in state 3 and all traffic must stop. The final transition is when the light changes back to green, reentering state 1.

RULES DEFINITION

All rules-based systems require the use of some kind of rules language as a descriptive formalism for describing all the aspects of the business process, including the system states, the actors, the inputs and events, the triggers, and the transitions between states. A rules language is a framework for describing sets of rules. Because our description of a rule includes both a condition and an action, any standard programming language, such as Java or C++ containing conditional branching logic (such as IF-THEN-ELSE constructs), can be used as a rules language.

But the standard procedural programming languages impose a sequential order of execution, so their use as rules languages is limited. This is because nondeterminism is associated with events and assertions in the modeled world. A procedural language will impose an artificial dependence on the event sequence and can lead to unexpected results if those events take place in different orders. Instead, rules languages, by virtue of their declarative syntax, provide a way to express a set of rules without imparting any order of execution.

Frequently, rules definition is being embodied within a visual interface. The benefit of the graphical user interface (GUI) is the inclusion of syntax-directed editing that prevents the user from entering ill-formed rules.

RULES ENGINES

A rules engine is an application that takes as input a set of rules, creates a framework for executing those rules, and monitors the system to ensure behavioral compliance with those rules. Rules engines work together with a rules language. A rules engine always acts abstractly, in that its operation is the same no matter what rules are being used; this reflects the separation of business logic from its implementation.

Complex rules engines allow for multiple concurrent evaluations of rules as well as parallel triggered execution. Other kinds of rules engines perform complex mathematical reductions to verify the continued truth values of the system. Simpler rules engines will (perhaps in a nondeterministic way) select a rule for evaluation and possibly execute an action if the condition evaluates to true.

Sources of Business Rules

There are many sources for rules, such as conversations with people, design documents, laws, regulations, and program codes, to name a few. Each of these sources may be rich in business rules, but because of the peculiarities of each source, the extraction of rules from each requires different skills.

PEOPLE

People drive conversations with subject matter experts to focus on understanding how the business processes work, specific decision points, and the logic employed to make those choices, and engage the subject matter experts to review data discrepancies. As an example, one client's data profile revealed some questionable values lurking within some of the columns. The mere mention of this to the subject matter expert immediately provoked a response that was indicative of an implicit business rule.

DOCUMENTATION

Business rules are often directly embedded within documents, such as requirements documents, system designs, as well as data dictionaries. For example, clear dependencies are often detailed within data element descriptions, such as where the description of valid values for data elements as well as relationships between different elements within the same table and across other tables were all hidden within text fields as part of a data dictionary spreadsheet. Documentation is a rich source of business rules, although you must be careful, because documentation frequently does not remain synchronized with what is being documented. Descriptive text is rich with rules, and you must gain a lot of experience in translating text into rules.

LAWS AND STANDARDS

Organizations that are bound by a governing board's set of regulations may find that regulations are an excellent source of business rules. Clearly, laws and regulations, directives, and even suggestions by governing organizations or industry consortia are good sources for business rules. Reading through regulations requires the finely tuned eye of an SME who can reasonably extract the rule from the text.

APPLICATION CODE

One stickier problem in rule discovery is extracting business rules from existing application programs. Because all application code logic is likely to be related to some business directive, the amount of time it would take to collect and analyze an entire software system might prove to be a resource sink. Alternatively there have been some suggested tools to perform what could be called "code mining," which would:

■ Analyze program control structure;
■ Look for code fragments where conditions are being tested;
■ Extract those conditions;
■ Look for actions being taken based on the truth of conditions;
■ Extract those actions.

The extracted conditions and actions could then be presented to an analyst to determine whether business rules are encapsulated within that program logic.

TURNING LANGUAGE INTO RULES

A major benefit of the business rules approach is that analyzing a business process provides a mechanism for extracting knowledge from program logic and allowing it to be treated as content. The rule analysis process leads toward the ability not just to isolate rules that are relevant to the operations of a business process or decisions about the process that must be made, but also to identify terms, facts, and assertions about the business entities that are typically modeled in a database. By accumulating business rules, routing them into sets, naming those sets, and managing those as actionable content, we gain some control over our business processes that was missing when all the logic was buried in the implementation.

THE VALUE OF SUBJECT MATTER EXPERTS

A challenging part of this process is learning enough of the language that is specific or particular to an organization or an industry that is implicit in the selected sources of rules (people, documentation, legislation, etc.) and figuring out how to translate it into rule syntax. This is particularly valuable in an environment where knowledge needs to be published to a number of players throughout an organization, especially where context or subject matter expertise is required. This is a good example of a process that takes advantage of the BI team's technical and business knowledge diversity. Having business-savvy subject matter experts on the team will ease that process.

Consider this excerpt from an extension to Securities Exchange Commission (SEC) rule 17a-25, of the Securities Exchange Act of 1934.

> *For a proprietary transaction, the broker-dealer must include the following information: (1) clearing house number or alpha symbol used by the broker-dealer submitting the information; (2) clearing house number(s) or alpha symbol(s) of the broker-dealer(s) on the opposite side to the trade; (3) security identifier; (4) execution date; (5) quantity executed; (6) transaction price; (7) account number; and (8) identity of the exchange or market where each transaction was executed. Under the proposed rule, if a transaction was effected for a customer account (as opposed to a proprietary account), the broker-dealer would have been required to also include the customer's name, customer's address, name of the customer's employer, the customer's tax identification number, and other related account information.[2]*

From this example, an expert in understanding SEC regulations would be able to describe what goes into an electronic submission; the BI professional must prompt that SME to define those components, such as alpha symbol, clearing house number, security identifier, account numbers, and tax identification number (which we then add to our knowledge base), as well as the relationships between those components before any advantage can be gained through rule translation.

Management Issues

When deciding to develop a system using the business rules approach, we have to invert our thinking process by imagining what the state of the universe is when we have arrived at the end state. In other words, consider what the system should look like after it is built, and enumerate all the rules that specify our expectations about how that system works. These expectations are the seeds of our business rules.

What this means is that we have to envision our business process in operation and enumerate all animate and inanimate participants (people, events, data sources, etc.) in that process. Having done so, we then articulate all of our expectations of that business process and how those expectations are affected by inputs, people, and changes in state. Last, we look at ways to specify those expectations within the rule definition framework, as well as evaluating our system to ensure that we can handle all potential business events within the system.

Political Issues

Similar to other components of a BI program, a barrier to a successful business rule implementation is a social issue, not a technical one, for a number of reasons.

1. **Risk assessment.** When migrating to a new technology, there is always a measure of risk. Although rule-based systems have been available for a long time, their use in production systems is limited, and this will naturally lead to suspicion about the technology's effectiveness.
2. **Territorial concerns.** Trying to extract business logic from programmer code for the sake of automatically building applicationware is likely to stir concerns among the people working on the original code. They are likely to be resistant to the introduction of a technology that will render their positions obsolete.
3. **High expectations.** Because the use of a rules system dictates that a system will be built employing rules, instead of traditional procedural programming languages, this might imply a decrease in the need for programmers. In reality, business rule analysts are as specialized as programmers, and care must be taken not to set unrealistic expectations.

Limitations of the Approach

There are of course limitations to the use of business rules, often having to do with the "hockey-stick" growth of complexity as more individuals, systems, and expectations enter the mix. Some management issues include:

- **Detail management.** Associated with any set of rules is the specter of a rule base gone wild, filled with meaningless trivialities and stale rules that only clog up the system. When using a rules system, we must be detail oriented to the extent that the rules engineer is willing to commit to understanding the rule definition system and the rule management system. The rules approach requires a dedication to detail, because all objects operating in the business process as well as all attributes of each object must be specified. This requires a dedication to detail as well as an understanding of business process analysis.
- **Inflated expectations.** Enthusiastic adopters of rules-based technology may have expectations that a converted set of complex business policies into a rules-based system will always be faster to implement, easier to maintain, and efficient in execution. Although this may be true for some applications, the fact is that business policies themselves frequently are poorly specified, and the business process of converting a policy statement into a rules base can be very complicated.
- **Programmers are not eliminated.** Because of the nice "natural language" qualities of rule descriptions, there is a general impression that a business process application can be built by nonprogrammers and that the IT resources and

association can be eliminated. This is a naïve impression, because rule specification itself is dominated by strict syntactical structure; even if it is not called "programming," the skill and experience required match those of a programmer.

To Learn More

Business rules provide a nice mechanism for encapsulating discovered BI to be integrated into an ongoing operational framework. Some examples of this kind of application include ongoing fraud detection, customer behavior analysis and alerting, and customer attrition. In addition, business rules can be used as the basis for the data preparation process, such as information compliance, data cleansing, data profiling, and data integration.

Endnotes

1. Business Rules—What are They Really? http://www.businessrulesgroup.org/first_paper/br01c1.htm.
2. This material is taken from a proposed rule 17–25a of the Securities Exchange Act of 1934, the text of which can be found at www.sec.gov/rules/proposed/34-42741.htm.

Chapter 12

Data Quality

Good Decisions Rely on Quality Information

In Chapter 7 we described a process for soliciting data requirements from among the potential consumers of business intelligence (BI) and analytics, and part of that process yielded expectations for the quality of the source data to be used for analytics. Of course, if there are suspicions about the quality of the source data, that will lead to suspicions about the results, which can derail any decision-making process. Yet there is a difference between what is meant by managing the quality of data prior to its incorporation into a data analysis environment such as a data warehouse and cleansing data that has already been destined for the analytical platform.

In fact, we might say that there are some severe limitations to data cleansing that is performed outside of the originating systems. Although many data cleansing products can help in applying data edits to name and address data or help in transforming data during the data integration processes, the results will typically create an inconsistency with a data source, which (unless that cleansing is made in the source system) may eventually lead to confusion. Therefore, it is important to keep in mind that cleansing data in a data warehouse is almost a last resort—instead, ensure the quality of the data as it enters the environment, and that will help in reducing inconsistencies downstream.

Improved data quality is the result of a process for identifying and subsequently eliminating the root causes of data flaws. A critical component of improving data quality is being able to distinguish between "good" (i.e., valid) data and "bad" (i.e., invalid) data. But because data values appear in many contexts, formats, and frameworks, this simple concept devolves into extremely complicated notions as to what constitutes validity.

However, what is intended by the concept of data value validity *must* be evaluated and defined within the contexts in which that data value is used. For example, there may be many ways in which customers refer to a corporation, but there is only one legal name under which the corporation is officially registered. In most contexts any of the corporate aliases may be sufficient, whereas in other contexts only the legal name is valid.

This chapter centers on the importance of defining data quality expectations and measuring data quality against those expectations. We will also look at the general perception of data quality and what the savvy manager needs to know to distinguish between data cleansing and data quality.

What is particularly interesting is that some of these assessments of the commercial costs of poor data quality are based on relatively simple metrics related to incorrect names and addresses. Although I don't want to minimize the value of correct names and addresses, the realm of invalid data spans much more than the question of whether the catalog is being sent to the right person at the right address. In other words, data quality is more than just names and addresses.

The Virtuous Cycle of Data Quality

Data quality management incorporates a "virtuous cycle" in which continuous analysis, observation, and improvement lead to overall improvement in the quality of organizational information across the board (see Figure 12.1). The objective of this cycle is to transition from being an organization in which the data stewards react to acute data failures into an organization that proactively controls and limits the introduction of data flaws into the environment.

In turn, this virtuous cycle incorporates five fundamental data quality management practices, which are ultimately implemented using a combination of core data services. Those practices are:

1. **Data quality assessment**, as a way to understand how data issues affect business processes performance.
2. **Data quality measurement**, in which the data quality analysts synthesize the results of the assessment and concentrate on the data elements that are deemed

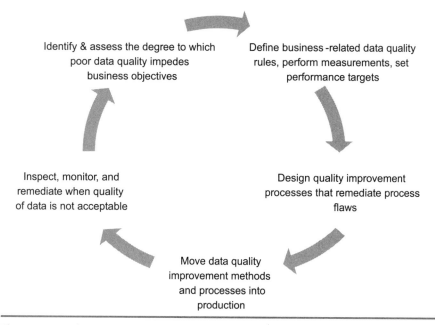

Figure 12.1   The virtuous cycle of data quality management.

critical based on the selected business users' needs. This enables data quality reporting and scorecards.

3. **Integrating data quality into the application infrastructure**, by integrating validation of data requirements into applications as part of the system development life cycle.

4. **Operational data quality improvement**, where data governance procedures are used to manage identified data quality rules along with conformance at targeted levels of acceptability.

5. **Data quality incident management**, which allows the data quality analysts to review the degree to which the data does or does not meet the levels of acceptability; report, log, and track issues; and document the processes for remediation and improvement.

These practices help in laying the groundwork for continuous improvement of data quality, which, as we will see later in this chapter, is particularly critical in the data warehouse and business analytics environment.

Types of Data Flaws

A good way to internalize the types of issues to be dealt with is to consider some common error paradigms. Here we look at some common data flaws.

Inconsistent Number of Records

Data exchanges may be executed in a variety of ways, of which a large percentage involve batch or bundled transfers of sets of data instances or records. A gross-level data flaw occurs when the number of records in the bundle is not the same as the number of records purported to have been transferred.

Data Element Granularity Issues

Physical representations of similar data elements in different data sources can be designed to capture different amounts of information. For example one data set may use a data element that holds a large character string with a customer's full name (first name, middle name, and last name), while that same information is captured in a different data set using three discrete data elements. The inclusion of multiple name components within a single data element may be relevant in analyses attempting to resolve multiple instances of individual identities that appear in more than one data set that is being incorporated into the analytical framework. Therefore, differences in the granularity of information managed can impact identity resolution.

Invalid Values

A significant amount of information is encapsulated using code sets and reference tables. The validity of a code value can be directly related to its use within a business process context and the existence of a valid mapping to additional reference information. In fact, invalid codes can significantly impact BI and analytics due to the integral hierarchical relationship between the code sets and domain dimensions, especially when the hierarchy is embedded within the code values (a good example is industry classification codes). Values may be invalid because they are not enumerated within the code set or because they are inconsistent with other dependent data element values.

Transcription Errors

Many data errors are introduced as a result of the need to transcribe or copy data from one medium to another, and this often happens at the entry points for data creation or acquisition. When typing data into a form or web page, data entry staff members are likely to introduce variations in spellings, abbreviations, phonetic similarities, transcribed letters inside words, misspelled words, miskeyed letters, among others. Often, data values are subjected to copying from one application to another via "cut-and-paste" editing, which also is prone to occasional errors. Call center personnel often misspell personal and location names, *even when a proper spelling is provided!*

Sometimes there are mechanical issues that can introduce transcription errors as well. As an example, in one data environment, where many of the company names used an ampersand (&) character as part of the name (e.g., Johnson & Smith), a frequent error was the appearance of a 7 instead of the ampersand (e.g., Johnson 7 Smith). This is an apparent shift-key problem, because the "&" is the "7" key shifted. Another example is the pervasive "auto-correct" features provided within web browsers and smart-phone apps, in which a presumed incorrect keying is mapped to an alternative character string.

FORMS AND FLOATING DATA

Business applications are often designed so that their internal models are mapped within the context of the business process to produce forms for data entry and interaction. However, imprecision in the metadata modeling may result in lack of clarity as to whether certain kinds of data go into specific fields. For example, some applications may have data elements for "address1" and "address2," referring to the first and second lines of a party's address. Yet without a standard as to what went into the first line and what went into the second line, suite/apartment/floor information floated into address1 and street number/name/type floated down into address2 (the typical standard prescribes the opposite).

Another common error is floating data—data that inadvertently flows into the wrong element. In a similar example, the street address field was insufficiently sized, so the entry person just continued entering street address data that subsequently floated into the city field.

ABSENT AND (IMPLICITLY) NULL VALUES

The question of nullness is interesting, because the absence of a value may provide more fodder for making inferences than the presence of an incorrect value. The ability of modern relational database systems to impose "not null" constraints on columns may actually create problems that it attempts to solve. The question becomes: If I do not have a value for a specific column that requires a value, what value should be assigned?

The result of this conundrum, as you have probably encountered, is the appearance of a variety of nonstandard values meant to represent different kinds of null values. For example one data assessment might uncover the frequent use of "NA" in many columns, but this is an artifact in incorrect application design: the system would not allow a form to be submitted unless all fields had a value, so the data entry person would just input the "X" to make sure the transaction would be accepted. Some examples are shown in Figure 12.2.

Telephone number	Names	Dates
000-000-0000 0000000000 999-999-9999 X No phone number provided	NA N/A na n/a Unknown UNKNOWN ? ?? ??? X	99/99/9999 XX/XX/XXXX 99/99/99 9/9/99

Figure 12.2   Different kinds of explicit nulls.

UNSTRUCTURED AND SEMISTRUCTURED VALUES

Data records in regular databases are formatted in a structured way, with values assigned to named data elements. However, the content embedded within free text is said to be unstructured (with no imposed formats), or sometimes semistructured, which is essentially free text with some conceptual connectivity. Understanding that connectivity allows for intelligently extracting information embedded within the semistructure.

To reuse one of our earlier examples, a data set that uses a single field for customer name would allow different semistructured formats for representing names. Another example is a data set containing "comments" fields where the data provider is able to insert rambling chunks of free text with no hope of automated extraction. Yet a third example is the streaming of content through social media channels such as social networks, blogs, and so on, where the author has few if any constraints on content format.

FORMATTING ERRORS

We naturally tend to view information in patterns, and data modelers will employ this knowledge to impose a pattern or set of patterns on a set of attributes that may actually prevent those fields from being properly filled in. For example, our expectation that telephone numbers always consist of a three-digit area code, a three-digit exchange number, and a four-digit line number may be generally correct, but it is not correct if we are entering European or Japanese telephone numbers, nor is it necessarily correct if we are viewing US telephone numbers from your office desk in Tokyo. The imposition of strict format compliance may capture correctly formed data a large part of the time and prevent the proper capture the rest of the time!

FLAWED TRANSFORMATION RULES

Errors may be introduced when rules for data integration are incorrectly applied—if the transformation rules are not completely correct or if there is a flaw in the transformation application, errors will be created where none originally existed. For example, in an interesting case, a database of names was found to have an inordinately large number of high-frequency word fragments, such as "INCORP," "ATIONAL," "COMPA." It turned out that the field had been reconstructed from data extracted from a legacy database, which had a limit on the size of an attribute, forcing the data modeler to use more than one actual field to make up one virtual field. During the integration process the merging application inserted a space between each of a set of concatenated fields from the source, and because some of the original data spanned two physical fields, the insertion of the space created a collection of fragments that did not appear in the original data.

ATTRIBUTE OVERLOADING

Either as a reflection of poor data modeling or as a result of changing business concerns, there is information that is stored in one data field that actually contains more than one data value. Examples of this are prevalent in the financial industries, where companies are moving from an account-oriented view to a customer-oriented view. Typically, account names are the official names associated with a financial account, and they may include many combination forms with many associated context terms. The context terms represent business relationships that may need to be exposed in a customer or party's database. Here are some examples.

- John Smith and Mary Smith
- John and Mary Smith
- John Smith in Trust for Charles Smith
- John and Mary Smith UGMA Charles Smith
- John and Mary Smith Foundation, John and Mary Smith Trustees

In each of these examples, we actually see more than just entity names—we may see bound relationships (e.g., the appearance of a male and a female name together, implying a marriage relationship) and business-related attributions (e.g., UGMA = Uniform Gift to Minors Act account) embedded within a single field.

UNIT OF MEASURE ERRORS

Is it measured in feet or in meters? In minutes, hours, or days? Data elements that contain magnitudes must be aligned with the correct unit of measure, which would be documented as part of its metadata. Incorrect presumption of unit of measure can have serious impacts to delivering the appropriate aggregations.

Business Impacts of Data Flaws

Numerous attempts have been made to assign some objective cost to data errors, usually through the presumption of increased costs. Many of these "ROI calculators" are founded on commercial costs of poor data quality related to incorrect names and addresses. Although maintaining high-quality identifying information is critical, there are many types of data errors with different types of information that can impact all sorts of business processes leading to increased costs as well as decreased revenues, increased risk, or decreased productivity. In other words, data quality is more than just names and addresses.

In Chapter 2, we discussed the value drivers for an organization, and how those guided the development of relevant performance metrics. We can similarly consider how data errors can impact both our perception of business performance (based on incorrect results) as well as the performance itself (when data flaws impair business process success).

That suggests that the question of data quality is not one of standardized names and addresses, but rather of fitness for the potentially many purposes to which that data will be put to use. In practicality, almost everyone has a different understanding of what data quality is; each definition is geared toward the individual's view of what is fit and what is not. This leads to the conclusion that there is no hard and fast definition of data quality, nor can there be a single source of "truth." Rather, data quality is defined in terms of how each data consumer wishes to use the data, and to this end we must discuss some dimensions across which data quality can be measured.

Dimensions of Data Quality

A dimension of data quality effectively describes a method for quantifying the level of compliance with defined expectations. There are many possible dimensions of data quality that are relevant within particular business activities, and this is related to the ways that the data will be used downstream. Some of the more typical dimensions include:

- **Completeness**. This dimension measures the degree to which attributes are assigned a nonnull value. Completeness rules can be assigned to a data set in varying levels of constraint—mandatory attributes that require a value, data elements with conditionally optional values, and inapplicable attribute values. Completeness may also be seen as encompassing usability and appropriateness of data values.

- **Consistency**. This dimension refers to ensuring that data values in one data set are consistent with values in another data set, are managed in a consistent representation, or are presented in a consistent manner. The concept of consistency is relatively broad; it can include an expectation that two data values drawn from separate data sets must not conflict with each other, or define consistency with a set of predefined constraints. More formal consistency constraints can be encapsulated as a set of rules that specify consistency relationships between values of attributes, either across a record or message, or along all values of a single attribute. Consistency is not the same as "correctness" or "accuracy," although consistency with a system of records is often the "closest guess" we might have to measuring accuracy. Consistency may be defined between one set of attribute values and another attribute set within the same record (record-level consistency), between one set of attribute values and another attribute set in different records (cross-record consistency), or between one set of attribute values and the same attribute set within the same record at different points in time (temporal consistency).

- **Unique Identifiability**. This dimension refers to requirements that entities modeled within a data set (or across more than one data set) are represented uniquely and are uniquely found within a selected data set. Asserting uniqueness of the entities within a data set implies that no entity exists more than once within the data set and that there is a key that can be used to uniquely access each entity (and only that specific entity) within the data set. Essentially, uniqueness states that no entity exists more than once within the data set, and that the single record can always be located.

- **Currency**. This dimension refers to the degree to which information is current with the world that it models. Currency measures whether data is considered to be "fresh," and its correctness in the face of possible time-related changes. Data currency may be measured as a function of the expected frequency rate at which different data elements are expected to be refreshed, as well as verifying that the data is up to date. Currency rules may be defined to assert the "lifetime" (or correspondingly, the "expiration") of a data value before it needs to be checked and possibly refreshed.

- **Timeliness**. This dimension refers to the time expectation for accessibility and availability of information. As an example, one aspect of timeliness can be measured as the time between when information is expected and when it is readily available for use.

- **Accuracy**. Data accuracy refers to the degree with which data correctly represents the "real-life" entities it is intended to model. In many cases, accuracy is measured by how the values agree with an identified reference source of correct information, such as comparing values against a database of record or a similar corroborative set of data values from another table, checking against dynamically computed values, or perhaps applying a manual process to check value accuracy.

- **Validity**. This dimension refers to whether data instances are stored, exchanged, or presented in a format that is consistent with the domain of values, as well as consistent with other similar attribute values. Each column has numerous metadata attributes associated with it: its data type, precision, format patterns, use of a predefined enumeration of values, domain ranges, underlying storage formats, and so on.

- **Reasonableness**. This dimension is used to consider expectations regarding whether the values make sense within the business context. Often, reasonableness is a catch-all set of dimensions for various defined business rules.

- **Referential Integrity**. Assigning unique identifiers to objects (customers, products, etc.) within your environment simplifies the management of your data, but introduces new expectations that any time an object identifier is used as a foreign key within a data set to refer to the core representation, that core representation actually exists. Rules associated with referential integrity often are manifested as constraints against duplication (to ensure that each entity is represented once, and only once), as well as other relational integrity rules, which assert that all values used as keys actually refer to existing records in another table.

These provide a starting point for measuring the quality of data to be subjected to reporting and analysis. They also provide a categorization for potential issues that can be uncovered through a data quality assessment.

Data Quality Assessment

In order to establish some quantification of the quality of data in a data warehouse, an assessment can be performed using data profiling tools and other statistical methods to help identify potential issues, review the significance or potential impacts associated with the identified issues, and determine the mitigation and remediation tasks to ensure that the data warehouse data is trustworthy enough to satisfy the reporting and analysis needs.

PREPARATION AND DATA ANALYSIS

The typical process of data profiling and statistical analysis is undirected, allowing the tool to drive the activity, with the analyst drilling through various measurements with little forethought, seeking any potential anomalies that may indicate a data flaw. Therefore, we need to assess the quality of the data in the context scoped by the expectations for the downstream BI consumers. This means that the focus is limited to evaluating the quality of the data elements associated with identified business performance value drivers and corresponding measures. This can include:

- **Isolation of critical data elements**. Reducing the scope of the data elements to be examined to those that are critical to producing the results that are impacted;
- **Definition of data quality measurements**. Reviewing the issues that are reported by the business users to provide specific types of data quality expectations, what is to be measured, and how those measurements reflect the business impacts;
- **Prepare data analysis environment**. Prepare the environment to be used for assessment, typically data profiling and statistical analysis tools;
- **Analysis to capture measurements**. Analyzing the data and then capture analysis statistics and measures.

DATA ASSESSMENT

Analysts will first review the column profile of the selected tables/files for frequency-based statistics for the purpose of identifying potential issues. The information potentially derived from column profiling includes inferred metadata, statistical details of value distribution, and frequency of values in columns of interest. Some common column statistics and measures include:

- The number of distinct values
- The highest (maximum) values
- The lowest (minimum) values
- The mean and median value (for numeric data)
- The standard deviation (for numeric data)
- Number of nulls
- Discovered patterns, if any
- Potential overloaded use
- For each column's set of values, verification that inferred data type is consistent with documented data type
- For each column's set of values, verification of the validity of values
- The most frequently occurring values
- The least frequently occurring values
- A visual inspection for consecutive values, similar values, incorrect values

Table profiling focuses on dependencies across the entire table, either between sets of columns or across all records in the data set, such as candidate keys. Identification of functional dependence between sets of attributes may indicate some general correlations, the existence of some (potentially implicit) business rules, or some frequently occurring error conditions that require attention.

Cross-table profiling looks at the relational structure inherent in a collection of data tables, such as:

- **Assessing referential integrity**. Identify any orphaned records in the related table.
- **Reference data validation**. Validate that data elements that are expected to draw their values from existing code tables comply with the expectations.
- **Seek cross-table (Join) duplicates**. Identify overlapping records across multiple tables where only one record should exist.

The analysts reviewing the data statistics are on the lookout for situations in which potentially flawed data values could skew analytical results. The assessment can result in a listing of potential issues for review, such as completeness, consistency, timeliness, and so on, as well as any special processes (other than profiling) used for measurement. The values or results that are of concern or require additional review are noted along with any additional details and suggestions for further investigation.

SYNTHESIS OF ASSESSMENT RESULTS

Even with constraining profiling to those critical data elements, any conclusions regarding the quality of data within the specific business context require review of the analysis results synthesized into a coherent enumeration of potential anomalies, annotated with descriptions indicating their potential relevance. The goal is to organize a list of potential problems along with reasons for suspecting that the issues will affect the BI activity. This phase includes these steps:

- **Review assessment results**. Examine the results of the analysis statistics within the context of the business value drivers.
- **Enumeration of potential anomalies**. Specifically describe the potential anomalies along with the notes explaining why those anomalies are related to business impacts.
- **Potential drill-down for additional detail**. Some discovered items may require additional drill-down or review, perhaps using other analytic tools.
- **Enumeration of items for remediation**. This provides a tangible artifact detailing the potential data flaws in preparation for review with the business data consumers.

REVIEW WITH BUSINESS DATA CONSUMERS

The last part of the assessment is to meet with the business data consumers to review the discovered issues and explore options for remediation. This phase includes these steps:

- **Present analysis report and associated measurements**. Walk through the anomalies, explain what measurements were performed, the scores, and why those scores may be related to identified business impacts.
- **Prioritize discovered issues**. Based on the business client input, prioritize the issues based on significance, business relevance, and feasibility of remediation.
- **Identify remediation tasks**. List specific tasks to be performed to correct data, evaluate root causes, mitigate immediate issues and remediation steps to eliminate the root causes of the introduction of flawed data.

Data Quality Rules

The framework for articulating quality expectations considers how that data is used and how we can express rules from this holistic approach. This can be decomposed into the definition of metadata-like reference data sets and assertions that relate to values, records, columns, and tables within a collection of data sets.

There are many explicit and implicit rules embedded in the use of reference data, and these rules can be documented using a formal metadata definition of nulls, domains, and mappings. Once these collections of data have been identified and their semantics assigned, we begin to get a better understanding of what information is being used in the organization, who is using it, and how that information is being used. Although the values that make up the domains and the mappings may have actually been derived from transactional data, the reference value sets can be categorized as value domains related to conceptual domains, and the relations as mappings. At that point meaning can be ascribed to the collections, the reference data sets can be properly documented and made available for reuse.

Assertions revolve around specifying some business constraint on the relationship between the abstract data instance and the values bound to individual data attributes. Defining these assertions captures the contextual knowledge that governs true data quality by imposing a semantic metadata layer on top of the data format description.

CONCEPTUAL DOMAINS AND VALUE DOMAINS

By assigning an attribute a data type, we indicate that it draws its values from a specific set of allowed values. Further, we expect that any value is taken from a value set that has some structural (i.e., syntactic) rules and explicit semantic rules governing validity. Either way, these expectations restrict the values that an attribute takes. Whether these rules are syntactic or semantic, we can define an explicit set of restrictions on a set of values within a type and call that a *domain*. Some examples of domains include US states, country codes, country currency codes, credit card numbers (they have a predetermined length and there are semantic rules governing validity based on a high-level parity calculation), and colors.

MAPPINGS

We also look at relationships between pairs of values that are taken from different domains. A *mapping* is a relation between domain A and domain B, defined as a set of pairs of values $\{a, b\}$ such that a is a member of domain A and b is a member of domain B. There is an intuitive meaning to this mapping relationship. A familiar example of a mapping is the relationship between ZIP code and city. Every ZIP code belongs to a named area covered by a small post office or postal zone.

NULL CONFORMANCE RULES

There are different data quality rules regarding nulls. One is whether or not an attribute allows nulls at all. Another kind of rule relates previously defined null representations. If nulls are allowed, the rule specifies that if a data attribute's value is null, then it must use one of a set of defined null representations.

VALUE RESTRICTION RULES

A value restriction describes some business knowledge about a range of values, such as "test score is greater than 200 and less than 800." A value restriction rule constrains values to be within the defined range.

DOMAIN AND MAPPING MEMBERSHIP RULES

Domain membership asserts that an attribute's value is always taken from a previously defined data domain. For example, an online catalog vendor may specify a domain of fabric colors and then assert that all sweaters that can be ordered online must be of one of the named colors. A *mapping membership* rule asserts that the relation between two attributes or fields is restricted based on a named mapping. An example enforces the mapping from US state name to its corresponding two-letter postal abbreviation.

Completeness and Exemption Rules

A completeness rule specifies that when a condition is true, a record is incomplete unless all attributes on a provided list are not null. An example in the financial world would specify that if the security being traded is a stock option, the trade is incomplete unless a strike price and expiration date are provided. An exemption rule says that if a condition is true, then those attributes in a named list should not have values. For example, if the customer's age is less than 16, then the driver's license field should be null.

Consistency Rules

A consistency rule indicates that if a particular condition holds true, then a following consequent must also be true. An example in a credit analysis application might say that the amount allowed for a monthly mortgage payment must be no more than 35% of the monthly gross income.

Continuous Data Quality Monitoring and Improvement

We iteratively improve data quality by identifying sources of poor data quality, asserting a set of rules about our expectations for the data, and implementing a measurement application using those rules. In operation, a set of rules is instantiated at each point in the information flow where data quality conformance is to be measured. Each data instance is tested against all associated rules; if no nonconformities are detected, the data instance is deemed to be valid; otherwise, it is said to be invalid. Data instances that fail the rules give us clues as to the sources of the nonconformance, which are then isolated and remedied.

Given a set of rules that define fitness for use and a mechanism for determining conformance of data instances to those rules, we have a measurement framework for data quality. Each data instance tested against a rule set can be scored across multiple dimensions. As we define more rules, we build a rule base that defines the basic expectations of data fitness against which each data instance (record, message, etc.) is measured, thereby providing an ongoing process for improved data quality.

Considerations Regarding Data Quality for Business Analytics

As we have discussed, once candidate data sets have been selected for analysis, it is incumbent upon the data analysts to ensure that the quality of the data sets satisfies the needs of the consumers of the analytical results. It is valuable to focus attention on some specific, related issues:

- Quality vs. correctness
- Precision of quality
- Supplier management (or the lack thereof)
- Data correction vs. process correction

QUALITY VERSUS CORRECTNESS

The first issue involves establishing the difference between what is meant by "perfection" or "correctness" versus defining and adhering to the levels of quality that are sufficient to meet the business needs. Some data quality analysts seem to suggest that data quality assessment should focus on characterizing the "correctness" or "incorrectness" of critical data attributes. The theory is that any obviously incorrect data attribute is probably a problem, and therefore counting the number (or percentage, if that is your preference) of records that are not "perfect" is the first step in identifying opportunities for data quality improvement.

The flaw in this line of thinking is the presumption of what can be inferred to be "obviously incorrect." In some cases, a value that is potentially incorrect might be truly inconsistent with expectations when taken out of context, yet might not have any negative business impact for any number of reasons. And when it comes to business analytics, sometimes the right result can be delivered even in the presence in "imperfect" data.

PRECISION OF QUALITY

This leads into the second issue: how good does the data need to be? The effectiveness of quality improvement, like almost any activity, reflects the Pareto principle: 80% of the benefit can be achieved by 20% of the effort, and consequently, the last 20% of the benefit is achieved with 80% of the effort. If we need our quality rating to be 100%, that is going to have a high demand on resources to eke our way from 80% to 100%. But if a quality score of 80% is sufficient, that is a much smaller hill to climb.

For operational reporting requiring accurate statistics that will be compared to original source systems, the quality of the data must reflect a high consistency between the data for analysis and the original source. On the other hand, when analyzing very large data sets for unusual patterns or to determine relationships, a small number of errors might not significantly skew the results. For example, many large online retailers might seek to drive increased sales through relationship analysis and the appearance of correlated items within a market basket. If they are looking at millions of transactions a day, and a few show up as incorrect or incomplete, the errors are probably going to be irrelevant. This question of precision (i.e., how precise do we need to be in demanding adherence to our target scores for our dimensions of data quality?) may be an objective question but relies on subjective opinions for the measures.

SUPPLIER MANAGEMENT

As we have noted, the level of quality of data used for analysis is directly dependent on the quality of the original sources. As long as the data sets are produced or managed within the same organization, it is not unreasonable to impose an operational governance framework in which flawed data items are investigated to determine the root causes that might be eliminated. But, as we have discussed, there may be a real issue if the data sets used for analysis originate outside your organization's administrative domain and the quality is not up to snuff.

The "supplier management" concept for data quality basically states that as a "customer" of data, you have the right to expect that the data "supplier" will meet your level of expectation for a quality "product." There is a general concept of this unstated contract when we buy things in stores—if the item is no good, we can bring it back for a replacement or refund. If we were paying for the data, the same contract should be in place.

But in many cases, that is not the situation—we use someone else's data, with no exchange of value, and therefore we are not in a position to demand that the supplier put forth effort to meet our needs if this goes beyond their needs. This is even more of an issue when using data taken from outside the organization, especially if the data is "out in the open" such as government data published through data.gov, or even screen-scraped data sets resulting from web queries.

DATA CORRECTION VERSUS PROCESS CORRECTION

This leads to our fourth issue: if we have no leverage with which to induce the data producer to make changes to meet our analytical usage needs, we must be left to our own devices to ensure the quality of the data. It is great to suggest that producer processes be evaluated and improved, but when push comes to shove, we cannot rely on the producer's data quality. Therefore, if corrective action is needed to make the data usable, it might not be unreasonable to presume that is done by the user.

In essence, our four issues provide some level of balance for managing the quality of data that originates outside the administrative domain. In other words, to ensure the data is usable, understand the needs of the users for reporting and analysis, engage the data suppliers if possible to contribute to improving the quality of provided data, and if that is not possible, then you may need to take the matters into your own hands to ensure that the quality of the data is sufficient to meet your needs.

Data Cleansing

In essence, the conclusion we might draw from this discussion is the criticality of ensuring the quality of data prior to its being used for analytical purposes. That suggests a need for encouraging assurance of cleansed data in the originating source systems, suggesting a need for *data cleansing* to be applied early in the process if possible.

However, in the circumstances in which there is a desire to incorporate data that does not meet quality standards into the analytical environment, a decision must be made to either clean the data or load the data set as is. That being said, it is valuable to review the methods used for data cleansing.

PARSING

Often, variations or ambiguity in data value representation may confuse individuals as well as automated applications. For example, consider these different data values: {California, CA, Calif., US-CA, Cal, 06}. Some of these values use character strings, another uses digits, and some use punctuation or special characters. For the most part, a human would read these and recognize that they all represent the same conceptual value: the state of California. Yet automating the process of determining whether these values are accurate or investigating whether duplicate records exist, the values must be parsed into their component segments and then transformed into a standard format.

Parsing is the process of identifying meaningful tokens within a data instance and then analyzing token streams for recognizable patterns. A token is a conglomeration of a number of single words that have some business meaning; with customer data, these tokens may refer to components of a person or business name, parts of an address, or a part of some other domain-specific data item. For example, we might refer to a "title" token that represents a list of frequently used titles, such as "Mr.," "Mrs.," and "Dr.," and any time we see a word that is in our "titles" list, we can refer to that word as a title for subsequent pattern analysis.

The parsing process segregates each word and then attempts to determine the relationship between the word and previously defined token sets and to form sequences of tokens. Token sequences are submitted to a pattern-matching application that searches for similar patterns. When a pattern is matched, a predefined transformation is applied to the original field value to extract its individual components, which are then reported to the driver applications. Pattern-based tools are flexible in that they can make use of predefined patterns and absorb newly defined or discovered patterns for ongoing parsing.

STANDARDIZATION

Parsing uses defined patterns, regular expressions, or grammars managed within a rules engine along with table lookups to distinguish between valid and invalid data values. When patterns are recognized, other rules and actions can be triggered to transform the input data into a form that can be more effectively used, either to standardize the representation (presuming a valid representation) or to correct the values (should known errors be identified). To continue our example, each of our values for the state of California {California, CA, Calif., US-CA, Cal, 06} can be standardized to the United States Postal Service standard two-character abbreviation, CA.

Standardization is the process of transforming data into a form specified as a standard, and is a prelude to the cleansing process. Standardization builds on the parsing service, which can be combined with a library of data domains to split data values into multiple components and rearrange the components into a normalized format. Standardization can also change full words to abbreviations, or abbreviations to full words, transform nicknames into a standard name form, translate across languages (e.g., Spanish to English), as well as correct common misspellings.

Standardization will incorporate information-reduction transformations during a consolidation or summarization application, and can eventually be used as a means of extracting specific entity information (e.g., person, company, telephone number, location) and assigning it semantic value for subsequent manipulation. For example, consider these two customer records:

1. Elizabeth R. Johnson, 123 Main Street, Franconia, NH
2. Beth R. Johnson, 123 Main Street, Franconia, NH

Our intuition upon reviewing this pair of records allows us to infer an entity match, because there seems to be enough heuristic data to take that leap: We know that "Beth" is a short version of "Elizabeth," and the street address is a match. Heuristics such as matching a nickname to a full-version name (and others like these) can be collected as simple transformations that can be applied generally to parsed names.

There are many different data types that fall into a semantic taxonomy that provides some intuitive set of content-related standardization rules. For example, first names in many cultures have variant forms (nicknames, etc.) that all can relate any name to at least one standard form. For instance, "Bob," "Rob," "Bobby," and "Robbie" are all different forms of the name "Robert"; "Liz," "Lizzie," and "Beth" may all be forms of the name "Elizabeth."

Once a name with a number of variants is identified, the standardization process may augment a data value with a chosen standard form to be used during the linkage stage. Note that standardization is not restricted to names or addresses. Other abstract data types that can be standardized include business words, telephone numbers, industry jargon, product codes, and transaction codes. And it doesn't even matter if the standard form is applied in a manner that is not consistent with real life. For example, "Beth Smith" might not be named "Elizabeth," but we can assign the standard "Elizabeth" to the records anyway, because this standardization is being used purely as a means to a different end: linkage and cleansing.

ABBREVIATION EXPANSION

An abbreviation is a compact representation of some alternate recognized entity, and finding and standardizing abbreviations is another rule-oriented aspect of data cleansing. There are different kinds of abbreviation. One type shortens each of a set of words to a smaller form, where the abbreviation consists of a prefix of the original data value. Examples include INC for incorporated, CORP for corporation, and ST for street. Another type shortens the word by eliminating vowels or by contracting the letters to phonetics, such as INTL or INTRNTL for international, PRGRM for program, and MGR for manager. A third form of abbreviation is the acronym, where the first characters of each of a set of words are composed into a string, such as USA for United States of America and RFP for Request for Proposal. Abbreviations must be parsed and recognized, and then a set of transformational business rules can be used to change abbreviations into their expanded form.

DATA CORRECTION

Once components of a string have been identified and standardized, the next stage of the process attempts to correct those data values that are not recognized and to augment correctable records with the corrected information. Obviously, if we can recognize that data is in error, we want to be able to fix that data. There are a few different ways to automatically correct data, and these all rely on some sort of intelligent knowledge base of rules and transformations or some heuristic algorithms for recognizing and linking variations of known data values. It is important to realize that the correction process can only be partially automated; many vendors may give the impression that their tools can completely correct invalid data, but there is no silver bullet.

In general, the correction process is based on maintaining a set of incorrect values and their corrected forms. As an example, if the word International is frequently misspelled as "Intrnational," there would be a rule mapping the incorrect form to the correct form. Some tools may incorporate business knowledge accumulated over a long period of time, which accounts for large knowledge bases of rules incorporated into these products; unfortunately, this opens the door for loads of obscure rules that reflect many special cases.

This approach is flawed, because the effect of accumulating correction rules based on analyzing certain kinds of data (usually names and addresses) will bias the corrective process to that kind of information. In addition, a large part of one organization's data is different than any other organization's data, and consequently the business rules that govern the use of that data are also different. Relying on the business rules from other organizations will still add value, especially if the data content is similar, but there will always be some area where humans will need to interact with the system to make decisions about data corrections.

Last, data can be perceived as incorrect only when there are rules indicating correctness. Inaccuracy or imprecise data values may exist within a set, yet there is no way to determine that invalidity without a source of correct values against which to compare. Relying on other sets of correctness rules can lead to a bad problem: What might already be good data may inadvertently be changed to something incorrect. An example of this in address correction is the famous East-West Highway in suburban Washington, DC. Because the expectation with addresses with the word "East" at the beginning is that the word is being used as a direction prefix and not as part of the street name itself, some applications inappropriately "correct" this to "E. West Highway," which is not the name of the road.

An even worse problem is the perception that the data is correct although it really is not. Sometimes, the only way to identify incorrect data is for an analyst to manually review the data directly.

UPDATING MISSING FIELDS

One aspect of data cleansing is being able to fill fields that are missing information. Missing values may carry more information than we might suspect; the absence of a value may be due to one of the following reasons.

- It is known that there is really no value for this field.
- It is known that there is a value that should go into a field, but for some reason the value is unknown at this point, and it is not clear if the value will ever be known.
- It is known that there is a value for this field, and at some point in the future that value will be obtained and filled in.
- There is no applicable value for this based on some constraint dependent on other attribute values.
- There is a value for this field, but it does not conform to a predefined set of acceptable values for that field.

This is just a short list of the kinds of null values that exist. Depending on the null type, there may be ways to impute the missing value, although some approaches are more reliable than others. For example, we might try to fill in a person's sex field based on his or her first name, but this will not necessarily work with a person with a transgender name.

In some other cases, the reason for the missing value may be due to errors in the original data, and after a cleansing process, we may have enough information to properly fill out the missing field. For unavailable fields, if the reason for the omissions has to do with the dearth of data at the time of record instantiation, then the consolidation process may provide enough information leverage to make available data that had been previously unavailable. For unclassified fields, the reason for the inability to classify the value may be that erroneous data in other attributes has prevented the classification. Given the corrected data, the proper value may be filled in. For unknown attributes, the process of cleansing and consolidation may provide the missing value.

It is important to understand, though, that without a well-documented and agreed-to set of rules to determine how to fill in a missing field, it can be (at the least) counterproductive and (at the worst) dangerous to fill in missing values. Maintain strict caution when automating the replacement of absent values.

DUPLICATE ANALYSIS AND ELIMINATION USING IDENTITY RESOLUTION

Because operational systems have grown organically into a suite of enterprise applications, it is not unusual that multiple data instances in different systems will have different ways to refer to the same real-world entity. Alternately, the desire to consolidate and link data about the same business concepts with a high level of confidence might convince someone that a record might not already exist for a real-world entity when in fact it really does. Both of these problems ultimately represent the same core challenge: being able to compare identifying data within a pair of records to determine similarity between that pair or to distinguish the entities represented in those records.

Both of these issues are addressed through a process called identity resolution, in which the degree of similarity between any two records is scored, most often based on weighted approximate matching between a set of attribute values between the two records. If the score is above a specific threshold, the two records are deemed to be a match, and are presented to the end client as most likely to represent the same entity. Identity resolution is used to recognize when only slight variations suggest that different records are connected and where values may be cleansed, or where enough differences between the data suggest that the two records truly represent distinct entities. Since comparing every record against every other record is computationally intensive, many data services use advanced algorithms for blocking records that are most likely to contain matches into smaller sets in order to reduce computation time.

Identity resolution provides the foundation of a more sophisticated core data service: duplicate record analysis and elimination. Identifying similar records within the same data set probably means that the records are duplicated, and may be subjected to cleansing and/or elimination. Identifying similar records in different sets may indicate a link across the data sets, which helps facilitate merging or similar records for the purposes of data cleansing as well as supporting analytical applications that expect to see a unified view of key entities, such as product/pricing models or customer profiling initiatives.

Summary

The length and depth of the material in this chapter should be an indication as to the criticality of ensuring data quality as part of the data warehousing, BI, and business analytics processes. The BI projects in which data quality is an afterthought tend to disintegrate because the consumers become frustrated with the inability to trust the results. Therefore, when developing your BI capability, concentrate on the data quality plan as a key enabler, and measurably-high quality data as a critical success factor.

Chapter 13

Data Integration

Improving Data Accessibility

Clearly, the advent of increasing data volumes, the desire to take advantage of high-performance business intelligence (BI) and analytics architectures, and the broadening community of knowledge consumers all contribute to the need for reusing and repurposing data in different business processes and applications. However, there are two core concepts anyone developing BI and analytics applications requiring data reusability will need to be aware of: accessibility and latency.

ACCESSIBILITY

Most applications developed to support siloed or business function-related processes are built with the presumption that the data sets are persisted in some system organization. Whether that organization is simplistic (files with fixed-field columns) or more sophisticated (such as entity-relationship models, etc.), the application programmer can depend on the accessibility of the data to support the acute business needs. Data reuse and data repurposing change the rules somewhat, especially when the data sets are sourced from alternate persistent or streamed models.

For example, you may want to employ your BI applications to aggregate and analyze data taken from a number of different sources. That implies that methods must be created and invoked to extract the data from those sources and migrate that data into some target mechanism for analysis and/or reporting. And recognizing that the data sources may originate from a wide variety of systems or streams, software vendors evolved tools for accessing data from the original source in preparation for transformation and loading into data warehouses that would then feed the analysis and reporting engines.

As long as each piece of the analysis and reporting framework is distinct (and in many cases that remains true), solving the accessibility challenge using extraction, transformation, and loading (ETL) tools is "good enough." This first generation of data integration techniques (at this point, at least) has effectively become a commodity, becoming bundled with other data management tools, or independently developed via open source channels. But as the expected time frame for analysis becomes more compressed, the diversity of data source formats expands, and the volumes of data increase, this "phased extraction and transformation" for the purposes of data integration begin to seem insufficient.

LATENCY

Meeting performance needs is yet another fundamental challenge, especially with increased demands for absorption of data sources whose sizes are orders of magnitude greater than that experienced in the past. The issue is not necessarily the ability to extract and transform the data, but rather the ability to extract and transform the data within the narrowed time frame for discovery and subsequent exploitation of actionable knowledge. More simply, the second challenge involves reducing *data latency*, or eliminating the throttling effects of limited I/O channels and network bandwidth through which ever-increasing data volumes need to be pushed.

Data latency is not a new issue, but is one that has been ever present throughout the history of computing. There have always been delays in moving data from larger and slower platforms to smaller and faster ones. A primary example involves looking at the microprocessor itself: a CPU unit with a small number of registers that needs to make its calculations of data streamed into main memory (which is slower than the registers) from its storage on disk (which is way slower than main memory).

The need to balance increased accessibility against the performance issues relating to data latency effectively frame the disciplines associated with data integration. Essentially, we are beginning to redefine the concept of data integration—it is not limited to extracting data sets from internal sources and loading them into a data warehouse, but focuses on effectively facilitating the delivery of information to the right places within the appropriate time. Data integration goes beyond ETL, data replication, and change data capture, although these remain key components of the integration fabric.

Some of the key factors in this redefinition include:

- **Volume**. Petabyte and exabyte data volumes are becoming the norm, not the exception;
- **Performance**. Emerging demands for high-performance data integration capabilities are based on the need for linear scalability, the use of parallelism, and high-bandwidth data channels;
- **Lineage**. Or rather, the exposure of lineage, namely transparency when desired, and opacity otherwise;
- **Speed of delivery**. Reduced latency for accessing data from across nonuniform, heterogeneous platforms;
- **Semantic consistency**. Collaborative methods for managing and utilizing metadata shared across communities of interest;
- **Quality**. Embedded controls to ensure quality of the data; and
- **Security**. Guarantees of data protection no matter where data lives.

In this chapter we will examine how these drivers have molded and shaped the broad capabilities for different aspects of data integration.

Extraction/Transformation/Loading

A basic concept for populating a data warehouse is that data sets from multiple sources are collected and then added to a data repository from which analytical applications can source their input data. This sounds straightforward, but actually can become quite complex. Although the data warehouse data model may have been designed very carefully with the BI clients' needs in mind, the data sets that are being used to source the warehouse typically have their own peculiarities. Yet not only do these data sets need to be migrated into the data warehouse, they will need to be integrated with other data sets either before or during the data warehouse population process.

This *extract/transform/load* (commonly abbreviated to ETL) process is the sequence of applications that extract data sets from the various sources, bring them to a data staging area, apply a sequence of processes to prepare the data for migration into the data warehouse, and actually load them. Here is the general theme of an ETL process.

1. Get the data from the source location.
2. Map the data from its original form into a data model that is suitable for manipulation at the staging area.
3. Validate and clean the data.
4. Apply any transformations to the data that are required before the data sets are loaded into the repository.
5. Map the data from its staging area model to its loading model.
6. Move the data set to the repository.
7. Load the data into the warehouse.

STAGING ARCHITECTURE

The first part of the ETL process is to assemble the infrastructure needed for aggregating the raw data sets and for the application of the transformation and the subsequent preparation of the data to be forwarded to the data warehouse. This is typically a combination of a hardware platform and appropriate management software that we refer to as the *staging area*. The architecture of a staging process can be seen in Figure 13.1. Note that the staging architecture must take into account the

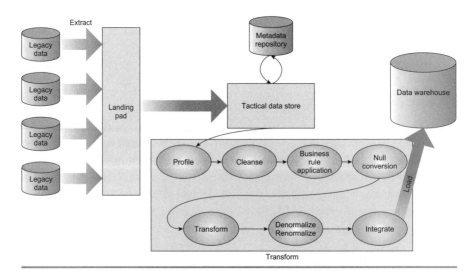

Figure 13.1   Staging data in preparation for loading into an analytical environment.

order of execution of the individual ETL stages, including scheduling data extractions, the frequency of repository refresh, the kinds of transformations that are to be applied, the collection of data for forwarding to the warehouse, and the actual warehouse population.

EXTRACTION

Extraction essentially boils down to two questions:

- What data should be extracted?
- How should that data be extracted?

Realize that the first question essentially relies on what the BI clients expect to see ultimately factored into their analytical applications, and will have been identified as a result of the data requirements analysis process that was covered in Chapter 7. But it is a deeper question, because the data that we want to flow into the repository is likely to be a subset of some existing set of tables. In other words, for each data set extracted, we may only want to grab particular columns of interest, yet we may want to use the source system's ability to select and join data before it flows into the staging area. A lot of extracted data is reformulated or restructured in different ways that can be either easily manipulated in process at the staging area or forwarded directly to the warehouse.

How data should be extracted may depend on the scale of the project, the number (and disparity) of data sources, and how far into the implementation the developers are. Extraction can be as simple as a collection of simple SQL queries, the use of adapters that connect to different originating sources, yet can be as complex as to require specially designed programs written in a proprietary programming language. There are tools available to help automate the process, although their quality (and corresponding price) varies widely.

Automated extraction tools generally provide some kind of definition interface specifying the source of the data to be extracted and a destination for the extract, and they can work in one of two major ways, both of which involve code generation techniques. The first is to generate a program to be executed on the platform where the data is sourced to initiate a transfer of the data to the staging area. The other way is to generate an extraction program that can run on the staging platform that pulls the data from the source down to the staging area.

TRANSFORMATION

Chapter 10 discussed data profiling and how that can be used as a way to capture the metadata of a data set. What is discovered during the profiling is put to use as part of the ETL process to help in the mapping of source data to a form suitable for the target repository, including the following tasks.

- **Data type conversion**. This includes parsing strings representing integer and numeric values and transforming them into the proper representational form for the target machine, and converting physical value representations from one platform to another (EBCDIC to ASCII being the best example).
- **Data cleansing**. The rules we can uncover through the profiling process can be applied as discussed in Chapter 10, along with directed actions that can be used to correct data that is known to be incorrect and where the corrections can be automated. This component also covers data-duplicate analysis and elimination and merge/purge.
- **Integration**. This includes exploiting the discovery of table and foreign keys for representing linkage between different tables, along with the generation of alternate (i.e., artificial) keys that are independent of any systemic business rules, mapping keys from one system to another, archiving data domains and codes that are mapped into those data domains, and maintaining the metadata (including full descriptions of code values and master key-lookup tables).
- **Referential integrity checking**. In relation to the foreign key relationships exposed through profiling or as documented through interaction with subject matter experts, this component checks that any referential integrity constraints are not violated and highlights any nonunique (supposed) key fields and any detected orphan foreign keys.
- **Derivations**. Any transformations based on business rules, new calculations, string manipulations, and such that need to be applied as the data moves from source to target are applied during the transformation stage. For example, a new "revenue" field might be constructed and populated as a function of "unit price" and "quantity sold."
- **Denormalization and renormalization**. Frequently data that is in normalized form when it comes from the source system needs to be broken out into a denormalized form when dimensions are created in repository data tables. Conversely, data sourced from join extractions may be denormalized and may need to be renormalized before it is forwarded to the warehouse.
- **Aggregation**. Any aggregate information that is used for populating summaries or any cube dimensions can be performed at the staging area.
- **Audit information**. As a matter of reference for integrity checking, it is always useful to calculate some auditing information, such as row counts, table counts, column counts, and other tests, to make sure that what you have is what you wanted. In addition, some data augmentation can be done to attach provenance information, including source, time and date of extraction, and time and date of transformation.

■ **Null conversion**. Because nulls can appear in different forms, ranging from system nulls to explicit strings representing different kinds of nulls (see Chapter 9), it is useful to have some kind of null conversion that transforms different nulls from disparate systems.

LOADING

The loading component of ETL is centered on moving the transformed data into the data warehouse. The critical issues include the following.

■ **Target dependencies**, such as where and on how many machines the repository lives, and the specifics of loading data into that platform.
■ **Refresh volume and frequency**, such as whether the data warehouse is to be loaded on an incremental basis, whether data is forwarded to the repository as a result of triggered transaction events, or whether all the data is periodically loaded into the warehouse in the form of a full refresh.

ETL SCALABILITY

There are two flavors of operations that are addressed during the ETL process. One involves processing that is limited to all data instances within a single data set, and the other involves the resolution of issues involving more than one data set. For example, the merge/purge operation compares pairs of records taken from different data sets to determine if they represent the same entity and are therefore candidates for merging. In the most naive method, this process requires each instance from one data set to be compared with all the instances from the other set; as more data sets are added to the mix, the complexity of this process increases geometrically.

The story is basically this: The more data sets that are being integrated, the greater the amount of work that needs to be done for the integration to complete. This creates two requirements: (1) More efficient methods must be applied to perform the integration, and (2) the process must be scalable, as both the size and the number of data sets increase.

EXTRACT, LOAD, AND TRANSFORM (ELT)

Increased data volumes pose a problem for the traditional ETL approach in that first accumulating the mounds of data into a staging area creates a burst-y demand for resources. When the data sets are being extracted and transformed, the storage and computational needs may be high (or actually, *very* high), but during the interim periods, those resources might be largely unused. This is undesirable from both the performance and utilization standpoints.

A different approach seeks to take advantage of the performance characteristics of the analytical platforms themselves by bypassing the staging area. In other words, the data sets are extracted from the sources, loaded into the target, and the transformations are applied at the target. This modified approach, Extract, Load, and Transform (ELT), is beneficial with massive data sets because it eliminates the demand for the staging platform (and its corresponding costs to manage).

However, once the data is loaded into the target system, you may be limited by the capabilities of executing the transformation. For example, applications for transformation can be much more flexible dealing with data streamed directly out of files. In the ELT approach, you may have to use an RDBMS's native methods for applying transformation. These may not be as complete and may run slower than custom-designed transformation applications.

Data Latency and Data Synchrony

The perception that the ability to absorb and analyze ever-growing heterogeneous collections of data will increase the precision (and therefore, the accuracy) of decision-making implies that the time to deliver actionable knowledge must be compressed. The notion of "real-time" is often stretched in this context and slightly modified into what is referred to as "right-time" delivery of knowledge. Right-time delivery implies that the appropriate pieces of information are provided to the necessary parties within a timeframe that allows them to make decisions in a manner that is consistent with optimal results.

However, the tolerance for what is meant by the "right" time varies based on the consumer of the results. In turn, the factors that are relevant to the timeliness of knowledge delivery must influence the design characteristics for all aspects of data integration, both into the analytical platform and then from the analytical platform to each consumer.

This suggests two aspects to the data integration challenge. The first has to do with data acquisition and absorption. The second involves providing a consistent view to the consumers. These two factors are bound together, as the details associated with the *latency* of data access from heterogeneous sources will impact the *synchronization* of collected data instances, entities, and values in preparation for analysis and presentation to the users. Our next sections will look at these two factors and consider end-user expectations in light of balancing one against the other.

THE PERVASIVENESS OF THE DATA ACCESS BOTTLENECK

The history of computing is tightly bound with the struggle between speed of computation and the relative sloth of access latency. Hardware architectures at the

CPU level are engineered around the delays associated with streaming data from disk to core memory, then to cache before the data is accessible by the CPU without delays. Data architectures have evolved in a similar manner, whether we are discussing optimized data layouts for high-performance analytical engines or software caches meant to speed access to nonuniform data sources. Most of these approaches are clearly intended to smooth out the potential delays associated with latency, or the time it takes to move data from a slower source to a faster layer of the memory hierarchy.

In the best of all possible worlds, all the data streamed into your analytical platforms would not just be consistent from a structural and semantic perspective, but also from a temporal perspective. That means that the data associated with an entity pulled from one data source is not out of synchronization with the data associated with the same entity pulled from a different data source. Yet because of the differences associated with heterogeneous sources (and their corresponding data access characteristics), the time it may take to access, transform, and load data from the first source may be significantly longer (or shorter) than the time it takes to access, transform, and load from the second source. The result is the potential that once both sources have been published to the analytical applications, there are potential inconsistencies as a result of the data delays.

That is the emerging challenge for data integration: balancing the latency issues on the source side with the synchronization issues on the delivery side. Because there are no silver bullets as of yet for completely solving this dichotomy, it is best to consider the variables upon which the decisions are dependent.

Characteristics Governing Data Synchrony

There is a need to balance between navigating the challenges of variable data access latency on the source side with the need for synchronizing the view for analytical purposes. It is worth attempting to assert some measurement framework for characterizing the dependencies between high-performance data access and the delivery of consistent results, especially if inconsistency in aggregate values (such as counts, sums, and averages) on reports will lead to interminable demands for repeated reconciliations. Therefore, here are some dimensions to consider:

- **Timeliness**. This refers to the ability to ensure the availability of analytical data to the client applications and stakeholders within a reasonable window from the time that the originating data sources were initially created or introduced into the enterprise. Timeliness is essentially a gauge of the maximum time it takes for accessed data to propagate across the system, as well as the time window in which the underlying replicas or copies of data have potentially inconsistent values.

- **Currency.** This corresponds to the degree of "freshness" of the data in the data warehouse, which measures the update times and frequency associated with any "expiration" time of data values.
- **Delivery time.** This refers to the time between an application's request for information and the time of its delivery.
- **Consistency.** Consistency is a measure of the degree to which each end-user application's view of warehouse data is not different than any other operational or analytical application's view.
- **Coherence.** This is the ability to ensure the maintenance of predictable synchronization between data in the original sources, data in the data warehouse, and any local copies of data pushed to analytical applications (such as those driven off data marts or even big data applications).
- **Determinism/idempotence.** This reflects the idea that when the same query is performed more than once, both return the same result.

The upshot is that each of these measures is somewhat interdependent on the others. For example, a need for exact coherence means that all the data must be available from all sources at the same time, which might force a delay on one source until others are available, thereby effectively decreasing that source's currency (since it sits around waiting for the other sources to show up). Alternatively, if the users are willing to accept decreased determinism, we can potentially decrease the level of coherence to reflect the natural access times for any of the data sources. In essence, this means that the consumer requirements for each of these measures must be solicited and considered when determining the systemic requirements for different aspects of data integration.

Data Replication and Change Data Capture

A root cause of increased latency is the sheer volume of data that must move between and among transactional systems, operational data stores, staging areas, data warehouses, data marts, and increasingly, cloud-based environments. The commoditization of storage is somewhat tracked to computational performance, and distributed data stores are often linked with parallel computing platforms. Yet often the corresponding networking bandwidth remains a bottleneck.

You can reduce that bottleneck in one of two ways: increase the width of the pipes (i.e., improve the network bandwidth to accommodate large amounts of data) or decrease the payload (by reducing the amounts of data that are pushed through the pipes). The latter suggestion turns out to be a good one in those situations that require initial data loads that are large but subsequently only require incremental updates, where extracting large source data sets would impact production system performance, or where the source data sets are not physically local to the destination systems.

At the hardware level, an engineered method for reducing data access latency is a device called a *cache*, which is a smaller memory module that provides much more rapid access to data. By prefetching data into the cache, streaming accesses go much quicker, since the data has already been delivered close to where it needs to be. The data values that are in the cache basically mirror what is on disk, and the values in the cache need to be updated when the corresponding values on disk are updated.

At the software level, we can get the same effect by doing the same thing: making mirror images of data values close by to where they need to be. When the underlying data source changes, the copy needs to be updated also. This caching concept is relatively high level, but there are different infrastructure implementations that rely on this approach. One is called *data replication*—the approach has been around for a long time, and was used in earlier times to make copies of files in remote locations. For example, if transaction processing took place in New York and that data needed to be accessible in Hong Kong, a replica was created in Hong Kong. Instead of repeating every transaction in both places, the changes in the original were tracked and propagated to the replica via a process called *change data capture*, or CDC. Change data capture is a process that monitors the logs of transaction systems and propagates the changes made to the transaction database along to the analytical platform.

When implemented the right way, data replication services can provide extremely rapid access mechanisms for pulling data from one or more sources and creating copies that can satisfy different business analytics needs, especially when there is a mixed workload for reporting and analysis. Separate data replicas can be used for complex queries, knowing that rapid data access can reduce the drag on multiway joins. Data replication also enables faster reporting, thereby accelerating the analyze/review/decision-making cycle.

Data replication coupled with change data capture enables more rapid alignment of transactions into the analytical environment, and this provides synchronized visibility without increasing demand on production transaction systems. In turn, the replication process eliminates the need for batch extracts and loading into the data warehouse, allowing decisions to be synchronized with current data.

In addition, replication allows data sets to be rapidly cloned and propagated to a number of different targets, which can map nicely to different computational models for analysis and reporting. Pushing data out might mean a combination of distribution (of some of the data) and multiple copies of others—a feat that is easily done by a data replication framework.

Data Federation and Virtualization

An alternative approach to data sharing is data federation, which allows the data to remain in its primary data source until required for specific downstream needs. Data virtualization provides layers of abstraction between the consuming applications and the primary data sources, and these abstraction layers present data taken from its original structures using standardized or canonical representations (Figure 13.2). This approach is meant to simplify data reuse while enabling common data services to meet downstream consumer performance and data quality expectations.

Data federation techniques help mitigate both the accessibility and the latency issues. From a business application perspective, the abstraction provided through federation reduces complexity by standardizing the representations. This not only reduces the complexity for accessing data from heterogeneous systems, it also allows you to incorporate data transformations and data quality techniques directly into these layers of abstraction.

Within the ETL world, data inconsistencies and inaccuracies are dealt with through a separate data profiling and data quality phase. This works nicely when the data has already been dumped into a separate staging area. But with federation, not all the data is situated within a segregated staging area. Loosely coupled integration with data quality tools may address some of the problem, but loosely coupled data quality can't eliminate those situations in which the inconsistencies are not immediately visible.

This becomes even more of an issue when considering use cases. In many scenarios, the role of the data virtualization layer is providing homogenized access to heterogeneous sources from a semantically consistent perspective. The consumers of that data want to execute queries directly against the view, without having to qualify the underlying sources. The data virtualization layer must enable those views with

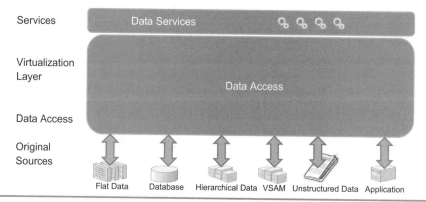

Figure 13.2   Layers in a data virtualization framework.

high performance, integrating optimizations into the query engine that do not violate any underlying semantic constraints.

A comprehensive data virtualization solution has to provide a deeper level of knowledge about the structure, formats, and the semantics associated with the data sources. This type of solution will go beyond just delivering data and become a provision layer that identifies data inconsistencies and inaccuracies from the structural and semantic perspectives and, more importantly, can distinguish issues and fold their resolution *directly into the data virtualization layer.*

In other words, to truly provision high-quality and consistent data with minimized latency from a heterogeneous set of sources, a data virtualization framework must provide at least these capabilities:

- Access methods for a broad set of data sources, both persistent and streaming
- Early involvement of the business user to create virtual views without help from IT
- Software caching to enable rapid access in real time
- Consistent views into the underlying sources
- Query optimizations to retain high performance
- Visibility into the enterprise metadata and data architectures
- Views into shared reference data
- Accessibility of shared business rules associated with data quality
- Integrated data profiling for data validation
- Integrated application of advanced data transformation rules that ensure consistency and accuracy

What differentiates a comprehensive data virtualization framework from simplistic layering of access and caching services via data federation is that the comprehensive data virtualization solution goes beyond just data federation. It is not only about heterogeneity and latency, but must incorporate the methodologies that are standardized within the business processes to ensure semantic consistency for the business.

Embedding the transformation and data quality management as part of data federation integrates data management best practices directly into the application infrastructure, identifies data issues early in the information production process, and enables cleansing or other remediation processes to be performed before material impacts can be incurred.

Data Integration and Cloud Computing

Cloud services are generally understood to refer to employing virtualized computing services in a utility service model. A cloud service provider may enable alternative means for managing enterprise computing resources, and is increasingly being adopted for managing platforms upon which an organization may deploy its own environment as well as more sophisticated services such as applicationware (AKA "Software as a Service," or SaaS), or even "information as a service."

The evolution toward simultaneously exploiting both on-premise and cloud-based environments implies a need for greater agility for data acquisition, integration, and absorption. Moving data beyond the corporate firewall goes beyond solely extracting data from existing internal legacy data sources. The challenge becomes more acute as you look at the different scenarios where data instances and data sets cross the enterprise boundary. Some examples include:

- Incorporating analytical results with cloud-based systems (such as SaaS-based sales, marketing, and contact management applications);
- Incorporating external data into an analytical platform (such as social network graph analysis that examines continuous data streams);
- When exposing reporting services to customers (such as account statements and analysis in the financial industry); or
- Collaborative data analysis in which data sources are pooled from different enterprises (such as comparative effectiveness research in the healthcare industry).

Sharing data across enterprise boundaries has implications for data exchange and integration. This suggests some key characteristics for "cloud-enabled" data exchange for the purposes of BI such as:

- The ability to seamlessly access a variety of large data sets inside the organization (such as transaction data from different operational systems, or data in an enterprise data warehouse);
- The ability to seamlessly access a variety of large data sets *outside* the organization (including licensed data sets, public domain data sets, data in the cloud, data feeds, and streamed data);
- The ability to provide a harmonized view of data to each data consumer in the organization; and
- The ability to share data with applications and environments hosted outside the organization (again, with a focus on interfacing with cloud-based systems and applications).

Extra-enterprise data integration must enable these types of exchanges by providing data standards, canonical models, exchange schemas, as well as high-performance methods for cloud-based data access and integration as services for information availability with different levels of transparency (or opacity, if necessary) to reduce the effort for application development.

Information Protection

There has always been an awareness of the need for locking-down access to data warehouse data. However, the historical focus of information protection within a BI framework has most closely been aligned with the typical approaches to system or IT security, largely centered on two facets of protection: intrusion prevention and data classification. The first deals with system monitoring, while the second specifically looks at defining policies for managing or restricting client access to specific data sets within the RDBMS, and specification and assignment of roles, employing standard data access control and IT security methods.

In retrospect, because of the expectation of provisioning reports using data accumulated from across the enterprise, when you look at the architectures and the flows of information within a BI framework, you begin to see that data warehousing may introduce additional risk factors for data exposure. Some issues in particular include:

- **Deemphasized security**. Data warehousing is facilitating reporting and analysis, and the efforts focus on data integration; security is generally *not* a focus of data warehouse design.
- **Heterogeneous yet uncharted lineage**. Data in the warehouse comes from multiple systems, each potentially having its own set of protection directives, but the absence of tracking of lineage means that some of the security expectations of the sources may be "lost along the way."
- **Integration and privacy**. Because the nature of consolidation merges data sets together, a source table with protected data may "infect" a nonprivate data source during the integration process.
- **Increased exposure through data movement**. Protecting data at rest is one thing, but typical methods of consolidation extract, move, transform, and load data across multiple platforms, increasing the potential for exposure when data is "in the air," especially as BI users are prone to "cutting and pasting" results into unsecured frameworks (such as desktop productivity software).
- **Data inferencing**. One result of consolidation is that inferences can be made when records are linked together, allowing presumably protected facts to be revealed.
- **Regulations**. There is a growing portfolio of laws detailing constraints for protection and penalties for data exposure, thereby increasing the risk.

As the barrier between what is or is not subject to access control becomes blurred, expectations for protecting the data must be evaluated in greater detail. Essentially, integrating multiple source data sets into a single repository increases the complexity of access control and information protection.

Intrusion prevention and role-based access control are both approaches to prevent unauthorized access to the protected resource, but once the system is breached, all bets for protecting the content are off. This means that you must consider alternate approaches for directly protecting the data. One approach is data encryption, which is an algorithmic process of transforming the original form of the data ("free text") into a form that is unreadable ("cipher text"), yet can use the same algorithm to reverse the transformation so that the encrypted data can be read.

With broad awareness of the potential failure points of existing means of pene-tration prevention, satisfying the requirement for information protection means presuming that existing system security frameworks and approaches to data access control are insufficient. A data-centric approach to protection is necessary to augment the traditional IT security plan, especially in the context of data integration for data warehousing, BI, and analytics. It is worthwhile to consider the benefits of locking down the content using approaches like encryption to protect sensitive information and knowledge.

More on Merge/Purge and Record Consolidation

Consolidation is a catch-all term for those processes that make use of collected metadata and knowledge to eliminate duplicate entities and merge data from multiple sources, among other data enhancement operations. That process is pow-ered by the ability to identify some kind of relationship between any arbitrary pair of data instances.

There are different kinds of relationships that we look for. One is *identity*— determining that two data instances refer to the exact same entity. This is what we look for when searching for duplicate entries in one database or searching for multiple instances of the same entity when merging databases. Another is *equiva-lence classing*, which refers to grouping entities together based on some set of similar attributes. An example of this is finding people from the same family or people who work for the same company.

The key to record linkage is the concept of *similarity*. This is a measure of how close two data instances are to each other, and can be a hard measure (either the two records are the same, or they are not) or a more approximate measure (based on some form of scoring), in which case the similarity is judged based on scores above or below a threshold.

As an example, similarity scoring for names might parse each name into its individual components (first name, last name, title, suffix, etc.) and then compare the individually parsed components to see how many match and how closely they match. Consider comparing "H. David Loshin" with "David Loshin." The first string has a first initial, a middle name, and a last name; the second has a first name and a last name. A naive similarity scoring approach might conclude that this is not a close match, because the first initial of the first string does not match the first name of the second string. A more savvy algorithm would recognize that the match between the middle name of the first string and the first name of the second string represents a close match.

SCORING PRECISION AND APPLICATION CONTEXT

One of the most significant insights into similarity and difference measurements is the issue of application context and its impact on both measurement precision and the similarity criteria. Depending on the kind of application that makes use of approximate searching and matching, the thresholds will most likely change.

For example, in a simple direct mail sales program, our goal is to find duplicate entries. But if a pair of duplicates is not caught, the worst that can happen is that some household gets more than one catalog. In this case, we might prefer that any borderline matches be assumed to be mismatches so that our coverage is greater (Figure 13.3).

On the other hand, if we are evaluating potential matches during a criminal investigation, then if a person's name matches one of the names on the list of known criminals, that person can be isolated and a full investigation performed to determine whether there are any reasons for further detention. In this instance, where safety and security are concerned, we all know the worst that can happen if there is a missed match. We might prefer to err on the side of caution and lower the match threshold so that any borderline matches are brought to the attention of the criminal investigators.

Although the basic application in both of these cases is the same (matching names against other names), we can, depending on the expected results, group our

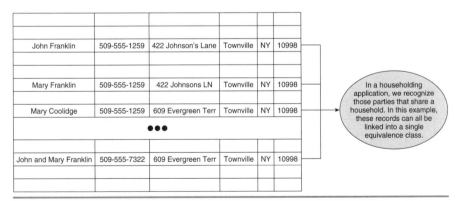

Figure 13.3   Different degrees of search precision.

applications into those that are *exclusive* searches, which are intended to distinguish as many individuals as possible, and *inclusive* searches, which want to include as many potential matches into a cluster as possible. The direct marketing duplicate elimination would be an exclusive application, whereas the criminal intelligence application is an inclusive application (Figure 13.4).

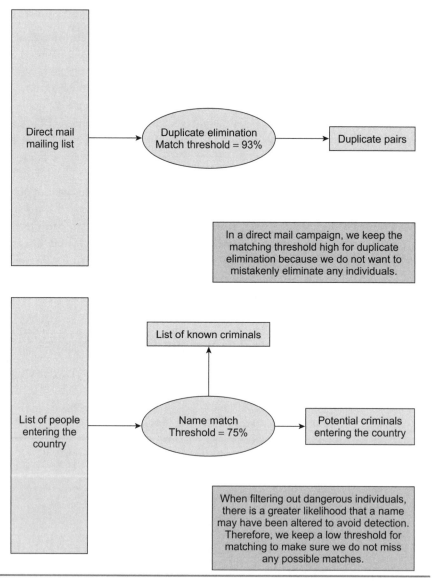

Figure 13.4 Eliminating duplicates.

ELIMINATION OF DUPLICATES

The elimination of duplicates is a process of finding multiple representations of the same entity within the data set and eliminating all but one of those representations from the set. In some instances, such as with a primary key in a relational database table, duplicates are not allowed, and so it is imperative that duplicate records be found and reduced to a single entity. When duplicates are exact matches, they can be discovered through the simple process of sorting the records based on the data attributes under investigation. When duplicates exist because of erroneous values, we have to use a more advanced technique, such as approximate searching and matching, to find and eliminate duplicates.

The elimination of duplicates is essentially a process of clustering similar records together and then reviewing the corresponding similarity scores with respect to a pair of thresholds. Any scores above the higher threshold are automatically deemed to be a match; any scores below the lower threshold are automatically deemed not to be a match. Scores between the thresholds are to be pulled for human review.

MERGE/PURGE

Merge/purge is similar to the elimination of duplicates, except that whereas duplicate elimination is associated with removing doubles from a single data set, merge/purge involves the aggregation of multiple data sets followed by eliminating duplicates (Figure 13.5). Data from different sources will tend to have inconsistencies and inaccuracies when consolidated, and therefore simple matching is insufficient during an aggregation phase. Again, approximate matching can be used to cluster similar records, which can either have a reduction phase automated or be passed through human review, depending on the application.

HOUSEHOLDING

Householding is a process of reducing a number of records into a single set associated with a single household. A *household* could be defined as a single residence, and the householding process is used to determine which individuals live within the same residence.

Householding is more than just finding all people with the same last name living at the same address. Associated with householding is a more advanced set of facts, such as marital status, family structure, and residence type (single- vs. multifamily home vs. apartment). As in other areas that we have discussed, the goal of the application determines the result of the householding process.

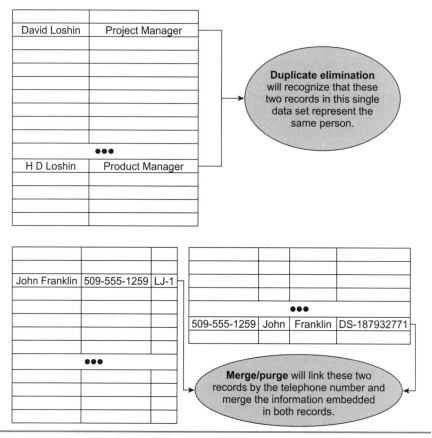

Figure 13.5 Householding.

For example, a mail-order catalog company might want to ensure that only one catalog was being sent to each residence. In that case, the householding process is meant to aggregate records around a particular delivery address, attempting to recognize those names that all belong to the same address, whether or not they belong to the same family. Alternatively, an application that is targeting only the teenagers in a household would want to identify all members of the same family as well as each family member's role. A third application might be to find unmarried individuals living together. In each of these applications, the process is similar, but the details of which attributes are used in the process may differ.

The general approach for householding naturally revolves around the address. All addresses are cleansed and standardized, and then groups are clustered based on the same address. Addresses are enhanced based on their location status, such as single-family home, two-family home, multifamily dwelling, small apartment, large apartment, storefront, and business address.

The clusters now represent sets of entities residing at the same location. Any distinction based on individual occupancy unit (e.g., apartment number, floor, suite) is done at this time. Within each cluster, each entity is considered as to its relation to other entities within the cluster. Two entities are related if some connection can be established between them using corroborating data. This might include sharing a last name, having the same telephone number, the existence of a third record that contains both names, and so on. When two entity records are determine to be related, that relation is documented as a virtual link between them.

RELIABILITY OF AUTOMATED LINKAGE

Although our desire is for automated processes to properly link data instances as part of the integration process, there is always some doubt that the software is actually doing what we want it to do. In the case of record linkage, thresholds are set—a higher one above which we assume there is a match, and a lower one below which there is no match. Two issues arise from this. The first is that similarity scoring attempts to reduce the complexity of assessing the sameness between two objects across multiple dimensions down to a single number; in certain instances, biases creep into the computation to unduly skew that number, which potentially links two records that should not be linked (*false positives*) or misses linking a pair of records that should be linked (*false negatives*). Trying to find these false results is a matter of exhaustive review, which may be approached via sampling, although you may never be sure that the process is doing exactly what is desired.

The second problem is the result of setting too wide a gap between the upper threshold and the lower threshold, which allows a large number of records to fall between those thresholds. Because those records are forwarded to staff members for clerical review, the more records that are shunted into the manual review process, the more work that must be done by people instead of computers.

Thoughts on Data Stewardship and Governance for Integration

In a world with growing needs for data reuse and repurposing, who is responsible for accommodating the collective requirements for a data set? This seemingly straightforward question has relatively deep ramifications, because the issue of stewardship and governance becomes much more relevant when more than one business process employs data that is either purchased, created, controlled, or managed by a specific group within the enterprise. The question is not really about ownership but, rather, about the limits of data management responsibility: governance and stewardship. This is particularly important when the business functions that acquire or create the data are not among the pool of consumers of the results of BI and analytics (such as front-line operational systems).

To illustrate the issues, consider a BI group designing and building a data warehouse that wants to accumulate and integrate data sets from different groups within the organization. The source data sets are designed and used with respect to particular (functional) transactional purposes. The business processes and applications that produce the data to be consumed have been in production for a long time, and their clients are completely satisfied with their system performance. As soon as many of these data sets are examined and profiled by the BI/data warehouse team, a number of anomalies, errors, and inconsistencies between the different data sets appear as a by-product of the integration process. Essentially, if you were to continue integrating these data sets, you would knowingly have a data warehouse with questionable data.

As the manager of the BI and analytics program, you are now faced with a dilemma: How are you to direct your team to maintain a high level of data quality within the warehouse? There are three ways to address this: Correct the data in the warehouse, try to effect some changes to the source data, and leave the errors in the data. The third choice is the least desirable, and therefore this is where stewardship and governance become issues.

Choosing to fix the data in the warehouse means that not only will you be continually correcting the same bad data over and over again as part of the integration process (which will occupy time and computational resources), but the warehouse data will be inconsistent with one or more group's view. Choosing to effect the correction at the data source is also a challenge if there is no positive value added to each group's application by fixing the data (or, better, the process responsible for the flawed data). A savvy manager will arrange for the institutionalization of data management standards, practices, and a responsibility chain that provides for the resolution of problems that are hampered by the absence of formalized data governance practices.

High-Performance
Business
Intelligence

The Need for Speed

Recall our discussion in Chapter 3 of the different types of consumer of business intelligence (BI) and analytics:

■ Power users (experienced, sophisticated analysts);
■ Business users (relying on domain-specific reporting and analyses prepared by power users, but also execute ad hoc queries and drill-down);
■ Casual users (those who represent cross-functional areas of the business, and rely on rolled-up metrics from across functional or operational areas);
■ Data aggregators or Information Providers (collectors and publishers of data);
■ Operational analytics users (who indirectly rely on the results of analytics embedded within operational applications);
■ Extended enterprise users (comprising external parties, customers, regulators, external business analysts, partners, suppliers, or anyone with a need for reported information for tactical decision-making); and
■ IT users (involved in the development aspects of BI).

211

In a successful BI and analytics environment, there is bound to be growth in the demand for applications and solutions. When there is a demand for the mixed workload of BI applications, there will be a corresponding strain on resources. The potential degradation in performance introduces a risk of being overwhelmed by success—the more users and the more varied their uses, the greater the need for scalable performance.

In this chapter we examine some approaches to ensuring high performance for your BI applications. The key concepts are computational parallelism and data distribution, and the chapter will look at some ways these ideas are integrated into high performance BI environments.

The Value of Parallelism

If we were to assess the size of the data sets that are common in any major industry, we would not be surprised at how much data is being created, collected, and stored, even before considering aggregating this data into any sort of data warehouse. It would not be unusual to see large customer databases accompanied by transaction data sets such as point-of-sale orders, online product searches, online orders, call detail records (CDRs), or insurance claims that are one or two orders of magnitude larger. For example, it would not be unreasonable to expect a telecommunications company to log millions, if not billions, of CDRs each day. According to comScore, there were 18.7 *million* web transactions on Cyber Monday 2011;[1] in fact, online activities can account for great volumes of transactions in many different industries. Add in party reference data, customer service detail records, order transactions, service orders, billing, shipping, and more, and we have the makings of a huge data integration and analysis problem.

When we combine all that information into an analytical framework, we are presented with two major barriers to the timely capture, analysis, and exploitation of information. The first is that the sheer amount of information available overwhelms any individual's ability to understand it, and the second is that the time to complete the amount of processing needed to digest that information is likely to exceed the window of opportunity for exploiting any results.

A successful BI and analytics strategy encompasses more than just the desired analytical functionality. It must also incorporate expectations about the timeliness of the applications. Fortunately, evolving approaches to optimizing system perfor-mance like massive parallelism, improved networking, data distribution, as well as other techniques for performance improvement can be applied to improved system scalability.

THE NEED FOR SCALABLE SYSTEMS

Maintaining large amounts of transaction data is one thing, but integrating and subsequently transforming that data into an analytical environment (such as a data warehouse or any multidimensional analytical framework) requires a large amount of both storage space and processing capability. And unfortunately, the kinds of processing needed for BI applications cannot be scaled linearly. In other words, with most BI processing, doubling the amount of data can dramatically increase the amount of processing required.

For example, consider a simple customer name-matching application for duplicate analysis. Given two data sets, each containing 10,000 names, the brute-force approach is to compare each name in the first data set against each name in the second data set, resulting in $10,000 \times 10,000 = 100,000,000$ comparisons. If the two data sets each contains 20,000 names, suddenly we are faced with 400,000,000 comparisons; doubling the size of the problem quadruples the amount of work! But let's say we break the first data set into four subsets of 5000 names each and then farm out each subset to one of four identical processing systems to be compared to the 20,000-name second data set. Although the amount of work is the same, each of the four systems performs 100,000,000 comparisons, and because this processing can operate in parallel, the elapsed time for completion is actually one-fourth of the time that a single system would require. By scaling our resources to meet the size of the problem, we have achieved a scalability that could not have been made explicit in the application.

This then poses another issue—as BI projects succeed, the demand for more analytical services increases, which in turn increases the size of the project. Whether the size of the input grows or the number of applications grows, the demands on the system may potentially be met by making use of parallel processing.

Within certain constraints, there is an appeal to exploiting multiple processor execution, for a number of reasons, such as:

- Computer hardware is increasingly sophisticated, with multicore processors becoming the norm, and multiple node machines available are reasonable price points.
- Loosely coupled parallel systems can be configured using commodity parts; for example, large numbers of homogeneous workstations can easily be networked using high-speed switches.
- Software frameworks can be instituted on top of already available resources to make use of underused computer capability. For example, grid configurations are able to virtualize multiple processor systems and thereby increase return on hardware investment.
- Cloud computing is rapidly becoming a feasible solution for applications with elastic resource requirements at different times of the day.

- Small-scale multiple processor systems are readily available at reasonable prices in configurations that can be expanded by incrementally adding processors and memory.
- Programming languages and libraries (such as in C++ and Java) have embedded support for thread- or task-level parallelization, which eases the way for implementation and use.
- More sophisticated programming environments such as MapReduce and HPCC enable more programmers to develop parallel applications, taking advantage of distributed storage resources.

PARALLELISM AND GRANULARITY

Whenever we talk about parallelism, we need to assess the size of the problem as well as the way the problem can be decomposed into parallelizable units. The metric of unit size with respect to concurrency is called *granularity*. Large problems that decompose into a relatively small number of large tasks would have *coarse granularity*, whereas decomposing a process into a large number of very small tasks would have *fine granularity*. In this section we look at different kinds of parallelism ranging from coarse-grained to fine-grained parallelism. Ultimately, our goal is to be able to achieve a speedup that correlates to the resources we have allocated to the problem.

A sequence of operations that are collected together is called a *unit of work*. Each concurrent unit of work can be allocated as a job to be performed by a computational executor, but these executors have different characteristics, depending on the granularity of the unit of work. The decision boils down to the amount of overhead required for each kind of executor. For example, coarsely grained work may be allocated to a high-overhead process, a medium-grained unit of work may be allocated to a lightweight process, or *task*, and finely grained units may be integrated directly into function calls to a parallel runtime system.

SCALABILITY

When we decompose a problem into smaller units of work, we expect to gain speedup when concurrently executing those units of work allocated to multiple-execution resources. *Scalability* refers to the situation when the speedup linearly increases as the number of resources is increased. For example, if the time for a program halves each time the number of processors increases, that program exhibits linear scalability.

TASK PARALLELISM

Imagine that you are preparing a three-course dinner, with an appetizer, a main course, and a dessert. Although our cultural bias constrains the order of *eating* those courses, there are no rules about the order of *preparing* the courses. In other words, you can make the dessert before cooking the main course, because there is nothing inherent in dessert preparation that depends on main course preparation.

How long does it take to prepare this meal? If there is only one chef, then the total time to prepare the meal is the sum of the times to prepare each course. But if we assume that there are three competent chefs in the kitchen, then each one can take on the task of preparing one of the courses. If all the participants start at the same time, then the total time to prepare the meal is bounded by the longest preparation time of each of the three courses. By delegating each independent task to an available resource, we reduce the overall preparation time, possibly by two-thirds of the original time requirement (Figure 14.1).

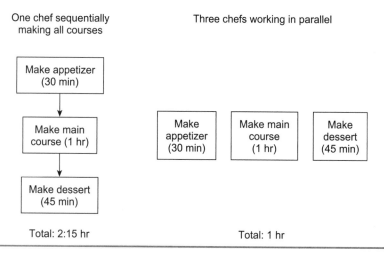

Figure 14.1   Task parallelism in the kitchen.

This is an example of task parallelism, which is a coarsely grained parallelism. In this case, a high-level process is decomposed into a collection of discrete tasks, each of which performs some set of operations and results in some output or side effect.

PIPELINE PARALLELISM

Let's consider a different example that can inherently benefit from a different kind of parallelism. In an automobile assembly line, a car is incrementally built in a sequence of stages. At each stage, another set of parts is added to the developing product, until the final stage, when a working car rolls off the line. What is nice about this process is that it forms what we call a pipeline, and it is appealing because the different teams can execute their stages of the pipeline on many partially completed cars all at the same time. In other words, while one group is fitting the chassis for one car, another group is inserting the engine on another car. In fact, the beauty of the assembly line is its inherent parallelizability, because many partial tasks can be in process simultaneously.

This kind of parallelism is called *pipeline parallelism* (or *pipelining*); any process that can be broken up into a discrete sequence of stages can benefit from pipelining. Pipelining is an example of medium-grained parallelism, because the tasks are not fully separable (i.e., the completion of a single stage does not result in a finished product); however, the amount of work is large enough that it can be cordoned off and assigned as operational tasks (Figure 14.2).

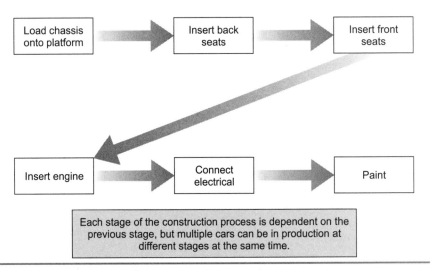

Figure 14.2   Pipeline parallelism example.

DATA PARALLELISM

Data parallelism is a different kind of parallelism that, instead of relying on process or task concurrency, is related to both the flow and the structure of the information. An analogy might revisit the automobile factory from our example in the previous section. There we looked at how the construction of an automobile could be transformed into a pipelined process. Here, because the construction of cars along one assembly has no relation to the construction of the same kinds of cars along any other assembly line, there is no reason why we can't duplicate the same assembly line multiple times; two assembly lines will result in twice as many cars being produced in the same amount of time as a single assembly line.

For data parallelism, the goal is to scale the throughput of processing based on the ability to decompose the data set into concurrent processing streams, all performing

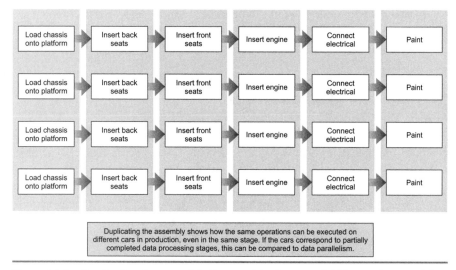

Duplicating the assembly shows how the same operations can be executed on different cars in production, even in the same stage. If the cars correspond to partially completed data processing stages, this can be compared to data parallelism.

Figure 14.3   Duplicating the assembly line provides linear scalability—a feature of data parallelism.

the same set of operations. For example, a customer address standardization process iteratively grabs an address and attempts to transform it into a standard form. This task is adaptable to data parallelism and can be sped up by a factor of 4 by instantiating four address standardization processes and streaming one-fourth of the address records through each instantiation (Figure 14.3). Data parallelism is a more finely grained parallelism in that we achieve our performance improvement by applying the same small set of tasks iteratively over multiple streams of data.

COMBINATIONS

Note that these forms of parallelism are not mutually exclusive. For example, the data parallel address standardization process discussed earlier may be one stage of a pipelined process propagating data from a set of sources to a final target. We can embed pipelined processing within coarsely grained tasks or even decompose a pipe stage into a set of concurrent processes. The value of each of these kinds of parallelism is bounded by the system's ability to support the overhead for managing those different levels.

Parallel Processing Systems

In this section we look at some popular parallel processing architectures. Systems employing these architectures either are configured by system manufacturers (such as symmetric multiprocessor or massively parallel processing systems), are managed as external services and utilities (such as clouds), or can be homebrewed by savvy technical personnel (such as by use of a network of workstations).

Symmetric Multiprocessing

A symmetric multiprocessing (SMP) system is a hardware configuration that combines multiple processors within a single architecture. All processors in an SMP machine share a single operating system, input/output (I/O) devices, and memory, and each processor (or CPU) maintains its own cache related to the shared memory. In an SMP system, multiple processes can be allocated to different CPUs within the system, which makes an SMP machine a good platform for coarse-grained parallelism.

An SMP machine can also be formulated for pipelined execution by allocating each CPU a different stage of an application and propagating partial results through communication via the shared memory system.

MULTICORE MACHINES

A multicore processor incorporates multiple processors on the same chip, sharing main memory and sometimes second level caches and bus. Each processor will have its own level 1 cache. The different processors execute independently, allowing for embedded task- or thread-level parallelism. However, the different processors can also be configured to execute the same program at the same time on different data, enabling data parallelism as well.

MASSIVELY PARALLEL PROCESSING

A massively parallel processing (MPP) system consists of a large number of small homogeneous processing nodes interconnected via a high-speed network. The processing nodes in an MPP machine are independent—they typically do not share memory, and typically each processor may run its own instance of an operating system, although there may be systemic controller applications hosted on leader processing nodes that instruct the individual processing nodes in the MPP configuration on the tasks to perform.

Nodes on MPP machines may also be connected directly to their own I/O devices, or I/O may be channeled into the entire system via high-speed interconnects. Communication between nodes is likely to occur in a *coordinated* fashion, where all nodes stop processing and participate in an exchange of data across the network, or in an *uncoordinated* fashion, with messages targeted for specific recipients being injected into the network independently.

Because data can be streamed through the network and targeted for specific nodes, an MPP machine is nicely suited for data parallel applications. In this case, all processors execute the same program on different data streams. In addition, because individual processors can execute different programs, an MPP machine is nicely suited to coarse-grained parallelism and can be configured for pipelined execution as well.

NETWORKS OF WORKSTATIONS

A network of workstations is a more loosely coupled version of an MPP system; the workstations are likely to be configured as individual machines that are connected via network. The *communication latencies* (i.e., delays in exchanging data) are likely to be an order of magnitude greater in this kind of configuration, and it is also possible for the machines in the network to be heterogeneous (i.e., involving different kinds of systems). Because of the configuration, a network of workstations is better suited to coarse-grained parallelism, although any data parallel application without a lot of communication could be nicely adapted to this configuration.

CLOUD COMPUTING

Cloud computing allows for high performance computing as a utility: clusters of computing nodes can be harnessed and a layer can be employed to provide a virtualized high-performance framework. In effect, a cloud-based environment leverages a potentially elastic collection of available processing nodes plus available storage as a utility instead of a capitalized hardware acquisition. Clouds are often managed by external providers, although we can implement a cloud behind your corporate firewall for the benefit of internal consumers.

HYBRID ARCHITECTURES

A hybrid architecture is one that combines or adapts one of the previously discussed systems. For example, system manufacturers will connect multiple SMP machines using a high-speed interconnect to create a hybrid system with a communications model involving two different levels of service. *On-node* communication (where a node is a single SMP machine) is significantly faster than *cross-node* communication. Another configuration might connect small MPP (i.e., 16-node) machines, each of which shares some memory with other small MPP machines within a single box. The use of a hybrid architecture may be very dependent on the specific application, because some systems may be better suited to the concurrency specifics associated with each application.

▌ Parallelism and Business Intelligence

At this point it makes sense to review the value of parallelism with respect to a sample of the BI-related applications we have discussed so far. In each of these applications, a significant speedup can be achieved by exploiting parallelism. First we look at one example of query processing, which is integral to most analytical data functions. In this example, the right kind of parallelism can provide linear scalability. Our second example shows how the column analysis of data profiling can be sped up through task parallelism, and our third example discusses coarse-grained parallelism and the ETL process.

QUERY PROCESSING

Although the complexity of query optimizations may be beyond the scope of this book, a very simple query example can demonstrate the scale of the problem. Consider a database system with a customer table and an orders table. To make things simple, each order entry refers to a specific quantity order of a single product by the referenced customer, along with the total for that order. Assume that there are 100,000 entries in the customer table, that each customer has some dollar rating indicating the minimum order total for which an order is profitable, and that there are 2 million entries in the orders table. We want to identify those customers who have made at least one order whose total is greater than that customer's dollar rating. This request can be configured as a query joining the customer table to the orders table, by selecting any customers from the customer table where there exists an order placed by that customer in the orders table and that order's total is greater than the customer's dollar rating.

The brute-force approach to implementing this join requires examining each of the orders for every customer, which results in $100,000 \times 2,000,000 = 200,000,000,000$ comparisons. If we can execute 1 million comparisons per second on a single processor, it would still take more than two days to finish this query.

In this case, each comparison between the customer table and the orders table is not related to any other comparison—in other words, no comparison is data dependent on any other comparison. If we had eight processors, we can replicate the customer table at each processor and distribute equal-sized chunks of the orders table to each processor. Then each processor is executing $100,000 \times 250,000 = 25,000,000,000$ comparisons. At the same execution speed, this cuts the overall time down to just under seven hours to complete the entire task. Doubling the number of processors decreases the time by one-half again; in fact we could achieve a linear speedup that is proportional to the number of processors participating.

Of course, relational database management systems (RDBMS) will most likely have taken advantage of internal query optimization as well as user-defined indexes to speed up this kind of query. But even in that situation there are different ways that the query can be parallelized, and this will still result in a speedup.

DATA PROFILING

The column analysis component of data profiling is another good example of an application that can benefit from parallelism. Every column in a table is subject to a collection of analyses: frequency of values, value cardinality, distribution of value ranges, and so on. But because the analysis of one column is distinct from that applied to all other columns, we can exploit parallelism by treating the set of analyses applied to each column as a separate task and then instantiating separate tasks to analyze a collection of columns simultaneously. As each task completes, its results are reported, and then the resources used by that task can be allocated to a new task operating on the next available column.

EXTRACT, TRANSFORM, LOAD

The ETL component of data warehouse population is actually well suited to all the kinds of parallelism we have discussed in this chapter. Because we are collecting data from multiple independent sources, the extraction of data from each data source can be configured as a separate task, yielding coarse-grained parallelism as a result of all those extractions that are being performed concurrently. The ETL process itself consists of a sequence of stages that can be configured as a pipeline, propagating the results of each stage to its successor, yielding some medium-grained parallelism. Last, many of the stages performed during the ETL process exhibit data parallel characteristics (i.e., record-by-record transformations are data independent), which can then take advantage of fine-grained parallelism.

Performance Platforms and Analytical Appliances

Recalling the BI user types, we can consider the fact that the demands from the different types of users suggest a general mix of uses for BI and analysis systems. A large percentage of the user community is solely reliant on typical reporting and analysis, which consists of a mixed load of rolled-up and predesigned reports, reporting and analytics prepared by power users, ad hoc queries, interactive analysis, as well as interactive drill down into the supporting data sets. In the decision-making and information management usage, scenarios of the extended user community demonstrate a dependence on four basic classes of information applications that are well suited to an analytic database server:

1. **Traditional reporting.** Together, the business users, casual users, and extended enterprise users comprise the significant majority of the user community, and generally use reporting that conceivably depends on massive amounts of data, whether that is a result of aggregate reporting of transactions, online analytical processing (OLAP) along various predefined dimensions, or summarized reporting through scorecards or dashboards. The lion's share of the processing for most of these activities is either predesigned ("canned") reports or selective ad hoc querying performed by business users, which often default to parameterized versions of similar information requests.

2. **Complex and advanced analytics.** Despite the small percentage of power users, the growth in expectations from large scale analytics and "data scientists" suggest that both the size and prominence of the power user community are growing. There is significant momentum driving increasing development of complex and "big data" analytics, which are designed as a sequence of developing quantitative models that use large data sets that are subjected to statistical analyses, data mining, and other sophisticated, computationally intensive algorithms. These models are then incorporated as evaluation, scoring, or segmentation techniques applied to input data and to data in the data warehouses as a way to improve decision-support processes.

3. **Data aggregation.** There is a growing number of organizations that accumulate data from multiple sources and make that data available for hundreds or thousands of simultaneous ad hoc queries to support customer-facing data services. Data aggregation applications perform tasks such as the generation of reports and analyses of managed data, to collecting, organizing, and provisioning the delivery of news, weather, financial, transportation, and many other types of streamed data. In turn, both the aggregated data sets as well as analytical results provide revenue streams for the aggregator organizations.

4. **Data life cycle management.** This infrastructure usage scenario incorporates managing of security roles, user authentication, role-based access control, data archiving, integration of trickle data feeds (such as streamed point-of-sale transactions, call detail records, and security transactions), and generally maintaining operational data availability as data collections are rolled off main transaction systems. Increasingly, the expectation of availability of longer historical views of data means that these systems have utility in maintaining access to archived data as well.

ARCHITECTURAL APPROACHES FOR ANALYTICAL SYSTEMS

Clearly, most of these applications require a level of performance that can be addressed using multiple processor systems. The primary performance driver for traditional reporting is scalability, with respect to both potentially massive data volumes as well as the number of simultaneous users. Savvy managers and technical leaders must consider scalability requirements to help in the determination of a specific architectural approach.

As we have seen, there is a range of multiprocessor architectures, and they essentially vary in ways that the different resources (such as CPUs, cache memory, core memory, flash memory, temporary disk storage areas, and persistent disk storage) contribute to maximizing system performance. These resources constitute a "memory hierarchy," which hardware architects employ in varying configurations to find the right combination of memory devices with varying sizes, costs, and speed to provide optimal results by reducing the latency for responding to increasingly complex queries and analyses.

Nonetheless, different architectural configurations address different scalability and performance issues in different ways, so when it comes to deciding which type of architecture is best for your analytics needs, don't adopt the automatic reaction of advocates of particular architectural styles, who might reflexively recommend either symmetric multiprocessor (SMP) systems or massively parallel processing (MPP) systems as a prerequisite to implementation. Rather, the determination of the most appropriate architectural style for reporting and analytics must always be based on *clearly defined criteria used to evaluate which approach best meets the business needs in the right context.*

This means that you should consider all aspects of the performance needs of the collections of different types of applications that will be in flight across the organization. This must include data scalability, user scalability, the need for workload isolation, reliance on parallelization and optimization, reliability in the presence of failures, the dependence on storage duplication or data distribution and replication, among other performance expectations. Once the expectations and needs have been assessed, you can then examine how the performance needs of the different types of applications can be addressed by different architectural configurations; some common configurations are presented here.

SHARED-NOTHING

In this variant of the MPP architecture, each independent processing unit is connected to its own memory and communicates directly with its own disk system (Figure 14.4). The processing units can communicate with each other via a network interconnect.

Because the independent processing units do not contend for any shared resources, this type of architecture is nicely suited for applications that are eminently parallelizable. In those cases, we can achieve almost linear scalability in performance in relation to the number of processing units, making this framework an excellent choice for very large-scale *data parallel* tasks. However, because any data

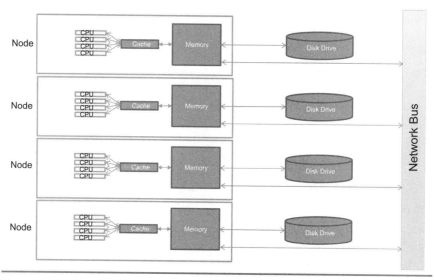

Figure 14.4 Shared-nothing architecture.

sharing must be facilitated via the shared network interconnect, the decreased bandwidth becomes a performance bottleneck for any application that needs to access data that is not stored locally.

In this architecture, one processing node is selected as the *master* node, which often controls the allocation and invocation of parallel tasks across the remainder of the processing nodes. While this approach benefits the computation of results for individual queries requested sequentially, a single master node can be a bottleneck for multiuser concurrent queries, and attempting to overlay multiple parallel tasks simultaneously may lead to node saturation, which also degrades performance. Also, the dependence on a single master process for controlling parallel activities limits fault tolerance because it is a potential point of failure.

SHARED-DISK

In a shared-disk multiprocessor architecture (Figure 14.5), each independent processing unit is connected to its own memory, but differs from the shared-nothing approach in that all processing units access a common disk system. The processing units can communicate with each other via a network interconnect.

The ability to access data directly from various levels of the memory hierarchy eliminates the burden on the processing unit for accessing, packaging, sharing, and then unpackaging data sets. As a result, in most circumstances applications can maintain a high level of processing performance even when data is shared, because the bottlenecks are eliminated.

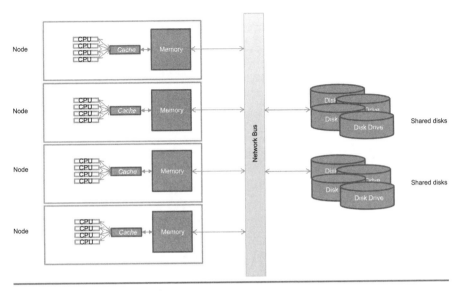

Figure 14.5 Shared-disk architecture.

As we will see, this effect is multiplied when coupled with storage-efficient, column-oriented data layouts, compression, and large page sizes. The requirement for a master computation node acting as a controller is eliminated, which means that individual queries can be directed to different computational nodes for isolation, leading to dramatic improvements in concurrent query stream processing (which is the case for most large scale, multiuser, real-world situations). On the other hand, as more processing units are added to this framework, the demand on shared resources grows, which suggests limits to this approach's scalability.

SHARED-EVERYTHING

In this architectural approach, usually implemented using a traditional symmetric multiprocessing (SMP) architecture, every processing unit has access to a shared memory system as well as access to shared disk storage (Figure 14.6). With predictable memory access latencies, this approach is nicely suited to applications that will need access to shared data, as long as that need does not flood the data access network in an attempt to stream data to many processing units at the same time.

However, there is a need for cache management strategies to maintain coherent views across the processing unit caches, as well as a need for locking to prevent direct contention for shared resources. Yet even the indirect contention for those resources can become a performance bottleneck. So although this approach may be

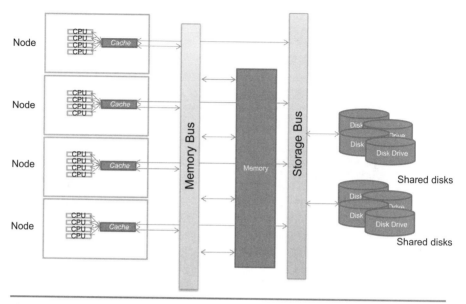

Figure 14.6 Shared everything architecture.

more scalable than the shared-disk approach, there still is a limit to the number of sockets this style can accommodate.

Data Layouts and Performance

The orientation of data on disk contributes significantly to the performance of analytic database applications. The traditional row layout may work well for transactional systems, which largely focus on specific records associated with a limited number of transactions (or transaction steps) at a time. But since analytic applications aggregate and summarize over large data sets, often in the presence of filters manifested as query join conditions, accessing whole rows at a time when only the values of single columns are needed may increase the memory bottleneck.

PERFORMANCE CHARACTERISTICS OF A ROW-ORIENTED DATA LAYOUT

Most database management systems employ a row-oriented data layout; the benefit of this orientation for transactional systems is that operations often require access to many of the attributes associated with a single record. However, most reporting and analytic applications join data from multiple tables, compose reports concentrated on accessing specific columns from each record, or summarize and aggregate data from specific columns in the table.

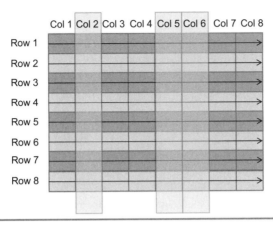

Figure 14.7   In a row-oriented database, accessing specific columns requires reading all records.

Most analytical queries only need to access a subset of the attributes, usually to satisfy join conditions. With row-oriented layouts, the entire record must be read in order to access the required attributes, with significantly more data read than is needed to satisfy the request (Figure 14.7). Also, the row-oriented layout is often misaligned with the characteristics of the memory hierarchy, leading to increased access latencies. A row-oriented data layout is not amenable to the high performance needed for the types of joins or aggregations typical of analytic queries.

COLUMN-ORIENTED DATA MANAGEMENT SYSTEMS

Some performance-oriented analytical architectures will employ a columnar layout to mitigate the poor performance of a row-oriented data layout. Because each column can be stored separately, for any query, the system is able to selectively access those values requested from the specific columns (Figure 14.8). And instead of requiring separate indexes for optimally tuned queries, the data values themselves within each column form the index, speeding data access and reducing the overall database footprint, while dramatically improving query performance.

The simplicity of the columnar approach provides many benefits, especially for those seeking a high-performance environment to meet the growing needs of extremely large analytic data sets, such as:

■ **Engineered for access performance.** Row-oriented systems are limited in supporting many simultaneous diverse queries; column-oriented systems are engineered to enable selective traversal of the required columns aligned along commonly used caching strategies, which increases data access speed.

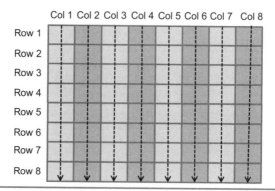

Col 1 Col 2 Col 3 Col 4 Col 5 Col 6 Col 7 Col 8

Row 1
Row 2
Row 3
Row 4
Row 5
Row 6
Row 7
Row 8

Figure 14.8 In a column-oriented database, only the columns in the query need to be retrieved.

- **Rapid joins and aggregation.** Data access streaming along column-oriented data allows for rapid join condition evaluation as well as incrementally computing the results of aggregate functions. Multiple processing units accessing and aggregating different columns in parallel increases overall query performance.
- **Suitability for enumeration compression.** The columnar alignment exposes opportunities for compressing data that results in a significant decrease in storage needs while maintaining high performance. When employing an enumeration approach, there is no associated decompression burden, thereby not incurring additional computational load.
- **Rapid data loading.** The typical process for loading data into a data warehouse involves extracting data into a staging area, perform transformations, load denormalized representations into the warehouse fact and dimension tables, and create the collection of required indexes and views. In a row-based arrangement, all the data values in each row need to be stored together, but the columnar arrangement effectively lets us segregate storage by column. This means that each column, in principle, could be stored separately, which would allow the database system to load columns in parallel using multiple threads.

MapReduce and Hadoop

At the same time that data management professionals are transitioning high-performance computing technologies like cloud computing and analytical databases into the mainstream, a growing community of analytical programmers are adapting programming models for massively parallel programming to enable more flexibility in analyzing both structured and unstructured data and integrating the results of both approaches as part of the BI and analytics program.

Paradigms like Google's MapReduce have become the center point for parallel application development, and programmers are gravitating toward the use of implementations such as Hadoop, which is an open source framework with an implementation of MapReduce as well as a distributed file system to support the development of high-performance data analysis applications.

WHAT IS MAPREDUCE?

MapReduce, which is typically used to analyze web logs on hundreds, sometimes thousands of web application servers without moving the data into a data warehouse, is not a database system. Rather, it is a programming model introduced and described by Google researchers for parallel, distributed computation involving massive data sets (ranging from hundreds of terabytes to petabytes). As opposed to the familiar procedural/imperative approaches used by Java or C++ programmers, MapReduce's programming model mimics functional languages (notably Lisp and APL), mostly due to its dependence on two basic operations that are applied to sets or lists of data value pairs:

- **Map**, which describes the computation or analysis applied to a set of input key/value pairs to produce a set of intermediate key/value pairs, and
- **Reduce**, in which the set of values associated with the intermediate key/value pairs output by the *Map* operation are combined to provide the results.

With some applications applied to massive data sets, the theory is that the computations applied during the *Map* phase to each input key/value pair are independent from one another. Combining both data and computational independence means that both the data and the computations can be distributed across multiple storage and processing units and automatically parallelized. This parallelizability allows the programmer to exploit scalable massively parallel processing resources for increased processing speed and performance.

A COMMON EXAMPLE

A simple example can demonstrate MapReduce's scalability: counting the number of times that each word appears in a massive collection of web pages. A recursive approach to solving this challenge considers incrementally smaller data "chunks" for analysis:

- The total number of occurrences of each word in the entire collection is equal to the sum of the occurrences of each word in each document.

- The total number of occurrences of each word in each document can be computed as the sum of the occurrences of each word in each paragraph.
- The total number of occurrences of each word in each paragraph can be computed as the sum of the occurrences of each word in each sentence.

From a functional perspective, the programmer's goal is to ultimately map each word to its number of occurrences in all the documents. This suggests the context for both the *Map* function, which allocates a data chunk to a processing node and then asks each processing node to map each word to its count, and the *Reduce* function, which collects the word count pairs from all the processing nodes and sums together the counts for each particular word.

The basic steps are simple, and the implementation of the program is straightforward. The programmer relies on the underlying runtime system to distribute the data to be analyzed to the processing nodes, instantiate the *Map* and *Reduce* directives across the processor pool, initiate the *Map* phase, coordinate the communication of the intermediate results, initiate the *Reduce* phase, and then collect and collate the final results. Some example applications include:

- **Document aggregations**, such as sorting, word counts, phrase counts, and building inverted indexes for word and phrase searching;
- **Real-time statistical web log and traffic analysis**, to facilitate offer placement and dynamic product recommendations;
- **Data enhancements**, associated with data migration, data extraction, content tagging, standardization, and other types of transformations;
- **Data mining algorithms**, such as clustering, classification, market basket analysis, or abandoned cart analysis;
- **Data profiling**, to assess data value frequencies, cross-column dependencies, referential integrity, potential data anomalies, and data validation;
- **Semantic text analytics**, for entity extraction and network analysis; and
- **Social network analyses**, associated with social media webs and interactive behavior assessment.

In the past, the programmer was responsible for considering the level of granularity for computation (document vs. paragraph vs. sentence) and the mechanics of data distribution and intermediate communication. In the MapReduce model, though, the mechanics of data distribution and communication are handled by the model, freeing the application programmer to focus on solving the problem instead of its implementation details. In fact, the simplicity of MapReduce allows the programmer to describe the expected results of each of the computations while relying on the compiler and runtime systems for optimal parallelization while providing fault-tolerance.

Assessing Architectural Suitability for Application Performance

Each of the application types has its own particular expectations for performance:

- **Traditional Reporting.** The users of what we called traditional reporting fall into two categories. The first category includes the informed individuals who review the results of predesigned reports, or aggregates rolled up and presented through scorecards, dashboards, or direct notifications. The analyses performed to satisfy the needs of these information consumers may depend on massive amounts of data. However, prior knowledge of the queries used to generate these reports allows for both query optimization for the processing component of the query and locality optimization for the placement of the data.

- The second category of user includes the interactive analysts. Instead of perusing selected analytic results, these information consumers are more likely to be directly analyzing data presented via an OLAP tool or an interactive mash-up framework, or performing numerous, repetitive ad hoc queries, often at different times throughout the day, with an expectation of rapid results. Because of the dynamic nature of the interactions, there is not a lot of prior knowledge that can be used for preoptimization. Also, in this user community there is likely to be a mixed workload, combining the queries to generate the canned reports operating simultaneously with a number of interactive analysts and their variety of processing demands.

- **Complex and Advanced Analytics.** The community of power users for advanced analytics is often focused on "big problems," such as distributed number crunching, complex statistical analyses, model development using data mining tools, and large-scale filtering and reduction, as a way of evaluating massive data sets, possibly a mixture of structured and unstructured data. The developed analytical results and corresponding predictive models are then applied in operation, potentially in relation to many simultaneous streams of information (such as news feeds, logged securities transactions, or web traffic analysis) for real-time operational activities. These users are likely to employ a variety of analytical techniques operating on embarrassingly parallel tasks, such as combining data warehousing with data mining algorithms or crafted Map-Reduce/Hadoop applications. However, there still remain opportunities to reduce the complexity associated with MapReduce/Hadoop programming, and there are ongoing development projects seeking to improve scripting and SQL processing.

- **Data Aggregation.** In situations where the aggregation is focused on scanning data in existing tables, or scanning and aggregating values resulting from complex queries, there is a need for rapid access to data, as well as the need for optimized access and storage. Other applications may be preprocessing unstructured data as a prelude to aggregation—consider the example of counting the number of times that each word appears in a massive corpus of documents. These may rely on a combination of specially developed applications (again using a programming model such as MapReduce) that then performs the aggregation and saves the results to persistent storage.

- **Data Lifecycle Management.** For data access and lifecycle management, these applications are likely to be accessing data associated with security policies, roles, storage policies, data access permissions, and so on.

Summary of performance drivers

Table 14.1 provides a summary of the performance drivers by application type.

TABLE 14.1 Summary of Application Characteristics and Performance Drivers

Application Type	Application Characteristics	Performance Drivers
Traditional Reporting	Predefined reports Parameterized reports Dashboards Scorecards OLAP analysis Ad hoc queries	Delivery of predesigned reports within a designated time frame Combination of predesigned and ad hoc queries Must be able to satisfy ad hoc needs (including potentially complex data access patterns) within real-time constraints Very large to massive amounts of data Need to accommodate a variety of often concurrent users Mixed workload throughout the day
Complex and Advanced Analytics	Aggregation and summarization Potentially complex queries Massive amounts of data Complex algorithmic computations Embarrassingly parallel tasks	Rapid access to data Optimized access of locally accessible data Data parallelism
Data Aggregation	Scanning column data across tables Aggregation and summarization Potentially complex queries Massive amounts of data	Rapid access to data Optimized data exchange for complex joins when necessary Rapid access to data being aggregated Need to accommodate a variety of often concurrent users
Data Lifecycle Management	Data lookup Data access	Rapid access to data

ARCHITECTURAL SUITABILITY

We can speculate as to the suitability of the architectural approaches based on the performance drivers for each of the application types:

- **Traditional Reporting.** The need for producing predesigned reports that aggregate large amounts of data would be served by an architecture that rapidly scans columns. For the interactive information consumers, there is a need to be able to quickly run ad hoc queries that may involve changing data access patterns, and this is best served by a system that does not impose a performance penalty for data sharing such as the shared-disk approach. With these kinds of workloads for large (but perhaps not massive) amounts of data, a shared-disk system using a columnar layout is going to perform well. When there is a demand for massive (exabyte and higher orders of magnitude) data scalability, the shared-nothing platform may be better, but only presuming that the queries are preoptimized, we limit any ad hoc queries, and we do not allow mixed workloads. However, in most environments and circumstances, and with the right data orientation, any of the architectural approaches are going to satisfy the performance expectations.

- **Complex and Advanced Analytics.** When users employ a variety of analytical techniques operating on embarrassingly parallel tasks, such as combining data warehousing with data mining algorithms or MapReduce applications, their applications are often data independent, require massive amounts of storage, and expect linear (if possible) scalability. If the users are only executing programmed applications without any need for persistent structured "database" storage (such as text analytics processing large volumes of documents), a shared-nothing approach is only disk-bound at the initial time of loading. However, in most situations, there will still be a need to capture aggregated results, and if the persistent database storage is deployed within the same architectural environment, in most cases any of the three approaches we have reviewed should perform reasonably well.

- **Data Aggregation.** When the aggregation requires specially developed algorithms and applications, such as those produced in Hadoop, we must contrast the benefits of algorithmic data parallelism with the need for concurrent access to assess both the benefits and limitations of any of the three models. In the circumstance of aggregation of columnar data in existing tables, the performance expectations match the performance characteristics of the shared-disk and shared-everything models, especially with the column-oriented data layout.

- **Data Lifecycle Management.** When it comes to operational management, especially in a time-critical context such as validating access rights to information, the need is for rapid access to persistent data. For this family of applications, any of the architectural styles is satisfactory, so the selection criteria might focus on cost of ownership and simplicity of execution.

QUESTIONS FOR SELECTING A PERFORMANCE ARCHITECTURE

An examination of the performance requirements for each of the classes of analytic applications helps outline the expectations critical to satisfying the needs of the different types of information consumers. In turn, this evaluation provides insight into the key differences between the ways that each of the architectural approaches satisfies the performance and scalability needs. Certain patterns of BI use are best suited to systems that can optimize query execution aligned with data layout, others reflect a broad audience with diverse querying activities, some continually generate the same types of reports with predictable frequency, while other environments may have a diverse set of users that together do not fit into any specific mold. Organizations with massive (exabyte and higher orders of magnitude) data volumes might be better suited to certain architectural approaches, but in general, any environment with a relatively mixed workload is going to benefit from analytic applications using *any* of the parallel architectures.

However, determining the most appropriate architecture is directly related to the degree each approach satisfies clearly articulated business needs. To help in that evaluation, here is an augmented set of parameters that can help in determining the performance expectations and corresponding performance requirements:

- Types of reporting (for example "canned" vs. interactive or OLAP)
- Types of queries (simple aggregations vs. complex multiway joins requiring data sharing)
- Size and growth rate of data volumes
- User community (casual users vs. power analysts, size of the community)
- Types of analyses (query-based vs. algorithmic-based)
- Workload mix (similar analyses vs. variety of users and application types)
- Fault-tolerance and recoverability
- Total cost of operations
- Flexibility in adjusting deployments as workloads evolve
- Real-time constraints (such as required response times for interactive users)
- Sustainability and power efficiency

Asking and answering questions about the application mix can drive the decision process regarding the selection of an architectural approach toward analytic database servers. However, we see that organizations are increasingly transitioning their BI and analytics demands from being solely focused on specific outcomes ("canned reporting") to ones that need to address a broad variety of predefined vs. ad hoc reporting, support mixed-load operations, enable a broad application mix, and scale to meet rapidly growing user demand for simultaneous access to massive amounts of data.

Endnote

1. See press release. "Cyber Monday Spending Hits $1.25 Billion to Rank as Heaviest U.S. Online Spending Day in History," November 29, 2011, downloaded from. http://www.comscore.com/Press_Events/Press_Releases/2011/11/Cyber_Monday_Spending_Hits_1.25_Billion.

Chapter 15

Deriving Insight from Collections of Data

Introduction

An interesting aspect of the business intelligence (BI) process is that although to a large degree it relies on relatively well-defined methods, architectures, and techniques, much of the success of a BI program stems from insight and intuition related to the use of data. Sometimes it is valuable to consider how typical data domains and associated collections (such as customer or product data sets) are used together with other sources of information to lead the analyst in drawing inferences and implications that can lead to profitable action.

For example, by itself geographical data may not be of great interest, but merging customer transactions with rolled-up psychographic profiles associated with geographic data may provide insight into the hows and whys of your customers' behavior. And while we will look at spatial analysis and location intelligence in much greater detail in Chapter 16, there is value in considering how geographic data (as well as many other types of data sets) all contribute to deriving insight in the context of data discovery. **237**

In this chapter we examine alternate information contexts—what kind of data is available, what its value is, and how to plan to integrate that information into your enterprise.

We will also discuss some of the more interesting issues and applications associated with the BI program: the use of demographics (i.e., nonqualitative descriptions, such as age and marital status) and psychographics (i.e., qualitative descriptions of lifestyle characteristics) for enhancement.

A lot of the bits of knowledge we can uncover through a BI application are not actionable unless we have some idea of what to do once we have discovered them. Making use of other data to tell us what to do with our knowledge not only provides insight into how to convert knowledge into dollars, it also continues to leverage our use of data in the first place. The kinds of data uses described in this chapter focus on the thought processes we can employ to help in not only answering questions, but helping in figuring out what the questions should be in the first place.

Customer Profiles and Customer Behavior

If the intent of BI and analytics is optimizing business opportunities, then most business scenarios involving revenue generation as well as managing the customer experience must reflect what can be learned from interactions with customers. There are at least three aspects to this consideration: who the customers are, how they behave, and how you can influence changes to customer behavior that benefit both you and the customer.

CUSTOMER KNOWLEDGE AND CUSTOMER PROFILES

The first aspect is "customer knowledge," implying awareness of key customer characteristics that are relevant to your organization's business processes. Your analytical framework will most likely want to capture these characteristics in a "customer profile" to help in both analyzing the different archetypes of customers you have and how each of the archetypes interact with the business.

The phrase "customer profile" is used in similar contexts with different meanings. In one sense, a profile provides a general overview of the customer incorporating details about inherent characteristics (such as "name," or "birth date"), descriptive demographic characteristics (such as where the individual lives, whether the individual is married), preferences (such as the customer's favorite sports team), as well as analytical characteristics such as purchasing patterns or credit-worthiness.

A slightly adjusted view of a customer profile is mapped to your business and the way your business interacts with customers. In this view, there are classes of customer profiles into which each customer entity is grouped. The value of each customer type is calculated in terms of specific variables relevant to creating value, such as the number of products purchased, or the frequency of store visits, or the variety of products bought.

CUSTOMER BEHAVIOR

Customer behavior is also a somewhat fuzzily defined term; for our purposes let's suggest that "customer behavior" models are intended to capture information about the actions a customer performs under specific circumstances.

As an example, let's say that a retail company emailed a special coupon for an in-store purchase of a particular item. There are a number of specific circumstances associated with this scenario: the presentation of the offer, the method of presentation, the time at which the offer was presented, the time the customer took an action, the timeframe associated with the offer, a particular retail location. Given this scenario, the retailer can track customer actions in relation to the circumstances—the customer ignored the offer, or took advantage of it at some specific time and location.

DEVELOPING BEHAVIOR MODELS

In essence, the initial objective of capturing and analyzing customer behavior is to develop models reflecting customer decision-making processes. In turn, these models are expected to help predict behaviors associated with the different customer archetypes. To continue the example, the company can link a tracking mechanism to the email campaign such as a bar code to be scanned at the point of sale. After the conclusion of the campaign, statistics can be collected about which customers responded. That data set can then be subjected to dimensional analysis based on the customer profile characteristics. This will allow some segmentation to suggest any correlation between selected variables and purchasing the product, such as showing predispositions like:

- Customers between the ages of 30 and 40
- Customers living within 2.5 miles of the retail location
- Customers with an income between $80,000 and $100,000 per year
- Customers who vacation in Florida during December

Remember, though, that correlation does not necessarily imply causation. Identifying potentially dependent variables may suggest a predisposition, but establishing the predictive nature of this suggestion requires additional research. The bottom line is that there is a need feeding the *insight* back into the process, and you should ask questions such as:

- Can the correlation be validated using additional campaigns?

■ Can you verify the causal nature of the correlation? Does this require some alternate investigation such as surveys or focus groups?

■ Can the variable dependences be refined to better target the customer profiles?

INFLUENCING CHANGE

If the first objective is to understand who the customers are and what they do, the next objective is to apply what you believe about customer archetypes and behaviors to influence changes in relation to customer behavior. There may be many approaches to behavior change, and that effort can be directed inside the organization or outside to the customer community.

As one approach, the analytical results of customer profile analysis might highlight a gap in a business process in which the intended target customer audience is not being reached. In that case, the process can be adjusted to broaden the reach to the targeted customer types. An example is determining that a particular age segment is not responding as expected, and altering the marketing and advertising plan to insert television advertisements on channels or networks with the desired age-group audience.

In another approach, you might see that one specific customer segment is predisposed to taking some action. In this case, you might determine if there are other customers who might be easily moved from one segment to the desired one through a sequence of engagement. An example is an airline seeking to engage more business travelers by offering "elite status" incentives for purchasing air travel. At some point, travelers with improved elite statuses will have ratcheted into the desired customer segment.

There can be some variety in the approaches to influencing change, some of which are hybrids of changing both internal processes and external characteristics. The common thread, though, is that analyzing customer profiles and behavior will prove to be a meaningless task unless actions are taken in reaction to what is learned.

Customer Lifetime Value

At the most basic level, *customer lifetime value* (CLV) is a theoretical financial value of a customer over the duration of the relationship with your business. There are many theories on how this value is calculated. For example, one approach is that CLV is calculated as the net present value of the average predicted profit expected from sales to (or cash flow attributed to) any customer.

From a practical perspective, the concept of customer lifetime value is appealing because it not only provides a tangible value to be associated with customer acquisition, it also directs the key stakeholders in the company to take a long-term view associated with managing and maintaining the customer relationship. There are many models for calculating customer lifetime value that incorporate many different variables, although many models incorporate key concepts such as:

- **Acquisition cost**. This incorporates the costs associated with convincing a prospective customer to purchase your product or service.
- **Customer lifetime**. This is the duration of the company's relationship with the customer.
- **Retention rate**. The annual retention rate is the percentage of customers who remain engaged with your company.
- **Retention cost**. These include any costs incurred related to actively maintaining the customer relationship, such as rebates or elimination of service fees.
- **Revenue per customer**. The annual average revenue per customer is the cumulative amount of revenue divided by the total number of (engaged) customers.
- **Servicing cost**. These costs include ones associated with supporting the customer and providing service.
- **Gross profit**. This is the difference between what is brought in as revenue and the cost of creating and providing the product and/or service prior to deducting the operating expenses (including overhead, direct costs, taxes, etc.).
- **Discount rate**. In this context, this is the rate used to calculate the current value of future cash flows.

A customer's lifetime value is then a function of the net present value of the revenue per customer over the customer's lifetime minus the acquisition, retention, and servicing costs. There may be other variables as well, such as attrition costs (incurred when a customer severs his or her relationship), as well as revenues (such as penalties a customer must pay for severing contracts early).

The customer lifetime value concept can also provide guidance into strategies for dealing with different kinds of customers. One example involves understanding the value proposition for customer acquisition. There is typically a cost associated with acquiring new customers. If that cost is greater than the customer lifetime value, there would have to be some motive other than profitability that drives customer acquisition!

A different example relies on more comprehensive customer segmentation. This allows you to be more precise when differentiating between the average customer lifetime value across the entire customer base and analyzing customer lifetime value within discrete customer segments in ways that may influence marketing and sales. For example, a company's overall average customer lifetime value may be $25, but if the customer lifetime value of males between the ages of 18 and 34 is $50, then we might draw the conclusion that the product base skews younger. In this case, it may make sense to orient the marketing budget toward individuals meeting that specific demographic profile because the return on investment is much greater.

One more use is examining processes within the organization that can be adjusted to help increase customer lifetime value. This can be done by focusing on optimizing the dependent variables, such as lowering the associated costs, increasing customer lifetime, or increasing the profitability.

Yet one big challenge for calculating and managing customer lifetime value is accumulating the right data needed for each of the dependent variables. As an example, let's look at one of these variables: duration of the customer lifetime. Calculating customer lifetime requires historical data detailing all customer transactions across all areas of the business. You cannot just depend on the dates of the sales transactions, especially when the sales cycle requires numerous steps each time the customer is engaged. At the same time, there may be other customer touch points that indicate engagement (such as calls to the call center), while monitoring of service usage could signal a reduction in use, signifying an imminent disengagement.

In each case, coming up with a definition for customer engagement and determining what data is necessary to confirm that a customer continues to be engaged requires both defined policies and directed data management effort. The same can be said about any of the other variables: what are the actual costs of acquisition? Does that include the costs of manufacturing the product, marketing, general administrative costs allocated to each customer? What are the ongoing servicing costs? Do those include specific service and maintenance activities for each customer, or do we also allocate part of the infrastructure charges (such as placing a new cell tower) to service costs?

Customer lifetime value is a very powerful concept that can help drive specific actions, both strategic and tactical. And the need to present the appropriate collections of data to help analysts formulate the right types of questions lends credibility with our recurring themes of clarifying business term definitions, understanding business user requirements, and ensuring quality and governance for the source data sets used for driving the data discovery and analysis.

Demographics, Psychographics, Geographics

Our customer profiles help the business know who the customers are, but as we have seen, there may be interest in knowing more than just customer names and locations. You might want to use those profiles to understand the kind of people your customers are—how old they are, what kinds of foods they like, what styles of car they drive, what their hobbies are, or how they like to have fun. Knowing this kind of information can enhance the way that products and services are marketed, especially when analyzing customer characteristics for market segmentation.

By analyzing demographic data (corresponding to the inherent characteristics) and the psychographic data (corresponding to habits, desires, preferences, affinities) of those people who populate each market segment, the business analyst can try to formulate a profile of characteristics that model or represent each segment. Chapter 17 discusses how this segmentation is performed, as well as how new individuals are mapped into the previously defined segments. In this section we look at those characteristic details that can help describe people as a prelude to segmentation.

DEMOGRAPHICS

Demographics represent a quantitative statistical representation of the *nonqualitative* characteristics of a human population. Demographics can include a person's age, marital status, gender, race, religion, ethnicity, income level, and such. Demographics incorporate that information about a person that is not necessarily a result of a lifestyle choice, but rather is more likely to be some attribution related to some external set of variables. For example, people do not choose their age; age is related to the difference between the date they were born and today's date. Similarly, people do not choose their race.

Typically, demographics are used to demonstrate the similarity between people. For example, a population is grouped by membership within certain characteristics (e.g., ages 18–34, 35–49, 50–75). The intent is examining the behavior of customers grouped into similar populations.

PSYCHOGRAPHICS

Psychographics refer to the quantitative representation of the *lifestyle* characteristics of a segmented population, mostly in terms of attitudes, interests, passions, and values. Whereas demographics measure those attributes that are not chosen, psychographics measure chosen attributes related to lifestyle, such as food and beverage preferences, the types of television programs someone watches, vacation location choices, chosen hobbies, leisure activities, and so on.

Psychographics are often used to differentiate people within a population. For example, psychographic information can be used to segment the population by component lifestyles based on individual behavior.

DEVELOPING THE CUSTOMER PROFILES

As discussed previously in this chapter, demographic and psychographic information is used in combination to enhance customer profiles. Demographic and psychographic information is frequently presented in a summarized, comparative form. An example is "75% of males between the age of 18 and 34 have sampled at least four kinds of French wine." A statement like this relates a demographic population (males between the age of 18 and 34) with a lifestyle characteristic (wine drinking) through some metric (75%).

Historically, psychographic data originated from a variety of sources, such as surveys, contest forms, customer service activity, registration cards, specialized lists, and even magazine subscriptions. However, the explosion of online interaction has created an incredible wealth of potential sources of psychographic information, both at an aggregate level and at a personal level. Consider these potential sources of data:

- **Online subscriptions**. Data about the types of online services to which an individual pays for service, such as streamed entertainment, online gaming, or news services.
- **Interactive sites**. Online businesses can monitor web transactions to look at user/visitor behavior patterns.
- **Social networks**. Self-declared interests and connections are mined to assemble information about hobbies and interests.
- **Ad servers**. These are businesses that insert and present advertisements via browser sessions. Installment of "tracking devices" (such as cookies) enables tracking of presentation and click-throughs, even across different web sites and browser sessions over time.
- **Content servers**. Companies running these services see patterns of traffic that provide insight into trends of interests by served IP addresses.
- **Search engines**. Again, patterns of interest in different topics can be aggregated, as well as pinpointed to individuals, households, or business by IP address.
- **Media channels**. Online content providers can aggregate information about topics of relevance by IP addresses served based on the topics of their content.

There is a wealth of this kind of information available, and this can be provided at an aggregate level or can often be isolated to specific locations, even down to the machines used for surfing the web.

Linking personalized psychographics relies on the kind of data enhancement capabilities discussed in Chapter 13 and again in Chapter 16, but having done so can provide fuel for the automated clustering and segmentation that can be provided by data mining software. At that point, you can begin the process of data discovery for developing customer profiles and then using those to drive profitable actions.

Geographic Data

There is a lot of value to incorporating the analysis of BI in the context of location—where your customers live, where they shop, what the closest warehouses to your retail locations are, and so on. Geographic data is largely available, and spatial analytics tools will provide creative visualization methods for extracting actionable knowledge from your data when it is enhanced with geographic data, as we will see in the next chapter.

The informative power of integrated data sets is improved when demographic and psychographic attributes are combined with geographic ones. Certainly, a large source of geographic attribution data is the U.S. Census Bureau, which publishes the results of each 10-year census. This data details all sorts of demographic information about geographic regions as small as a *census tract* (on the order of a few thousand people).

For example, consider the information displayed in Table 15.1, which is derived from data from the 2010 U.S. Census. When presented with a customer record whose address was located within census tract 7006.07, there is a high probability that the individual owns their own home (89.8% of the homes are owner-occupied), is likely to be carrying a mortgage (since only 13.1% of the homes are owned free and clear), and the homeowner is likely to be white (41.5%) or Asian (42.5%). The more information we have to enhance the customer record, the better position we are in to make these inferences.

GEOGRAPHICAL CLUSTERS

Census data can be used for more than the kind of attribution just described. Enhancing the census data itself with data from other sources can provide significant information about the kinds of people who live within a specific area. For example, let's enhance our previous example and see what else we can learn about our customer.

- We know that 82.3% of the households are owner occupied. By integrating average home sale prices over the last 5 years along with the average mortgage interest rates for the same time period, we can determine the average monthly mortgage payment a homeowner makes. Because mortgage brokers typically lend money as a function of a set of ratios of monthly debt to monthly salary, we can calculate an educated guess as to the average monthly salary of homeowners within the geographic area, which in turn can contribute to a geographic clustering profile.
- If our customer record contains a business or daytime telephone number, we can locate where the customer works and then determine the distance between home and work.
- By integrating this data with geographic data about transportation options between the two locations, we can also infer how the customer travels to work. By enhancing that with details of transportation schedules (which may also be available electronically), we can infer the length of time of the customer's commute to work.

For the most part, similar people tend to aggregate in the same areas (e.g., rich people live among other rich people); we can take advantage of this by purchasing

TABLE 15.1 Example of US 2010 Census Housing and Occupancy Statistics

Subject	Number	Percent
Occupancy Status		
Total housing units	2,519	100.0
Occupied housing units	2,487	98.7
Vacant housing units	32	1.3
Tenure		
Occupied housing units	2,487	100.0
Owner occupied	2,234	89.8
Owned with a mortgage or loan	1,908	76.7
Owned free and clear	326	13.1
Renter occupied	253	10.2
Vacancy Status		
Vacant housing units	32	100.0
For rent	6	18.8
Rented, not occupied	2	6.3
For sale only	6	18.8
Sold, not occupied	1	3.1
For seasonal, recreational, or occasional use	5	15.6
For migratory workers	1	3.1
Other vacant	11	34.4
Tenure by Hispanic or Latino Origin of Householder by Race of Householder		
Occupied housing units	2,487	100.0
Owner-occupied housing units	2,234	89.8
Not Hispanic or Latino householder	2,165	87.1
White alone householder	1,032	41.5
Black or African American alone householder	48	1.9
American Indian and Alaska Native alone householder	1	0.0

TABLE 15.1 Example of US 2010 Census Housing and Occupancy Statistics
—(*Continued*)

Subject	Number	Percent
Asian alone householder	1,056	42.5
Native Hawaiian and Other Pacific Islander alone householder	0	0.0
Some Other Race alone householder	2	0.1
Two or More Races householder	26	1.0
Hispanic or Latino householder	69	2.8
White alone householder	55	2.2
Black or African American alone householder	4	0.2
American Indian and Alaska Native alone householder	2	0.1
Asian alone householder	2	0.1
Native Hawaiian and Other Pacific Islander alone householder	0	0.0
Some Other Race alone householder	4	0.2
Two or More Races householder	2	0.1
Renter-occupied housing units	253	10.2
Not Hispanic or Latino householder	233	9.4
White alone householder	83	3.3
Black or African American alone householder	43	1.7
American Indian and Alaska Native alone householder	0	0.0
Asian alone householder	104	4.2
Native Hawaiian and Other Pacific Islander alone householder	0	0.0
Some Other Race alone householder	1	0.0
Two or More Races householder	2	0.1
Hispanic or Latino householder	20	0.8
White alone householder	16	0.6
Black or African American alone householder	0	0.0

(Continued)

TABLE 15.1 Example of US 2010 Census Housing and Occupancy Statistics
—(*Continued*)

Subject	Number	Percent
American Indian and Alaska Native alone householder	1	0.0
Asian alone householder	0	0.0
Native Hawaiian and Other Pacific Islander alone householder	0	0.0
Some Other Race alone householder	3	0.1
Two or More Races householder	0	0.0
Subject	Number	Percent

additional demographic and psychographic data and performing these kinds of enhancements to specially attribute geographic regions to much greater detail. Fortunately, there are a number of companies that package and sell this kind of geographic detail. These data sets will provide not only detail but also essentially a reverse mapping between profile characterization and the places in which people live, and we will explore this in greater detail in the next chapter.

Behavior Analysis

The behavior analysis is a combination of the collection of actions or transactions, an analysis looking for patterns that have business relevance, and the use of the identified patterns for process improvement or for predictive purposes. We can illustrate this using an example of web-based transactions.

Practically every web-based transaction carries relevant information and practically every transaction is seen by a multitude of parties. Every web page you request is seen by your Internet service provider, other Internet service providers, content servers, numerous ad servers, numerous social networking sites, owners of the network infrastructure, as well as the owner of the web site you are requesting. There is a tremendous amount of data generated and generally accumulated as web statistics, page visit logs, time stamps, and so on.

Each of these parties can track the movements of visitors to various web sites. This provides an opportunity to analyze the correlation between content and individuals (based on their IP addresses) and potentially use that behavior information themselves or package it for the purposes of developing marketing strategies through the combination of traditional demographic and psychographic information with online behavioral data. This information can be used in the creation of rich customer profiles, and the mining of these profiles for useful behavioral patterns and the application of the knowledge inherent in those patterns can help solve numerous business problems. Particularly exciting is the potential to convert Web visitors from browsers to purchasers. Profiling customers in the context of an e-business intelligence strategy can assist in providing micro-segmentation for targeting value-added products and services for cross-sell and up-sell opportunities.

TRACKING WEB ACTIVITIES

Tracking user behavior involves more than just collecting server log files. Instead of relying on the traditional server log data, we can incorporate a more meaningful characterization of user activity. First, it is necessary to specify the kinds of actions that a user may perform while browsing at your site. This is more than just page views; rather, we want to superimpose business meaning on top of appropriate page views and to ignore meaningless ones. Behavior modeling then becomes a process of analyzing the sequence of actions that users perform, within what context those actions are performed, and whether any particular behaviors can be generalized for later predictive purposes.

Although each e-business's list of user actions may vary, here is a short list of some user actions that are interesting to log:

- Content request, asking for a specific page to be served
- Content impression, when a Web page containing specific content is served
- Content read, when served content is read
- Hyperlink click-through
- Advertisement impression, when an advertisement is served
- Advertisement click-through
- Social network click-through (such as a "like" button)
- Social network login
- Social network posting
- Social network repost (such as the "retweet" feature on Twitter)
- Comment posting (such as a comment on an interactive page)
- Comment read (such as clicking on a "more" button to expose the full text of a comment)
- Syndicated posting (such as content pushed through an RSS feed or forwarded from a page to a social network site)
- Initial registration, when a user registers
- Subsequent registration, when a user reregisters
- User login
- User logout

- Password change
- Password request, when a user forgets a password
- Input of new profile information (any time a user voluntarily enters new profile information)
- Forced data input accepted (when a user is asked to input new information and that request is followed)
- Forced data input rejected (when a user is asked to input new information and does not follow through)
- Information query (the user searches for information)
- Select product for purchase, such as when using a shopping basket and a product is selected for purchase
- Purchase sequence initiated, when purchase information is requested
- Purchase sequence completed, when enough information has been collected to complete a purchase
- Purchase sequence aborted, when a user does not complete the purchase sequence ("abandoned cart")

A specific data mart can be constructed to capture this kind of activity for later analysis.

CUSTOMER BEHAVIOR PATTERNS

Now, after having captured customer actions for a period of time, the information in the user activity data set will represent a collection of time series of the ways that all the web visitors act when they are visiting the site. We can analyze this time series data to look for particular user behavior patterns. If these patterns represent desired business activity, we have discovered actionable knowledge that can be used in influencing visitor behavior.

One analysis framework presumes a desired outcome, and it looks for patterns that lead to that outcome. For example, we might want to explore how viewing a specific content item correlates to making an online sale. Or we may want to see how well the placement of advertising affects click-through rates associated with browsing sequences. This is actionable knowledge, because it gives us information about how well our expectations are converting into good business practices.

A different analysis framework looks for behaviors that are not known a priori. For example, we might extract activity sequences that lead to a completed purchase and then look for patterns in those sequences. We might discover that a purchase-completed action takes place 25% of the time that a specific order sequence of content views take place. This becomes actionable knowledge, because it suggests different ways to configure the browsing experience to accelerate a customer's purchase.

Consideration When Drawing Inferences

When presented with a palette of information about a particular topic, an analyst can apply his or her own experiences, thought processes, and intuition to make judgments and develop insights. But we must also be careful when drawing inferences and not confuse inferences with "facts." Data analysis can suggest new insights, but data analysis does not "create facts." For example, market basket analysis might suggest a discovery that a person exhibits purchasing behaviors that are consistent with pregnancy, but that does not necessarily make that person pregnant. Granted, though, there may be situations in which people will mistake analytical results for facts; however, that can happen with any inference, such as guessing that a celebrity is pregnant based on the exposure of her bump in pictures printed in the tabloids.

On the other hand, though, certain inferences may suggest very strong correlations with what may be factual. In these cases, though, your organization must be careful in using those inferences. Using the same example, we can be relatively sure that a person's purchasing behavior is consistent with someone who is pregnant, but you might still want to exercise some care in attempting to send out marketing material to that individual. Aside from the individual's desire for protecting her own privacy, the perception that a retailer has this level of visibility into an individual's personal world could be seen as invasive.

Chapter 16

Creating Business Value through Location-Based Intelligence

The Business Value of Location

Even with the growth of virtual businesses, online companies, and electronic commerce, it is still true that any business transaction or event, ranging from sales, customer service, maintenance, supply chain, and so on, involves parties that are physically at some set of locations. As companies seek to drive improved profits, reduced costs, or improved productivity from the "virtualized space" of the World Wide Web, the ever-growing volume of data can yield interesting and surprising insight in relation to the location of events, transactions, and behaviors. Whether we are looking for operational efficiencies, revenue growth, or more effective management, many individual decisions on a minute-by-minute basis can be informed as a result of location-based intelligence.

In other words, there is value in understanding how location influences both operational and analytical applications. This chapter provides an introduction to location-based intelligence as it relates to the common view of an address, and provides an overview of geocoding and geographic data services. We will then examine how geocoding can be used within business applications, and consider analytical techniques that can be applied across many types of industries and organizations. The chapter provides examples of some specific usage scenarios for selected vertical industries, presents an overview of some types of geographic data services, and discusses how those services satisfy the needs of those business applications, without the need of an actual "map."

Demystifying Geography: Address Versus Location

Often people are confused by the term "location," and equate it with the concept of an "address." But in fact there are some key differences that are worth reviewing.

An address is a text string formatted according to a definition provided by a postal authority intended for direct mail delivery. While an address often maps to a physical place, there are addresses (such as post office boxes or military addresses) that are used for mail delivery but do not truly correspond to a location. The ability to map an address associated with an identified physical place to its specific location is critical in many industries, such as insurance, financial services, and utility provision, among numerous others.

Sometimes there is ambiguity inherent in the concept of an address, especially with respect to the degree of precision to which it can be directly related to a physical location. For example, an address can refer to the front door of an office building, the center of the rooftop of a house on a specific property, a suite on some floor of a high-rise office, or even the position of a property's mailbox.

However, the meaning of location is much more precise—it describes a specific point in a dimensional space, most frequently two dimensions on the surface of the earth, and sometimes even adding a third, vertical dimension. In this context it is useful to consider the simplicity of locating a specific point on the globe. Every point on the earth can be represented as a combination of two numbers: the latitude and the longitude. The *latitude* is the measure of angular distance (in degrees) between the equator and the poles of the earth, and the latitude lines run horizontally across the globe. The *longitude* lines are perpendicular to the lines of latitude, and measure the angular distance (in degrees) from an arbitrarily selected Prime Meridian assigned the value of 0 degrees. A latitude and longitude pair defines a specific point on the earth's surface. The pair of numbers is often represented using a standardized all-natural number representation format called a *geocode*. The word geocode is also used as a verb, meaning to find the latitude and longitude (and sometimes altitude) of a specific location.

Geocoding and Geographic Enhancement

The geocode is a straightforward concept that captures the latitude and longitude coordinates (often referred to as a *latlong*). The geocode is the core building block for implementing geographic data services, which combine geographic and topological features (such as points, lines between points, and polygons representing areas on a map) with interesting attributes assigned to those features (such as median income, proximity to points of interest, or average prices for goods and services) to provide insight into both operational and analytical application contexts. Geographic data services are essentially built to leverage core functionality for spatial relationships and analysis, such as:

- **Geocoding.** Identifying the latitude and longitude coordinates for the location of an object or an address;
- **Reverse geocoding.** Mapping a set of coordinates to a specific address or region; and
- **Data enhancement.** Appending value-added attribution associated with a location.

These geographic data services are able to leverage information at different levels of precision, ranging from a wide area (such as the area contained within a ZIP code) to more precise (such as the interpolated location based on street address) to even greater levels of precision and granularity (such as the center of a manhole cover located in the street in front of a residential property).

For the most part, the consumers of geographic data services had been limited to a relatively small cohort of expert users with great depth of knowledge in the use of complex geographic information system (GIS) tools. This community of GIS tool users consists of individuals with deep backgrounds in spatial analysis, being conversant in the analysis of location information, as well as expert in the extraction of data from a variety of sources and the manipulation and preparation of data for loading into the stand-alone GIS tool. In other words, the GIS community effectively replicates a large part of what the business intelligence (BI) community does, but may be constrained by the specifics of the interfaces and limitations of stand-alone GIS tools.

Yet the availability and growing popularity of portable devices that interface with the Global Positioning Satellites (also known as GPS devices) has broken down the walls to what you might call the "GIS ivory tower." As more information consumers are becoming aware of the value of location-based intelligence and analysis provided by geographic data services, there is a greater need for providing *spatial analysis* and *location intelligence* applications and enabling the rapid integration of the resulting actionable knowledge about different attributes of location into operational environments.

Interestingly, while individuals may directly benefit from the availability of precise location information, GPS positioning, and specialty applications for direction deployed on hand-held devices, many location intelligence applications no longer consider location only with respect to visualizing specifics on a map. Rather, there is business value in growing awareness of the *context* of location—communicating actionable knowledge about preferences, characteristics, behavior, and events based on where the objects or individuals are, their proximity to each other or other points of interest, or where transactions or events take place and whether their locations can influence the outcomes.

And these ideas are becoming more pervasive, especially in terms of delivery to that same smart hand-held device. For example, an individual's search for a new home can be radically improved when the individual's demographic profile can be matched with neighborhoods whose residents share similar characteristics. Introducing geographic data services into the enterprise allows the integration of location information to augment operational activities (such as real-time proximity searching for points of interest closest to the consumer) while greatly enhancing BI and analysis through the addition of a geographical dimension to the data.

Fundamentals of Location-Based Intelligence for Operational Uses

Geographic data services enable the analysis of objects (such as individuals, members of a logical cohort or community of interest, businesses, points of interest, or geographic regions), their location attributes (such as average age, median income, average driving distance, or average educational attainment), and on occasion, temporal events, all within a number of application scenarios. This combined *location-based intelligence* informs operational and analytical applications, workflows, and decision-making, and can add value by increasing revenues, decreasing costs, or improving productivity and satisfaction. This section looks more closely at fundamental geographic data services including address cleansing and standardization, mapping, distance calculations, calculating nearest points of interest, risk assessment, real-time traffic and routing updates, emergency or accident routing, and other typical use cases for operational purposes.

MAILING ACCURACY

At least within the United States, there are two aspects of business benefits derived from increasing mailing accuracy through address standardization. This first is reduction of mailing costs; the US Postal Service incentivizes standardizing addresses for delivery, which in turn relies on geographic data services. Postage rates are reduced for high volume mailings with standardized addresses (including bar codes), thereby reducing costs. At the same time, ensuring high quality and accurate addresses eliminates the risk of expenditures on undeliverable or incorrectly delivered mail.

The second aspect reflects improved opportunities. While increasing mailing accuracy reduces redundant costs, you also get the ability to target accurate delivery with greater precision, with the result that more pieces reach the intended audience. So while additional mailing costs are eliminated, we can simultaneously increase prospect and customer response rates.

FINDING THE NEAREST LOCATION

There are many operational instances that benefit from real-time calculation of the nearest locations or assets. Some examples include:

- **Expedite call routing**, such as mobile emergency (E-911) calls that can be routed to the proper authorities based on origination point coordinates provided by the mobile device;
- **Optimize allocation of assets**, such as routing mobile telephone calls based on proximity to cell towers and antennas;
- **Find closest points of interest**, such as hotels, restaurants, or entertainment;
- **Optimize dispatch services**, such as dispatching the closest service vehicle to the point of service, such as taxicabs, roadside assistance, or utility installation and/or repair;
- **Maximize customer contact**, such as a sales representative visiting a client in one location who is able to schedule additional client visits within the same vicinity; or
- **Provide emergency assistance**, such as directing the police or emergency medical staff, especially for locations unreachable by standard emergency vehicles.

Finding the nearest location builds directly on geocoding, reverse geocoding, potential access to a knowledge base of points of interest, and the ability to calculate distances.

NONADDRESSABLE LOCATIONS

Most people are accustomed to thinking about location in the context of deliverable addresses, but they may not be aware that there are many infrastructure assets whose physical locations do not necessarily resolve to a "standardizable" address (Figure 16.1). Storm drains, bridges, telephone poles, electrical wires, fences, wireless towers, railways, and airport hangars are all examples of nonaddressable locations. Typically we would not send a letter to any of these items, yet each of these

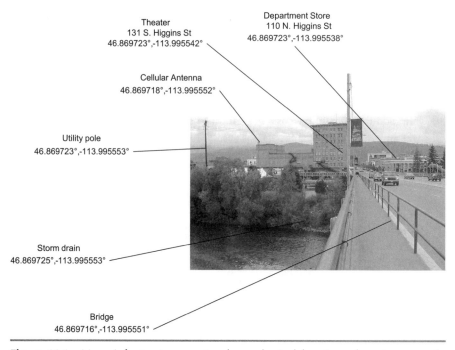

Figure 16.1   Many infrastructure assets whose physical locations do not necessarily resolve to a "standardizable" address.

examples represents one or more assets situated at a physical location that requires attention and maintenance on a regular basis. Combining geocoding with a knowledge base of different classes of points of interest allows precision in finding the geographic coordinate for any of these assets as well as the best methods and routes for accessing them.

ELIGIBILITY AND PROVISIONING

Eligibility for acquiring some services may be constrained based on the consumer's location. Consider these examples:

- **Determine government assistance eligibility**, such as determining if a homeowner is within an area that is eligible for government assistance in the aftermath of an emergency, or if a business is located within an area that qualifies for government-supported capital investment, municipal tax incentives, preference in contracting engagements, and for subsidies for economic development;
- **Calculate service boundaries**, such as determining which is the correct supplier to service a particular region, or whether a location is close enough to a telecommunications central office to be wired for DSL Internet service;

- **Determine service eligibility**, such as determining whether a residential area is served by public water and sewage systems or if a service location is served by fiber optic telecommunication lines;
- **Isolate sources of system failures**, such as determining where a damaged wire in an energy grid has caused a power outage;
- **Differentiate service charges**, such as distinguishing between covered wireless service areas and those areas for which roaming charges are incurred; or
- **Comply with zoning ordinances**, such as observing regional zoning restrictions for construction of new housing developments.

LOCATION-BASED CONTENT PROVISION

Organizations with a web presence are increasingly crafting their content and advertising presentation to web surfers in relation to the geographic location to which the surfer's IP (internet protocol) address resolves. Content provision based purely on location can highlight businesses that are in close proximity to the surfer's physical location, such as advertising local restaurants or the circulars for local supermarkets.

Fundamentals of Location-Based Intelligence for Analytical Uses

Content provision that combines location information with corresponding demographic data allows placement of targeted advertising of specific goods and services customized to specific customer profiles. This is a good example where analyzing historical transactions, object profiles, events, and location attributes to identify deeper insights provides an analytic avenue for applying geographic data services. This allows the user to inform decision-makers looking for answers to more sophisticated questions, such as:

- Which side of the street is preferable for opening a new drive-through restaurant?
- Which branch offices can be merged without risking significant customer attrition?
- How can a mortgage company optimally distribute its risk of borrower defaults based on location-based payment histories and geo-demographic similarities?
- What are optimal staff resource allocations to reduce crime within specific neighborhoods?
- Are people living in certain regions at greater risk of contracting communicable diseases?
- Are mortality rates by disease in different parts of the country impacted by proximity to environmental hazards?
- Will municipal street planning objectives align with regional growth patterns?

- How many supermarkets are within a reasonable walking distance for residents within low-income areas?
- How much time should a political candidate allocate to canvassing in specific neighborhoods?

Every business event or transaction happens at some specific location, and an analyst can look for patterns associated with geography that can be effectively used to improve business performance. Here we present some examples that use geographic location for analytic purposes, such as geographic targeting, fraud detection, site location, risk assessment and determination of premiums for insurance, dead zone analysis for telecommunication utilities, and other typical analytical use cases. We consider both "horizontal" use cases that can be generally applied across many industries, as well as "vertical" use cases specific for particular industries.

HORIZONTAL ANALYSIS

Horizontal analyses are areas of focus that are common across many different types of businesses that can be applied in many industries, and often focus on operational analytics to optimize general activities such as communications and fraud analysis.

Geographic Targeting

Our previous example of location-based content provision is a special case of more generalized approaches to targeted marketing. This use case uses geocoding and data enhancement to select specific locations and methods for targeted communications. Some examples include:

- **Direct advertising**. Directed media advertising placement, such as customized circular inserts for newspaper delivery or targeted radio and television advertisements;
- **Identify sites of high-volume traffic**. Identifying regions whose residents share desirable demographics and placing billboard advertisements along key commuting corridors;
- **Monitor voter sentiment**. Evaluating areas of voter sentiment to optimize concentration of candidate canvassing; or
- **Target mass communications**. Communicating emergency event notifications to specified first responders.

Property and Asset Management

There are many organizations that operate out of a collection of sites and facilities, such as universities, retail chains, health care networks, and hospitality companies.

Not only do these businesses deal with physical buildings, they must also manage interactions taking place at a variety of places within each building (such as receiving goods at a loading dock intake at an emergency room entrance, or managing waste management points) as well as managing the distribution of assets (such as beds, computers, desks, or other devices) to specific locations.

Knowing the location of each facility and asset benefits the organization when it comes to planning and maintenance, and organizing goods and services procurement around locations in close proximity can enable better pricing while reducing staff allocation and transportation costs. In addition, rental properties can be continually assessed to determine whether their rents are in line with fair market prices for the region and help with maintaining high levels of continuous occupancy.

Fraud Detection

Location data adds much value to analyzing events and transactions and looking for unusual patterns indicative of fraudulent behavior. Some (of many!) examples include:

- **Prevent identity theft**. Using location information to validate customer identification at inbound call centers to reduce identity theft;
- **Flag stolen credit cards**. Discrepancies between the location of a credit card transaction and the location of the holder of that credit card;
- **Discover insurance claim fraud**. Evaluating residential addresses of patients and dates of service in comparison to the health care providers to determine whether "runners" are importing patients from one location to providers in another location for identifying health insurance claim fraud; or
- **Identify public assistance fraud**. Looking for grocery stores with unusual numbers of food-stamp transactions or unusual concentrations of whole-dollar transactions indicative of patterns of food-stamp fraud.

Site Location

Physical facilities are still common across many different industries, particularly retail, banking, healthcare, and hospitality, as well as public sector and social services. There are many factors that contribute to a company's decision process for selecting a site for a physical facility. In each case, the decision depends on the degree to which characteristics of the proposed locations meet a set of defined criteria aligned with the organization's business needs.

For example, a professional home builder may want to create smart housing strategies that will ensure the right housing plans are built for the right neighborhoods. The company wants to carefully study the surrounding points of environmental interests before selecting that location and needs answers to the following questions:

- Is the area served by public water, sewage, natural gas, electricity utilities?
- Is the location in close proximity to shopping and other services?
- Are there any nearby environmental issues that could impact home sale prices?
- What are the hazard risks associated with the plot?

Some other examples of site location include:

- **Retail sites.** Retail site analysis may consider sites to be the most desirable sites based on centrality and accessibility within a region whose residents share certain demographic and behavioral attributes;
- **Development sites.** For urban development, location selection for new housing subdivisions may be impacted by proximity to points of environmental interest; or
- **Telecommunication tower sites.** For a wireless telecommunications tower selection of a location depends on zoning, usage permitting, and community restrictions for utility facilities.

VERTICAL APPLICATIONS

The horizontal applications provide a general set of analytical capabilities that can be used across many different industries. Industry-oriented (or "vertical") analytical applications also benefit from geographic data services and spatial analysis, and this section provides some usage scenarios for selected vertical industries.

Logistics and Delivery

Value drivers within the logistics and delivery industries are a mixture of improving efficiency and productivity while reducing fuel costs and safety risks. This presents opportunities for employing spatial analysis such as:

- **Reduce searching time.** Reducing the time spent searching for the right delivery location by combining address standardization, cleansing, and enhancement to correct inaccurate or invalid addresses, and to resolve incomplete locations due to out-of-date maps;
- **Increase delivery speed.** Increasing delivery speed by using a routing service that suggests the optimal route that minimizes the overall driving time;
- **Lower fuel costs.** Reducing expensive fuel costs by using a routing service that suggests the optimal route that minimizes the total distance driven; or
- **Improve safety.** Maximizing safety by using a routing service that suggests the route that ensures that each delivery point is always positioned to the right of the vehicle, which reduces the risk of accidents to the driver.

In each of these situations, combining data quality and geographic data services provides efficient routing to accurate addresses, which increases driver productivity, reduces costs, and increases customer satisfaction.

Insurance

High-quality geographic information is critical to the insurance industry. Policy premiums are related to risks, many of which are directly tied to location. For example, premiums for a home insurance policy are definitely influenced if the property is situated within a high crime area or natural hazard zone and is potentially subjected to earthquakes, flooding, tornados, hurricanes, or wildfires.

In addition, while location data is necessary to complete the underwriting process, location intelligence is especially critical to many other insurance activities such as

- Evaluating (and subsequently balancing) exposure to aggregate risk across different areas;
- Managing risk inventory and potentially adjusting premium rates in relation to shifting location characteristics;
- Catastrophe management, to not only ensure that adjusters are able to help insureds in times of crisis, but also to foresee the stockpiling of materials in anticipation of or prior to potential disasters that are subject to prediction, such as hurricanes or floods;
- Managing the portfolio in relation to demographics associated with risk of theft and damage;
- Mandatory reporting to regulatory and oversight boards such as state insurance commissions; and
- Assessing additional expenses and responsibilities such as taxes and fees.

Interestingly, in most of these activities, location information is used without the need for visualizing a point on a map. For example, we do not need to see the location of a parcel on a map to determine if it is situated within a hazard zone. Instead, the context is driven using spatial analytics that calculate whether a specific set of coordinates are contained within a polygonal region. This is a very important point: geographic data services go way beyond simplistic queries that are typically satisfied via maps presented through popular web sites.

Telecommunications

We have already seen uses of horizontal analytics leveraging geographic data services for the telecommunications industry for tasks like site selection for physical assets (e.g., wireless telecommunications towers), for service eligibility (as is needed for DSL service), and for facility and asset management. Yet location can play many more roles within the telecommunications industry for other tasks as well.

Since many mobile telephones and other personal digital assistant devices either have integrated GPS hardware that provides geocodes or can interpolate location with some degree of precision by triangulation across nearby cell towers, wireless telecommunications providers can serve content to subscribers based on location. By reviewing call detail records and surveying the originating points of dropped calls, wireless companies can analyze "dead zones" where there are interruptions in continuous service, helping to identify candidate locations for cellular communication equipment or deployment of new services. And traditional telephone providers can align their targeted marketing and communications efforts with staged installation of new infrastructure such as fiber optic lines to specific neighborhoods and subdivisions.

In addition, spatial analysis can be used to help in analyzing location-based pricing sensitivity that can suggest ways that product and service bundling could improve profitability while potentially decreasing consumer costs. For example, assessing the technical savviness of a community could help a telecommunication company in marketing new services such as remote home automation.

Government

Location is relevant to almost all areas and levels of government, ranging from the federal level down to distinct municipalities. Government agencies and businesses share many of the same challenges associated with communications, logistics, and facility and asset management that have already been addressed in this paper. It would be challenging to list the many other government uses of geographic data services, but here are some additional examples:

- **Persons of interest**. Locating persons of interest such as terrorists, drug dealers, money launderers, and others involved in criminal or regulated activities for the purposes of observation and monitoring;
- **Social services**. Effective management and provision of social services, including analysis of service coverage and availability by region;
- **Environmental interest**. Oversight of facilities involved in activities of environmental interests for monitoring substance emissions;
- **Military analysis**. Geographic analysis for optimal military defense; or
- **Transportation planning**. Medium and long-term planning for transportation infrastructure such as airports, railways, and interstate highways.

Geographic Data Services

Both the operational and the analytical business applications of geographic information and spatial analysis depend on a qualified set of underlying geographic data services. We can see that the realm of possibilities for exploiting location may seem endless; however, these applications rely on a relatively compact set of geographic data services, as described next.

GEOCODING

The fundamental task for geographic intelligence is geocoding, which translates a named location to specific coordinates on a map of the earth's surface. Given a conceptual location such as an address, the geocoding service provides the corresponding latitude and longitude coordinates. In concert with a provided knowledge base of points of interest, the geocoding service might be able determine the latitude and longitude coordinates given a named point of interest, the name of a region, a description of a street intersection, an airport code, using text analysis to decode unstructured text (such as "15 miles north of the Golden Gate Bridge"), or even through interactively clicking on a web-based map. In addition, the geocoding process can work in reverse: Given a set of latitude and longitude coordinates, the geocoder can provide the nearest address.

A geocoding service can be adapted to the precision expectations of the consuming business application. For example, an address can be geocoded to a *parcel rooftop*, which is the center point of a specific land tract referred to as a parcel. If there is not enough information to resolve the location to the parcel rooftop, the geocoder can provide the *interpolated rooftop* latitude and longitude coordinates by estimating the parcel's location within a range of addresses whose starting and ending coordinates are known. Even less precise is providing the coordinates of the *centroid* of the postal code area.

REVERSE GEOCODING

This service looks at a set of latitude, longitude coordinates and searches for the closest addresses within a given radius.

ADDRESS CLEANSING AND STANDARDIZATION

Another valuable geographic data service relies on underlying data quality services such as parsing, standardization, matching, and third-party data for enhancement to meet published standards for postal addressing.

DATA ENHANCEMENT

By combining geocoding and address standardization, an enhancement service provides value-added benefits by appending additional information (such as address corrections, demographic data imports, psychographic data imports, and household list appends) to existing records. This is particularly valuable when it comes to appending geographic information associated with risk assessment, identification of municipal taxing authorities, and standardized representations of regional hierarchies (such as place/township/city/county/state).

MAPPING

The desire to track the locations at which business transactions occur suggests a fundamental need for a mapping service that notes the positions of spatial data (e.g., location, a point of interest, a route, or an address) on a map. A mapping service enables positioning points on a map as well as editing, analyzing, and displaying value-added associated information on a map.

A mapping service essentially combines the geocoding capability with reporting and visualization tools. Often, a mapping service is assembled through tight integration with business intelligence toolsets to leverage the underlying geocoding capability, enhancement, and reporting and analytics to address operational and analytical expectations.

INCLUSION

This service takes a point and a region and tells you whether the point is or is not contained within the region.

DISTANCE

From the spatial perspective, there are a variety of methods for calculating the distance between two points. The most basic distance is a Euclidean distance, which is the "straight line" distance between two sets of coordinates. Practically, there are many versions of "distance" between two location coordinates, including ones based on driving distance, driving time, minimized fuel-costs, or even the number of left turns, among others. Distance calculations support proximity matching and geographic searches for close-by points of interest.

ROUTING

A routing service yet again leverages the underlying geocoding and distance capabilities, and is primarily used to plan routes between two points. Routing may rely on the different distance calculations to evaluate and present the most efficient paths along a set of points using a variety of weighting criteria such as direct distance, driving distance, drive time, number of turns, or speed limits. In turn, the routing service can then present the optimal paths based on shortest distance or shortest driving times.

Proximity Matching

A mapping service can support interactions in which the end-user may consider alternate or additional locations or points of interest within some close proximity to known locations. Proximity matching allows for a spatial search of objects within a defined radial range or via specific routes or corridors in relation to either a specified point, or even in relation to named locations (such as "all fast food restaurants within the city of Tulsa, OK"). Proximity matching incorporates a knowledge base of categorized points of interest and matches spatial analysis with that reference data to perform proximity searches along defined categories (such as a restaurant guide or a list of bank branch offices) to provide a list of matches within the closest vicinity.

An alternate use of proximity matching incorporates location as characterization information for resolving unique identities. For example, when considering whether two name/address records refer to the same individual, we can use the proximity matching service to determine "closeness" of the geocoded addresses; if two addresses have latitude and longitude coordinate pairs that are within a specified range, they can be considered as duplicates, contributing to the overall similarity score for the pair of records.

Challenges and Considerations

Recognizing that there is a growing need for pervasive geographic data services and spatial analytics establishes the imperative of integrating geographic data services as part of the enterprise information management framework. Yet the need for quick turnaround, trustworthy information, and interoperability is diametrically opposed to the approaches of using traditional GIS tools or risking exposure of private data while attempting to squeeze the most out of the limited functionality of web-based mapping interfaces. Therefore, if the growing demand for geographic intelligence is to be met, it means that the traditional model of geographic information processing using standalone GIS tools or web-based interfaces is not sustainable.

That being said, an alternative approach to traditional GIS would be more direct integration within a business intelligence and analytical environment. In fact, since there is a need for tight integration across the analytical and operational scenarios, more "agile" geographic data services must become the standard. This means the same geographic data services should be integrated directly into both operational and analytic systems as a core component of any enterprise information management framework. Therefore, consider these specific criteria for evaluating capabilities or tools that provide geographic data services, such as:

- **Breadth of functionality.** We've examined a number of fundamental geographic data service capabilities, and functionality can be assessed in terms of its overall ability to provide the core services such as geocoding, reverse geocoding, distance, and address cleansing, as well as layered capabilities such as mapping, routing, locating points of interest, and more sophisticated analytics.

- **Usability.** Traditionally, mapping and geographic information systems users have been specifically trained in the use of standalone GIS tools, and have evolved their own approaches to data extraction and transformation in preparation for analysis. But as the community of users becomes broader, there is a need for reducing the complexity associated with the traditional tools. This implies a need for ease-of-use and increased simplicity of data integration, and full functional integration within both analytical and operational applications.

- **Data integration.** As more attention is given to the variety of concepts subjected to spatial analysis, the demands for many different kinds of data continue to grow. To meet these demands, the tools and techniques must accommodate integration of data pulled from existing structured data sets derived from operational and transactional systems, as well as accessing, parsing, and aggregating spatial, nonspatial, operational, and analytic data from multiple, nonstandard sources.

- **Functional integration.** Expectations for both real-time operational geographic data services and corresponding spatial analytics means that the services cannot be totally embedded within a standalone environment. Alternatively, there is a need to encapsulate these capabilities as services and enable interoperability across transactional, operational, and analytical environments. This encapsulation simplifies the integration of the functionality with analysis, reporting, and visualization tools, which again improves ease of use while reducing complexity.

- **Data enhancement.** Many of the applications explored in this chapter rely on a combination of geocoding techniques and access to data sources for information appending, location characteristics, as well as providing characterization and classification based on demographics across geographic regions. In other words, the value proposition for geographic data services is greatly increased in concert with data enhancement and enrichment capabilities.

- **Data trustworthiness.** Last, and absolutely not least, is the fundamental need for high-quality data for *any* kind of business intelligence or analytics technique. Interestingly, the techniques described in this chapter both rely on and contribute to improvement in the quality of data. However, the expectation for transparent interoperability of geographic data services across the application infrastructure means that data quality processes and procedures should be tightly coupled with geographic data services.

Where to Next?

Organizations that rely solely on traditional approaches to geographic data services will be ultimately limited by the repetitive processes employed by the pool of GIS experts. In addition, unoptimized data integration and cleansing will lead to poor performance. These issues are often dwarfed by the types of inaccuracy, inconsistency, incompleteness, and other data quality issues that continually plague most organizations. Geographic data services and the tools that are tightly coupled with data integration, data cleansing, and data quality techniques are bound to enhance the actionable knowledge resulting from spatial analysis and location intelligence.

Competitive organizations are aware of the business value of geographic data services and spatial analytics. Key stakeholders are reevaluating the place of geographic intelligence as part of an enterprise information strategy, and they are aggressively incorporating these capabilities into their services infrastructure. Instituting location-based intelligence is a straightforward way to add both breadth and depth to operational activities and business analytics, and there are few industries that are not positively impacted when geographic data services are added to the mix.

Knowledge Discovery and Data Mining for Predictive Analytics

The term *data mining* evokes an image of the old-time panner for gold—sifting through mounds of dirt trying to find those elusive valuable nuggets that make the whole process worthwhile. The translation into the information world is the data analyst sifting through terabytes of data looking for the corresponding knowledge nugget. This image is so powerful that the original meaning of data mining has been lost in the media hype that surrounds information exploitation. Now any information worker with a query tool connected to a database running ad hoc queries is called a "data miner," and the concepts that I discuss in this chapter are lost in that translation.

As an alternative to proactive business intelligence (BI) operations, the knowledge discovery process is a means for finding new intelligence from collections of data. Although the methods discussed in this chapter have traditionally been referred to as *data mining*, that term has become overloaded and so we will use the more correct term, *knowledge discovery*. Knowledge discovery refers to the process of discovering patterns that lead to actionable knowledge from large data sets through one or more traditional data mining techniques, such as market basket analysis and clustering. A lot of the knowledge discovery methodology has evolved from the combination of the worlds of statistics and computer science.

In this chapter, a lot of which is adapted from the very fine writings of Michael Berry and Gordon Linoff, we will look at the business use of knowledge discovery techniques and the kinds of methods used. In addition, we will look at some of the management issues associated with this process, as well as how to properly set expectations for the results of an iterative proactive process whose results may not be measurable right away.

Business Drivers

Of the analytical processes we have discussed in this book, most have been focused on specific a priori drivers, such as the manifestation of visualization of key performance indicators appearing on a business executive's desktop browser and building reports via an online analytical processing (OLAP) tool to allow a data client to examine and drill down through cross-dimensional metrics. Essentially, the resulting analytical frameworks have always been to allow the data consumer either to verify that things are going the way they should or to look for situations where they are not so that the process and, correspondingly, the business can be improved.

Data mining will often fill a niche in the BI arena where the data consumer is not necessarily sure what to be looking for. The kinds of knowledge that are discovered may be directed toward a specific goal (e.g., finding out why you are losing customers) or not (e.g., finding some interesting patterns), but the methods of data mining are driven by finding patterns in the data that reflect more meaningful bits of knowledge. And those discovered bits of knowledge can then be fed into the more general areas of BI. For example, you may discover some new business rules that predict a business situation requiring an action. Those rules can then be integrated into a business rule system as well as the intelligence portal that notifies the proper person when some condition suddenly becomes true.

Data mining algorithms used to be relegated to the supercomputers attached to the large-scale data systems because of the computational complexity and storage requirements of the data mining process. A combination of improved algorithms, high-performance platforms, and integration of data mining techniques into the mainstream means that what used to be a boutique operation is not only accessible to a broad spectrum of users; the ability to develop, test, and deploy predictive models is fully integrated into many database management, SQL, and BI tool suites. It would be unwise to engage in building a BI program and ignore the promise of a data mining component.

Data Mining, Data Warehousing, Big Data

Knowledge discovery is a process that requires a lot of data, and that data needs to be in a reliable state before it can be subjected to the data mining process. The accumulation of enterprise data within a data warehouse that has been properly validated, cleaned, and integrated provides the best source of data that can be subjected to knowledge discovery. Not only is the warehouse likely to incorporate the breadth of data needed for this component of the BI process, it probably contains the historical data needed. Because a lot of data mining relies on using one set of data for training a process that can then be tested on another set of data, having the historical information available for testing and evaluating hypotheses makes the warehouse even more valuable.

Perhaps the democratization of data mining and analytics algorithms through direct integration with existing platforms, the availability of high-performance analytical platforms, and the ability to stream many data sources into an analytical platform have created a "perfect storm" for large-scale "big data" analytics applications development.

Basically, the availability, ease-of-use, and scalability of systems like Hadoop has created the environment for development of rich data mining and analytics algorithms. As we discussed in Chapter 14, programming environments such as the one provided by Hadoop and MapReduce provide a straightforward framework for parallel and distributed application development. These applications will eventually be robust enough to handle large-scale applications absorbing both structured and unstructured data access from multiple sources and streamed at variable rates.

The Virtuous Cycle

As Berry and Linoff state in their book, *Data Mining Techniques*, the process of mining data can be described as a virtuous cycle. The virtue is based on the continuous improvement of a business process that is driven by the discovery of actionable knowledge and taking the actions prescribed by these discoveries.

IDENTIFY THE BUSINESS PROBLEM

One of the more difficult tasks is identifying the business problem that needs to be solved. Very often, other aspects of the BI program can feed into this process. If you recall our "analysis spectrum" from Chapter 1, the first step is awareness of an issue (what happened), which is then followed by understanding the root causes (why it happened).

For example, an OLAP report may indicate that sales of one class of product in the Northeast region may lag behind sales in other regions or that the average wait time at the inbound call centers peaks at certain times of the day. After being alerted to this situation, it would be useful to understand why this sales lag exists, and this type of question provides a starting point for formulating the business problem to be examined.

Other kinds of business problems are actually part of the general business cycle. For example, planning a new marketing campaign and understanding customer attrition are frequent business problems that can be attacked through data mining. Once the problem has been identified and a goal set (e.g., lower the attrition rate by 50% or relieve the issues that are causing sales to lag in particular areas), you must assemble the right data needed for analysis and then move on to the next stage.

MINE THE DATA FOR ACTIONABLE INFORMATION

Depending on the problem, there are a number of different data mining techniques that can be employed to develop models for predictive purposes. But no matter what techniques are used, the process is to assemble the right set of information, prepare that information for mining, apply the algorithms, and analyze the results to find some knowledge that is actionable. At the same time, the business processes must be adjusted to enable individuals to take action based on an identified trigger as well as continuously measuring for improved business performance.

For example, it may be discovered that, with some degree of frequency, bank customers tend to close their checking accounts once they have been assessed bank fees more than three times in a single year. The embedded suggestion is that bank customers of high value who have been assessed a fee more than three times in a year are at risk.

TAKE THE ACTION

The next logical step is to take the actions suggested by the discoveries during the data mining process. To continue our example from the previous section, this sequence of events can be identified as an alert for bank managers—the third time that a high-value customer is assessed a bank fee within a 12-month period, a bank manager should be assigned to reach out to and engage the customer to identify opportunities or incentives that can help prevent attrition. There may be a number of different actions to take, and it is useful to try more than one. Here are a few possible actions.

- Remove the assessed fee(s).
- Perform an account review and suggest different checking account alternatives.

- Provide some alternate benefit on another product (such as a decreased interest rate on a home equity loan).

Keep track of which actions were taken, because that leads to the next stage.

MEASURE RESULTS

The importance of measuring the results of the actions taken is that it refines the process of addressing the original business problem. The goal here is to look at what the expected response was to the specific actions and to determine the quality of each action. To finish our attrition example, three different actions were suggested in the previous section. The goal was to reduce attrition among the high-value customers. Here we would measure the decrease in attrition associated with those customers offered each of the three suggested actions and see which provided the largest decrease in attrition. Perhaps another round of testing and measurement might be in order, but the ultimate result is to identify the precursor to attrition and offer the most effective promotion in attrition reduction to those high-value customers at risk.

Directed Versus Undirected Knowledge Discovery

There are two different approaches to knowledge discovery. The first is when we already have the problem we want to solve and are applying knowledge discovery and data mining methods to uncover the relationship between the variables under scrutiny in terms of the other available variables. Our earlier desire to research the root causes of lagging sales is an example of this approach, which we called *directed* knowledge discovery.

The alternative, *undirected* knowledge discovery, is the process of using data mining techniques to find interesting patterns within a data set as a way to highlight some potentially interesting issue, pattern, or opportunity. This approach is more likely to be used to recognize behavior or relationships, whereas directed knowledge discovery is used primarily to explain or describe those relationships once they have been found.

Six Basic Data Mining Activities

It is important to differentiate between the tasks employed for mining data, the methods by which these tasks are performed, and the techniques that use these activities for uncovering business opportunities. We can essentially boil the most significant methods down to a set of six tasks, some of which we have already briefly introduced in other chapters.

CLUSTERING AND SEGMENTATION

Clustering is the task of taking a large collection of entities and dividing that collection into smaller groups of entities that exhibit some similarity (Figure 17.1). The difference between clustering and classification is that during the clustering task, the classes are not defined beforehand. Rather, it is the process of evaluating the classes after the clustering has completed that drives the determination or definition of that class.

Clustering is useful when you are not really sure what you are looking for but want to perform some kind of segmentation. For example, you might want to evaluate health data based on particular diseases along with other variables to see if there are any correlations that can be inferred through the clustering process. Clustering can be used in concert with other data mining tasks as a way of identifying a business problem area to be further explored. An example is performing a market segmentation based on product sales as a prelude for looking at why sales are low within a particular market segment.

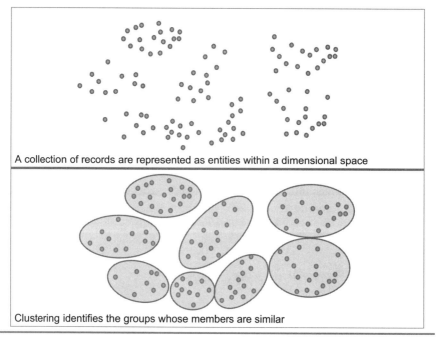

A collection of records are represented as entities within a dimensional space

Clustering identifies the groups whose members are similar

Figure 17.1 Example of clustering.

The clustering process collects data instances into groups such that each group is clearly different from all others, and that the members of each group are recognizably similar. The records in the set are organized based on similarity; since there are no predefined specifications for classification, the algorithms essentially "select" the attributes (or "variables") used to determine similarity. Someone with business context knowledge might be called upon to interpret the results to determine if there is any specific meaning associated with the clustering, and sometimes this may result in culling out variables that do not carry meaning or may not have any relevance, in which case the clustering can be repeated in the absence of the culled variables.

CLASSIFICATION

The world is divided into two groups of people: those who classify the world into two groups, and those who do not. But seriously, our natural tendency is to assign things into groups based on some set of similar characteristics. For example, we break up groups of customers by demographic and/or psychographic profiles (e.g., marketing to the lucrative 18- to 34-year-olds), or divide products into product classes, and so on.

Once you have completed a segmentation process, the values of identified dependent variables can be used for *classification*. Classification is the process of organizing data into predefined classes (Figure 17.2). Those classes may be described using attributes selected by the analyst, or may actually be based on the results of a clustering model. During a classification process, the class definitions and a training data set of previously classified objects is presented to the application, which then attempts to build a model that can be used to accurately classify new records. For example, a classification model can be used to evaluate public companies into good, medium, and poor investments, assign meta-tags to news articles based on their content, or assign customers into defined market segments.

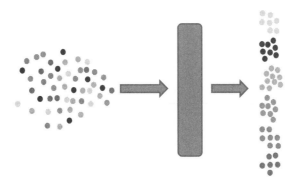

Figure 17.2   Classification of records based on defined characteristics.

ESTIMATION

Estimation is a process of assigning some continuously valued numeric value to an object. For example, credit risk assessment is not necessarily a yes/no question; it is more likely to be some kind of scoring that assesses a propensity to default on a loan. Estimation can be used as part of the classification process (such as using an estimation model to guess a person's annual salary as part of a market segmentation process).

A value of estimation is that because a value is being assigned to some continuous variable, the resulting assignments can be ranked by score. So, for example, an estimation process may assign some value to the variable "probability of purchasing a time-share vacation package" and then rank the candidates by that estimated score, making those candidates the best prospects.

Estimation is used frequently to infer some propensity to take some action or as a way to establish some reasonable guess at an indeterminable value. An example is customer lifetime value, discussed in Chapter 15, in which we sought to build a model reflecting the future value of the relationship with a customer.

PREDICTION

The subtle difference between *prediction* and the previous two tasks is that prediction is the attempt to classify objects according to some expected future behavior. Classification and estimation can be used for the purposes of prediction by using historical data, where the classification is already known, to build a model (this is called *training*). That model can then be applied to new data to predict future behavior.

You must be careful when using training sets for prediction. There may be a risk of an inherent bias in the data that may lead you to draw inferences or conclusions that are relevant in relation to the bias. Use different data sets for training and test, test, test!

AFFINITY GROUPING

Affinity grouping is a process of evaluating relationships or associations between data elements that demonstrate some kind of affinity between objects. For example, affinity grouping might be used to determine the likelihood that people who buy one product will be willing to try a different product. This kind of analysis is useful for marketing campaigns when trying to cross-sell or up-sell a customer on additional or better products. This can also be used as a way to create product packages that have appeal to large market segments. For example, fast-food restaurants may select certain product components to go into a meal packaged for a particular group of people (e.g., the "kid's meal") and targeted at the population who is most likely to purchase that package (e.g., children between the ages of 9 and 14).

DESCRIPTION

The last of the tasks is *description*, which is the process of trying to characterize what has been discovered or trying to explain the results of the data mining process. Being able to describe a behavior or a business rule is another step toward an effective intelligence program that can identify knowledge, articulate it, and then evaluate actions that can be taken. In fact, we might say that the description of discovered knowledge can be incorporated into the metadata associated with that data set.

Data Mining Techniques

Although there are a number of techniques used for data mining, this section enumerates some techniques that are frequently used as well as some examples of how each technique is used.

MARKET BASKET ANALYSIS

When you go to the supermarket, usually the first thing you do is grab a shopping cart. As you move up and down the aisles, you will pick up certain items and place them in your shopping cart. Most of these items may correspond to a shopping list that was prepared ahead of time, but other items may have been selected spontaneously. Let's presume that when you check out at the cashier, the contents of your (and every other shopper's) cart are logged, because the supermarket wants to see if there are any patterns in selection that occur from one shopper to another. This is called *market basket analysis*.

Market basket analysis is a process that looks for relationships of objects that "go together" within the business context. In reality, market basket analysis goes beyond the supermarket scenario from which its name is derived. Market basket analysis is the analysis of any collection of items to identify affinities that can be exploited in some manner. Some examples of the use of market basket analysis include:

- **Product placement**. Identifying products that may often be purchased together and arranging the placement of those items (such as in a catalog or on a web site) close by to encourage the purchaser to buy both items.
- **Physical shelf arrangement**. An alternate use for physical product placement in a store is to separate items that are often purchased at the same time to encourage

individuals to wander through the store to find what they are looking for to potentially increase the probability of additional impulse purchases.

- **Up-sell, cross-sell, and bundling opportunities**. Companies may use the affinity grouping of multiple products as an indication that customers may be predisposed to buying the grouped products at the same time. This enables the presentation of items for cross-selling, or may suggest that customers may be willing to buy more items when certain products are bundled together.
- **Customer retention**. When customers contact a business to sever a relationship, a company representative may use market basket analysis to determine the right incentives to offer in order to retain the customer's business.

MEMORY-BASED REASONING

A sick visit to a doctor typically involves the patient's describing a collection of symptoms and the doctor's review of documented history to match the symptoms to known illnesses, come up with a diagnosis, and then recommend ways to treat the patient. This is a real-world example of memory-based reasoning (MBR, which is sometimes also called case-based reasoning or instance-based reasoning), in which known situations are employed to form a model for analysis. New situations are compared against the model to find the closest matches, which can then be reviewed to inform decisions about classification or for prediction.

Memory-based reasoning is a process of using one data set to create a model from which predictions or assumptions can be made about newly introduced objects. This is implemented in two steps. The first is to build the model using a training set of data and specific outcomes. The model is then used for comparison with new data instances, resulting in an entity's classification or with suggestions for actions to take based on the new data instance's value. The main component of the technique involves the concept of measuring similarity between pairs of objects, both during the training process and later, trying to match the new object to its closest neighbor within the classified set.

There are two basic components to an MBR method. The first is the *similarity* (sometimes called *distance*) *function*, which measures how similar the members of any pair of objects are to each other. The second is the *combination function*, which is used to combine the results from the set of neighbors to arrive at a decision.

Memory-based reasoning can be used for classification, presuming that an existing data set is used as the basis for determining classes (perhaps by clustering) and then using the results to classify new objects. It can also be used for prediction, via the same method as the matching process to find the closest match. The resulting behavior of that matching object can be used to predict the outcome of the new object.

As an example, consider a database that tracks cancer symptoms, diagnoses, and treatments. Having already performed a clustering of the cases based on symptoms, MBR can be used to find the cases closest to a newly introduced one to guess at the diagnosis as well as propose a treatment protocol.

CLUSTER DETECTION

Given a large set of heterogeneous objects, a common data mining task is to divide that set into a number of smaller, more homogeneous groups. Automated clustering applications are used to perform this grouping. Again, as in memory-based reasoning, we must have a concept of a function that measures the distance between any two points based on an element's attributes. An example where clustering is useful would be segmenting visitors to an e-commerce Web site to understand what kinds of people are visiting the site.

There are two approaches to clustering. The first approach is to assume that a certain number of clusters are already embedded in the data; the goal is to break the data up into that number of clusters. A frequently used approach is the K-Means clustering technique, which initially designates clusters and then iteratively applies these steps: Identify the exact middle of the clusters, measure the distance of each object to that exact middle, assign each object to the cluster owning that exact middle, then redraw the cluster boundaries. This is repeated until the cluster boundaries no longer change.

In the other approach, called *agglomerative clustering*, instead of assuming the existence of any specific predetermined number of clusters, every item starts out in its own cluster, and an iterative process attempts to merge clusters, again through a process of computing similarity. In this case, though, we will need a way to compare similarity between clusters (as opposed to points within an *n*-dimensional space), which is a bit more complicated. The result of the agglomerative method is ultimately to have composed all clusters into a single cluster. But as each iteration takes place the history is recorded, so the data analyst can choose the level of clustering that is most appropriate for the particular business need.

LINK ANALYSIS

Link analysis is the process of looking for and establishing links between entities within a data set as well as characterizing the weight associated with any link between two entities. Some examples include analyzing telephone call detail records to examine links established when a connection is initiated at one telephone number to a different telephone number, determining whether two individuals are connected via a social network, or the degree to which similar travelers select travel on specific flights. Not only does this form a link between a pair of entities, but other variables or attributes can be used to characterize that link. For telephone connectivity, some examples include the frequency of the calls, the duration of the calls, or the times at which those calls are made.

Link analysis is useful for analytical applications that rely on graph theory for drawing conclusions. One example is looking for closely connected groups of people. In other words, are there collections of people that are linked together where the linkage between any pair within that set is as strong as the link between any other pair? Answering this question might uncover information about the existence of illegal drug rings or perhaps about a collection of people who can exert strong influence on one another.

Another analytical area for which link analysis is useful is process optimization. An example might be evaluating the allocation of airplanes and pilots (who are trained for flying specific kinds of airplanes) to the many routes that an airline travels. Every flight represents a link within a large graph, and the assignment of pilots to airplanes is guided by the goal of reducing both lag time and extra travel time required for a flight crew, as well as any external regulations associated with the time a crew may be in the air.

A third use is in assessing viral influence of individuals within a social networking environment. One participant might not necessarily account for a significant number of product purchases directly, but her recommendation may be followed by many individuals within her "sphere of influence."

RULE INDUCTION USING DECISION TREES

Chapter 11 discussed business rules and how those rules can be used as part of the BI and analytics program. Part of the knowledge discovery process is the identification of business (or other kinds of) rules that are embedded within data. The methods associated with rule induction are used for this discovery process.

Many situations can be addressed by answering a series of questions that increasingly narrow down the possibilities of a solution, much like the game "Twenty Questions." One approach to rule discovery is the use of decision trees. A decision tree is a decision-support model that encapsulates the questions and the possible answers and guides the analyst toward the appropriate result, and can be used for operational processes as well as classification.

A completed decision tree is a tree where each node represents a question and the decision as to which path to take from that node is dependent on the answer to the question. For example, we can have a binary decision tree where one internal node asks whether the employee's salary is greater than $50,000. If the answer is yes, the left-hand path is taken, but if the answer is no, the right-hand path is taken.

Decision tree analysis looks at a collection of data instances and given outcomes, evaluates the frequency and distribution of values across the set of variables, and constructs a decision model in the form of a tree. The nodes at each level of this tree each represent a question, and each possible answer to the question is represented as a branch that points to another node at the next level. At each step along the path from the root of the tree to the leaves, the set of records that conform to the answers along the way continues to grow smaller.

Essentially, each node in the tree represents a set of records that conform to the answers to the questions along the path one traverses to the specified node. Each of these questions bisects the view into two smaller segments, and every path from the root node to any other node is unique. Each node in the tree also represents the expression of a rule, and at each point in the tree we can evaluate the set of records that conform to that rule as well as the size of that record set.

The analyst uses the model to seek a desired result as the decision support process traverses the tree and stops when the traversal reaches the leaf of the tree. A nice aspect of decision tree models is that the "thought process" used by the model is transparent, and it is clear to the analyst how the model reached a particular conclusion.

RULE INDUCTION USING ASSOCIATION RULES

Another approach to rule induction is the discovery of association rules. *Association rules* specify a relation between attributes that appears more frequently than expected if the attributes were independent. An association rule describes a relationship between sets of values occurring with enough frequency to signify an interesting pattern. A rule usually takes the form of "If {X} then {Y}," where X is a set of conditions regarding a set of variables upon which the values of set Y depend. An example is the canonical data mining story regarding the frequency of the purchase of diapers and beer together. The cooccurrence of the variable values must have *support*, which means that those values occur together with a reasonable frequency, and the apparent codependent variable(s) must show a degree of *confidence* indicating that of the times that the {X} values appear, so do the values for {Y}. Basically, an association rule states that the values of a set of attributes determine the values of another set of attributes, with some degree of *confidence* and some measure of *support*.

An association rule is specified as {source attribute value set} → {target attribute value set}. The source attribute set is also referred to as the *left-hand side* (for obvious reasons) and the target attribute set as the *right-hand side*. The confidence of the association rule is the percentage of the time that the rule applies. For example, if 85% of the time that a customer buys a network hub she will also buy a network interface card (NIC), the confidence of the rule {item1: Buys network hub} → {item2: Buys NIC} is 85%. The support of a rule is the percentage of all the records where the left-hand side and right-hand side attributes have the assigned values.

In this case, if 6% of all the records have the values set {item1: Buys network hub} and {item2: Buys NIC}, then the support for the rule is 6%.

NEURAL NETWORKS

A neural network is a data mining model that is used for prediction. The neural network model is trained using data instances and desired outcomes, and the algorithms for building neural networks encapsulate statistical artifacts of the training data to create a "black box" process that takes some number of inputs and produces some predictive output. Originally envisioned as a way of modeling human thought, neural network models are based on statistics and probability, and once trained are very good for prediction problems. However, the knowledge embedded in the training set becomes integrated into the neural network in a way that is not transparent—the neural network model is very good at prediction, but can't tell you why it came up with a particular answer.

A neural network essentially captures a set of statistical operations embodied as the application of a weighted combination function applied to all inputs to a neuron to compute a single output value that is then propagated to other neurons within the network. Ultimately, the input values are connected as the initial inputs, and the resulting output(s) represent some decision generated by the neural network. This approach is good for classification, estimation, and prediction.

Sometimes the representation of data needs to be modified to get the kinds of values required for proper value calculation. For example, historical data represented as dates may need to be transformed into elapsed days, and continuous value results may need to be rounded to 0 or 1 when looking for a discrete yes/no answer.

Technology Expectations

When data mining first emerged as a viable technology, the computational demands of the algorithms coupled with the necessary requirements for expertise kept the barrier to entry high for most organizations. The most significant challenges lie in reducing the barrier to entry in two different ways: reducing the computational strain and eliminating the need for data mining algorithm expertise. The first challenge has essentially gone away, as the availability of computing power and the necessary storage systems have become increasingly affordable to almost every kind of business.

The second challenge is a technical one in incorporating the right kind of "business smarts" into the predictive analysis utilities to make the processes pervasive in a way that supports the bottom-up approach. Achieving this goal leads to three expectations that business and data analysts would have of technology suppliers:

- **Availability of the utilities**. Availability of the tool set is critical, and it involves providing predictive analysis services in a way that is easily accessed across the analyst spectrum (senior managers, mid-level managers, business analysts, super-users, as well as developers).
- **Education and training**. Availability is of limited value if the target audience is not aware of the tools or how those tools can be employed to build predictive models. Any technology innovations must be accompanied by the corresponding educational collateral to operationalize the value proposition of bottom-up analytics.
- **Ease of use**. Yet another barrier to entry has been the difficulty in developing models and applying them in the proper context. Pervasive predictive analysis is dependent on reducing the complexity of analyzing data sets, building models, and employing those predictive models in tactical and operational contexts.
- **Embedding and integration**. The best way to meet all of these expectations is through full integration of the technology directly into the productivity tools used on a daily basis. Many analysts interact with databases that can be subjected to analysis in order to build predictive models. Embedding the capability to build the model into the database fabric effectively eliminates the middleman, enabling the analyst to invoke the right services at his or her own convenience to build predictive models for daily use.

This last point defines the technical opportunity, and this is one that has become increasingly commonplace with the desire for integrated predictive analytics: embedding data mining capabilities and packaging their use in business analytic packages within the existing infrastructure. This includes incorporation of data mining services directly integrated at various levels in applications, at either the data level (e.g., integrated within the query environment), the management level, the developer level (embedded APIs within development platforms), or the desktop level (e.g., as part of desktop tools such as spreadsheets, database tools, project planning tools, presentation development tools, etc.). This allows for data preparation, model training, evaluation of discovered knowledge, and integration of pattern-based business rules or predictions back into operational applications while staying within a unified information architecture.

Summary

Data mining is not magic. It is, rather, a disciplined approach to exploring patterns within data, determining actionable knowledge from those patterns, and putting that knowledge to use. Data mining techniques make use of data in the data warehouse in a way that augments the other analytical techniques, such as business reporting and

OLAP analysis. The basic tasks of data mining are to use existing models for either classifying objects within a data set, predicting future behavior, or exposing relationships between objects. In addition, data mining can be used to help identify classes as a prelude to future classification by automatically clustering heterogeneous data into more homogeneous groups.

At the same time, the emergence of embedded predictive analytics may be a significant boon to anyone interested in exploiting the benefits of data mining to improve the results of everyday activities. Anyone across the organization willing to invest some time to learn the basics of predictive analysis may be able to improve business processes, whether those are strategic decision-making processes or decision support to supplement ongoing operational work flows. Improved marketing, sales, customer service, reduction in attrition, fraud, and improved satisfaction for customers and staff members can result from fine-tuning business processes through the filter of advanced analytics.

Putting the power of analytics in the hands of different individuals across the organization is the key driver to success in this endeavor. Instead of relying on a select few individuals in the organization entrusted with this predictive power, everyone in the organization can exploit these tools by employing a radically different approach to developing analytic models. Instead of using a top-down approach with *a priori* knowledge of statistics and probability to develop the "right model," let anyone in the organization use embedded data mining capabilities using a bottom-up approach to use many different analysis techniques to see how different kinds of models ultimately provide the most value to the enterprise.

Chapter 18

Repurposing Publicly Available Data

This book has emphasized the value of collecting and repurposing data sets to facilitate querying, reporting, and analysis that can improve performance and corporate value. And while we have largely focused on extracting data from internal sources, it turns out that not only are there numerous external data sources that can be used, many of them are available with little or no cost. We can refer to these data sets as publicly available data, which comes in a variety of sizes, shapes, and forms. In addition, you can also use publicly available data sets that are packaged and sold by value-added information resellers.

Here is an example: I once participated in a conversation with an entrepreneur in the business of buying and selling large construction equipment to different companies around the world. He tracked all the information that was relevant to his business in his own data managed systems, including data about construction companies, new projects, locations, equipment manufacturers, ownerships, financing, and corporate relationships. When he was alerted to the fact that a company might be engaging a construction contractor to begin a new project, he would contact them and see what kind of equipment they might need, and he was **287** then able to search the database for those companies that owned that particular piece of machinery.

The interesting part is that he built this database by scanning through publicly available documents, such as corporate asset listings, and Uniform Commercial Code (UCC) lien filings, looking for references to an ownership relationship between a machine and a company. Every time he brokered a transaction, he also updated his own database. By doing this, not only was he able to keep track of who owned what, but he could also track the history of the machine, from its original construction (via serial number) through each subsequent owner. With this knowledge at his fingertips, he had successfully created a niche business in machinery exchange, enabling faster convergence on brokered deals. This is a good example of the exploitation of public data for business value.

Many public data sets are made available as a by-product of some legal or regulatory mandate capturing descriptive information, aggregate information, transaction data, survey data, and numerous other types of data. In some cases, personal data supplied directly by individuals is made available in both individual and aggregated forms. Many of these public data sets are made available by government bodies as a convenience to their constituents, specifically for public use. In any of these cases, depending on the context or source, significant value can be added to internal data sets by acquiring and integrating publicly available data.

The previous three chapters have already introduced the use of publicly available data; a good example was our example of merging geographic and demographic data made available by the Census Bureau. It is very simple to make the case for using publicly available data. Data that has been collected and made available by government resources or as a result of regulatory mandate (or any other reason!) is available at a low cost, requiring some minimal investment for storage, management, and integration with other business intelligence (BI) data. In any company that has set up a BI environment, the processes associated with importing, managing, and integrating data have already been streamlined for internal data set aggregation. And so the only increase is in those variable costs associated with executing those processes. On the other hand, in the right circumstances there can be significant value through data enhancement using publicly available data.

In this chapter, we look at publicly available data sets so that we can consider their value in terms of information integration and exploitation and hopefully show the value of acquiring and managing this kind of data. In addition, we will briefly discuss concerns of collecting and manipulating public data in a way that poses the perception of an invasion of privacy. Whether it is using individual entity detail, aggregate demographics, or historical trends, there is great value in linking internal data with publicly available data.

Using Publicly Available Data: Some Challenges

There are at least four major management issues associated with the use of publicly available data:

- **Integration.** The integration issue is similar to the general data integration problems discussed in other chapters, except that because data sets may be provided by some agency that has no vested interest in its use, the structure and the quality of the data may be called into question. In fact, there are a number of companies whose business is to enhance and improve public data sets and then resell them based on their added value.
- **Protected information.** There is a perception that any organization that collects data about individuals and then tries to exploit that information is invading a person's privacy. In fact, companies are now required to state their privacy policies explicitly to their customers, and much BI work can be done within the constraints described therein; we discuss this in greater detail in this chapter.
- **Absence of metadata.** For structured data sets, the format of the presentation of the data is often arbitrary and/or artificially constructed. Many data sets are extracted from existing transactional or operational systems in relational models, and when the data set is created, the records are linearized as a result of structured queries that may join two or more tables. Many times these data sets are provided with little description of the contents, leaving it to the consumer to reinterpret what is actually in the data.
- **Ambiguity in structure.** A lot of publicly available data is not always in a nicely structured form that is easily adaptable. Sometimes the data is semistructured, which means that the data requires some manipulation before it can be successfully and properly integrated. Most often, the data is unstructured, meaning there are no formatting standards for the data.

Public Data

Describing the entire realm of publicly available data could fill multiple books, and this chapter is not intended as a directory of public data resources. However, what is important to learn involves the different types of data, approaches for locating publicly available data sets, and ideas for how those data sets can be incorporated into your BI and analytics plan.

Linking the information from public data sets with the data in your corporate data warehouse may catalyze new business inferences and insights. For example, if we know the price a person paid for a house and whether that is the first house that person has bought, then based on the assumption that the person obtained a mortgage for 80% of the purchase price and knowing the current interest rates and the local tax rates, we can take a reasonable guess at his monthly mortgage and tax payments. This piece of information, along with the assumption that the lender would allow the buyer to pay 38% of his gross monthly income, allows us to infer his monthly salary!

In this section, we will look at different kinds of public data as examples of the exploitation process. There are many ways that data sets can be categorized, and each of the next sections details some specific examples.

REFERENCE INFORMATION

Publicly available reference data sets provide standard data enumerations used in common business contexts. For example, the International Organization for Standardization (ISO) publishes many reference data sets that are commonly employed in numerous business contexts, with common data sets for two-character country codes, three-character country codes, two-digit country codes, as well as alphanumeric and numeric versions of currency codes.

INDIVIDUAL INFORMATION

Any data that attributes the information about a person could be called personal information. For example, in most, if not all, of the United States, many life events, professional licenses, and other transactions are registered or recorded with government authorities. In some cases, the information is available for special purposes, but in other cases the data is truly made public, and can be accessed via requests, online queries, or can be purchased in aggregated form from the state or other designated providers.

In other cases, individuals willingly provide data that is accumulated into data products that are also made available through data aggregators. Some examples of individual attribution data sets include:

- **Real property sales and ownership.** In many states the data can be directly queried on a location-by-location basis, but often, for a small fee, the data can be provided in bulk.
- **Death records.** The Social Security Agency maintains a database of death records for holders of social security numbers (called the Social Security Death Index).
- **Voter registration data.** There may be usage restrictions on data sets like these to be limited to "the electoral process," but there are probably broad definitions for what that means, opening interesting opportunities for research and analysis.
- **Immigration records.** These may be accessible from the government or through alternate genealogy web sites.

- **Campaign finance donations.** Both state and the federal governments maintain records of donations to election campaigns, and these data sets contain identifying information.
- **Contact data.** There are vendors providing databases containing land-line telephone number, mobile telephone number, as well as email address data and social network handles.

There are many other examples in which publicly available data sets contain personally identifiable information.

BUSINESS/LEGAL ENTITY INFORMATION

Aside from personal information, there is a lot of data that can be used to enhance data representing business entities. These public records are frequently related to rules and regulations imposed on business operations by federal or state government jurisdictions. This kind of data includes the following.

- **Corporate web persona data.** This can include registered web domains, IP addresses, as well as social network names and URLs.
- **Incorporations.** Company incorporations fall under state jurisdiction, and the incorporation is registered with the state. Typical information that is in a statement of incorporation includes the name of the incorporated entity and the names of the principals involved.
- **Uniform Commercial Code (UCC).** A UCC filing is meant to document a security interest incurred by a debtor and to document liens held on consumer goods or personal property. A UCC filing may show that one person or company is using personal property as collateral for a loan. Perusing UCC filings lets you accumulate information about the types and values of an individual entity's assets, as well as loan amounts.
- **Bankruptcy filings.** Bankruptcy filings contain information about the entity's assets, creditors, and the amount of money owed to each creditor, the trustee that was assigned to the case, among other things. This kind of information allows for enhancement of relationship data by establishing a link between the individuals associated with the bankruptcy and all other named parties (creditors and trustees).
- **Professional licensing.** The establishment of a connection between a specific individual and a profession that requires licensing (of which there are many) provides multiple enhancement opportunities, such as adding to the psychographic profile, as well as possibly establishing a connection with other individuals with the same profession in the same geographic area.
- **Securities filings.** The Securities and Exchange Commission is a governmental body that enforces and manages federal securities regulations, which mandate

the filing of significant statements and events associated with public companies. There are many different kinds of filings, ranging from quarterly statements, to statements regarding percentage of beneficial ownership an individual or an organization holds in a different company. Although the bulk of the information contained in these filings is in an unstructured (i.e., free text) form (from which it is difficult to extract interesting data), a lot of the text may be in a structured or unstructured form, which may be amenable to entity extraction.

- **Regulatory licensing.** In areas of business that are regulated by government bodies, there may be requirements for individuals or companies to acquire a license to do certain kinds of business, and these license applications (and notification of license grant) are public data. Examples include the many uses associated with the radio spectrum that must be licensed through the Federal Communications Commission (FCC), such as radio and television stations, mobile telephone services, mobile telephone antenna construction and management, and so on.
- **Patents and trademarks.** The Patent and Trademark office (PTO) provides access to the text of a large number of granted patents, which provide a source of business and psychographic data, as well as linkage between individuals and sponsoring institutions.

LEGAL INFORMATION

A large number of legal cases are accessible online, providing the names of the parties involved in the cases as well as unstructured text describing the case. These documents, many of which having been indexed and made available for search, contain embedded psychographic and geographic enhancement potential, along with opportunities for entity extraction and entity linkage. Those linkages may represent either personal (such as family relationships) or business relationships.

GOVERNMENT DEMOGRAPHIC DATABASES

There is an abundance of what could be called "demographic" information provided in available data sets. Although there may be some restrictions on specific uses of some of this data, there is still much business value that can be derived from this data.

- **Census data.** Every 10 years, the Census Bureau counts all the people living in the United States. For the years following the census, a number of data products are generated and made available both interactively through the Census Bureau's web site and in raw form that can be downloaded via FTP. The example used in Chapter 15 demonstrated the use of geo-demographic data sourced from the Census Bureau.

- **Environmental data.** The Environmental Protection Agency is tasked with collecting information about sites and facilities for which there may be an environmental interest, as well as the substances that are covered under this rubric. The EPA provides open data sets for their facility registry, which contains business and location information, as well as a substance registry.
- **TIGER.** Another data product made available by the Census Bureau is a set of extracts from the Topologically Integrated Geographic Encoding and Referencing database, also known as TIGER. The TIGER/Line files contain selected geographic and cartographic information, including details of line features (e.g., roads, railroads) and landmarks (e.g., schools, cemeteries) as well as geographic entity codes for areas that link to the Census statistical data. These tables provide details of geographic attributes, such as the latitude and longitude of street segments. This kind of data can be used to identify the nearest physical neighbors to a particular street address or to provide geographic enhancement to the summary data referenced in SF1.
- **Federal Election Commission.** There are many laws that constrain political donations, and regulations require that most campaign contributions be reported to the Federal Election Commission (FEC). These contributions are logged in a database that details who made the contribution, from which address, to which candidate or political action committee, and the amount given. The data in this table can be used to track support of individual candidates over time, as well as review rolled-up aggregate views of political spending. This in turn can be used to infer geographical political preferences and trends.
- **Bureau of Labor Statistics (BLS).** The BLS provides summary historical information about many different item prices over long periods of time.
- **Pharmaceutical data.** Information about individual drugs, devices, delivery methods, and narcotic ingredients is available from both the Food and Drug Administration (FDA) and the Drug Enforcement Agency (DEA). This kind of data may be useful in the insurance industry as well as in individual criminal jurisdictions.

As far as data provided by the US government is concerned, there is a movement for government data transparency, based on the proposition that government data should be made available to the public. A portal web site, www.data.gov, is a good starting point for researching available data sets. However, the site is subject to the same issues we raised at the beginning of the chapter regarding the absence of metadata and the ambiguity in structure. In addition, data sets posted to data.gov are extracted and pushed to the portal; more current versions of the data may be accessed directly from the agencies, and may be accessed in different configurations.

CONTENT DATA SETS

With the maturation of text analysis algorithms (which we will look at in Chapter 20), there is growing interest in accumulating, scanning, and extracting information from unstructured data sources. This means that data sets whose utility might have previously been limited to purely publication are now subjected to analysis and reporting.

Some examples include news archives, job postings, professional descriptive databases (such as resume databases or online professional directories), obituaries, real estate listings, movie, music, or other entertainment databases, descriptions of posted images and videos, or requests for contract bids. Each of these examples contains individual entity information, location information, and other contextual information that can be scanned for demographic, geographic, and psychographic content.

STREAMED OR FILTERED DATA SETS

With the advent of online collaboration, continuous monitoring, blogging, and other forms of social connectivity and social networking, there are emerging data streams and feeds for which the content owners provide an application programming interface (API). Programmers may develop applications that connect to a subset (sometime the entire subset) of the data streams, filter for specific metadata tags or concepts, and forward the results into an analytical environment.

As an example, the National Weather Service provides access to current weather conditions as well as warnings that can be accessed via a variety of standard formats. An application can poll these feeds and stream new information as it is published to the appropriate consumers.

Data Resources

Having determined that we want to make use of publicly available data, how do we get it? There are basically two approaches: gather data from the original source, and pay a data aggregator for a value-added data set.

ORIGINAL SOURCE

As mentioned in the previous sections, the government is a very good source of publicly available data. On the other hand, be aware that there are so many agencies and divisions of international, federal, and state governments that source/supplier management becomes an additional management risk. Although the price may be right, there may be added costs associated with the process of internalizing the multiple external data models as well as creating the processes to exploit that data in the right way. In addition, because these data sets are being provided for general use for a low or no price, there is little leverage that a data consumer can use to enforce any levels of data quality or timeliness expectations.

Another source of publicly available information may be provided by third parties in a form that is not meant for exploitation. As we have pointed out already, a good example is a web site, which may have some data but not in a directly usable form. And don't forget the unstructured information that reflects some knowledge taxonomy, such as birth notices, wedding announcements, obituaries, death notices, legal notices, biographies, job descriptions, and resumes.

Surprisingly, another interesting source of publicly available data is the subject of that data itself. Frequently, individuals and even representatives of organizations are willing to provide very detailed information about themselves or their organization for little or no incentive. Telephone or online surveys, product registration cards, free magazine subscription applications, preferred customer programs, among others, are all sources for information that can be used to enhance an entity profile. I include this as publicly available data, although it is not necessarily public, because most frequently those providing the data are not aware of how the provided information is going to be used, making it effectively public data.

Data Aggregators

A *data aggregator* is an organization that collects data from one or more sources, provides some value-added processing, and repackages the result in a usable form. Sometimes the data comes directly to the client through a sales or licensing agreement, although frequently data aggregators will act as an agent to enhance the clients' data. This is typically done by giving a data set to the data supplier, who then enhances the data and returns it to the client.

Another method for providing aggregated data is through a query-and-delivery process. For example, an interface allows the client to request all data instances that relate to a particular party or entity. The aggregator will provide a list of matched records, and then the user can purchase any or all of the matched data instances.

The Myth of Privacy

As mentioned earlier, one of the major issues in using publicly available data is the concern for protecting private information. To explore this, let's perform a small thought experiment.

A friend of mine, Brian, recently moved to my neighborhood. Very excitedly, he told me all about his experience—how he was able to get a great deal on a mortgage because he borrowed the money from the bank holding his checking accounts. Brian had saved enough money to apply some of the proceeds of the sale of his previous home toward a vacation in Europe—the tickets were free because he applied frequent-flyer miles accumulated from using an affinity card associated with his favorite airline.

Brian loves living in my area, because he and his wife can manage the cost of living much better than in his previous neighborhood, especially because all the supermarkets have bonus cards that provide additional discounts off many food item purchases. They also love shopping at the local warehouse club, because there are a lot of rebate offers on the products they buy there. By using his credit card to buy groceries, he has quickly accumulated additional frequent-flyer miles.

Yet Brian is subject to the marketing tsunami that affects us all. He is inundated with junk mail offers of new credit cards. His family's dinner is interrupted by telemarketing phone calls. His morning at work is taken up with sifting through a flood of spam e-mails peddling discount life insurance and human growth hormone. "Where is my privacy protection?" Brian asks.

FEAR OF INVASION

Brian is not a real person, but his behavior strongly resembles reasonable behavior for a large percentage of the population. And, as reflected by Brian's question, there is a growing fear that some monolithic organizations sneak around collecting our deepest, darkest secrets and are using computers to invade our privacy.

According to the Federal Trade Commission (FTC), "Advances in computer technology have made it possible for detailed information about people to be compiled and shared more easily and cheaply than ever." At the FTC's Privacy Initiatives web site (www.ftc.gov/privacy/), there is a warning about allowing the misuse of personal information. The truth is, as BI professionals, we are somewhat responsible for collecting customer information and manipulating that information for marketing purposes, but are we really guilty of invasion of privacy?

Let's take a second look at Brian's behavior.

- The purchase of his home must be registered with the public agencies, because real estate transactions are recorded in public records.
- Publicly available information from the Census Bureau describes fine details about the area into which Brian has moved.
- The widely available regional cluster databases can accurately describe the demographics and psychographics of people who live in his neighborhood.

- His use of cross-marketed products from his financial institution provides a lot of information about his finances and lifestyle to his bank—information that is likely to be shared with all bank subsidiaries as well as affiliated third parties.
- Brian's use of an affinity credit card, along with his selection of destination for his vacation (as well as his choice of how and when to apply his frequent-flyer miles) also is registered as personal preference entries in some database.
- Their choice to use a supermarket bonus card not only registers the kinds of foods that he and his wife buy, but also allows someone to infer their preferred shopping time, their weekly food budget, the number of children they have, when they have company, and so on.
- Each time they fill out a rebate slip, they provide feedback to the vendor regarding the purchase patterns of their products and specific information about who buys what products and when.

Any of the activities in which Brian is engaged potentially generates *usable* information that could be construed as personal information. In reality, the data that feeds the marketing machine the consumers fear so much is most likely supplied by those very same consumers.

THE VALUE AND COST OF PRIVACY

This demonstrates an interesting model of information valuation, in that the consumer is being compensated in some way in return for providing information. For example, in return for the supermarket's ability to track every food item purchase, the consumer is rewarded with incremental coupon savings. In return for supplying information about the purchase of a product, the company will pay you a $5 rebate. In return for providing information about flight preferences and transactions, the airlines provide free air travel. There are second-order consumer benefits that are rarely articulated well, such as a better ability to provide products targeted only to those consumers who might be interested in those products and more efficient placement of products on supermarket shelves.

On the other hand, most organizations that collect data allow the consumer to prevent any misuse of that data by opting out. But opting out is an active process, requiring the consumer to take the action, which in turn generates some cost, perhaps in terms of time and energy spent (which can be lengthy, if waiting on hold). In other words, there is an incurred cost associated with managing personal information.

The public relations problem stems from the *perception* that because of the availability of fast computational resources along with knowledge discovery applications, companies are sifting through mounds of data eking out the smallest bits of private information. In reality, under the right circumstances (i.e., we all are obeying the law), companies are using provided personal information in a way that is consistent with the consumers' directives. Unfortunately, the onus for directing the prevention of the use personal information is placed on the consumer through the opt-out process.

Information Protection and Privacy Concerns

There are certainly some concerns about a perceived invasion of an individual's privacy, such as:

- **Elongated data retention.** The presumption that collected data will prove to be valuable at some point in the future, prompting even greater effort at collecting and keeping data;
- **Drawing incorrect inferences.** Discomfort with the idea that a corporation is drawing conclusions about individuals based on collected information;
- **Facilitating corporate economic disadvantages.** The creation of scenarios in which organizations that are capable of collecting more data will put smaller, less nimble organizations at a disadvantage;
- **Invalid risk models.** The uses of inferences and conclusions in place of facts for determination of services or provision of products as a way of reducing risk, such as increasing credit percentages or higher insurance premiums.

These are justified concerns, although we can address some aspects in the context of business always wanting to have deeper insight about their clients, even long before the creation of the computer, when customer information was noted on index or rolodex cards and sales people engaged in direct conversations to get to know their customers.

DATA RETENTION

It may seem true that more collection of data and longer retention might turn out to be of value, yet without a crystal ball to tell you exactly *what* data is going to be useful to you in the future, you'd have to store *all the data*. But even if organizations do feel incentivized to collect and retain data, few of these organizations have ironed out the gaps in their own process maturity to be effective at extracting much value. In the foreseeable future, the costs and efforts for capturing, managing, archiving, and ultimately, trying to *even find the data they need* is going to far exceed the value most businesses can derive.

As we have suggested throughout the book, a prerequisite to taking advantage of BI and analytics are openness to improving the associated business processes. When the organizations have a level of data management and business process maturity, they will be better able to not just manage the proper retention times for data, but be better at articulating their retention policies to their customers.

DRAWING INFERENCES

When it comes to organizations drawing conclusions based on the data available to them, we must be careful to differentiate between inference and fact. We will draw inferences and insights from the BI and analytics programs, but we still rely on human cognition to decide how to employ those insights. Yet recall, though, that most interactions (business or otherwise) involve an exchange of information. People who want to control what other people know and do not know about them must be aware of this fact. Alternatively, each of us derives some value from the interaction.

Instead of suggesting that people need to control information, a better approach might be to suggest that those people must weigh the value they get from the interaction and the cost of exposing the data. For example, when you search for information through using a search engine, you benefit by getting access to the information you were looking for. On the other hand, the search engine has to capture what you are looking for in order to help you, and the search histories help refine the algorithms and make the results more precise.

Simply put, in return for getting some information, you must share some information, and it is essentially an economic transaction. The same can be said for our example earlier in the chapter in which you share personal data with the supermarket to get discounts on purchases. It is up to each individual to decide whether he or she got a good deal or not.

ECONOMIC DISADVANTAGES

All sales processes are driven by the need for the sales person to influence the decision of the buyer, and therefore you could extrapolate that in every sales situation the buyer is being "manipulated." The use of BI and analytics does not change the core sales process, it merely informs the salesperson. In addition, the suggestion that a buyer is subject to manipulation is actually somewhat insulting to the buyer, who is also getting something out of the transaction, not just forking over the money.

If a company has a lot of insight but provides bad products, poor customer service, or limited warranty protection for their products or services, customers will still go to other places to get the things they want. On the other hand, if a company uses customer insight to provide better products and services, stock the kinds of products the customers want, and engage the customer in a relationship, customers will go there, even without the data mining.

Last, companies are usually in the business of generating profits, so it is ingenuous to fault them for wanting to extract the maximum profit. In fact, analyzing customer sensitivity to product pricing might show that *lowering* certain product prices might increase volume sales, leading to greater profits. In this case they are "extracting the maximum profit," but not necessarily through increased prices.

MANAGING RISK

An organization has a fiduciary responsibility to attempt to limit its risk, especially when it comes to offering credit or lending money. The models for risk analysis do (and probably should) take behavior characteristics into account. For example, parachuting out of airplanes probably impacts your life insurance premium. And you don't need data mining to figure that out, but rather the standard statistical and probability analysis that actuaries have been doing for a long time.

Identifying the characteristics of a pool of individuals that increase risk of defaulting on credit payments is a way of (1) protecting the corporate self-interest, but also (2) protecting the interests of those who don't choose to default on their payments but are the ones whose interest rates are raised to accommodate for loss and fraud.

That being said, poor data quality and invalid decision-making can account for unfair practices. Another anecdote shared with me deals with an insurance company imposing an increased premium on an individual due to his filling prescriptions for a chronic ailment. That decision did not take into account the fact that the medication was prescribed by a veterinarian for his pet cat!

THE "PRIVACY" POLICY

So what about all those privacy statements that we get in the mail each year? Under the Gramm–Leach–Bliley Act, any financial institution that collects nonpublic personal information must provide, both at the time of establishing a relationship and on an annual basis, a "clear and conspicuous disclosure to such consumer, in writing or in electronic form, … of that financial institution's policies and practices" with respect to disclosing nonpublic personal information to affiliates and nonaffiliated third parties.

But the issuing of a privacy statement does not imply that your data is being treated as private data. These statements actually are the opposite—they tell the consumer how the information is *not* being kept private. For example, one bank's privacy statement says, "We may share any of the personal information that we collect about you among companies within the <omitted> family." Later in the statement's text is an enumeration of 30 different companies within the family, including auto leasing, insurance, investment advisors, credit card, and real estate advisors.

Not only that, this privacy statement also says that the bank "may disclose any of the personal information that we have collected about you to:

- other financial institutions with whom we have joint marketing agreements; and
- companies that perform services, including marketing services, for us or for us and the financial institutions with whom we have joint marketing agreements."

This pretty much opens the door for sharing a consumer's personal data with just about anyone. So as long as the consumer does not actively opt out of participation, it is likely that personal information is being widely broadcast!

THE GOOD NEWS FOR BUSINESS INTELLIGENCE

There are a lot of benefits in society to the (limited) dissemination of personal information, such as the ability to track down criminals, detect fraud, provide channels for improved customer relationship management, and even track down terrorists. As BI professionals, we have a twofold opportunity with respect to the privacy issue. The first is to raise awareness regarding the consumer's value proposition with respect to data provision, leading to raised awareness about both the legality and the propriety of BI analysis and information use. The second is to build better BI applications. For example, if these darn computers are so smart, why are companies trying to sell long distance service to my children? And why do representatives of the company we use for our home alarm system keep calling us and asking if we want an introductory system?

All joking aside, junk mail and marketing calls are viewed as annoyances and invasions only because companies are *not* able to analyze that information as well as the populace thinks. When we can build better BI applications and use them properly, the perception of invasion will likely change.

Finding and Using Open Data Sets

There is a large body of publicly available information that is either free or inexpensive and that can add a lot of value to your data. Much of this data deals with either demographic or behavioral attribution associated with personal or organizational entities. Whether this data is provided by government resources or by separate data aggregator/packagers, there may be some issues with the quality of the data that will need to be addressed from within the organization.

The best places to start to learn more about public data are search engines and government web sites. There is a lot of public data available from the US government as well as from state governments. We will also seek to maintain a directory of good open data resources on this book's web site at www.businessintelligence-book.com.

Knowledge Delivery

One of the most alluring aspects of business intelligence (BI)—the graphic visualization—also presents a bit of a conundrum to the BI professional. Upon the initiation of a BI program, a common pattern is that the first task be the review and selection of tools, especially when visual fireworks triggered interest in instituting a BI program in the first place. In fact, the review and selection of front-end presentation tools is often seen as the gating factor for delivering value.

You would think that the ability to deliver and present analytical results would be top of mind for anyone beginning a BI and analytics program, yet we have delayed this discussion until almost the end of the book. The reason is that the introduction of presentation tools is a double-edged sword. Frequently, when the front-end tools are installed and put into production, many are still empty shells when the underlying data sets are not properly prepared for reporting and analysis. The perceived value of beautiful graphic presentations (as well as the simplicity of implementation) often masks the hard aspects of data requirements analysis, selection, validation, integration, and reorganization.

The attraction of delivery and presentation of actionable knowledge must be balanced with the effort necessary for preparing the data so that there is something **303** that can actually be delivered. That being said, once the key components of the data integration, data warehousing, and BI framework have been put in place, it is time to consider what types of questions the different BI users are looking to ask and have answered, and the best way of presenting results.

Review: The Business Intelligence User Types

In Chapter 3 we discussed seven different types of consumers of the results from the BI and analytics environment:

- **Power users**, who constitute a community of experienced, sophisticated analysts who want to use complex tools and techniques to analyze data and whose results will inform decision-making processes;
- **Business users**, who rely on domain-specific reporting and analyses prepared by power users, but who also rely on their own ad hoc queries and desire access to raw data for drilling down, direct interaction with analytics servers, extraction, and then further manipulation, perhaps using desktop utility tools;
- **Casual users**, who may represent more than one area of the business, and rely on rolled-up metrics from across functions or operational areas summarized from predesigned reports presented via scorecards or dashboards;
- **Data aggregators or Information Providers**, which are businesses that collect industry- or societywide data and enhance and reorganize that data as a way of providing value-added services to customers and subscribers. Some examples include database marketing services, financial and credit information services, real estate business information services, audience measurement services, market research providers, and national statistical agencies, among others;
- **Operational analytics users**, who indirectly rely on the results of analytics embedded within operational applications. Examples include call center representatives whose scripts are adjusted interactively in relation to customer profiles, predicted behavioral predispositions, and real-time customer responses, web site offers and ad placement, or users of retail shelf management systems that adjust stock levels based on demand across multiple regions;
- **Extended enterprise users**, comprising external parties, customers, regulators, external business analysts, partners, suppliers, or anyone with a need for reported information for tactical decision-making; and
- **IT users**, mostly involved in the development aspects of BI, and whose use of BI is more for supporting the needs of other information consumers.

Each of these user types has different expectations for his or her interactive experience, and each is framed within the context of the driving factors for delivery of actionable knowledge and the types of actions each would take based on the presented results. Some examples are provided in Table 19.1 for non-IT and non-aggregator users.

The upshot is that there are many different modes of presentation that are relevant to different user types. The next sections provide an overview of the typical methods employed for delivery and presentation.

Standard Reports

The most "generic" approach to presentation of information reflects a relatively basic, two-dimensional alignment of information, characterized within a grid of rows and columns. Standard, static reports derived from user specifications provide a consistent view of particular aspects of the business, generated in batch and typically delivered on a scheduled basis through a standard (web) interface.

The columns typically articulate the item or characteristic being measured, while the rows will generally correspond to the division and hierarchies for which those measures are provided. The intersection of each row and column provides the specific measure for the column's characteristic for the row's item. For example, let's examine a sample report provided by the US Census Bureau, shown in Table 19.2.

In this example, there are two measures (in the columns)—the estimate of owner-occupied housing units with a mortgage, and the margin of error associated with the measure. There are four groups of items being measured:

- The number of owner-occupied housing units with a mortgage
- Value of the houses
- Mortgage status
- Household income for the previous 12 months

Within some of these groups, there are further hierarchical breakdowns, such as the dollar groupings for value, or the categories for mortgage status. These are relatively generic categories/hierarchies, and this is reflected in the fact that these are indeed "canned" (or static) reports that have been already prepared for presentation. The presumption is that the static nature of standard reports will drive the need for alternative methods for additional insight. In other words, standard reports present analytical results, but may not provide enough information for analysts seeking actionable insight unless any of the reported numbers are perceived to be beyond the bounds of expectations. And in either case, the standard report only provides a view into what was intended to be shared, but is limited in providing answers to specific business questions.

TABLE 19.1 Example Usage Demands for Different Types of BI Users

User Type	Example Users	Actionable Knowledge	Type of Action	Example Usage Expectations
Power users	Data scientist, research analyst, "data miner"	Behavior patterns, statistical anomalies, analytical results, predictive models	Recommendations to corporate strategy, develop and deliver predictive models, adjustments to corporate tactics	Unencumbered access to data, ability to slice and dice dimensional data, integrated data mining models, ad hoc queries, access to analytical platforms and programming models
Business users	Operations managers, division managers	Operational reports, behavior that deviates from expectations within business function	Further drill-down, communication with front-line employees, recommendations to senior management	Periodically updated standard reports, notifications and alerts, presentation of current statuses within monitored business functions, ad hoc queries
Casual users	Senior managers	Deviation from expected behavior, outlier activity, pessimization across business functions	Alert business managers and users for further investigation and resolution	Monitoring of continuously updated reports and statuses across different business functions, notifications and alerts
Operational analytics users	Line or production managers, staff workers	Ongoing operational statuses, anomalous behavior	Mitigation or remediation of risks or emergent issues	Notifications and alerts, integration within existing applications
Extended enterprise users	Your business's customers	Current status of interactions with the business	Purchase or sale of assets, revising portfolio, payment	Secure presentation via the Web

TABLE 19.2 Example Standard Report for US Housing Characteristics, Taken from American Fact Finder, http://factfinder2.census.gov/

	United States	
	Owner-occupied housing units with a mortgage	
Subject	Estimate	Margin of Error
Owner-occupied housing units with a mortgage	50,339,500	±146,035
VALUE		
Less than $50,000	4.5%	±0.1
$50,000 to $99,999	13.3%	±0.1
$100,000 to $149,999	16.6%	±0.1
$150,000 to $199,999	16.2%	±0.1
$200,000 to $299,999	20.3%	±0.1
$300,000 to $499,999	17.8%	±0.1
$500,000 or more	11.1%	±0.1
Median (dollars)	197,300	±413
MORTGAGE STATUS		
With either a second mortgage, or home equity loan, but not both	21.7%	±0.1
Second mortgage only	5.7%	±0.1
Home equity loan only	16.1%	±0.1
Both second mortgage and home equity loan	0.9%	±0.1
No second mortgage and no home equity loan	77.4%	±0.1
HOUSEHOLD INCOME IN THE PAST 12 MONTHS (IN 2010 INFLATION-ADJUSTED DOLLARS)		
Less than $10,000	2.3%	±0.1
$10,000 to $24,999	7.4%	±0.1
$25,000 to $34,999	7.1%	±0.1
$35,000 to $49,999	12.6%	±0.1
$50,000 to $74,999	21.3%	±0.1
$75,000 to $99,999	16.8%	±0.1

(Continued)

TABLE 19.2 Example Standard Report for US Housing Characteristics, Taken from American Fact Finder, http://factfinder2.census.gov/ (*Continued*)

| | United States | |
| | Owner-occupied housing units with a mortgage | |
Subject	Estimate	Margin of Error
$100,000 to $149,999	18.9%	±0.1
$150,000 or more	13.5%	±0.1
Median household income (dollars)	73,892	±144

Interactive Analysis and Ad Hoc Querying

BI users looking for additional details regarding information delivered in standard reports may opt to drill into the data, either with broader visibility into the existing data or with a finer level of granularity. Both are intended to go beyond the relatively strict format of the standard report, even if they open up different views into the data.

The first option involves taking data formatted into a standard report and downloading it into a framework that allows you to slice and dice the existing data more freely. One example involves extracting data from the report into a desktop spreadsheet tool that provides organization around hierarchies. This precursor to dimensional analysis provides some level of interactive analysis, and is often manifested as a pivot table. These pivot tables enable broader flexibility in grouping data within ordered hierarchies, development of static graphs and charts, or just perusing the data from different angles.

The second option is more powerful in enabling finer granularity by allowing more sophisticated users to execute their own queries into the analytical data platform. Users with an understanding of the data warehouse's data inventory *and* who have some skill at articulating their queries can either run ad hoc queries directly using SQL or can use tools that help users describe the data sets they'd like to review. These tools reformulate those requests in SQL queries that are executed directly.

The result sets are also suitable for loading into desktop tools for further organization and analysis, as well as forming the basis for static charts and graphs. However, there are some caveats when allowing users to formulate and execute ad hoc queries; here are some:

- **Performance.** Writing efficient queries is a skill, and many queries involve joins across multiple tables that can bring a system's performance to its knees. The users would be expected to be highly trained before letting many loose in writing their own queries.

■ **Semantic consistency.** Allowing users to write their own queries implies they know and understand the meanings of the data elements they have selected to include in their result sets. However, without comprehensive, standardized business term glossaries and metadata repositories, users may see data element names and impute their definitions, potentially assigning meanings that are different than what was intended by the data creators. These discrepancies may impact believability of the results.

■ **Repeatability.** The ad hoc process involves a sequence consisting of multiple iterations of the two-phased query and review of the result set process. The operational process allows the analyst to effectively follow a thread or a train of thought, but without a means for capturing the thought processes driving the sequence, it is difficult to capture the intuition that drives the ultimate result. In other words, the sequence may yield some results, but it may be difficult to replicate that process a second or third time.

Standard reports can provide knowledge to a broad spectrum of consumers, even if those consumers must have contextual knowledge to identify the key indicators and take action. Ad hoc queries enable greater drill-down and potential for insight. However, given the growth of data into the petabytes coupled with the complexity and performance impacts of ad hoc queries, standard reporting is rapidly yielding to more organized methods for delivering results, through parameterized reporting, dimensional analysis, and notification, alerts, and exception reporting.

Parameterized Reports and Self-Service Reporting

After monitoring the types of ad hoc queries performed, it became apparent in many scenarios that users within similar categories were executing very similar queries. The problem was that despite the similarity of the queries, each was being executed in isolation, with each contributing to degradation of overall performance. However, knowledge of the similarity of query patterns allows the system managers to optimize the environment to help reduce system load but reorganizing the data to make it more amenable to the similar queries, preprocessing some aspects of those queries, or caching parts of the data to reduce memory access and network latency.

If the similar queries differ only by variables within the query conditions (such as "show me all the customers in New York" vs. "show me all the customers in Pennsylvania") or within different levels of dimensional hierarchies, then it is easy to develop template queries whose conditions can be filled in through selections from precomputed lists or even via form-based drop-downs. In other words, the queries are generally static, and differ only by a defined set of parameter values. Satisfying these parameterized reports bridges the gap between static, canned reports and free-flowing ad hoc queries. The parameterized approach is particularly beneficial in operational scenarios in which similar queries and drill-downs are done over and over again. For example, a call center manager may execute queries focusing on performance by location—the queries are always the same, they just differ by the location parameter.

Parameterized reports provide one approach to self-service business intelligence, or "self-service BI." In a self-service BI framework, tools simplify the different aspects of generating results and reports, including simplifying:

- The data discovery process by presenting a palette of data sets that the user can access and use;
- The data access methods by masking or virtualizing access to the data to be queried;
- The documentation of the "make-up" of the report via collaborative means so that the results, and more importantly, the process for generating the results, can be shared with other analysts; and
- The development of the presentation layer, whether that is simple row/column reports, or using more sophisticated visualization techniques (as we will explore in the next few sections).

Another benefit of self-service BI is that it is intended to reduce or eliminate the IT bottleneck. In many environments, the IT department is responsible for developing reports, and as the BI program gains more acceptance, there will be greater demand for IT resources for report development. This becomes a bottleneck when the time for responding to a request exceeds the window of opportunity for exploiting the actionable knowledge. For example, one group might want to evaluate how a product performs within its first week of release so that adjustments and tweaks can be made; if it takes three weeks for the report to be readied, it is already too late to take action.

Dimensional Analysis

Multidimensional analysis and online analytical processing (OLAP) add a layer on top of the pivot table approaches used within desktop spreadsheet tools. The multidimensional analysis provided by OLAP tools helps analysts "slice and dice" relationships between different variables within different levels of their own hierarchies. Some examples include reviewing "item sales by time period by region" (in which there are different types of items, different time period durations, and different levels of granularity for regions) or "product availability by product classification by supplier by location" (in which there are multiple layers of product classifications and different levels of granularity for locations).

The use of the word "by" suggests a pivot around which the data can be viewed, allowing us to look at items sold, grouped by item classification and then grouped by time periods, then by regions, or the other way around, grouped by regions then by time periods. OLAP lets the analyst drill up and down along the hierarchies in the different dimensions to uncover dependent relationships that are hidden within the hierarchies.

Since OLAP queries are generally organized around partial aggregations along the different dimensions, the data can be organized along the different dimensions in what is referred to as an OLAP cube, which basically enables rapid responses for queries that "slice" or "dice" the data. "Slicing" fixes the value of one dimension and provides all others; in our example, that could mean fixing the region (Northeast) and reviewing items sales grouped by classification and then by time period for the Northeast. "Dicing" subselects components of one or more dimensions, such as selecting a collection of item classifications and then presenting those selected items by time period and location.

Any of the dimensions can be drilled-through (also referred to as drill-down) by navigating along the different levels of a dimension's hierarchy. For example, once a region is selected (Northeast), sales by item by time period can be reviewed at the next level down in the regional hierarchy (such as by each of the states in the Northeast region).

OLAP environments present the data aligned along selected dimensions. The presentation layer often provides a palette from which dimensions can be selected for visualization, and those dimensions can be pivoted around each other. The data can be presented in the same grid format as the standard report, or can be visualized using graphical components (such as those we discuss later in this chapter). The slicing, dicing, and drill-through provided by the OLAP presentation provides much greater flexibility for the power user performing data discovery. Alternatively, the business user seeking to drill down into data to identify anomalous behavior or to look for potential patterns may also benefit through the use of the OLAP environment.

Alerts/Notifications

When you think about the ways that individuals usually review the data in the standard report's layout, you will recognize that in many cases, the individual's attention is only focused on one or two key pieces of information. In these situations, the individual's goal is examining some specific variable's value, and either verifying that the value is within an expected range, or determining that the value is outside the expected range and then taking some action.

For example, a national call center manager might review average hold times by regional call center. As long as the average hold time is between 30 and 60 seconds, the averages remain within the acceptable level of service. However, once an average hold time for any region exceeds 60 seconds, the call center manager will need to reach out to the regional call center manager to investigate why the hold times are longer than expected.

Of course, you can envision many similar scenarios in which the action needs to be triggered only when certain variables hit specific values. And in each of these cases, reviewing the entire report is overkill—the business user only needs to know the specific variable's value, and only when that value would need to trigger an action; otherwise, the variable's value can be ignored. This realization means that instead of presenting an entire report, alerts or notifications can be an alternative method for delivering actionable knowledge.

This method is nicely suited to operational environments in which notifications can be delivered via different methods. Some examples include email, instant messages, direct messages delivered through (potentially internal) social networking sites, smartphones, other mobile devices, radio transmissions, or even visual cues (such as scrolling message boards, light banks, or visual consoles). In these situations, the notification method can embody the context; for example, a flashing amber light provides the medium for notification as well as the message. This approach not only simplifies the delivery of the critical piece of information, it reduces the effort for inspecting the critical value and thereby enables actions to be taken in a rapid manner.

Visualization: Charts, Graphs, Widgets

The methods discussed so far in this chapter have largely focused on the means of *delivery* of the analytical results, but less on the *presentation*. Yet our conclusion at the end of the previous section suggested that presentation methods for specific pieces of information might be better in conveying a message or triggering the appropriate actions. This idea can be extended to different methods of visualizing, and then *comparing* analytical results.

There are many different types of visualization modes for data, and while this is not intended to provide a comprehensive overview of visualization techniques, it is meant to provide an overview of a handful of ways to present actionable knowledge:

- **Line chart.** A line chart maps points on a grid connected by line segments. A line chart can be used to show a series of connected values, such as a time series. An example would be mapping the rise and fall of gas prices per gallon using the price of a gallon of gas on the first day of each month for the previous 36 months.

- **Bar chart.** A bar chart maps values using rectangles whose lengths correspond to the charted values. Bar charts are good for comparing different values of the same variable across different contexts. An example would be a chart of the average life expectancy in years across different countries.

- **Pie chart.** A pie chart is conveyed as a circle that is broken out into sectors representing some percentage of a whole. A pie chart is good for showing distributions of values across a single domain. An example is showing the relative percentages of owner-occupied homes by ethnicity within a Zip code area. The total of all the components always will add up to 100%, and each slice of the pie represents a percentage of the whole.

- **Scatter plot.** A scatter plot graphs points showing a relationship between two variables. Typically one variable is fixed (the dependent variable) and the other is not (the independent variable). In a two-dimensional scatter plot, the x axis represents the independent variable value and the y axis represents the dependent variable. A scatter plot is used to look for correlation between the dependent and independent variable. An example graphs an individual's age (the dependent variable) and the individual's observed weight (the independent variable).

- **Bubble chart.** A bubble chart is a variation on a scatter plot in which a third variable can be represented using the size of the item in the chart. An example would graph the dollar sales volume by the number of items sold, and the bubbles could represent the percentage of the overall market share.

- **Gauge.** A gauge is an indicator of magnitude in the context of critical value ranges. A gauge is good for conveying relative status of critical variables and points that should trigger some action. A traditional example is an automobile's fuel gauge, which indicates the relative fullness of the tank, as well as an area close to the "empty" measure marked as red to indicate the need for refueling.

- **Directional indicators (arrows up or down).** These are also indicators that are used for comparison to prior values. Often these are represented using three images—one to indicate improvement, one to indicate no change, and one to indicate degradation of the value. For example, directional indicators can be used as part of a time series presentation of stock prices to indicate whether the end of day price is higher, the same, or lower than the previous day's price.

- **Heat map.** This is a graph that tiles a two-dimensional space using tiles of different sizes and colors. A heat map is good for displaying many simultaneous values yet highlighting specific ones based on their values. As an example, a heat map can display the number of times each particular link on a web page was clicked, and can highlight the areas of greatest activity.

- **Spider or radar chart.** A spider chart displays a series of variable values across a collection of dimensions. Each dimension is represented as an axis emanating from the center with specific gradations. A set of observations can be mapped as points (and connected with lines). Different observations can be graphed using different colors. An example using a spider chart looks at a number of different characteristics of products (price, height, width, weight, mean time between failure), and relative success, allowing the analyst to quickly compare different products and look for correlations of the variable values.

- **Sparkline.** Sparklines are small line graphs without axes or coordinates. Many sparklines can be used in relative comparison regarding trends. As an example, the trends of different stock price histories for similar companies can be compared to determine of there are industry trends relating to stock price.

There are many other types of visual "widgets" that can be used for presentation of information. A good resource for understanding graphic visualization is the classic set of books by Edward Tufte, particularly the first (*The Visual Display of Quantitative Information*).

Scorecards and Dashboards

Beginning with notifications and alerts, we can extend the concept of carefully crafting the visual presentation of broader collections of relevant analytical results. In other words, if a trained eye is required to scan key performance metrics from standard reports, simplifying the presentation of key performance metrics may better enable the knowledge worker to transition from seeing what has already happened to understanding the changes necessary to improve the business process.

Scorecards and dashboards are two different approaches for consolidating the presentation of reported results to a particular user type. A scorecard usually presents the values of key performance indicators as well as indicators reflecting whether those KPI values are acceptable or not. The scorecard presentation may also be enhanced with historical trends and indications if the KPIs have been improving or not over time. Scorecards are often updated on a periodic basis (e.g., daily or hourly).

Dashboards provide some degree of flexibility to the user in crafting the presentation that is most relevant to the way he/she operates. Given an inventory of presentation graphics (such as those described in the previous section), an analyst and business user can work together in selecting the most appropriate methods of presentation. Dashboards can connect to real-time sources, and allow the business data consumer to customize an up-to-date presentation of summarized performance metrics, allowing continuous monitoring throughout the day.

Pervasive delivery mechanisms can push dashboards to a large variety of channels, ranging from the traditional browser-based format to handheld mobile devices. Through the interactive nature of the dashboard, the knowledge worker can drill down through the key indicators regarding any emerging opportunities, as well as take action through integrated process-flow and communication engines.

Another approach to dashboards is the concept of a mashup, which allows the knowledge consumers themselves the ability to identify their own combination of analytics and reports with external data streams, news feeds, social networks, and other Web 2.0 resources in a visualization framework that specifically suits their own business needs and objectives. The mashup framework provides the "glue" for integrating data streams and BI with interactive business applications.

Geographic Visualization

In Chapter 16 we discussed aspects of location intelligence and spatial analytics, and the results of that type of analysis can be presented within the context of a map. Instead of using the standard graphical widgets described in a previous section, aggregate values and totals can be attributed to a visual representation of a map. For example, population statistics for each country in the European Union can be superimposed on top of a map of Europe.

These maps can satisfy the desire to drill down; interactive selection or clicking on one segment of the map can zoom in from a geographic standpoint. In addition, spatial analysis results can be layered within the mapping interface. For example, in an insurance management application, hazard zones can be superimposed on top of regions potentially affected by weather events to help guide determination of heightened risk areas that will command additional insurance premiums in a way that balances risk across the company's customer base. Another example employs the heat map concept to geographic regions using sizes and colors to present a collection of variable values.

Often dashboards will link more than one visualization component to others, and this can be easily applied to geographic visualization. For example, a dimensional analysis presentation (such as a pivot table) for a geographic hierarchy can be presented in one frame while the aggregated values are displayed within a map. Realigning the dimensions in the grid will automatically update the map, and drilling through regions on the map will trigger a reload of the drilled-through data within the grid.

Integrated Analytics

As specific analytic values trigger specific actions within well-defined business processes, employing a combination of alerts and notifications with visualization tools reduces the need for the end users to have deep training in the use of the BI tool set. In other words, when the analytical results are fed directly into operational activities, the end-user may be a consumer of BI and *may not even be aware of it!*

Some characteristics of business processes that are nicely suited to integrated analytics include:

- The business process has distinct performance objectives.
- The business process involves decision points by one or more actors.
- The process's performance can be impaired by absence of information.
- The process's performance can be impaired by ill-informed decisions.
- The process can be improved with well-informed decision-making.
- Participants do not need to be "tech-savvy" to be informed.

Yet in order to make integrated analytics work, the implementers must make sure that all the information necessary can be delivered to the appropriate person with the right time frame to facilitate the best decisions. That might imply the need for real-time integration of data from multiple sources of both analytics results and operational data. In turn, the delivery of the actionable knowledge must be seamlessly presented in a way that is best suited to business operations and is seamlessly integrated with the common suites of desktop productivity tools. This type of event-driven notification allows analytics to be directly embedded within operational processes and supporting applications across multiple channels. As this approach gains popularity, more widespread adoption of BI services coupled with lowered barriers to deployment will open new opportunities for integrating BI results.

Considerations: Optimizing the Presentation for the Right Message

In this chapter we have covered the range of presentation from the traditional grid-style report all the way to fancy graphic visualizations, all intended to help convey the results of analyses that should trigger actions to benefit the business. However, the wide palette of available graphs, charts, indicators, dials, knobs, and such can, at times, detract from the content when the presentation overwhelms the values that are being presented. Here are some quick guidelines to keep in mind when laying out a BI dashboard:

- **Choose the right visualization graphic.** Don't let the shiny graphics fool you into using a visual component that does not properly convey the intended result. For example, line charts are good for depicting historical trends of the same variable over time, but bar charts may not be as good a choice.
- **Manage your "real estate."** The available screen space limits what can be displayed at one time, and this is what is referred to as screen "real estate." Different

delivery channels allow different amounts of real estate. A regular desktop screen affords more presentation area than the screen on a laptop, while both trump the screen of a portable tablet and especially a smartphone. When considering the channel and the consumer, employ the right visualization components that fit within the available space yet still deliver the actionable knowledge.

- **Maintain context.** You must recognize that the presentation of a value is subject to variant interpretations when there is no external context defining its meaning. For example, presenting a value on a dial-gauge conveys the variable's magnitude, but not whether that value is good, bad, or indifferent. Adjusting the dial gauge with a red zone (to indicate a bad value) and a green zone (to indicate a good value) provides the context of the displayed magnitude.

- **Be consistent.** When the power of self-service dashboard development is placed in the hands of many data consumers, their own biases will lead to an explosion of variant ways of representing the same or similar ideas. The result is that what makes sense to one data consumer has less meaning when presented to another, and the confusion only grows with wider dissemination. Consistent representations and presentations (and corresponding selection of standard visualization graphics) will help to ensure consistent interpretations.

- **Keep it simple.** Don't inundate the presentation with fancy-looking graphics that don't add to the decision-making process. Often the simpler the presentation, the more easily the content is conveyed.

- **Engage.** Engage the user community and agree on standards, practices, and a guide book for developing visualization parameters for delivery and presentation.

Chapter 20

Emerging Business Intelligence Trends

Discussing new and emerging technologies poses the risk of putting a conceptual "freshness date" on this book. However, the techniques described in this chapter focus on a combination of methods that, when combined with business process improvements and governed data management practices, will open new vistas in which actionable knowledge can be put to profitable use. And to mitigate the risk of diminished shelf life, we will continue to present new and emerging concepts and trends on the book's companion web site, http://www.businessintelligence-book. com.

Search as a Business Intelligence Technique

Search engines have largely fueled the way people use the World Wide Web, mostly due to their ability to present a seamless index to an almost inexhaustible supply of constantly morphing content. But what is the objective of a content search? At the simplest level, anyone making use of a search capability is performing a data discovery activity, looking for a refined set of items that most closely match the provided search terms.

It is intriguing to consider the different goals people have for their searches. At the same time, the search process itself guides the data discovery in terms of the reaction of the searcher to the delivered results, sometimes influencing the next iterations of the search query until the content that was sought after is sufficiently "found." In effect, the search cycle is in its own right a business intelligence (BI) activity, especially when you consider the different "classes" of information that can be inferred from a content search, as well as the framework of presentation of search results.

It is worthwhile to consider the various meta-attributes of a search result, since the information that is presented to the searcher provides different characteristics and bits of value depending on the values of these attributes. For example, querying a search engine with a set of search terms results in the presentation of candidate documents ordered by a score representing their similarity to the requested search terms. In some cases, a section that is particularly relevant is excerpted and presented as well.

The presentation of these "slices of information" is important, since it is possible that these slices will contain the relevant results with the specific infor-mation that was sought after. In other cases, the researcher will drill down into the presented document to scan for the desired information. Either way, we start to see that the data discovery process provided by searching is essentially similar to the ad hoc querying a data analyst performs on structured data in a data ware-house, as is shown in Figure 20.1. The analyst selects search terms, reviews the results, and either refines the search terms and reiterates, drills down, or is finished. Once the drill-down is complete, the researcher either refines the search terms and starts again, goes back to review the remainder of the last query's results, or completes.

At the same time, enabling high-precision searching is the result of an analytical activity involving big data analytics: absorbing massive amounts of source content, indexing both the content values (such as individual words or collections of words as phrases), the semantic concepts associated with those values, and the collections of semantic concepts within defined hierarchies within a document, as well as their relative proximities. These semantic indexes are used in scoring the match between the collection of search query terms and the corpus of documents, thereby improving the precision of results.

Last, the search capabilities for unstructured data can be combined with the traditional BI activities so that the types of reports and dashboards discussed in Chapter 19 can be enhanced with links to relevant documents. For example, a recruiting application's report can be organized around skillsets and enhanced with resumes selected based on their similarity to the hierarchy of skills.

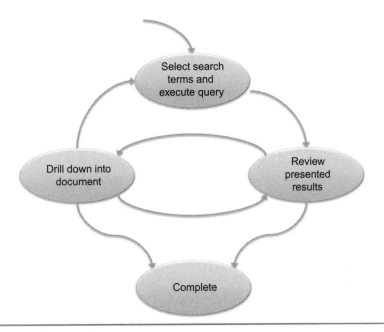

Figure 20.1   The search cycle.

Text Analysis

Search capabilities enable you to incorporate aspects of unstructured data into your BI environment, but the onus of scanning and interpreting the content served via search still lies with the information consumers. Yet there is an overwhelming recognition of the potential value locked within the growing body of unstructured data, and there is a desire to automate aspects of scanning and extracting information from text. An emerging technique, called text analysis, is increasingly integrated within the BI program to incorporate knowledge discovery from unstructured data.

Text analysis can be used to isolate key words, phrases, and concepts within semistructured and unstructured text, and these key text artifacts are analyzed semantically, modeled, and their source documents correlated based on recognized concepts. This implies the need for concept taxonomies in which like terms can be collected and aggregated at different levels of precision, such as car makes, models, as well as alternative versions resulting from the presence or absence of specific features.

Algorithms for entity recognition, entity extraction, and text analysis need to be more sophisticated in relation to the text's structure. While simple, pattern-based unstructured entities (such as telephone numbers) can be scanned using techniques such as regular expression parsing, more complex pattern and context sensitive techniques are increasingly used. A standard for content analytics called the Unstructured

Information Management Architecture (UIMA) was established by OASIS in 2009, and guides the development of a framework for the integration of text analysis components and rules to drive the development of unstructured analysis software.

These components allow you to analyze documents and identify terms that appear with relative frequency, identify statistically improbable terms, determine sentinel or signal terms, build concept hierarchies, create dictionaries, and document rules for phrase recognition and for concept extraction, among other techniques. Once this analysis is completed, the information contained within the documents can be clustered, categorized, and organized to support intelligent searches, and filtering concepts from streaming text helps identify important text artifacts that can be routed directly to individuals with a particular interest in the supplied content. Once the concepts have been ordered, identified, extracted, and organized, they can be subjected to data mining and other types of analysis to help the knowledge worker draw conclusions from actionable information.

Entity Recognition and Entity Extraction

A consequence of the growing flood of unstructured artifacts is the challenge in isolating key terms in text (such as people, places, and things) and establishing linkages and relationships among those concepts. "Real-time" entity identity recognition has traditionally been a batch process, but time-critical operations relating to online comments, customer service, call center operations, or more sensitive activities involving security, bank secrecy act/anti–money laundering, or other "persons of interest" applications become significantly more effective when individual identities can be recognized in real time.

Entity recognition in text is a specific pattern analysis task of scanning word sequences and isolating phrases and word combinations that represent recognized named entities (either parties, named locations, items, etc.). While this may sound simplistic, the challenge goes beyond scanning text strings and looking for name patterns in sequential text. The complexity increases in relation to the desire to isolate entity relationships embedded (and sometimes *implicit*) within the text.

This builds on natural language processing concepts coupled with semantics and taxonomies to expose explicit relationships (such as an individual's affinity for a particular charity), causal relationships (such as correlation of product issues within geographical regions), or multiple references to the same entity (such as the introduction of pronouns like "He" or "It" that refer to named entities with proper nouns such as "George Washington"). It also requires matching string patterns to items within organized hierarchies (such as recognizing that "electric drill" is a concept contained within a set of items referred to as "power tools").

In fact, entity recognition and extraction is not limited to text; there are entity recognition algorithms that can be applied to visual media (such as streaming video or images) and to audio as well. Real-time identity recognition enables rapid linkage between individuals and their related attributes, characteristics, profiles, and transaction histories, and can be used in real-time embedded predictive models to enhance operational decision-making.

Sentiment Analysis

With the plethora of platforms for individuals to express ideas and opinion, many companies believe that these media channels also create scenarios in which customers express positive or negative sentiment regarding the company or its products. Social media sites, social networks, online collaborative environments, content farms, articles, videos, and blogs provide ample opportunity for a wide variety of individuals to post subjective reviews, product evaluations, service ratings, experiences, and other opinions, often ones that influence a broad spectrum of other individuals within the author's network. As opposed to idly reflecting on what has been presented, organizations seek to take advantage of these growing networks of influence by rapidly addressing negative sentiment or exploiting positive sentiments.

Sentiment analysis takes text analytics to the next level through the analysis of unstructured text to review and evaluate subjectivity in the attitude of the material's author. For example, a product's manufacturer may analyze call center reports for part names appearing frequently with negative interactions such as product failures. Doing so can help identify common failure patterns, thereby allowing for proactive actions to reach out to product owners before the part fails. Sentiment analysis presents other opportunities as well, such as identifying emerging consumer trends, identifying customer preferences, or finding unhappy customers. This allows businesses to manage their online reputation by highlighting positive opinions while reducing impacts due to negative opinions.

Sentiment analysis is a culmination of a number of techniques discussed in this book—analyzing term frequency, deducing taxonomies and hierarchies, tagging document artifacts with their corresponding concept tags, organizing concepts in relation to alternate structured data, and applying data mining analyses to look for patterns, associations, causality, and other types of relationships.

Mobile Business Intelligence

In Chapter 19 we discussed different approaches for delivery of actionable knowledge, including mobile devices; in fact, what is referred to as mobile BI is an emerging technique that warrants further consideration for two reasons. The first is the determination of the appropriate means for presentation: is there a mobile presentation layer on the mobile device and is the data streamed to the device where it can be directly reviewed, sliced and diced, and so on? Or is the device just a conduit for attaching to a hosted or cloud-based data repository, providing a window to a BI application running on a remote platform?

The answer to these questions is relevant to the second critical issue, having to do with management and oversight of the mobile devices themselves. For the most part, individuals seeking to attach to their corporate BI environments are doing so using their own private devices. This approach, called BYOD (Bring Your Own Device), raises issues of corporate oversight and protection of information, with questions like:

- Does downloading data to an individual's private device pose a corporate security and data protection risk?
- Is delivering data that is protected by privacy laws to private devices designated as a violation of those laws?
- Are there connectivity and performance issues if the private device must connect to a hosted solution?
- What level of control is provided to the owner of the device for viewing and manipulating corporate data?

As more key staff members demand full-service mobile BI, we will see how these and similar questions are answered to satisfy both the needs of the information consumers as well as complying with best practices for information and data protection.

Event Stream Processing

Whether business processes are fully encompassed within an enterprise or include events and inputs that originate outside the organization, most business processes cross both functional and organizational boundaries. And while many dependencies exist based on events that take place within the organization, there is a potential order of magnitude more influence from events occurring beyond organizational boundaries. Analysis of these events after they have been logged and transmitted from operational systems to a data warehouse may provide some level of insight, yet the latency of that information transmission coupled with the need for analyzing the data once it has been moved to a separate, essentially static repository means an abdication of the ability to respond to predictive events as they occur in real time. In other words, traditional BI reporting and ad hoc queries are insufficient to address the active capturing, monitoring, and correlating of event information into actionable knowledge. A technique called event stream processing (ESP, also referred to as complex event processing, or CEP) enables real-time monitoring of patterns and sequences of events flowing through many simultaneously streamed sources of information.

Traditional queries are performed against data sets that are managed within a persistent store. While the query processing engine can conceptually access the entire data sets, from a performance perspective this is limited to environments that can provide rapid random access. In most cases, complex queries such as those involving sorting and/or aggregations will pull the data from disk storage into memory, possibly multiple times and with multiple scans through the data, in order to generate the result set. We can improve performance through parallelization and disk partitioning, and there are various partitioning schemes intended to address scalability. And although different users can request results to different types of queries, the data set against which the queries are made remains relatively static.

To enable the ability to rapidly respond to emerging opportunities that can result from the confluence of multiple streams of information, we must have the capability to:

- Model expected behavior of the (both human and automated) actors within a specific business process or workflow in relation to the myriad input streams;
- Analyze and identify the patterns in high volumes of streaming data that are common to the activity;
- Continuously monitor (in real time) all potentially influential streams of events against the expected patterns;
- Provide low-latency combination and processing of events within defined event windows;
- Recognize diversion or variance from the defined expectations that might indicate the need for intervention or a new opportunity; and
- Generate alerts in response to identified triggers and notify the right personnel within the organization who can take action within a reasonable time frame.

Event stream processing enables an alternative to series of queries against static data sets. An ESP framework can be configured to monitor high volumes of data flowing through multiple continuously flowing input data sources with very low latencies for event processing. The application developer can configure a "data flow" network of state-preserving processing stages (such as that shown in Figure 20.2), each with actions triggered as a result of the arrival of information coupled with integrated business rules. The flexibility of the configuration of this data flow network allows rapidly changing data from the different input streams to be subjected to multiple rule sets at the same time.

The ESP engine can evaluate both transient events as well as events that are retained within a virtual cache. Input streams are continuously pushed to a query

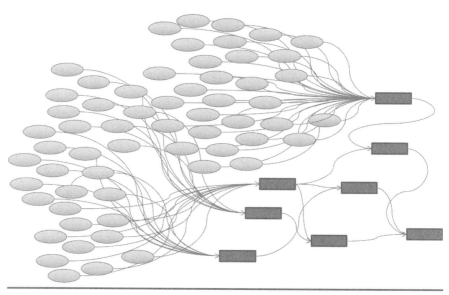

Figure 20.2 An example of an event stream network.

processor that essentially "reacts" to arriving data. Multiple patterns can be scanned simultaneously, because as new events arrive, they are routed through a set of continuous queries. The asynchronous and independent nature of the different sets of queries means that the system can be scaled through distribution of processing and drawing from a pool of available computational units.

The ability to continuously monitor a wide variety of streaming inputs in a scalable manner allows you to respond to emerging scenarios through the recognition of actionable knowledge because of the lower latencies and turnaround time for analysis. In essence, instead of running dynamic queries against static data, we can look at ESP as a method for *simultaneously running multiple stored queries against massive amounts of dynamic data.*

The event streams are not limited to external data feeds. Rather, those data feeds can be accompanied by application outputs, data pulled from existing databases, as well as sensor network data streams. An ESP engine can combine its internal event windows and states to perform different types of continuous queries, including aggregations, correlations and joins, computations (using internal native calculations or user defined functions and procedures), filtering and pattern-matching, as well as expressed limitations on the internal retained state.

The types of business problems that can be addressed using an ESP solution share a number of common characteristics, such as:

- Multiple streams of inputs of events or logged transactions;
- Potentially very large data volumes;

- Relationships among different inputs and events, either by virtue of the objects affected (such as customers), events that take place within a specified time frame, or events that take place in a particular sequence or with unusual frequency;
- Knowledge of particular sequences or patterns that would have some particular business interest;
- An expectation of correlation across different event streams;
- The need to perform computations and queries against the streams;
- The need to trigger a reactive event within a real-time window.

This becomes particularly valuable in business environments in which it is important to detect any variation from expected behavior and react in a timely manner that adds value. Not only are there numerous use cases that are common across different industries, a number of verticals have specific dependencies for an ESP-style solution.

Some example business scenarios that have these characteristics include:

- **Customer sentiment monitoring.** The "voice of the customer" is getting increasingly louder as a result of the explosion of social networking environments and collaboration mechanisms that span multiple corporate web sites, social networking applications, online retailer product reviews, independent opinion sites, blogs, review sites, and so on. Companies can benefit from early identification of emerging customer problems, product failures, safety risks, or general market disapproval. An ESP model can be configured to connect to social networking feeds, the logs of customer call center transactions, real-time point-of-sale data streams, and email streams and filters to look for particularly correlated events such as increased complaints, increased returns, and decreased sales, all coupled with a rise in negative comments from social network streams, and then generate a notification to the right customer support and public relations teams with guidance indicating the sources of potential issues.
- **Inventory management.** In anticipation of customer product demand, retail businesses will establish inventory positions in a variety of items, which are delivered to warehouses and then distributed to retail locations for sale. However, significant amounts of cash are tied up in inventory, and unsold items are often relegated to lot sales at significant discounts in order to make room for new product. Reducing inventory can lead to other issues such as when there is customer demand for items that are out of stock, which may encourage the customers to purchase the product elsewhere. Any analyses that can help the company manage the proper balance of inventory are desirable, especially if transitory or regional product demands can be satisfied from existing stock instead of triggering additional orders. An ESP model can be designed to continuously monitor product inventory across the company's network, aggregated at different levels (store, region, county, state, etc.). The model can monitor when anticipated

demand exceeds a location's available inventory and can trigger deliveries or a between-store transfer, generate orders for replenishment at the warehouse to enable the stores to meet customer needs, and help optimize the supply chain processes.

■ **Utilities monitoring.** As the utilities industry changes and adopts smart grid technologies employing smart meters, these businesses are able to monitor metering and usage as the smart power meters calculate usage on an almost continuous basis, thereby generating and communicating mounds of data every second about energy delivery and residential consumption. This can help in rapidly identifying anomalies in the power grid, even across relatively small regions. Incorporating additional information streams such as continuous feeds of meteorological data helps to monitor demand, potentially predict emergent outages, and then trigger conservation events and transmit directives to residential digital control units to cycle down air conditioning compressors, balance the region's demand for energy, and potentially avert blackouts.

Each of these scenarios exhibit characteristics of those problems that are nicely suited to an ESP solution: multiple input streams, very large data volumes, correlation across events, real-time computations and queries applied to streaming data, and the need to trigger events within a real-time window.

Embedded Predictive Analytic Models

We have already discussed pervasive or integrated BI in which the results of BI and analytics are fed directly into operational applications. While this approach has gained traction, the field is still opportune for adoption, which is why we review it in this chapter on new and emerging techniques.

The predictive models developed using a variety of data and text mining algorithms can be integrated into business processes to supplement both operational decision-making as well as strategic analysis, using the patterns that have been revealed to predict future events or help in achieving a particular goal. For example, customer profiles created though the application of a clustering analysis can be used for real-time classification based on specific demographics or other characteristics. These profiles can be used to recommend opportunities for cross-selling and up-selling, thereby leading to increased revenue. Embedded predictive models can be used to address all of our value drivers, and are used in many different scenarios, including customer retention, acquisitions and procurement, supply chain improvements, fraud modeling, improving forecasting accuracy, clinical decision-making, credit analysis, and automated underwriting.

Big Data Analytics

Similar to embedded analytics, we have discussed big data analytical platforms such as Hadoop and its use of MapReduce, but as it still qualifies as an emerging technique, we revisit it in this chapter. It is safe to say that the exploitation of massive amounts of data sourced from a variety of locations, each with its own idiosyncrasies, is still in its infancy, even if the core techniques have been around for dozens of years. Yet Hadoop is still a moving target, with new capabilities being introduced into both the programming models and the distributed file systems, as well as the supporting technologies such as distributed queries and programming environments. In addition, there are alternate frameworks for parallel and distributed BI and analytics applications.

There is no doubt that the excitement around big data analytics is reaching a fevered pitch, yet this mania is still technology-driven. Without a clear process for asserting a value proposition for big data, though, there is a risk that it will remain a fad until it hits the typical milestones of the hype cycle, in which disappointment sets in because the basis for the investments in the technology are not grounded in expectations for clear business improvements.

That being said, a scan of existing content on the "value of big data" shed interesting light on what is being promoted as the expected result of big data analytics and, more interestingly, how familiar those expectations sound. A prime example is provided within the CEBR's economic study on the value of big data (titled "Data Equity—Unlocking the value of big data"), which speaks to the cumulative value of:

- Optimized consumer spending as a result of improved targeted customer marketing;
- Improvements to research and analytics within the manufacturing sectors to lead to new product development;
- Improvements in strategizing and business planning leading to innovation and new start-up companies;
- Predictive analytics for improving supply chain management to optimize stock management, replenishment, and forecasting;
- Improve the scope and accuracy of fraud detection.[1]

These are the same types of benefits we have always expected to get out of our BI and analytics activities. So what makes big data different? The answer must lie in the characteristics of the big data analytics application development environment, which largely consists of a framework for elastically harnessing parallel computing resources and distributed storage along with data exchange via high-speed networks. The result is improved performance and scalability, which suggests that of the

TABLE 20.1 Examples of Applications Suited to Big Data Analytics

Application	Criteria	Sample Data Sources
Energy network monitoring and optimization	Data throttling Computation throttling Large data volumes	Sensor data from smart meters and network components
Credit fraud detection	Data throttling Computation throttling Large data volumes Parallelization Data variety	Point-of-sale data Customer profiles Transaction histories Predictive models
Data profiling	Large data volumes Parallelization	Sources selected for downstream repurposing
Clustering and customer segmentation	Data throttling Computation throttling Large data volumes Parallelization Data variety	Customer profiles Transaction histories Enhancement data sets
Recommendation engines	Data throttling Computation throttling Large data volumes Parallelization Data variety	Customer profiles Transaction histories Enhancement data sets Social network data
Price modeling	Data throttling Computation throttling Large data volumes Parallelization	Point-of-sale data Customer profiles Transaction histories Predictive models

limited scenarios discussed as big data success stories. The framework is mostly suited to addressing or solving business problems that are subject to one or more of the following criteria:

- **Data-restricted throttling.** There is an existing solution whose performance is throttled as a result of data access latency, data availability, or size of inputs.
- **Computation-restricted throttling.** There are existing algorithms, but they are heuristic and have not been implemented because the anticipated computational performance has not been met with conventional systems.
- **Large data volumes.** The analytical application combines a multitude of existing large data sets and data streams with high rates of data creation and delivery.
- **Significant data variety.** The data in the different sources varies in structure and content, and some (or much) of the data is unstructured.
- **Benefits from data parallelization.** Because of the reduced data dependencies, the application's runtime can be improved through task parallelization applied to independent data segments.

So how does this relate to the business problems whose solutions are suited to big data analytics applications? Some examples are shown in Table 20.1.

However, we must anticipate that there are opportunities for employing big data analytics for developing algorithms and solutions that are not new implementations of old algorithms, but rather are new paradigms for using parallel execution and data distribution in innovative ways.

Considerations

The techniques covered in this chapter are emerging as of the writing of this book, but we can anticipate continued research and development that will lead to innovative ways of analyzing data and presenting results. And, as mentioned in the beginning of this chapter, for ongoing updates and ideas, please visit this book's companion web site at http://www.businessintelligence-book.com.

Endnote

1. "Data Equity—Unlocking the value of big data," Center for Economics and Business Research Ltd., April, 2012, downloaded from http://www.cebr.com/wp-content/uploads/1733_Cebr_Value-of-Data-Equity_report.pdf

Quick Reference Guide

This Quick Reference Guide encapsulates some of the more important topics covered in the book. The treatment here sometimes mimics and sometimes summarizes the material. Most sections give an overview and a pointer to where in the book you should look for more detail.

Analytics Appliance

Large-scale query/reporting/OLAP systems and big data analytics applications require a level of performance that can be addressed using analytics appliances, which are multiple processor systems that are sometimes customized systems and sometimes configured using commodity components. The primary performance driver for traditional reporting is scalability, with respect to both potentially massive data volumes as well as the number of simultaneous users. Savvy managers and technical leaders must consider scalability requirements to help in the determination of a specific architectural approach.

There is a range of analytics appliance architectures, and they essentially vary ways that the different resources (such as CPUs, cache memory, core memory, flash **333** memory, temporary disk storage areas, and persistent disk storage) contribute to maximizing system performance. These resources constitute a "memory hierarchy" that hardware architects employ in varying configurations to find the right combination of memory devices with varying sizes, costs, and speed to provide optimal results by reducing the latency for responding to increasingly complex queries and analyses.

Different architectural configurations address different scalability and performance issues in different ways. The determination of the most appropriate architectural style for reporting and analytics must always be based on clearly defined criteria to use to evaluate which approach best meets the business needs in the right context, and that may help in deciding which types of architectural styles are best suited to the organization.

Business Analytics

Business analytics refers to the applications used as part of a business intelligence (BI) program to provide insight and to deliver actionable knowledge that can help key stakeholders make decisions regarding business value creation. Business analytics can incorporate applications associated with different aspects of the business in ways that promote increased revenues, decreased risk, more efficient cost management, and improved customer experiences, such as analyzing

- **Customers and their behaviors**, including customer profiling, call center effectiveness, targeted marketing, personalization of presentation (such as for a web site), customer lifetime value estimations, and customer loyalty. Customer relationship management (CRM) covers a large number of these topics and is the process of understanding who your customers are, what they like and don't like, and how to manage your relationship with them.
- **Human productivity analytics**, such as call center utilization, process optimization, and productivity effectiveness metrics. This can be applied in trying to understand when and where the best productivity is achieved within an organization and perhaps why this is true.
- **Business productivity analytics**, such as defect analysis, capacity planning, financial reporting, risk management, credit management, resource planning, asset management, and inventory risk assessment. What is usually referred to as financial reporting can be grouped into this category.
- **Sales channel analytics**, including the creation and analysis of marketing campaigns, evaluating sales performance, and looking at sales channel effectiveness.
- **Supply chain analytics**, used to characterize and benchmark a company's supply channels from various vendors and suppliers, including supplier management, shipping effectiveness, inventory control, and the analysis of the distribution network.

- **Behavior analysis**, which deals with evaluating activity trends as a way to identify interesting or predictive behavior, relating to purchasing trends, Web activity, fraud detection, customer attrition analysis, and social network analysis.

Business analytic applications use or extract data from the central data warehouse and either formulate an interactive analytical process by providing access to different focused aspects of the data (as separated into individual subject area data marts) or manage their own views of the data internally.

Business Intelligence

The Data Warehousing Institute, a provider of education and training in the data warehouse and BI industry, defines *business intelligence* as:

> *The processes, technologies, and tools needed to turn data into information, information into knowledge, and knowledge into plans that drive profitable business action. Business intelligence encompasses data warehousing, business analytic tools, and content/knowledge management.*[1]

This is a great working definition, especially because it completely captures the idea that there is a hierarchy imposed on the different scopes of intelligence. In addition, this definition also exposes two critical notions:

- A BI program encompasses more than just a collection of software products and visualization tools. The value of BI comes from the processes for delivering actionable knowledge to the end users, the processes for acting upon that knowledge, and the right people willing to take action. This means that without the processes and the right people, the tools are of little value.
- The value of BI is realized in the context of profitable business action. This means that if knowledge that can be used for profitable action is ignored, the practice is of little value.

Unfortunately, the words *data* and *information* are frequently used interchangeably. At the risk of clashing with any individual's understanding of the terms *data*, *information*, and *knowledge*, for the purposes of this book we will use these conceptual definitions:

- **Data** is a collection of raw value elements or facts used for calculating, reasoning, or measuring. Data may be collected, stored, or processed but not put into a context from which any meaning can be inferred.
- **Information** is the result of collecting and organizing data in a way that establishes relationships between data items, which thereby provides context and meaning.

- **Knowledge** is the concept of understanding information based on recognized patterns in a way that provides insight to information.

Business Rules

A business rule is a directive that is intended to influence or guide business behavior, in support of business policy that is formulated in response to an opportunity or threat. From the information system perspective, a business rule is a statement that defines or constrains some aspect of the business. It is intended to assert business structure or to control or influence the behavior of the business.[2]

From a practical standpoint, a business rule asserts a statement about the state of a business process or a directive describing changes in the state of a business process. More simply, a business rule dictates what happens when a sequence of inputs is applied to one or more well-described scenarios. A rule is a statement that asserts some truth about the system, along with optional actions to be performed, depending on the assertion's truth value. Rules can be classified as falling into one of the following areas:

- **Definitions and specifications**, which provides a well-defined vocabulary for more complex rule specification. Rules in this class should enumerate the descriptive figures of speech used in describing business processes.
- **Assertions**, which are statements about entities within the system that express sensible observations about the business. Assertions describe relationships between entities and activities within the framework. Together, the definitions and assertions drive the construction of the logical data model within which the business rules operate.
- **Constraints**, which express unconditional conformance to a business statement; compared to a constraint, a data instance either conforms to that constraint or violates it. An event that violates a constraint will be rejected by the system; therefore, by definition, no action can be taken that will violate a constraint.
- **Guidelines**, which express a desire about the state of the system or a warning about a potential change in the system.
- **Actions**, which are operations that change the system state, typically as a result of the violation of some constraint or guideline.
- **Triggers**, which specify a collection of conditions and the initiation of an action contingent upon the conditions' values.
- **Inferences**, which specify a collection of conditions establishing a fact that becomes true as a by-product of changes within the states of the system.

A business rule system encapsulates sets of states, variables, and rules that reflect business processes and policies and provides a means for defining and managing business rules while creating an environment in which a rules engine will execute those rules. For more information see Chapter 11.

Dashboards and Scorecards

Scorecards and dashboards are two different approaches for consolidating the presentation of reported results to a particular user type. A scorecard usually presents the values of key performance indicators as well as indicators reflecting whether those KPI values are acceptable or not. The scorecard presentation may also be enhanced with historical trends and indications if the KPIs have been improving or not over time. Scorecards are often updated on a periodic basis (e.g., daily or hourly).

Dashboards provide some degree of flexibility to the user in crafting the presentation that is most relevant to the way he or she operates. Given an inventory of presentation graphics (such as those described in the previous section), an analyst and business user can work together in selecting the most appropriate methods of presentation. Dashboards can connect to real-time sources, and allow the business data consumer to customize an up-to-date presentation of summarized performance metrics, allowing continuous monitoring throughout the day.

Pervasive delivery mechanisms can push dashboards to a large variety of channels, ranging from the traditional browser-based format to handheld mobile devices. Through the interactive nature of the dashboard, the knowledge worker can drill down through the key indicators regarding any emerging opportunities, as well as take action through integrated process-flow and communication engines.

Data Cleansing

Data cleansing is the process of finding errors in data and either automatically or manually correcting the errors. A large part of the cleansing process involves the identification and elimination of duplicate records; a large part of this process is easy, because exact duplicates are easy to find in a database using simple queries or in a flat file by sorting and streaming the data based on a specific key. The difficult part of duplicates elimination is finding those nonexact duplicates—for example, pairs of records where there are subtle differences in the matching key. Data cleansing, which we discuss in Chapter 12, employs a number of techniques, with some of the most prevalent being:

- **Parsing**, which is the process of identifying tokens within a data instance and looking for recognizable patterns. The parsing process segregates each word, attempts to determine the relationship between the word and previously defined token sets, and then forms patterns from sequences of tokens. When a pattern is matched, there is a predefined transformation applied to the original field value to extract its individual components, which are then reported to the driver applications.

- **Standardization**, which transforms data into a standard form. Standardization, a prelude to the record consolidation process, is used to extract entity information (e.g., person, company, telephone number, location) and to assign some semantic value for subsequent manipulation. Standardization will incorporate information reduction transformations during a consolidation or summarization application.

- **Abbreviation expansion**, which transforms abbreviations into their full form. There are different kinds of abbreviation. One type shortens each of a set of words to a smaller form, where the abbreviation consists of a prefix of the original data value. Examples include "INC" for incorporated and "CORP" for corporation. Another type shortens the word by eliminating vowels or by contracting the letters to phonetics, such as "INTL" or "INTRNTL" for international. A third form of abbreviation is the acronym, where the first characters of each of a set of words are composed into a string, such as "USA" for "United States of America."

- **Correction**, which attempts to correct those data values that are not recognized and to augment correctable records with the correction. Realize that the correction process can only be partially automated; many vendors may give the impression that their tools can completely correct invalid data, but there is no silver bullet. In general, the correction process is based on maintaining a set of incorrect values as well as their corrected forms. As an example, if the word *International* is frequently misspelled as "Intrnational," there would be a rule mapping the incorrect form to the correct form. Some tools may incorporate business knowledge accumulated over a long period of time, which accounts for large knowledge bases of rules incorporated into these products; unfortunately, this opens the door for loads of obscure rules that reflect many special cases.

Data Enhancement

Data enhancement is a process to add value to information by accumulating additional information about a base set of entities and then merging all the sets of information to provide a focused view of the data. There are two approaches to data enhancement. One focuses on incrementally improving or adding information as data is viewed or processed. *Incremental* enhancements are useful as a component of a later analysis stage, such as sequence pattern analysis or behavior modeling. The other approach is *batch* enhancement, where data collections are aggregated and methods are applied to the collection to create value-added information. Data can be enhanced in different ways, pulling information from alternate types of sources, such as:

- **Auditing information**, which provides some kind of historical tracking information through which the sequence of business processes applied to data can be traced.
- **Temporal information**, where data is enhanced by incrementally adding timestamps noting the time at which some event occurred. With data, this can refer to the time at which a transaction took place, the time at which a message was sent or received, the time at which a customer requested information, and so on.
- **Contextual information**, which describes the place where some action was performed.
- **Geographic information**, which provides location information, such as locality coding, neighborhood mapping, latitude/longitude pairs, and other kinds of regional codes.
- **Demographic information**, such as customer age, marital status, gender, or ethnic coding.
- **Psychographic information**, which describes lifestyle preference information for people, such as product and brand use and preferences, leisure activities, and vacation preferences.

Data enhancement is a value-adding component of a BI program, especially in the areas of increasing competitive intelligence, improved CRM, micromarketing and focused targeting, personalization, and cooperative marketing, among other areas. Data enhancement frequently makes use of publicly available data sets that provide additional rolled-up demographics or psychographics, and this is discussed in greater detail in Chapters 15 and 16.

Data Governance

Data governance incorporates the policies, processes, and procedures for collecting data requirements, defining and approving data policies and data standards, and ensuring compliance with any defined and agreed-to policies and standards. Data governance dovetails with metadata management and data quality management, and is critical in ensuring level of trust in the utility of data streamed into an analytical environment such as a data warehouse.

Data Integration

Data integration covers the spectrum of methods for facilitating the provision of data from one or more sources to one or more targets, and includes flowing data from operational systems into a data warehouse as well as delivering information from an analytical environment to the different members of the BI user community. Data integration is not limited to extracting data sets from internal sources and loading them into a data warehouse, but focuses on effectively facilitating the delivery of information to the right places within the appropriate time. Data integration goes beyond ETL, data replication, and change data capture, although these remain key components of the integration fabric. Some of the key factors that must be considered when detailing any component of the data integration framework include:

- **Volume.** Petabyte and exabyte data volumes are becoming the norm, not the exception;
- **Performance.** Emerging demands for high-performance data integration capabilities are based on the need for linear scalability, the use of parallelism, and high-bandwidth data channels;
- **Lineage.** Or rather, the exposure of lineage, namely transparency when desired, and opacity otherwise;
- **Speed of delivery.** Reduced latency for accessing data from across nonuniform, heterogeneous platforms;
- **Semantic consistency.** Collaborative methods for managing and utilizing metadata shared across communities of interest;
- **Quality.** Embedded controls to ensure quality of the data; and
- **Security.** Guarantees of data protection no matter where data lives.

Data Mart

A data mart is a subject-oriented data repository, similar in structure to the enterprise data warehouse, but holding the data required for the decision support and BI needs of a specific department or group within the organization. A data mart could be constructed solely for the analytical purposes of the specific group, or it could be derived from an existing data warehouse. Data marts are built using a dimensional data model.

There are differences between a data mart and a data warehouse, mostly because of the different natures of the desired results. There is a school of thought that believes that data warehouses are meant for more loosely structured, exploratory analysis whereas data marts are for more formalized reporting and for directed drill-down. Because data marts are centered on the specific goals and decision support needs of a specific department within the company, the amount of data is much smaller, but the concentration is focused on data relevant to that department's operation. This implies that different departments with different analytical or reporting needs may need different kinds of data mart structures (which may account for the diverse set of data mart products on the market).

A data mart is likely to be configured for more generalized reporting for the specific business users within the department. Standard reports are more likely to be generated off of the data mart, which will be much smaller than the data warehouse and will provide better performance.

Data Mining

Data mining, or knowledge discovery, is a process of discovering patterns that lead to actionable knowledge from large data sets through one or more traditional data mining techniques, such as market basket analysis and clustering. A lot of the knowledge discovery methodology has evolved from the combination of the worlds of statistics and computer science. Data mining focuses mostly on discovering knowledge in association with six basic tasks.

- **Clustering and segmentation**, which is the task of dividing a large collection of objects into smaller groups of objects that exhibit some similarity. The difference between clustering and classification is that during the clustering task, the classes are not defined beforehand. Rather, the process of evaluating the classes after the clustering has completed drives the determination or definition of that class.
- **Classification**, which involves examining the attributes of a particular object and assigning it to a defined class. Classification can be used to divide a customer base into best, mediocre, and low-value customers, for instance, to distinguish suspicious characters at an airport security check, identify a fraudulent transaction, or identify prospects for a new service.
- **Estimation**, which is a process of assigning some continuously valued numeric value to an object. For example, credit risk assessment is not necessarily a yes/no question; it could be some kind of scoring that assesses a propensity to default on a loan. Estimation can be used as part of the classification process (such as using an estimation model to guess a person's annual salary as part of a market segmentation process).
- **Prediction**, which is an attempt to classify objects according to some expected future behavior. Classification and estimation can be used for prediction by applying historical data where the classification is already known to build a model (this is called *training*). That model can then be applied to new data to predict future behavior.
- **Affinity grouping**, which is a process of evaluating relationships or associations between data elements that demonstrate some kind of affinity between objects.
- **Description**, which is the process of trying to describe what has been discovered, or trying to explain the results of the data mining process.

There are a number of techniques that are used to perform these tasks: market basket analysis, memory-based reasoning, cluster detection, link analysis, rule induction, neural networks, and so on. For more information see Chapter 17.

Data Modeling

Practically all modern business applications that employ a data subsystem represent their data sets using data models. A data model is a discrete structured data representation of a real-world set of entities related to one another. Each entity (most often represented using a *table*) carries a set of characteristic attributes (described as *data elements*). Yet over time, our understanding of the ways that real-world objects and events are captured within a structured representation must adapt to the context in which the data sets are used and the ways the information satisfies the needs of the business processes.

Transaction processing systems need to have visibility into all aspects of a limited number of data instances at a time (such as a single *customer* buying a particular *product*). Analytical systems may need to support rapid aggregation to quickly respond to ad hoc queries relating to many data instances (such as "how many customers bought this specific product?"). In other words, there is bound to be a significant difference between how we use data in an operational/tactical manner (i.e., to "run the business") and the ways we use data in a strategic manner (i.e., to "improve the business").

The traditional modeling technique for operational systems revolves around the entity-relationship model. Unfortunately, reporting and analytical applications are generally less well-suited to utilizing data structured in the entity-relational form (although there are emerging environments that make this less true). The alternative is to restructure transaction or event data using what is called "dimensional modeling" that is better organized to provide rapid responses to different types of queries and analyses.

Data Profiling

The goal of profiling data is to discover metadata when it is not available and to validate metadata when it is available. Data profiling is a process of analyzing raw data for the purpose of characterizing the information embedded within a data set. Data profiling incorporates column analysis, data type determination, and cross-column association discovery. The result is a constructive process of information inference to prepare a data set for later integration.

Data profiling is a hierarchical process that attempts to build an assessment of the metadata associated with a collection of data sets. The bottom level of the hierarchy characterizes the values associated with individual attributes. At the next level, the assessment looks at relationships between multiple columns within a single table. At the highest level, the profile describes relationships that exist between data attributes across different tables.

Data profiling, discussed in Chapter 10, includes (among others) the following activities:

- **Data model inference**, which attempts to derive the data model from undocumented data.
- **Type inference**, a process to determine the data types associated with the data in each column of a table.
- **Value range analysis**, which explores the possibility that the values within a column fall within a defined value range (such as 0 to 100).
- **Cardinality and uniqueness**, where *cardinality* refers to the number of discrete values that appear within a column, and *uniqueness* tests to see that each row in a table has a unique value for any particular set of attributes.
- **Frequency distribution**, which yields the number of times each distinct value appears in a value set.
- **Nullness**, which evaluates the existence of null values, whether they are explicit system nulls or represented null values (such as 999-99-9999 for a Social Security number) extant in the data.
- **Domain analysis**, which is a process of identifying and isolating collections of data values that have some specific business value.
- **Functional dependency analysis**, which looks for relationships between columns within the same table and across different tables.
- **Key discovery**, which looks for candidate keys within a single table, and foreign keys that link different tables.

Data Quality

Data quality differs from data cleansing—whereas many data cleansing products can help in applying data edits to name and address data or in transforming data during the data integration process, there is usually no persistence in this cleansing. Each time a data warehouse is populated or updated, the same corrections are applied to the same data.

Data cleansing is an action, whereas data quality describes the state of the data. A data cleansing process can contribute to improving the quality of data. Improved data quality is the result of a business improvement process that looks to identify and eliminate the root causes of bad data. A critical component of improving data quality is being able to distinguish between "good" (i.e., valid) data and "bad" (i.e., invalid) data. But because data values appear in many contexts, formats, and frameworks, this simple concept devolves into extremely complicated notions as to what constitutes validity. This is because the validity of a data value *must* be defined within the context in which that data value appears.

There are many dimensions of data quality. The ones that usually attract the most attention are dimensions that deal with data values:

- **Accuracy**, which refers to the degree with which data values agree with an identified source of correct information.
- **Completeness**, which refers to the expectation that data instances contain all the information they are supposed to. Completeness can be prescribed on a single attribute, can be dependent on the values of other attributes within a record, or can even be defined with respect to all values within a column.
- **Consistency**, which refers to data values in one data set being consistent with values in another data set; formal consistency constraints can be encapsulated as a set of rules that specify consistency relationships between values of attributes, either across a record or message or along all values of a single attribute.
- **Currency and timeliness**, which refers to the degree to which information is current with the world that it models. *Currency* can measure how up-to-date information is and whether it is correct despite possible time-related changes. *Timeliness* refers to the time expectation for accessibility of information.

In essence, the level of data quality is determined by the data consumers in terms of observing the acceptability criteria of their defined expectations. In practice, this means identifying a set of data quality objectives associated with any data set and then measuring that data set's conformance to those objectives. Business rule systems (see Chapter 11) can be used to encapsulate data quality expectations as abstract rules that can be used to validate data as it moves from one location to another. For more information on data quality, see Chapter 12.

Data Warehouse

A "data warehouse" is the location from which BI reporting and analytics will be served. Basically, a data warehouse is the primary source of information that feeds the analytical processing within an organization. In Chapter 2 we discussed a number of different analytic applications that are driven by business needs, yet most, if not all of these applications are driven by the data that has been migrated into a data warehouse.

There are conflicting ideas about the formal definition of a data warehouse, but there is general consensus on some fundamental aspects, such as:

- A data warehouse is a centralized repository of information.
- A data warehouse is organized around the relevant subject areas important to the organization.
- A data warehouse provides a platform for different consumers (both human and automated) to submit queries about enterprise information.
- A data warehouse is used for analysis and not for transaction processing.
- The data in a data warehouse is nonvolatile.

■ A data warehouse is the target location for integrating data from multiple sources, both internal and external to an enterprise.

A data warehouse is usually constructed using a dimensional model. Information is loaded into the data warehouse after a number of preprocessing steps. Initially, as we discussed in the previous chapter, the BI consumers will have been engaged to provide their requirements, after which the candidate data sources will have been selected. The quality of those data sets can be assessed through data profiling. At the same time, the data analysts and modelers will design and build the dimensional models for the analytical platform.

Once the candidate sources have been selected, the data is extracted, cleansed, potentially transformed, and then prepared to be loaded into the warehouse model. This may incorporate business rules as well. That data is subsequently reformulated into dimensional form and loaded into the target warehouse. These processes compose what is referred to as the data warehouse's *back end.*

Once the data is in the warehouse, it may be used for any of the reporting and analysis purposes we will explore in subsequent chapters. Certain tools may draw their input directly from the data warehouse or from data marts that are extracted for specific purposes. The data warehouse can also act as a data source for algorithmic analytics performed on specialty analytical frameworks, as well as provide an "anchor point" for collecting and storing additional analytical results from these algorithms.

Dimensional Modeling

The challenge in using the standard entity-relationship model for reporting and analysis lies in the interconnectedness of the entities and the corresponding complexity in accumulating the information necessary for hierarchical aggregations. The alternative dimensional modeling technique captures the basic unit of representation as a single multikeyed entry in a slender *fact* table, with each key exploiting the relational model to refer to the different *dimensions* associated with those facts.

A maintained table of facts, each of which is related to a set of dimensions, is a much more efficient representation for data in a data warehouse and allows for information to be represented in a way that is more suitable to high-performance access. This is due to the ability to efficiently create aggregations and extractions of data specific to particular dimensional constraints quickly while being able to aggregate information. The representation of a dimensional model is straightforward in that each row in the fact table represents a unique observable transaction or event within a specific business context.

This representation captures both entity data and quantifiable data. The entity data items, such as *customer* or *location* are not the actual values but instead are references (or foreign keys) to the dimension tables. The quantifiable items (such as *quantity* or *unit price*) are specific pieces of information relevant to the fact and are captured in the fact record. This data is typically numeric so that it is amenable to aggregate functions (sum, max, min, etc.). Each fact represents the total quantity of a product sold to a specific customer at a particular point-of-sales location at a particular point in time.

ELT (Extract, Load, Transform)

Increased data volumes pose a problem for the traditional approach of extracting data, transforming it, and then loading the data in the data warehouse because first accumulating the mounds of data into a staging area creates a burst-y demand for resources. When the data sets are being extracted and transformed, the storage and computational needs may be high (or actually, *very* high), but during the interim periods, those resources might be largely unused. This is undesirable from both the performance and utilization standpoints.

A different approach seeks to take advantage of the performance characteristics of the analytical platforms themselves by bypassing the staging area. In other words, the data sets are extracted from the sources, loaded into the target, and the transformations are applied at the target. This modified approach, Extract, Load, and Transform (ELT), is beneficial with massive data sets because it eliminates the demand for the staging platform (and its corresponding costs to manage).

However, once the data is loaded into the target system, you may be limited by the capabilities of executing the transformation. For example, applications for transformation can be much more flexible dealing with data streamed directly out of files. In the ELT approach, you may have to use an RDBMS's native methods for applying transformation. These may not be as complete and may run slower than custom-designed transformation applications.

ETL (Extract, Transform, Load)

A basic concept for populating a data warehouse is that data sets from multiple sources are collected and then added to a data repository from which analytical applications can source their input data. This sounds straightforward, but actually can become quite complex. Although the data warehouse data model may have been designed very carefully with the BI clients' needs in mind, the data sets that are being used to source the warehouse typically have their own peculiarities. Yet not only do these data sets need to be migrated into the data warehouse, they will need to be integrated with other data sets either before or during the data warehouse population process.

This *extract/transform/load* (ETL) process is the sequence of applications that extract data sets from the various sources, bring them to a data staging area, apply a sequence of processes to prepare the data for migration into the data warehouse, and actually load them. Here is the general theme of an ETL process.

- Get the data from the source location.
- Map the data from its original form into a data model that is suitable for manipulation at the staging area.
- Validate and clean the data.
- Apply any transformations to the data that are required before the data sets are loaded into the repository.
- Map the data from its staging area model to its loading model.
- Move the data set to the repository.
- Load the data into the warehouse.

Event Stream Processing

Event stream processing (ESP) is a set of methods that enables an alternative to series of queries against static data sets. An ESP framework can be configured to monitor high volumes of data flowing through multiple continuously flowing input data sources with very low latencies for event processing. The application developer can configure a "data flow" network of state-preserving processing stages, each with actions triggered as a result of the arrival of information coupled with integrated business rules. The flexibility of the configuration of this data flow network allows rapidly changing data from the different input streams to be subjected to multiple rule sets at the same time.

An ESP engine can evaluate both transient events as well as events that are retained within a virtual cache. Input streams are continuously pushed to a query processor that essentially "reacts" to arriving data. Multiple patterns can be scanned simultaneously, because as new events arrive, they are routed through a set of continuous queries. The asynchronous and independent nature of the different sets of queries means that the system can be scaled through distribution of processing and drawing from a pool of available computational units.

The ability to continuously monitor a wide variety of streaming inputs in a scalable manner allows you to respond to emerging scenarios through the recognition of actionable knowledge because of the lower latencies and turnaround time for analysis. In essence, instead of running dynamic queries against static data, we can look at ESP as a method for simultaneously running multiple stored queries against massive amounts of dynamic data.

Hadoop and MapReduce

A growing community of analytical programmers are adapting programming models for massively parallel programming coupled with methods for distributed file storage to enable more flexibility in analyzing both structured and unstructured data and integrating the results of both approaches as part of the BI and analytics program. Paradigms like Google's MapReduce have become the center point for parallel application development. Programmers are gravitating toward the use of implementations such as Hadoop, which is an open source framework with an implementation of MapReduce as well as HDFW, the Hadoop Distributed File System, to support the development of high-performance data analysis applications.

MapReduce is not a database system, but is a programming model introduced and described by Google researchers for parallel, distributed computation involving massive data sets (ranging from hundreds of terabytes to petabytes). As opposed to the familiar procedural/imperative approaches used by Java or C++ programmers, MapReduce's programming model mimics functional languages (notably Lisp and APL), mostly due to its dependence on two basic operations that are applied to sets or lists of data value pairs:

- **Map**, which describes the computation or analysis applied to a set of input key/value pairs to produce a set of intermediate key/value pairs; and
- **Reduce**, in which the set of values associated with the intermediate key/value pairs output by the *Map* operation are combined to provide the results.

Organizations are looking at using the programming model for parallel application development as well as the distributed file system's fault-tolerant capabilities to enable a scalable yet elastic platform for rich big data analytics applications.

Location Intelligence and Geographic Analytics

Geographic data services enable the analysis of objects (such as individuals, members of a logical cohort or community of interest, businesses, points of interest, or geographic regions), their location attributes (such as average age, median income, average driving distance, or average educational attainment), and on occasion, temporal events, all within a number of application scenarios. This combined *location-based intelligence* informs operational and analytical applications, workflows, and decision-making, and can add value by increasing revenues, decreasing costs, or improving productivity and satisfaction. Fundamental geographic data services include address cleansing and standardization, mapping, distance calculations, calculating nearest points of interest, risk assessment, real-time traffic and routing updates, emergency or accident routing, and other typical use cases for operational purposes.

Every business event or transaction happens at some specific location, and an analyst can look for patterns associated with geography that can be effectively used to improve business performance. Some examples that use geographic location for analytic purposes include geographic targeting, fraud detection, site location, risk assessment and determination of premiums for insurance, dead zone analysis for telecommunication utilities, and other typical analytical use cases. Content provision that combines location information with corresponding demographic data allows placement of targeted advertising of specific goods and services customized to specific customer profiles; this is a good example where analyzing historical transactions, object profiles, events, and location attributes to identify deeper insights provides an analytic avenue for applying geographic data services. In Chapter 16 we examined both "horizontal" use cases that can be generally applied across many industries and "vertical" use cases specific for particular industries.

Metadata and Metadata Management

We can consider metadata as a catalog of the intellectual capital surrounding the creation, management, and use of a data set. That can range from simple observations about the number of columns in a database table to complex descriptions about the way that data flowed from multiple sources into the target database or how unstructured data input streams are absorbed into a big data analytical platform. The concept of metadata has evolved over time from its origin in the data dictionary associated with mainframe database tables, and has become a key factor and component supporting a BI program.

Metadata has matured out of the data dictionary in relation to the increase in information sharing. Data warehousing and BI are two facets of a framework for information sharing. Aggregating data from multiple sources into a target data warehouse model is the "provisioning" side, while accessing data from the warehouse and delivering it in a usable form through BI presentation and visualization tools. In essence, for the purposes of BI and data warehousing, metadata is a sharable master key to all the information that is feeding the business analytics, from the extraction and population of the central repository to the provisioning of data out of the warehouse and onto the screens of the business clients.

Metadata management is probably one of the most critical tasks associated with a successful BI program, for a number of reasons, including these:

- Metadata encapsulates the conceptual, logical, and physical information required to transform disparate data sets into a coherent set of models for analysis.
- Metadata captures the structure of the data that is being used for data warehousing and BI.

- The recording of operational metadata provides a road map for deriving an information audit trail.
- Metadata management processes provide a way to segregate the different meanings associated with source data and provide methods for the analyst to ensure coherence once data has been made available for reporting and analytics.
- We can capture differences associated with how data is manipulated over time (as well as the corresponding business rules), which is critical with data warehouses whose historical data spans large periods of time.
- Metadata provides the means for tracing the evolution of information as a way to validate and verify results derived from an analytical process.

Mobile Business Intelligence

Mobile BI is an emerging technique for delivering actionable knowledge to portable/mobile devices, and it warrants further consideration for two reasons. The first is the determination of the appropriate means for presentation: is there a mobile presentation layer on the mobile device and is the data streamed to the device where it can be directly reviewed, sliced and diced, and so on? Or is the device just a conduit for attaching to a hosted or cloud-based data repository, providing a window to a BI application running on a remote platform?

The answer to these questions is relevant to the second critical issue, having to do with management and oversight of the mobile devices themselves. For the most part, individuals seeking to attach to their corporate BI environments are doing so using their own private devices. This approach, called BYOD (Bring Your Own Device), raises issues of corporate oversight and protection of information. As more key staff members demand full-service mobile BI, we will see how questions about delivery to the portable device are answered to satisfy both the needs of the information consumers as well as complying with best practices for information and data protection.

Online Analytical Processing (OLAP)

Online analytical processing is different from the typical operational or transaction processing systems. There are many proposed definitions of OLAP, most of which describe what OLAP is used for. The most frequently used terms are *multidimensional* and *slice-and-dice*. Online analytical processing tools provide a means for presenting data sourced from a data warehouse or data mart in a way that allows the data consumer to view comparative metrics across multiple dimensions. In addition, these metrics are summarized in a way that allows the data consumer to *drill down* (which means to expose greater detail) on any particular aspect of the set of facts.

The data to be analyzed in an OLAP environment are arranged in a way that enables visibility along any of the dimensions. Usually this is described as a *cube*, although the organization is intended to allow the analyst to fix some set of dimensions and then see aggregates associated with the other dimensional hierarchies. Let's resume our sales analysis from earlier in this chapter, and consider a sales fact table that records every sales transaction, including date, time, location, customer, item, quantity, price per product, sales clerk, sales promotion, and total sales. We might configure an OLAP cube with these dimensions:

- Customer
- Sales Location
- Product
- Time
- Clerk
- Sales Promotion

Within each of these dimensions is a hierarchical structure, such as time periods (hour, day, week, month, quarter, year), sales locations (point of sale, store, city, county, state, region), and item categories (including specialized products such as shampoo, which is contained within the hair-care product class, which is contained within the beauty aids product class). The OLAP environment provides an aggregate view of data variables across the dimensions across each dimension's hierarchy. This might mean an aggregate function applied to any individual column across all the data related to each dimension (such as "total dollar sales by time period by sales location" or "average price by region by customer class"). For example, the data analyst can explore the total sales of beauty aid products within the Western region and then drill down across another dimension, such as the product dimension (total sales of hair-care products within the Western region) or the region dimension (total sales of beauty aids in California).

Because of the cube structure, there is an ability to rotate the perception of the data to provide different views into the data using alternate base dimensions. This conceptual ability to pivot or rotate the data provides the "slice" part; the ability to drill down on any particular aggregation provides the "dice" part.

The value of an OLAP tool is derived from the ability to quickly analyze the data from multiple points of view, and so OLAP tools are designed to precalculate the aggregations and store them directly in the OLAP databases. Although this design enables fast access, it means that there must be a significant amount of preparation of the data for the OLAP presentation as well as a potentially large storage space, because the number of cells within the cube is determined by both the number of dimensions and the size of each dimension.

For example, an OLAP cube with two dimensions, customer (1000 values) and sales locations (100 entries), would need 100,000 cells. Add a third dimension, product (with 200 entries), and you suddenly need 20 million cells. Add that fourth dimension, time (52 weeks), and your space requirement jumps to 1.04 trillion! Not only that, computational requirements grow in this same manner, because those aggregations need to be calculated and stored. No wonder many vendors rely on parallel machine architectures to support the OLAP data environment.

Parallel and Distributed Computing

Maintaining large amounts of transaction data is one thing, but integrating and subsequently transforming that data into an analytical environment (such as a data warehouse or any multidimensional analytical framework) requires both a large amount of storage space and processing capability. And unfortunately the kinds of processing needed for BI applications cannot be scaled linearly. In other words, with most BI processing, increasing the amount of data results in dramatically increasing the demand for computational resources as well as the need for increased storage facilities.

A successful BI strategy encompasses more than just the desired analytical functionality. It must also incorporate expectations about the speed of the applications. Luckily, there have been significant innovations in the area of *parallel processing* that allow us to decompose a lot of the processing in ways that can be mapped to collections of commodity hardware components to enable scalability that addresses both computational demand and memory and disk space. Whether the size of the input grows or the number of applications grows, the demands on the system may potentially be met by making use of parallel and distributed computing.

Within certain constraints, there is an appeal to exploiting multiple processor execution frameworks for a few reasons, among them:

- Loosely coupled parallel systems can be configured using commodity parts; for example, large numbers of homogeneous workstations can easily be networked using high-speed switches.
- Software frameworks can be instituted on top of already available resources to make use of underused computer capability (*cycle stealing*), thereby increasing return on hardware investment.
- Small-scale multiple-processor systems (4–16 processors) are readily available at reasonable prices in configurations that can be expanded by incrementally adding processors and memory.
- Programming languages and libraries (such as C++ and Java) have embedded support for thread- or task-level parallelization, which eases the way for implementation and use.
- New, open programming models for parallel and distributed systems (such as Hadoop) are rapidly being adopted as standards.

Parallel computer systems make use of replicated computational and I/O resources to provide scalable improvement in the time required for many of the processes associated with BI: query processing, data profiling, extraction and transformation, data cleansing, and data mining. For more detail on high-performance BI, see Chapter 14.

Query and Reporting

It is useful to distinguish the packaging and delivery of information from the information that is expected to be inside these delivered reports. Typically, these are some of the kinds of reporting that would be expected in a BI environment.

- **Standard reporting**, which is meant to convey the status of the business in operation, such as P&L reports, budget versus actual spending, expense reports, and production reports.
- **Structured queries**, which result in exposing specific routine queries such as sales per region. These can be parameterized to allow different clients to modify aspects of the queries for their own personalized use.
- **Ad hoc query systems**, which allow the client to formulate his or her own queries directly into the data. Some systems will provide query builders to help those who are not familiar with the query language syntax assemble proper ad hoc queries.
- **Self-service reporting**, which allows the business users to configure a parameterized template or design their own formats for reports.
- **Notification-based reporting**, in which a triggered business rule directs a notification to a specific individual with actionable knowledge.
- **Exception-based reporting**, which alerts individuals to events that have taken place within the environment.

There are many sorts of query and reporting tools providing a visual interface that allows the data client to formulate the queries required for a particular business report and then to assemble the report presentation. These tools will mask out the technical details of the data access and configuration and can be used to manage and reuse canned queries or sequences of ad hoc queries.

Endnotes

1. The Data Warehouse Institute Faculty Newsletter, Fall 2002.
2. Retrieved May 5, 2003, from www.businessrulesgroup.org/brgdefn.htm.

Bibliography

There are many excellent resources for learning more about business intelligence, data warehousing, data quality, data mining, knowledge delivery and presentation, among the other topics covered in this book. I have drawn inspiration and knowledge from these books, and I will continue to share resources from the book's web site, http://www.businessintelligence-book.com.

Analytics at Work: Smarter Decisions, Better Results. Thomas Davenport, Jeanne G. Harris, Robert Morison. (2010). Harvard Business Review Press.

Building the Data Warehouse, 4e, W. H. Inmon. (2005). New York: John Wiley & Sons.

Business Intelligence Roadmap, the Complete Project Lifecycle for Decision-Support Applications. (2003). Moss. L. T., and Moss Atre, Addison-Wesley Professional.

Business Metadata, Inmon, William, O'Neil, Bonnie, & Fryman, Lowell (2008). Morgan Kaufmann Publishers.

Data Mining: Concepts and Techniques. (2011). (3rd ed.). Jiawei Han, Micheline Kamber, Jian Pei, Morgan Kaufmann.

Data Mining: Practical Machine Learning Tools and Techniques, 3e, Ian Witten, Eibe Frank. (2011). Mark Hall: Morgan Kaufmann.

Data Mining Techniques: For Marketing, Sales, and Customer Relationship Management, 3e. Michael Berry and Gordon Linoff. (2011). Wiley Computer Publishing.

Data Quality: The Accuracy Dimension, Jack Olson. (2002). San Francisco: Morgan Kaufmann.

Information Dashboard Design: The Effective Visual Communication of Data. (2006). Stephen Few. O'Reilly Media.

Key Performance Indicators (KPI): Developing, Implementing, and Using Winning KPIs, 2e. (2010). David Parmenter. Wiley.

Metadata Solutions: Using Metamodels, Repositories, XML, and Enterprise Portals to Generate Information on Demand. Adrienne Tannenbaum. (2001). Boston: Addison Wesley Professional.

Performance Dashboards: Measuring, Monitoring, and Managing Your Business, 2e. (2010). Wayne Eckerson. Wiley.

Successful Business Intelligence: Secrets to Making BI a Killer App. (2007). Cindi Howson, McGraw-Hill Osborne Media.

The DAMA Guide to the Data Management Body of Knowledge (DAMA DMBOK). (2010). Technics Publications, LLC.

The Data Model Resource Books (Vols. 1–3). (2001–2009). Len Silverston. Wiley.

The Data Warehouse Lifecycle Toolkit, Ralph Kimball, et al. (1998) New York: John Wiley & Sons.

The Profit Impact of Business Intelligence. (2006). Steve Williams and Nancy Williams. Morgan Kaufmann.

Three-Dimensional Analysis—Data Profiling Techniques. (2008). Ed Lindsey. Data Profiling LLC.

Index

Note: Page numbers with "f" denote figures; "t" tables.